The Philosophy of
Education

EDUCATION INFORMATION GUIDE SERIES

Series Editor: Francesco Cordasco, Professor of Education, Montclair State College, Upper Montclair, New Jersey

Also in this series:

BILINGUAL EDUCATION IN AMERICAN SCHOOLS—*Edited by Francesco Cordasco and George Bernstein*

HISTORY OF AMERICAN EDUCATION—*Edited by Francesco Cordasco, David N. Alloway, and Marjorie Scilken Friedman*

MEDICAL EDUCATION IN THE UNITED STATES—*Edited by Francesco Cordasco and David N. Alloway*

MUSIC EDUCATION—*Edited by Ernest E. Harris*

THE PHILOSOPHY OF EDUCATION—*Edited by Charles Albert Baatz*

THE PSYCHOLOGICAL FOUNDATIONS OF EDUCATION—*Edited by Charles Albert Baatz and Olga K. Baatz**

READING IN AMERICAN SCHOOLS—*Edited by Maria E. Schantz and Joseph F. Brunner*

SOCIOLOGY OF EDUCATION—*Edited by Francesco Cordasco and David N. Alloway*

U.S. HIGHER EDUCATION—*Edited by Franklin Parker and Betty J. Parker**

WOMEN'S EDUCATION IN THE UNITED STATES—*Edited by Kay S. Wilkins*

*in preparation

The above series is part of the

GALE INFORMATION GUIDE LIBRARY

The Library consists of a number of separate series of guides covering major areas in the social sciences, humanities, and current affairs.

General Editor: Paul Wasserman, Professor and former Dean, School of Library and Information Services, University of Maryland

Managing Editor: Denise Allard Adzigian, Gale Research Company

"The Philosophy of Education"

A GUIDE TO INFORMATION SOURCES

Volume 6 in the Education Information Guide Series

Charles Albert Baatz

Professor of Education
and
Chairman
Department of General Professional Education
School of Education
Seton Hall University
South Orange, New Jersey

Gale Research Company
Book Tower, Detroit, Michigan 48226

Library of Congress Cataloging in Publication Data

Baatz, Charles Albert.
    The philosophy of education.

    (Education information guide series ; v. 6) (Gale
information guide library)
      1. Baatz, Charles Albert. 2. Education—
philosophy. I. Title. II. Series.
LB885.B22A36   370'.1   80-14346
ISBN 0-8103-1452-5

For Olga K. Baatz
Wife and Colleague

VITA

Charles Albert Baatz is professor of education and has been elected, for a third time, chairman of the department of general professional education in the School of Education, Seton Hall University, South Orange, New Jersey. For nearly a decade, Professor Baatz chaired the department of psychology in the School of Arts and Sciences. At their invitation, he has taught graduate and undergraduate courses in philosophy, psychology, and education at such institutions as the Newark College of Engineering, Georgetown, Fordham, and New York Universities. In response to a personal request from the Association of Teacher Educators, Professor Baatz conducted a seminar for their 1978 convention in Las Vegas. Known as author, philosopher, psychologist, and religious educator, he is cofounder and board member of both the New Jersey Council of Educational Foundations and the World Youth Vocational Education Association.

Professor Baatz received his Licentiate in philosophy and psychology from Georgetown University and completed his doctoral studies in the philosophy of education under the direction of John Redden, Francis Ryan, John Adam, and John W. Donohue of Fordham University.

CONTENTS

Contents

Contents

Contents

ACKNOWLEDGMENTS

Martin J. Smith, a Jesuit scholar at both Georgetown and Fordham Universities who had himself written in the German language a major work on the moral philosophy of John Dewey, gave me the initial impetus for studying the philosophy and science of education. Father Smith, by exhortation and example, inspired the scholarly study of the educational classics in the original Greek, Latin, French, German, and other European languages. His inspirational scholarship, together with that of Jaime Castiello, Joseph C. Glose, John Courtney Murray, Joseph A. Slattery, Neil J. Twombly, Stephen L. O'Beirne, and others imbued with the same Jesuit ideals and charisma, has helped to give this work an ethos it would never have had but for their teaching and influence.

Chapter 1

THE HEART OF THE MATTER

At this time and circumstance, the intention is not to redefine concepts or to decree in any fashion the metes and bounds of education but rather to make available a bibliography in the philosophy of education useful to both beginners and specialists. Certain thinkers find it very meaningful to approach education from either its scientific or philosophical or theological foundations. Many actually conduct their research under the formality of the science or the philosophy or the theology of education. Some prefer the entry through methodology or linguistic analysis while others limit their interpretation of education to inferences from or application of premises believed to be unquestionably and universally true. Whatever the initial conviction or the consequent outcome, these specialists in education are very likely to travel over the same terrain, are apt to unearth findings often substantially similar, and frequently set out separately for newer horizons only to meet each other again similarly engaged in a search for solutions to problems they hardly suspect may be common to all of them. This phenomenon probably reflects or is created by the human tendency toward unity; the sphere of knowledge is conceivably globular so that every path of entry from the surface eventually crosses almost all the other paths of inquiry once the researchers are determined to follow their preferred ways to their ultimate philosophic destinations. This basically is the outlook that has governed the compiling of the present bibliography.

If questions, in educational theory or practice, do in fact require probing into the mystery of life or penetrating into the meaning of philosophy or investigating the nature of science, then this necessity becomes all the more true when the central quest is the philosophy of education. Inevitably, the inquiry into educational philosophy raises ultimate questions about science, philosophy, and life itself, about their mutual interrelationships, about the consequences or even the feasibility of the inquiry itself. This complication is itself a unique problem; differing conceptions of life, differing understandings of philosophy, differing applications of science--all relative to education--seem only to raise more issues than they solve. The intellectual exchange in educational philosophy would appear doomed to endless bickering. But this need not be the case.

Harry S. Broudy, in his PHILOSOPHY OF EDUCATION: AN ORGANIZATION OF TOPICS AND SELECTED SOURCES, reached basic conclusions that merit general acceptance:

(1) logic and history unmistakably establish the philosophy of education as an academic discipline with its own content not identical with, but very closely related to, philosophy and all the other sciences;

(2) among these manifold relationships, philosophy of education enjoys an interpretative function; educators can be made conscious of their assumptions about principles and causes of things, they can be obligated to evaluate these assumptions, they may even be expected to point out the consequences of a thought system or to argue for the specific application of principle;

(3) the logical organization of the philosophy of education as a field of study is not only possible but highly desirable whether ideas and principles are examined theoretically, or applied to practical situations, or required in courses and preparation of candidates for the helping professions.[1]

Helpful to this general dialogue is the attempt of Philip G. Smith to clarify some of the interconnections between philosophy and education. Among these relationships, Smith chooses to distinguish between philosophy and education, philosophy in education, philosophy for education, and philosophy of education. His explanations sharpen the understanding of these various connections and strengthen the arguments for acknowledging the philosophy of education as a systematic study.[2] The exploration of all these problems has been greatly facilitated by the bibliographic research of Broudy and Brickman and hopefully will be aided by the work now before you.

A FRAME OF REFERENCE

Broudy and his associates at Urbana have led the way in their pioneering effort to organize topics and selected sources in the philosophy of education. The schema (chart 1) used here is a modification of Broudy's suggested organization of materials. It attempts to account for the general treatments of the philosophy or philosophies of education as well as for the relationships of the philosophic, critical, human, and natural sciences to the philosophy of education. The schema and its suggested categories make no claim to adequacy or to completeness but are expected to raise further inquiries, to encourage critical analysis, and to bother the readers to the degree that they will devise more valid systems of classification.

Philosophies of Education

General, critical, or comparative studies of systematic philosophies of educa-

---

1. Cf. Harry S. Broudy et al., PHILOSOPHY OF EDUCATION: AN ORGANIZATION OF TOPICS AND SELECTED SOURCES (Urbana, Chicago, and London: University of Illinois Press, 1967), pp. 1-4.

2. Philip G. Smith, PHILOSOPHY OF EDUCATION: INTRODUCTORY STUDIES (New York, Evanston, and London: Harper and Row, 1965), pp. 51-71.

THE PHILOSOPHICAL SCIENCES AND THE HUMAN PERSON

PHILOSOPHY OF EDUCATION
Syntheses
Critical Issues
Critiques
Readings   ch. 3 PE

	The Problem of Knowing 1	The Problem of Being 2	The Problem of Man and Human					The Problem of Values 7
			Nature and Unity 3	Intellective Powers 4	Affective Powers 5	Aesthetic Powers 6		
Aims and Ideals ch. 4	A 1	A 2	A 3	A 4	A 5	A 6		A 7
Curriculum: Design and Content ch. 5	B 1	B 2	B 3	B 4	B 5	B 6		B 7
Personal Agencies: Teacher–Learner ch. 6	C 1	C 2	C 3	C 4	C 5	C 6		C 7
Societal Agencies: Formal and Informal ch. 7	D 1	D 2	D 3	D 4	D 5	D 6		D 7
Policy and Organization Schooling ch. 8	E 1	E 2	E 3	E 4	E 5	E 6		E 7
Process and Methods ch. 9	F 1	F 2	F 3	F 4	F 5	F 6		F 7
Philosophy of Education: Nature and Ethos ch. 10	G 1	G 2	G 3	G 4	G 5	G 6		G 7

	Epistemology P 1	Metaphysics P 2	Philosophical Psychology P 3 P 4 P 5			Aesthetics P 6	Ethics P 7
Philosophy ch. 11							
History ch. 12	History and Development of Educational Thought						
Theory and Research ch. 13	The Science of Education: Theory and Research						

THE PHILOSOPHY OF EDUCATION

CHART 1

	CRITICAL SCIENCES	HUMAN AND NATURAL SCIENCES				THE PHILOSOPHY OF EDUCATION
	The Problem of Thought and Language 8	The Problem of God TR	The Problem of the Cosmos NS	The Problem of Human Society HS	The Problem of Art and Culture AC	
Aims and Ideals	A 8					
Curriculum: Design and Content	B 8	Theology	Physical	Human	Humane	
Personal Agencies: Teacher–Learner	C 8	and	and	and	Arts	
Societal Agencies: Formal and Informal	D 8	Religion	Mathematical	Social	and	
Policy and Organization Schooling	E 8		Sciences	Sciences	Sciences	
Process and Methods	F 8					
Philosophy of Education: Nature and Ethos	G 8					

	Philosophical Analysis and Logic	Phil. of Religion PTR	Phil. of Science PNS	Phil. of Society PHS	Phil. of Culture PAC
Philosophy	P 8				
History		HTR	HNS	HHS	HAC
Theory and Research		TTR	RNS	THS	TAC

CHART 1 (Continued)

tion are located separately in chapter 3. This chapter is divided into four sections: (1) syntheses, (2) issues, (3) critical and comparative analyses, (4) anthologies and readings. Broudy had largely omitted this grouping because the discussions of systematic philosophies proved difficult to sort with a system of division according to problems. It still remains a problem.

THE PHILOSOPHICAL SCIENCES AND THE HUMAN PERSON

The pattern of chapters 4 to 10 is generated by relating the problems of philosophy to the causal explanations of education. The vertical columns 1 to 7 represent the philosophic studies as problems with specific regard to the human person. Sources concerned with the philosophic sciences and the human person are classified according to the problem of knowing or epistemology (column 1), the problem of being or metaphysics (column 2), the problem of man or philosophical psychology with respect to human nature and unity of person (column 3), human intellective powers (column 4), the affective powers together with will and emotions (column 5), and the aesthetic powers (column 6). Allocated to column 7 are writings on the problem of values or ethics or axiology if the latter is restricted to examining the nature, types, assumptions, and criteria of values and value judgments. Where axiology is conceived to include aesthetics as part of its domain, then such listings are to be found in either column 6 or AC.

THE CRITICAL SCIENCES

Much of the contemporary mood in educational philosophy rises from the genuine preoccupation with the logical and analytical laws of thought and language. This mood is evident in the work of Socrates and Plato, takes on a modern coloring from Wittgenstein and his followers, and is actually believed by many to have produced its own school of philosophical and educational thought. The critical sciences of logic and philosophical analysis help clarify many aspects of the problem of meaning, help thinkers express themselves more precisely and intelligibly, help uncover many unsuspected assumptions, and help discover the links and interactive influences between philosophical belief and educational practice. Since philosophical analysis partly overlaps the field of logic and is conspicuous for using the tools of critical thinking, it is bracketed with logic in column 8, both for ease of reference and its distinctive character. References that relate philosophical analysis to problems special to the other sciences are to be found listed in the appropriate columns.

THE HUMAN AND NATURAL SCIENCES

This designation is borrowed from Bernard Lonergan to provide a rubric for the grouping of investigations into the problems of God; matter and the cosmos; human society and associative relationships; poietic and creative expression in all its cultural forms. At the highest levels these sciences and arts are genuinely philosophic but very commonly come within range of empirical and intermediate levels of abstraction. Philosophers of education enter these fields of human thought and action for specific data, norms or applications of principle. Experts in these same fields often reach higher level conclusions that produce repercussions in the philosophy of education.

TR: Theology and Religion

Whether the philosopher of education is a religious believer or not, the problem of God does require a stance or a response of some kind. Religions, religious institutions, and theologians insist on having their voices heard in the discussions on the philosophy of education. To them, revelation, tradition, and the supernatural are not a leap from religious experience to ontology but a matter of true affirmation to which corresponds reality as it truly is--the reality of God and his saving counsel in human affairs. Many of these theological thinkers prefer to speak of a theology of education. Religious thinkers guard a font of knowledge that many may disclaim but no one has proven valueless. Belief in revelation and in teachings consequent to such revelation still affects all human living and therefore education as well. In fact, acquaintance with the nuances and developments of religious and theological reflection is no less a hard-earned achievement than is a thorough familiarity with the intricacies of philosophical analysis.

NS: Natural Sciences

Authorities in the humanities and education quite frequently find themselves unable to appraise, in their real value, the seemingly impressive "final truths" of the physical sciences and so either ignore or exploit them uncritically. C.P. Snow shudders at the dangers of this growing cleavage between the humanities and the natural sciences. The sciences of life, matter, and the cosmos mold history and culture not only by their discoveries but also by the state of mind they foster. To this degree, physicists, mathematicians, biologists, and other scientists may exercise either a benevolent or a malevolent influence on educational thought and practice. Those who genuinely cultivate and love science, however, know the limits of the legitimate application of scientific methods. They understand the cultivation of the natural sciences as a human act that reaches its highest beauty and fullest meaning only in the coordination of the part to the whole, of particular experiences to the totality and universality of human reality. Such universality is also the only key to culture, philosophy, or education, because harmony with each other and life itself demands coordination of parts in an all-pervading unity (Stanley Jaki). The listings are only suggestive of the great work that still lies ahead for harmonizing education and the other natural or physico-mathematical sciences with each other. If it be true that the rift between the two cultures is largely the result of a lack of concern on one hand and a lack of competence on the other, then the educators had better overcome their scientific illiteracy by upgrading their preparation and changing their attitudes. Philosophers of education have an important role in restoring unity to the world of the mind, to the comprehension of reality, to the schooling and understanding of the human person, and to the proper enjoyment of life.

HS: Human Sciences

If men and women are naturally social beings, then so must be their education. Among the specifically human sciences that study human beings and social structures in their societal and communal relationships, the following are surely of some significance to educational philosophy: anthropology, economics, history, jurisprudence, political science, psychology, and sociology. When joined with education, these social or human sciences spawn families of their own as, for example, the psychology of education, sociological education, law-focused education, and the like. Again, these fields are much too vast to be fully represented here, yet some listings are necessary to alert readers to the possibilities of the research into the common grounds these sciences share with education.

AC: Art and Culture

In the poietic domain of human activity, persons uniquely express their inner thoughts, feelings, wishes, and values artfully in an outward and often aesthetic form by way of music, dancing, painting, sculpture, architecture, poetry, literature, and the other arts. Humane arts and letters can embellish the style of human discourse, can turn learning into a graceful experience, and can clothe intellectual communication with delicacy and refinement. To ignore or to shut this gateway to reality is to hold oneself incommunicado from the beauties that are within and around us. When philosophers and educators sometimes fail to transmit the intellectual treasures of the human race, poets, artists, and writers often breach the gap by stimulating the speculative and creative powers of their fellowmen. The arts, defined by Thomas Aquinas as "the right way of making things" (SUMMA THEOLOGIAE, 1-11, q. 57, a. 3, c.), issue from the excellencies of both speculative intelligence and abiding dispositions and, therefore, afford an understanding and appreciation of reality and the human person obtainable nowhere else. The arts introduce the aesthetic element into the ordinary life and education of every man and woman. Hence, they must have meaning also for the philosophy of education.

EDUCATION ENVISIONED FROM PHILOSOPHIC CAUSES

The philosophic, critical, human, and natural sciences center on the major problems of human life and action. They also cross the boundaries of education as well. What some of these boundaries may actually be becomes, at this moment, the chief focus of attention.

In the tradition of Aristotle and Thomas Aquinas, the mainstay of the thinking expressed above has been that philosophy, and the philosophy of education, make use of the findings of all the sciences. According to that same tradition, if realities can be philosophically known through their ultimate causes, then writings that purport to give a philosophical insight into education may be classified in terms of the final, efficient, formal, material, exemplary, and instrumental causes of education. Thus the explanation of education in terms of its philosophic causes provides a rationale for chapters 4 to 10 as represented in chart 1, respectively, by the horizontal rows A to G. If it be accepted that in the natural order what is first in intention becomes actually the last in execution, then the ordering within the schema given below follows a logical and natural order.

A: Aims and Ideals of Education

Chapter 4 lists references according to the final cause of education, defined as that for or account of which education is said to exist, to function, or to reach perfect development. The end, purpose, or goal to which education leads may also embody an archetype or standard of perfection and excellence or model as an ideal or exemplar worthy of personal imitation. Here the final and exemplary causes of education, though remaining formally distinct, tend toward congruence: the exemplar specifies the educative effect to be produced or imitated, whereas the end moves the agent to action and invests the educative act or interaction with special qualities. Writings that fall into either of these categories are noted in chapter 4 in keeping with the divisions of row A.

B: Curriculum Design and Content of Education

The material cause of education includes both the educability of the learner or recipient in the helping relationship and the subject matters and guided experiences of formal and informal instruction. Chapter 5 catalogs, according to the divisions of row B, whatever is written about the capacities or receptivity of the learner and about the regimen, design, and structure of instructional content or curriculum theory. The discussions on the sequences of studies and course content are usually integrated but are separately noted where desirable.

C: Personal Agencies of Teaching and Learning

The agencies or efficient causes of education, by way of prescribed studies and experiences, transform the individual into an educated person. Of these, the primary and principle agent of education is the individual learner. In the Judeo-Christian concept of education, God is also conceived as the principal teacher coactive with the learner. The secondary agencies are then the family, the state and governmental school systems, and the church, as well as all other persons who singly and collectively contribute to the refinement of the individual. These agencies generally cooperate with each other in some mode of schooling where their educative activities are channelled and conditioned by teachers, instructors, facilitators, guidance counselors, or other educators. Note that students are seen primarily as self-actuating persons; they are the prime agents but also the material cause of their own education, for they both possess and actuate their own potentialities for a more cultured way of life. The subject matter for chapter 6 is itemized according to row C.

D: Formal and Informal Societal Agencies of Education

Works pertaining to the educative function of society through the formal agencies of the family, state, and the church or through such instrumentalities as television, newspapers, and similar media are inventoried in chapter 7. They are classified in row D as the social agencies of education whether they operate through schools or not.

E: Organization and Policy of the Educational System

An instrumental cause conditions or facilitates the operation of principal agencies. The organization and administration of an educational system are but means by which primary and secondary educative agents carry out their intentions, their philosophy of education. Vital to and at the heart of the entire educational organism is the school. Here, expert observers can monitor the system, note the empirical effects of policies and administrative procedures, and evaluate the learning outcomes of differential schooling and special programs. Authors who specialize in this branch of education are mentioned in chapter 8 and classified in row E.

F: The Process and Methods of Education

Methodology is also an instrumental cause of education. In the effort to answer the needs of learners, educative agents may vary didactic processes and techniques to achieve more or less control and freedom. Some methods are more humanizing than others; some are experimental and others are time honored and proven ways to self-actualization. Because the debate still fluctuates over the value of authoritarian and permissive instructional patterns, the advocates on either side are filed together in chapter 9, and according to the divisions of row F.

G: The Nature and Ethos of Education

To state unequivocally the distinguishing character of education is to define education in terms of its formal causality. It is the core problem in the philosophy of education. Is there such a reality? What is it? What is it able or supposed to do? In the thinking of Aristotle and Aquinas, efficient causes act on material causes, under the influence of final causes, to effectuate or educe within the learner that certain formality called an educated person. This most difficult of all inquiries in education preoccupies the writers and thinkers introduced in chapter 10 and classified in row G.

ASSOCIATED DISCIPLINES

Education, as does the philosophy of education itself, relies on the resources of several auxiliary or ancillary fields of research. Among these accessory studies, the analysis of relationships that exist between philosophy and education, between history and education, and those that arise from the "philosophy" of the philosophy of education--the inquiry into the ultimate causes of educational philosophy as an intellectual and scientific domain in its own right ought to be mentioned. These background studies are also partially related to each of the philosophic, critical, human, and natural sciences as well.

P: Philosophy and Education

Great philosophers have actually extended the boundaries of their study, research, and theories into education; they have raised issues or made declarations that affect education. For this reason, and for reason of its privileged relationship to education, philosophy is an intellectual territory that ought to be familiar to every educational philosopher. Chapter 11 and row P contain items that have originated in epistemology, metaphysics, philosophical psychology, aesthetics, ethics, philosophical analysis, and logic, but can be related to the problematics of education.

H: History and Education

An ancient Greek once called history the "mother-city of philosophy," because the search after analogous features and the elaboration of general rules or the extrapolation of theory can be so earnest that history must warn every "hunter after the truth" to examine all obtainable facts before daring to jump at a conclusion. By placing, in critical juxtaposition, different philosophies of education and by tracing their intellectual genealogies, the history of educational thought can bring to contemporary philosophical discussions in education the balanced perspective and wisdom of the past. For this reason row H and chapter 12 were included.

T: Theory and Research in the Philosophy of Education

Since the topography of educational philosophy is still very far from being definitely surveyed and charted, the continuing exploration into this realm is really testimony to the vigor, vitality, and hardiness of the probers themselves and to the richness of the land to be mined. The growing interest in what, from a methodological and scientific viewpoint, must be understood as a higher level of philosophical discussion makes chapter 13 and row T necessary for indicating the recent developments in the field of educational philosophy.

Any effort to integrate educational, scholarly, scientific, and human studies ought to correspond to the exigence of contemporary research in the philosophy of education. Such an effort ought to unite scholars and scientists with educators in the mutual search for ultimate explanations and philosophic solutions. If the thinking that has produced the schema and order of this bibliography meets these prerequisites, then the reader is asked to take up the challenge of going beyond the limits and vision of this present effort.

Chapter 2
THE FACTS OF THE MATTER

Besides the explanation of the structural plan already given in the previous pages, it may be helpful to describe the tasks, to state the aims and objectives, and to offer the reader some guidelines in using this bibliography. A concluding section on philosophers of education suggests several lines of thought and action.

THE GROUNDWORK

It seemed that the first important task was to build on the fundamental structure originally designed by Broudy and his associates at the University of Illinois. The publication in 1967 of Broudy's findings (PHILOSOPHY OF EDUCATION: AN ORGANIZATION OF TOPICS AND SELECTED SOURCES), followed by the supplementary edition in 1969, afforded a natural point of departure for the review of literature from that time to the present (1967-78). Broudy's organization of topics and materials appeared to be an adequate framework for the continuation of the research begun at Urbana.

But it soon became apparent that some restructuring of the basic organizational pattern was necessary and that a new schema would have to be devised with its own philosophical justification and rationale. This decision led to the following tasks: experiment with different network systems or models of classification, cross examine the intertwining interrelationships within the organization of topics and materials, and test the sorting system for clarity and adequacy in encompassing the professional field of educational philosophy. Broudy is more than likely correct in believing that the "philosophy of education is still largely in the pre-paradigmatic stage."[1] One may doubt his opinion, however, that studies in the philosophy of education suffer or benefit from too many suggested structures than from too few. To attempt to write a kind of "unity of

---

1. Harry S. Broudy et al., PHILOSOPHY OF EDUCATION: AN ORGANIZATION OF TOPICS AND SELECTED SOURCES (Urbana: University of Illinois Press, 1967), p. 11.

educational experience" after the specifications of Etienne Gilson's UNITY OF PHILOSOPHICAL EXPERIENCE (1965) may still be a project for the distant future. Nevertheless, you are urged to construct arrangements of your own, based perhaps on different theoretical assumptions or expectancies, if only to hasten the day when all fields of learning are more scientifically coordinated with the study of educational philosophy. Your own critical analysis of the schema suggested here can only initiate a healthier exchange of ideas and stimulate progress toward a more generally accepted organization of research.

The third task was carried out in three stages: (1) locate the major works written in the last decade on the philosophy of education; (2) catalog the items contained in the footnotes, references, and bibliographies of these sources; and (3) check each entry against those of the standard guides to books and periodical literature, but particularly with the listings of the Library of Congress and National Union Catalogs. This search was considerably moved along by the bibliographic study by Brickman (BIBLIOGRAPHICAL ESSAYS ON THE HISTORY AND PHILOSOPHY OF EDUCATION, 1975), on the history and philosophy of education. The entries in the publication now before you represent, for the most part, writings by authors most frequently cited in the major studies of educational philosophy printed since 1967.

AIMS AND OBJECTIVES

The obvious goal of compiling a bibliography is to provide a research tool that is helpful in assessing the content, the scope, and the trends of writing in the specialty. The immediate objective in this case is to take up where Broudy has left off and to continue the search for order and coherence in the data and principles germane to educational philosophy. The quest for some method or form of structuring the materials may still be, to many thinkers, nothing but an empty dream. But, until that goal be proven an impossible one, the human mind prefers order to none at all and will tolerate a useful or hypothetical scheme until it is replaced by a superior one. With this intent in mind, the survey of literature since 1967 was completed. Broudy and his team had held the view that if there were no possibility of organizing the field so that its content could be distinguished from that of other fields, then perhaps educational philosophy had no place as a distinctive discipline. The aims and objectives expressed here rest on a different assumption; if logic and tradition unmistakably indicate the necessity for a field of study commonly known as the philosophy of education, then the specialists in the field ought to be able to discover the principles of its fundamental unity. In fact, it would be a matter of professional obligation.

A second objective is to list not only professional writers widely acknowledged to be expert in the field, but also authors who are not usually considered mainstream philosophers of education. Given the broad conception of the philosophy of education advanced by James E. McClellan and others, the literature they may think relevant to the field can be made to include almost everything ever written! Even where the application of norms would reduce the sifting of sources, the scope is still overwhelming; the influence of philosophers, poets, scientists, and other creative thinkers is often greater than that of the professionals in the field. Like philosophy itself, the philosophy of education relates to all fields of learning that center on men and benefits from their contributions. Accordingly, this study tries partially to reflect these influences without neglecting what the professionals themselves have written.

A third purpose was simply to scratch the surface of foreign and international study in educational philosophy. While American and British thinkers are among the foremost leaders in the field, the growing need is for more systematic reading in the other languages. Latin, Greek, French, German, Russian, Chinese, Italian, and Spanish are indispensable languages for the scholarly review of what is going on elsewhere in the philosophy of education. Some of these sources have been annotated here but far fewer than this reviewer is in the habit of reading, and in no proportion whatever to their real importance and quality of scholarship. The commotion in educational theory, for example, occurring in the Third World nations and along the iron-curtained corridors of East and West, is barely known to anyone unfamiliar with the languages of these cultures. Since these movements are likely, sooner or later, to affect American ideas, leaders in the profession ought to be digesting the materials as they emerge in print. Furthermore, McClellan's advice is very much to the point: let the translators get busier and have the retrieval systems go international.

Lonergan has observed that the rich store of common meaning and exchange is not the work of isolated individuals or even of single generations. Common meanings have histories; they are transmitted to successive generations through training and education. Similarly, if various bibliographies in the history of educational philosophy were compared, the comparative analysis would uncover large gaps in the tradition of educational wisdom. Not only do inattention, irresponsibility, shoddy scholarship, political pressure, or ideologies corrupt the work of the mind, but topics, areas of interest, theoretical positions, and methods have a way of falling into or out of fashion. In these respects, the last decade has been no exception. For this reason, some works published before 1967 have been selected for annotation to draw the attention of the reader to an important line of thought deemed to have perennial value. For reasons of economy, the effort is limited, but the objective is to underscore the need for a science of intellectual transmission. A synopticon of great themes and ideas would be fine but not nearly enough to serve the purpose. Besides keeping track of truly important traditions, this science would foster confrontation of ideas, objective criticism, and historical-synthetic studies to bridge generations of scholarship. The young scholar thinking of the philosophy of education as the appropriate arena for engaging the great issues in education ought to contemplate as well the almost infinite possibilities for advanced research in the science of traditions in the philosophy of education. If McClelland can refer to a survey of some fifteen thousand entries as comprising only a fractional and whimsically chosen sample, then indeed imagine the great accomplishments yet to come. You are most cordially invited!

A GUIDELINE OR TWO

The easiest and most time-saving access to the materials is by way of the author index. The index, alphabetized by last names, contains the author of every bibliographic entry and should spare the reader endless rummaging through the pages. Works are classified according to their predominant theme or purpose. Broudy had begun to list the separate parts of a work in different cells or categories more appropriate to the special thrust of a specific chapter or section of an article. This was done in a few cases, but a complete indexing of such a nature must await the completion of a larger and more inclusive research project.

In addition to providing an author index, to further facilitate the use of this bibliographic guide a title index has been prepared. This index, pages 291-314, lists the titles to all books cited in the bibliography. Titles to articles which appeared in periodicals, titles of doctoral dissertations, and titles of unpublished reports have been excluded because of space limitations. The subject index, pages 315-44, includes concepts, individual names, places, and other subject areas contained within the text.

Scholars doing research within several hundred miles of New York City have at their command almost unbelievably superior search facilities and bibliographic resources. In such circumstances, when a publication has limitations, as this one does, the cause may be attributed to a lack of either genius, time, help, or financial support. Nevertheless, all the entries are familiar to the reviewer and ten thousand more that have gone unselected. Likewise, the annotations are first-hand evaluations formulated with as little bias as possible. Scrupulous care has been taken not to allow any school of thought or personal commitment to prejudice the selection of an entry or to skew the annotation unfairly in the direction of one or another philosophical position contrary to an author's expressed or known stance. In dividing the schema into horizontal rows according to the Aristotelian and Thomistic traditional explanations of ultimate causes, the prime intention is in no sense apologetic but philosophic: to probe the deepest reaches of the human mind for the most universal principles capable of undergirding a lasting yet creative methodology.

PHILOSOPHERS OF EDUCATION

An immediate issue concerning the relation of education to philosophy is to answer the question whether educators would derive values from the constant and explicit attention to the study and application of metaphysical thought. The existence of this bibliography assumes an affirmative answer. In brief, it is imperative that formal experience in philosophy and in the philosophy of education be mandated for all educators. This actually is the conclusion reached by a task force of the American Association of Colleges for Teacher Education. The Bicentennial Commission on Education for the Profession of Teaching

(AACTE), noting that teacher preparation programs are too often criticized for being too theoretical, "holds to the contrary, that they may not be <u>sufficiently</u> theoretical." Similarly, the commission shares Holbrook's view that all men have the prerogative to universal humanism, to certain commonalities and educational processes that remain constant across all human communities and groups.[2]

The scandal, of course, is the difficulty in securing universal assent to a set of philosophical propositions among the numerous varieties of metaphysics engaged in a relentless intramural fight (Stanley Jaki). Yet no one may validly dispense with philosophy without converting the world of knowledge into a chaotic morass of isolate fact, subjective sense experience, or eccentric speculation. Apart from considerations of gain and loss or apart from the Aristotelian conviction that sciences are prolongations of philosophy and further determinations of basic concepts supplied by philosophy, metaphysics and science and education originate in the very same source, call it "freshness of mind" or "interiority" or "capacity for self-transcendence."

Now this world of the mind is constructed solely through the use of mathematical, scientific, artistic, and commonsense knowledge and of both ordinary and technical language (Bernard Lonergan). To engage creatively and imperially in the realm of human wisdom, educators have no choice but to philosophize in education. It may mean refusal to accept one or another ready-made system because the variety of data and the plurality of intellectual and cultural viewpoints preclude for the moment a single adequate representation of reality. It certainly means that educators must undertake their own interchange with the arts and sciences and work out philosophical frameworks or positions that have advanced beyond those of the past. It means, in addition to full exposure to and experience with the humanities, more than a mere acquaintance with the philosophic sciences of metaphysics, epistemology, axiology, and the philosophic psychology of man. In the United States and on every continent, the twentieth century has seen the force of human events in the practical everyday exigencies of daily living compel individuals and human societies to find solutions, to reach a workable unanimity or singleness of purpose even before arriving at some kind of intellectual or ideological agreement.

Philosophers of education, perhaps more fortunately than most theoreticians or practitioners, may enjoy the best of both the practical and the speculative worlds. They can participate in the commonsense world of daily educational experience and thereby test their most cherished theories, and they can with equal propriety develop philosophical stances on the bases of actual problems. The philosophers of education enjoy a most dignified and exalted calling that embraces both the active and the contemplative life of men. Over and beyond the day-to-day operation of schools and educative processes, educational philosophers can exert a unique influence on the quality of American culture and

2. Robert B. Howsam et al., EDUCATING A PROFESSION (Washington, D.C.: American Association of Colleges for Teacher Education, 1976), pp. 88, 98.

schools by lending their genius to discovering, expressing, validating, criticizing, testing, correcting, developing, and improving the meaning and value of human living. The fundamental schema may even be recast or more soundly interpreted in terms of Lonergan's transcendental method. The functions of the philosophy of education are normative, critical, dialectical, systematic, heuristic, foundational, transcendental, and highly contributive toward finding the key to unified science.[3] This syllabus of functions suggests programs for many future generations of philosophers of education. In fact, it is not a moment too soon to join the action now.

3. Bernard J. Lonergan, METHOD IN THEOLOGY (New York: Herder and Herder, 1972), pp. 20-25.

Chapter 3

PHILOSOPHIES OF EDUCATION

SYNTHESES

Ammendola, Vincenzo. LA CONCEZIONE EDUCATIVA IN BENEDETTO CROCE. Naples: Loffredo, 1973. 236 p.

Anderson, Lewis Flint, ed. PESTALOZZI. 1931. Westport, Conn.: Greenwood Press, 1974. ix, 283 p.

Araneta, Salvador. EDUCATIONAL PHILOSOPHY OF A UNIVERSITY PRESIDENT, TERMINAL REPORT. Malabor, Philippines: Araneta Institute of Agriculture, 1971. xii, 246 p.

Arnstine, Donald. PHILOSOPHY OF EDUCATION: LEARNING AND SCHOOLING. New York: Harper and Row, 1967. xi, 388 p.

> Arnstine applies philosophy and psychology to the study of educational methods, learning, schooling, curricula, aesthetics, and epistemic curiosity.

Aquinas, Saint Thomas

Conway, Pierre H. PRINCIPLES OF EDUCATION: A THOMISTIC APPROACH. Exercises and annotated bibliography by Sister Mary Michael Spangler. Washington, D.C.: Thomist Press, 1960. xii, 204 p.

> Conway approaches Christian education from two vantage points: part 1, concerned with the principles of Christian education, analyzes the encyclical CHRISTIAN EDUCATION OF YOUTH by Pope Pius XI and the relationship of the sciences to education; part 2 examines the principles of education as aligned under the four classical causes. The conclusion tries to effect a harmony between the natural and supernatural elements of education as stated and clarified by the Roman Catholic Church.

Donohue, John W. ST. THOMAS AQUINAS AND EDUCATION. New York: Random House, 1968. 119 p. Bibliographic note. Paperbound.

Donohue argues rather cogently that St. Thomas Aquinas deserves consideration by persons with special interest in the history and theory of education. The sections on Thomistic themes for a philosophy of education and on the relevance of Thomism for education today conclude to Aquinas's affirmation of the dignity of intelligence, the genuine ontological growth of persons through the acquisition of abiding dispositions, the importance of bodily sensory experience for the life of the mind, the instrumental character of intellectual activity for all of life, the coalescence of religious and secular values, and the philosophy of politics as completing the philosophy of man. The bibliographic note (pp. 111-13) is a fine guide to sources, printed in English, about the educational thought of Aquinas.

Gulley, Anthony D. THE EDUCATIONAL PHILOSOPHY OF SAINT THOMAS AQUINAS. New York: Pageant Press, 1964. xxii, 153 p.

The introductory essay (pp. i-xxii) contains a review of sources and related literature rather difficult to find elsewhere. The study is directly aimed at dissipating the confusion that exists in American educational theory today concerning the role of the efficient causes of education in the teaching-learning-helping relationship.

Jaeger, Werner. HUMANISM AND THEOLOGY. 2d printing. Milwaukee, Wis.: Marquette University Press, 1967. vi, 87 p.

A gem too long and too often overlooked by bibliographers, this slim but scholarly volume discloses "the theocentric view of the world represented by St. Thomas and its relationship to the Greek ideal of culture and the classical tradition which is the foundation of all humanism" (pp. 1-2, 65).

Aristotle

Aristotle. ARISTOTELES UND DIE PAIDEIA. Edited and translated by Edmund Braun. Paderborn, W. Ger.: F. Schoeningh, 1974. 258 p.

_____. ARISTOTLE ON EDUCATION. Translated and edited by John Burnet. Cambridge: Cambridge University Press, 1967. 141 p.

Texts have been extracted from the ETHICS and POLITICS of Aristotle.

_____. ARISTOTLE ON EDUCATION. Edited with an introduction by George Howie. London: Collier-Macmillan, 1968. 184 p.

Braido, Pietro. PAIDEIA ARISTOTELICA. Zurich: Pas Verlag, 1969. 229 p.

Augustine, Saint Aurelius

This section is arranged alphabetically of works by Augustine, about Augustine, and then general works.

Augustine, Saint Aurelius. BIBLIOGRAPHIA AUGUSTIANA. Edited by C. Andresen. Darmstadt, W. Ger.: Wissenschaftliche Buchgesellschaft, 1973. ix, 317 p.

> Augustine's educational thought is usually interpreted from his DE DOCTRINA CHRISTIANA and DE MAGISTRO but genuine understanding requires familiarity with the entire corpus of his work. Unlike some "exhaustive" studies, this bibliography is notable for its plan, content, and contact with the actuality of Augustine's thinking as well as with the best scholarship on Augustine.

_____. CHRISTIAN INSTRUCTION. Translated by John J. Gavigan; ADMONITION AND GRACE. Translated by John Courtney Murray; THE CHRISTIAN COMBAT. Translated by Robert P. Russell; FAITH, HOPE AND CHARITY. Translated by Bernard M. Peeples. THE FATHERS OF THE CHURCH, vol. 2. New York: Fathers of the Church, 1947. 494 p.

> St. Augustine's CHRISTIAN INSTRUCTION (pp. 3-235) has footnotes that question Marrou's opinion that St. Augustine may not have read Quintilian and a helpful introduction. Even for the reader with no interest in Biblical studies, the work is valuable for understanding St. Augustine's teachings on Christian morality and moral development.

_____. CONCERNING THE TEACHER AND ON THE IMMORTALITY OF THE SOUL. Translated from Latin with preface by George G. Leckie. New York: Appleton-Century-Crofts, 1938. xxxviii, 88 p. Paperbound.

> The information-laden preface gives the import of Augustinian rhetoric, ethical doctrine, and the liberal disciplines to the diverse modes of signation. Christ is both the Physician of Grace and the Interior Master who educates through man's intrinsic nature. The liberal disciplines, with their formal means of perfecting human aptitudes, are instruments to man's perfection as man.

_____. DE MAGISTRO. Introduction, translation, and notes by Franco V. Lombardi. Padua, Italy: R.A.D.A.R., 1968. 110 p.

_____. ON EDUCATION. Selected and translated by George Howie. South Bend, Ind.: Gateway Editions, 1969; Chicago: Henry Regnery, 1970. vi, 407 p.

> Augustine conceives education as the search for truth that demands a most profound commitment to the art of teaching. Every mod-

ern educational theorist must grapple, as does Adeodatus, with the ultimate question that concludes the DE MAGISTRO.

_____. THE TEACHER, THE FREE CHOICE OF THE WILL, GRACE AND FREE WILL. Translated from Latin by Robert P. Russell. The Fathers of the Church, vol. 59. Washington, D.C.: Catholic University of America Press, 1968. vii, 331 p.

The translation and notes of THE TEACHER (pp. 7-61) are superior. The introduction points directly to the heart of the dialogue between Adeodatus and Augustine, his father: it is Christ, the "indwelling Truth" who alone teaches men truth.

Eggersdorfer, Franz Xaver. DER HEILIGE AUGUSTINUS ALS PAEDAGOGE UND SEINE BEDEUTUNG FUER DIE GESCHICHTE DER BILDUNG. [Saint Augustine as educator and his significance for the history of liberal education]. Freiburg, W. Ger.: Herdersche Verlagshandlung, 1907. ix, 238 p.

The chief reason for mentioning this remarkable work is that it gives the classic synthesis of St. Augustine's educational thought and is itself a treasury of citations from the Augustinian corpus of writings. This eighth volume of the STRASSBURGER THEOLOGISCHE STUDIEN uses only primary sources to state St. Augustine's philosophy of education.

Howie, George. EDUCATIONAL THEORY AND PRACTICE IN ST. AUGUSTINE. New York: Teachers College Press, 1969. ix, 338 p. Bibliog.

One of many around the world who believe that St. Augustine as a formative spirit in the development of educational thought has received too little recognition by modern educational theorists, Howie states the case in scholarly fashion for studying the Augustinian challenge to our age of doubt and confusion. The bibliography (pp. 323-28) notes the Latin texts, translations, books on St. Augustine, and sources on the classical, patristic, and medieval periods.

Kevane, Eugene. "Augustine's DE DOCTRINA CHRISTIANA: A Treatise on Christian Education." RECHERCHES AUGUSTINIENNES 4 (1966): 97-133.

_____. AUGUSTINE THE EDUCATOR. Westminster, Md.: Newman Press, 1964. xiv, 446 p. Bibliographic note.

Augustine's life, thought, and work are explicitly examined for their meaning in education. Kevane finds that the Augustinian approach to the humanities, which is directly in line with the tradition of Plato and Cicero, opens perspectives toward the richly varied development of a humanism yet to come. The bibliographic note (pp. 381-416) serves as an excellent entrance to Augustinian scholarship about education.

Marrou, Henri Irenee. ST. AUGUSTINE AND HIS INFLUENCE THROUGH THE AGES. Translated from French by Patrick Hepburne-Scott; texts of St. Augustine translated by Edmund Hill. London: Longmans, Green; New York: Harper and Brothers, 1957. 191 p. Paperbound.

> Short as this work is, Marrou reveals the superior quality of his scholarship in the artful manner of highlighting the presence of St. Augustine in the midst of the culture of the last few generations. and of our own. The guide and orientation to the works of St. Augustine (pp. 182-90) has been judiciously adapted from the French original by John J. O'Meara.

Portalie, Eugene. A GUIDE TO THE THOUGHT OF SAINT AUGUSTINE. Introduction by Vernon J. Bourke. Translated from French by Ralph J. Bastian. Chicago: Henry Regnery, 1960. xxxvii, 428 p. Bibliog.

> This translation is from the article, "Saint Augustin," which appeared in the DICTIONNAIRE DE THEOLOGIE CATHOLIQUE, published by Editions Letouzey et Ane, Paris, 1908. The acclaim of Portalie's article is truly international and, next to Augustine's own writings, a peak watershed for any modern research into the thought of St. Augustine. Selected bibliography (pp. 407-18) has been updated to 1960.

Ballauff, Theodor. SYSTEMATISCHE PAEDAGOGIK: EINE GRUNDLEGUNG. 3d ed. Heidelberg, W. Ger.: Quelle and Meyer, 1970. 194 p.

Barrett, William. WHAT IS EXISTENTIALISM? New York: Grove Press, 1964. 218 p.

Bayles, Ernest E. PRAGMATISM IN EDUCATION. New York: Harper and Row, 1966. x, 146 p.

> Pragmatism, experimentalism, and the concept of relativity are delineated in terms of human nature, culture, and education. Bayles shows that pragmatism gives truth, value, existence, and culture a special coloring in the actual working out of educational purpose and program.

Beck, Clive. EDUCATIONAL PHILOSOPHY AND THEORY: AN INTRODUCTION. Boston: Little, Brown, 1974. viii, 328 p.

Blehl, Vincent Ferrer. "The Patristic Humanism of John Henry Newman." THOUGHT 50, no. 198 (1975): 266-74.

> Newman's realism is not simply the humanism of Oxford but the humanism of a Christian gentleman, the Christian humanism of the Fathers of the Church. Only the supernatural grace of man's powers can effect the fulfillment and harmonization of man's native powers.

Bollnow, Otto Friedrich. EXISTENZPHILOSOPHIE UND PAEDAGOGIK. 3d ed. Stuttgart, Berlin, Cologne, and Mainz: Kohlhammer, 1965. 160 p.

Boyd, William. THE EDUCATIONAL THEORY OF JEAN JACQUES ROUSSEAU. New York: Russell and Russell, 1963. 368 p.

Brameld, Theodore. CULTURAL FOUNDATIONS OF EDUCATION: AN IN-TERDISCIPLINARY EXPLORATION. Foreword by Clyde Kluckholm. 1957. Westport, Conn.: Greenwood Press, 1973. xxi, 330 p.

_____. PATTERNS OF EDUCATIONAL PHILOSOPHY: DIVERGENCE AND CONVERGENCE IN CULTUROLOGICAL PERSPECTIVE. New York: Holt, Rinehart and Winston, 1971. xvii, 615 p.

> Brameld's positions are not yet finalized so that reliance on any single or earlier publication could be misleading. Still holding to his faith in democracy, he tempers his former emphasis on societal factors with special regard for individuals having a problem finding their own identities. From the contributions of philosophy, anthropology, and education, Brameld presents a reconstruction of his thought with comparison to progressive, essentialist, and perennialist positions.

_____. TOWARD A RECONSTRUCTED PHILOSOPHY OF EDUCATION. New York: Dryden Press, 1956; Holt, Rinehart and Winston, 1962. 417 p.

> Here Brameld has developed the reconstructionist outlook more fully and forcefully.

Broudy, Harry S. "Realism in American Education." SCHOOL AND SOCIETY 87 (17 January 1959): 11-14. Reprinted in READINGS IN THE FOUNDA-TIONS OF EDUCATION, edited by James C. Stone and Frederick W. Schneider, pp. 479-85. 2d ed. New York: Thomas Y. Crowell, 1971.

> Realists reject any thoroughgoing relativism, whether it be cultural, intellectual, aesthetic, or moral. The emphasis of realist educators is likely to be cultural, religious, or philosophical and on the constant structure of human nature. Thus the education of man leads to the good life and transcends all individual differences. Realism is probably, in the opinion of Broudy, at the core of the beliefs held by most public school teachers explicitly or implicitly.

Buber, Martin

This section is arranged alphabetically of works by Buber, about Buber, and then general works.

Buber, Martin. A BELIEVING HUMANISM: MY TESTAMENT, 1902-1965. Translated with introduction and explanatory comments by Maurice Friedman.

New York: Simon and Schuster, 1967. 252 p.

Weinstein, Joshua. BUBER AND HUMANISTIC EDUCATION. New York: Philosophical Library, 1975. 102 p.

Calo, Giovanni, et al. LA MIA PEDAGOGIA. Padua, Italy: Liviana, 1972. vi, 334 p.

Chambliss, Joseph James. BOYD H. BODE, A PHILOSOPHY OF EDUCATION. Columbus: Ohio State University Press, 1963. xii, 98 p.

> Chambliss presents Bode's understanding of pragmatism as the way to the education of every man.

Chanel, Emile. LES GRANDS THEMES DE LA PEDAGOGIE MODERNE: TEXTES FONDAMENTAUX. Paris: Le Centurion, 1970. 310 p.

Chapman, James Crosby, and Counts, George Sylvester. PRINCIPLES OF EDUCATION. 1924. Dayton, Ohio: National Cash Register, 1970. xviii, 645 p.

Chavardes, Maurice. LES GRANDS MAITRES DE L'EDUCATION. Paris: Editions du Sud et A. Michel, 1966. 255 p.

Childs, John Lawrence. EDUCATION AND THE PHILOSOPHY OF EXPERI-MENTALISM. 1931. New York: Arno Press, 1971. xix, 264 p.

Chu, Don-chean. PHILOSOPHIC FOUNDATIONS OF AMERICAN EDUCATION. Dubuque, Iowa: Kendall/Hunt Publishing, 1971. viii, 392 p.

Cirigliano, Gustavo F. FILOSOFIA DE LA EDUCACION. Buenos Aires: Humanitas, 1973. 286 p.

> This work also contains the author's ANALISIS FENOMENOLO-GICO DE LA EDUCACION first published in 1962 (pp. 7-145).

Cowie, Leonard W., and Cowie, Evelyn E. GREAT IDEAS IN EDUCATION. New York: Pergamon General Books, 1971. 160 p.

Crittenden, Brian C. EDUCATION AND SOCIAL IDEALS: A STUDY IN PHILOSOPHY OF EDUCATION. Don Mills, Ont.: Longman Canada, 1973. xvi, 253 p.

Dearden, R.F. THE PHILOSOPHY OF PRIMARY EDUCATION. London: Routledge and Kegan Paul; New York: Humanities Press, 1968. xi, 194 p.

Catholic Educational Philosophy

"Declaration on Christian Education (Gravissimum Educationis)." In THE DOCUMENTS OF VATICAN II, edited by Walter M. Abbott and Joseph Gallagher, pp. 637-51. New York: America Press, 1966.

> This outlines a Christian philosophy of education aimed at the formation of the human person with respect to his ultimate goal, and simultaneously with respect to the good of those societies of which, as a man, he is member, and in whose responsibilities, as an adult, he will share. The index, prepared for this edition by Joseph W. Sprug (pp. 748-92), is invaluable for locating themes in education.

Donohue, John W. CATHOLICISM AND EDUCATION. New York: Harper and Row, 1973. vii, 152 p.

> In this work, the Jesuit author combines a most profound spirituality with a highly realistic grasp of educational problems. There is not a trace of triumphalism: Donohue uses the latest findings of scholarship in scripture, theology, and education to sketch what he modestly believes is yet a tentative philosophy of education. His writing and research are truly models of how to approach the Catholic or any other philosophy of education.

Driscoll, Justin A. "A Philosophy of Catholic Education in a Time of Change." CATHOLIC SCHOOL JOURNAL 67, no. 9 (1967): 29-33.

> Driscoll summarizes the principles of educational philosophy discernible in Vatican II Decrees. The reader should consult the documents as well for other insights not expressed in this article.

Dupuis, Adrian Maurice, and Nordberg, Robert B. PHILOSOPHY AND EDUCATION: A TOTAL VIEW. 3d ed. Beverly Hills, Calif.: Benziger, 1973. xvi, 334 p.

> The authors of this educational synthesis have mined diverse Catholic educational and philosophical traditions. Helpful toward understanding the Catholic approach to the philosophy of education is the comparison of this work with the declarations of Vatican II and with Donohue's CATHOLICISM AND EDUCATION and ST. THOMAS AQUINAS AND EDUCATION.

Johnston, Herbert. A PHILOSOPHY OF EDUCATION. New York: McGraw-Hill, 1963. xv, 362 p.

> Johnston meticulously introduces the reader to the nature of philosophy and education, the nature of man and human virtues, the aims and agencies of education, liberal and vocational education, the process of learning-teaching, curriculum planning, the teacher's vocation. Chapter 9, "Some Contemporary Philosophies of

Education," gives a critical evaluation of the educational philosophy found in the thought of Philip G. Smith, Scheffler, Phenix, Gruber, Broudy, Ulich, and Van Cleve Morris.

Marique, Pierre Joseph. THE PHILOSOPHY OF CHRISTIAN EDUCATION. New York: Prentice-Hall, 1939. Reprint. Westport, Conn.: Greenwood Press, 1970. xv, 347 p.

Maritain, Jacques. THE EDUCATION OF MAN. Edited with an introduction by Donald and Idella Gallagher. Notre Dame, Ind.: University of Notre Dame Press, 1967. Reprint. Westport, Conn.: Greenwood Press, 1976. 191 p.

Redden, John D., and Ryan, Francis A. A CATHOLIC PHILOSOPHY OF EDUCATION. Rev. ed. Milwaukee, Wis.: Bruce Publishing, 1956. 601 p.

> While the outcomes of Vatican II require a restatement of the principles elaborated in this text, this classic does link metaphysics with education and derives a Catholic philosophy of education from a Catholic philosophy of life. Book 1 thoroughly analyzes basic philosophical principles and their educational applications; book 2 critically reviews the educational consequences of naturalism, socialism, nationalism, communism, and experimentalism. It is an important reference for purposes of comparative study.

Rombach, Heinrich. ASPECKTE DER PERSONALEN PAEDAGOGIK. [Aspects of education and the person]. Freiburg, W. Ger.: Verlag Herder, 1959. 81 p.

> Through his philosophy of education, Otto Willmann achieved a threefold synthesis between the personal and societal aspects of education, between the reality of an abiding human nature and historical tradition or transmission of human culture, and between subjective and objective values. Rombach also notes a threefold crisis in contemporary education that concerns the nature of human society, the nature of education itself, and the nature of human values. Willmann can still make significant contributions toward the solutions of each crisis.

Weinschenk, Reinhold. FRANZ XAVER EGGERSDORFER (1879-1958) UND SEIN SYSTEM DER ALLGEMEINEN ERZIEHUNGSLEHRE. [Eggersdorfer and his theory of general education]. Paderborn, W. Ger.: F. Schoeningh, 1972. x, 267 p.

> Eggersdorfer was a disciple of Otto Willmann and carried forward much of his mentor's thinking in elaborating a Catholic philosophy of education of his own. This study gives a critical review of his life and work, of his pedagogical synthesis, and of the philosophical presuppositions that led to his theory of general education.

Philosophies of Education

Comenius, John Amos

Sadler, John Edward. J.A. COMENIUS AND THE CONCEPT OF UNIVER-
SAL EDUCATION. London: Allen and Unwin; New York: Barnes and Noble,
1966. 318 p.

Schaller, Klaus. JAN AMOS KOMENSKY. [John Amos Comenius].
Heidelberg, W. Ger.: Quelle and Meyer, 1970. 147 p.

> The life and work of Comenius are assessed for the present in
> eleven essays written by educational thinkers from Czechoslovakia,
> Norway, Holland, Italy, and Germany. THE GREAT DIDACTIC
> of Comenius is at once the product of his genius as an educa-
> tional philosopher and of his humane and Christian character.
> Kingsley Price considers him an early and probably leading Protes-
> tant writer in the philosophy of education.

Dewey, John

This section is arranged alphabetically of works by Dewey, about Dewey, and
then general works.

Dewey, John. JOHN DEWEY ON EDUCATION: SELECTED WRITINGS.
Edited by Reginald D. Archambault. The Modern Library. New York: Random
House, 1964. 439 p.

> A collection, in systematic form, of Dewey's major writings in
> education, together with basic philosophic statements in regard to
> (1) philosophy and education, (2) ethics and education, (3) aes-
> thetics and education, (4) science and education, (5) psychology
> and education, (6) society and education, and (7) principles of
> pedagogy.

Baker, Melvin Charles. FOUNDATIONS OF JOHN DEWEY'S EDUCATIONAL
THEORY. Oxford and New York: King's Crown Press, 1955. 214 p.

Boydston, Jo Ann, ed. GUIDE TO THE WORKS OF JOHN DEWEY.
Carbondale: Southern Illinois University Press, 1972. 413 p.

Dewey, John. MY PEDAGOGIC CREED. With "The Demands of Sociology
upon Pedagogy," by Albion W. Small. 1897. New York and Chicago: E.L.
Kellog; Photocopy at Ann Arbor, Mich.: University Microfilms, 1972. 36 p.

_____. THE PHILOSOPHY OF JOHN DEWEY. 2 vols. Edited with intro-
duction, notes, and commentary by John J. McDermott. New York: G.P.
Putnam's Sons, 1973.

> Volume 1: THE STRUCTURE OF EXPERIENCE. xli, 354 p.
>
> Volume 2: THE LIVED EXPERIENCE. xli, 355-723 p.

"There remains a need for a sustained work which applies the critical perspectives of Feinberg and Karier to the thought and action
of . . .progressives like Dewey or Counts" (Wayne J. Urban,
HARVARD EDUCATIONAL REVIEW 45, no. 4 [1975]: 557).

_____. THE SCHOOL AND SOCIETY. 1899. Chicago: University of
Chicago Press, 1961. 158 p.

As an embryonic and miniature society, the school functions as a
community seeking to master the ways of common and productive
activity. Cooperation soon replaces competition, mutual exchange
rules out passivity, subject matter assumes social meanings,
learning becomes real life doing. In the solving of problems, the
young learn to live harmoniously in a spirit of service and to engage in effective self-direction. Jane M. Dewey believes this is
"the most widely read and influential of Dewey's writing," p. 28.

Thomas, Milton Halsey. JOHN DEWEY: A CENTENNIAL BIBLIOGRAPHY.
1929. Chicago: University of Chicago Press, 1962. xiii, 370 p.

This indispensable publication gives, in chronological order, the
published writings of Dewey and a second listing, alphabetically
by author, of writings about John Dewey. Most accept this bibliography as the best and most comprehensive.

Dilthey, Wilhelm. SCHRIFTEN ZUR PAEDAGOGIK. [Pedagogical writings].
Prepared by Hans-Hermann Groothoff and Ulrich Herrmann. Paderborn, W.
Ger.: F. Schoeningh, 1971. 422 p. Bibliog.

Reprinted are the texts of Dilthey's GESAMMELTE SCHRIFTEN and
his KLEINEN PAEDAGOGISCHEN TEXTE. His lectures on education are supplemented with the findings of more recent research
from psychology, ethics, and philosophy. The treatment is both
historical and systematic. The bibliography is on pages 366–403.

Dunkel, Harold Baker, comp. WHITEHEAD ON EDUCATION. Columbus:
Ohio State University Press, 1965. xvi, 182 p.

Frankena, William K. PHILOSOPHY OF EDUCATION. New York:
Macmillan, 1965. 116 p.

By way of introducing the reader to the thought of Dewey,
Maritain, Whitehead, and Peters, Frankena explores education
first philosophically, according to principles, nature, aims, and
then programmatically in terms of systems, methods, and problems.

Gribble, James. INTRODUCTION TO PHILOSOPHY OF EDUCATION.
Boston: Allyn and Bacon, 1969. 198 p.

Guil Blanes, Francisco. FILOSOFIA Y SOCIOLOGIA DE LA EDUCACION.
Madrid: Editorial Magisterio Espanol, 1969. 336 p.

Philosophies of Education

Hegel, Georg Wilhelm Friedrich. ANSICHTEN UEBER ERZIEHUNG UND
UNTERRICHT. [Views on education and curriculum]. 1853-54. 3 parts in
1 vol. Reprint. Selected and systematically arranged by Gustav Thaulow.
Introduction to Hegel's philosophy of education by Heinz-Joachim Heydorn.
Glashutten im Taunus: D. Auvermann, 1974.

Henry, Nelson B., ed. FORTY-FIRST YEARBOOK OF THE NATIONAL
SOCIETY FOR THE STUDY OF EDUCATION. Part 1. PHILOSOPHIES OF
EDUCATION. Chicago: University of Chicago Press, 1942. xi, 321 p.

> The essays by Reisner ("Philosophy and Science"), Kilpatrick
> ("Experimentalism"), Breed ("Realism"), Horne ("Idealism"), Adler
> ("In Defense of the Philosophy of Education"), McGucken
> ("Philosophy of Catholic Education"), and Brubacher ("Comparative
> Philosophy of Education") are required readings for a fuller under-
> standing of the antecedents and significance of modern philosophi-
> cal positions in education.

_____. FIFTY-FOURTH YEARBOOK OF THE NATIONAL SOCIETY FOR THE
STUDY OF EDUCATION. Part 1. MODERN PHILOSOPHIES OF EDUCATION.
Chicago: University of Chicago Press, 1955. x, 374 p.

> The chapters, written under the direction of John S. Brubacher,
> by Wild, Maritain, Greene, Geiger, Feigl, and Feibleman are
> primary sources for their thought.

Herbart, Johann Friedrich

This section is arranged alphabetically of works by Herbart, about Herbart,
and then general works.

Herbart, Johann Friedrich. ALLGEMEINE PAEDAGOGIK AUS DEM ZWECK
DER ERZIEHUNG ABGELEITET. [The science of education: its general prin-
ciples deduced from its aims]. Edited by Hermann Holstein. Bochum, W.
Ger.: Kamp, 1965. 202 p.

Wittenbruch, Wilhelm. DIE PAEDAGOGIK WILHELM REINS: EINE
UNTERSUCHUNG ZUM SPAETHERBARTIANISMUS. [The educational theory of
Wilhelm Rein: an investigation into late Herbartianism]. Ratingen, W. Ger.;
Kastellaun, W. Ger.; and Dusseldorf, W. Ger.: Henn, 1972. xii, 612 p.

> Contrary to the excessive individualism of Locke and Rousseau,
> Rein (1847-1915) elaborated a social philosophy of education
> rooted in the genius and ethical-religious character of the social
> agencies of education. Many leaders in American education
> attended Rein's lectures at the University of Jena.

Howick, William H. PHILOSOPHIES OF WESTERN EDUCATION. Danville,
Ill.: Interstate Printers and Publishers, 1971. 123 p.

Jarrett, James Louis, ed. PHILOSOPHY FOR THE STUDY OF EDUCATION. Boston: Houghton Mifflin, 1969. ix, 473 p. Bibliog.

Reprinted are whole works or quasi-autonomous selections of long works by Plato, Aristotle, Quintilian, Augustine, Aquinas, Montaigne, Comenius, Descartes, Locke, Rousseau, Kant, Froebel, Newman, Mill, Spencer, James, Dewey, Whitehead, Russell, Buber, and Ryle. The texts were chosen for their importance today and for the help they can furnish the reader with little previous experience in the study of philosophy.

Kanz, Heinrich. EINFUEHRUNG IN DIE PAEDAGOGISCHE PHILOSOPHIE. [Introduction to educational philosophy]. 2d ed. Wuppertal, W. Ger.; Ratingen, W. Ger.; and Kastellaun, W.Ger.: Henn, 1971. 228 p.

Klafki, Wolfgang. STUDIEN ZUR BILDUNGSTHEORIE UND DIDAKTIK. [Studies on the theory of liberal education and the art of teaching]. 8th and 9th eds. Weinhem/Bergstr., W. Ger.: Beltz, 1967. 153 p.

Kneller, George Frederick. INTRODUCTION TO THE PHILOSOPHY OF EDUCATION. 2d ed. New York: John Wiley and Sons, 1971. viii, 118 p.

Koenig, Eckard. THEORIE DER ERZIEHUNGSWISSENSCHAFT. [A theory of education]. 3 vols. Munich: Fink, 1975.

Volume 1: WISSENSCHAFTSTHEORETISCHE RICHTUNGEN DER PAEDAGOGIK. [Theoretical principles of education]. 1975. 221 p.

Volume 2: NORMATIVE SAETZE. [Normative theorems]. Forthcoming.

Volume 3: ERZIEHUNGSWISSENSCHAFT ALS PRAKTISCHE DISZIPLIN. [Education as a practical discipline]. Forthcoming.

Langford, Glenn. PHILOSOPHY AND EDUCATION: AN INTRODUCTION. London: Macmillan, 1971. 160 p.

Locke, John

This section is arranged alphabetically of works by Locke, about Locke, and then general works.

Locke, John. JOHN LOCKE ON EDUCATION. 1693. Edited by Peter Gay. Reprint. New York: Bureau of Publications, Teachers College, Columbia University, 1964. vi, 176 p.

Locke's empiricism and environmentalism are amply reflected in these thoughts concerning education. Locke's educational thinking is still an important factor in current discussions of educational philosophy.

Sahakian, William S., and Sahakian, Mabel Lewis. JOHN LOCKE. Boston: Twayne Publishers, 1975. 143 p.

Stille, Oswald. DIE PAEDAGOGIK JOHN LOCKE IN DER TRADITION DER GENTLEMAN-ERZIEHUNG. [John Locke and the education of a gentleman]. Erlangen, W. Ger.: Universitat Erlangen-Nurnberg, 1971. 521 p.

Mackie, Margaret. EDUCATION IN THE INQUIRING SOCIETY: AN INTRODUCTION TO THE PHILOSOPHY OF EDUCATION. Hawthorn and Melbourne: Australian Council for Educational Research, 1966. 147 p.

Magee, John B. PHILOSOPHICAL ANALYSIS IN EDUCATION. New York: Macmillan, 1969; Harper and Row, 1971. xii, 189 p. Paperbound.

> Develops an appreciation for the analytic philosophy of education with an understanding of some implications for teaching-learning, curriculum, values, and democracy.

Marler, Charles Dennis. PHILOSOPHY AND SCHOOLING. Boston: Allyn and Bacon, 1975. xii, 396 p.

> This commonly used text presents the basic philosophical systems in American education in terms of the problems of human and non-human reality (metaphysics), knowledge and truth (epistemology), value and morality (axiology), the individual and society (social philosophy and ideologies), the possibilities or implications for educational policy and practice (applied philosophy of education).

Martin, William Oliver. REALISM IN EDUCATION. New York: Harper and Row, 1969. x, 198 p. Paperbound.

> In the Aristotelian mode, Martin approaches the nature of learning and teaching through the material, formal, efficient, and final causes of education. This ultimately becomes the structure for an educational philosophy of realism.

Marx, Karl

This section is arranged alphabetically of works by Marx, about Marx, and then general works.

Marx, Karl. BILDUNG UND ERZIEHUNG. [Education in theory and practice]. Selected and edited by Horst E. Wittig. Paderborn, W. Ger.: F. Schoeningh, 1968. 392 p.

Ch'ien, Chuen-jui. EDUCATIONAL THEORY IN THE PEOPLE'S REPUBLIC OF CHINA. Commentary and translation by John N. Hawkins. Honolulu: University of Hawaii Press, 1971. 122 p.

Macdonald, John. A PHILOSOPHY OF EDUCATION. Glenview, Ill.: Scott, Foresman, 1965. viii, 285 p.; Toronto: W.J. Gage, 1965. viii, 279 p.

Part 1 states the universals or constants of educational philosophy; part 2 distinguishes the significant contemporary from the ephemeral values of educational philosophy; and part 3 contains notes on idealism, pragmatism, realism, materialism, scientism, logical positivism, Marxism, positivism, and their educational bearings. [Cf. Broudy-Smith (1969), cited in chapter 13, p. 8].

Morris, Van Cleve. EXISTENTIALISM IN EDUCATION: WHAT IT MEANS. New York: Harper and Row, 1966. x, 163 p. Paperbound.

Dwelling on human subjectivity, the paradox and anxiety of human living, the existentialist seeks to affirm the self by confronting nothingness, freedom, other men, and even God. Because the place from which the meaning of life begins is necessarily the self, existential education incurs the responsibility of awakening each individual to the full intensity of his own selfhood.

Munizaga, Aguirre Roberto. PRINCIPIOS DE EDUCACION. 3d ed. Santiago, Chile: Editorial Universitaria, [1965]. 252 p.

Netzer, Hans. ERZIEHUNGSLEHRE. [Educational theory and practice]. 10th ed. Bad Heilbrunn/Obb., W. Ger.: Klinkhardt, 1972. 220 p.

Nock, Albert Jay. THE THEORY OF EDUCATION IN THE UNITED STATES. 1932. New York: Arno Press, 1969. 160 p.

Ozmon, Howard, and Craver, Sam. PHILOSOPHICAL FOUNDATIONS OF EDUCATION Columbus, Ohio: Charles E. Merrill, 1976. xi, 239. Bibliogs.

Ozmon draws out the nature and consequences of educational prin-ciples by a study of idealism, realism, pragmatism, reconstruction-ism, behaviorism, existentialism, and analytic philosophy.

Peters, Richard Stanley, ed. THE PHILOSOPHY OF EDUCATION. London: Oxford University Press, 1973. 278 p.

Peterson, Francis Edwin. PHILOSOPHIES OF EDUCATION CURRENT IN THE PREPARATION OF TEACHERS IN THE UNITED STATES. New York: Bureau of Publications, Teachers College, Columbia University, 1933. Reprint. New York: AMS Press, 1972. v, 147 p.

This study involved four state teachers colleges, twelve normal schools, and nine liberal arts colleges.

Petruzzellis, Nicola. I PROBLEMI DELLA PEDAGOGIA COME SCIENZA FILOSOFICA. 6th ed. Naples: Giannini, 1973. 577 p.

Phenix, Philip H. PHILOSOPHY OF EDUCATION. New York: Holt, Rinehart and Winston, 1958. 623 p.

> The reader must remain ever alert to the author's form of monism and to his lack of documentation (in order not to distract from the ideas themselves), particularly when specific citations are required for the objective evaluation of sources and doctrines. The discussions on the school, the curriculum, and the profession of education are balanced and expert.

Plato

This section is arranged alphabetically of works by Plato, about Plato, and then general works.

Plato. THE COLLECTED DIALOGUES OF PLATO INCLUDING THE LETTERS. Edited by Edith Hamilton and Huntington Cairns with introduction and prefatory notes. Bollingen Series 71. Princeton: Princeton University Press, 1961. xxv, 1,743 p.

> The general excellence of the translations and the inclusion of all the writings of Plato believed to be authentic make this volume a required purchase. The Abbott-Knight index (pp. 1609-1743) has been entirely remade for the present edition and, outside the concordances in Greek, the cross references are superb for tracing any Platonic idea through all his dialogues. This writer has carefully checked the translations with the original Greek and rates them comparable to those of Cornford and Lee and better than most others.

_____. THE REPUBLIC OF PLATO. 2d ed. 2 vols. Edited with critical notes, commentary, and appendixes by James Adam. Introduction by D.A. Rees. Cambridge: Cambridge University Press, 1963.

> Volume 1: Introduction and books 1-5. lviii, 364 p.
>
> Volume 2: Books 4-10 and indexes. 532 p.
>
> For those who can or wish to read the Greek original, this work is a necessary purchase. It still remains the most detailed and valuable critical edition available in English. So many poor translations abound, in which Plato is made to speak as someone from the nineteenth century, that the effort to learn the Greek is self-compensating. The notes, commentary, appendixes, and indexes in both Greek and English make this work indispensable to the Platonic scholar.

Boyd, William. AN INTRODUCTION TO THE REPUBLIC OF PLATO. 1904. New ed. London: Allen and Unwin, 1962; New York: Barnes and Noble, 1963. 115 p.

Cushman, Robert E. THERAPEIA: PLATO'S CONCEPTION OF PHILOSOPHY.

Chapel Hill: University of North Carolina Press, 1958. xxii, 322 p.

Since the ignorance of man flows from a total disorientation of life and thought, therapeia seeks to effect a conversion, or transformation of man by reestablishing the harmony of the affections with the soul and by orienting the mind rightly with prime reality. The union of this highest knowledge with virtue distinguishes the person of wisdom and happiness. In this respect, paideia is the therapeutic means of redirecting the cognition of reality through the transformation of the affections. Cushman offers a most profound understanding of Plato's fundamental educational philosophy.

Pongratz, Ludwig J., ed. PAEDAGOGIK IN SELBSTDARSTELLUNGEN. [Educators present their views]. 3 vols.-- . Hamburg: Felix Meiner Verlag.

This work of primary source materials has so far appeared in three volumes:

Volume 1: CONTRIBUTIONS BY BLAETTNER, BOHNENKAMP, BOLLNOW, CASELMANN, FELDMANN, KEILHACKER, SIMON. 1975. ix, 342 p.

Volume 2: CONTRIBUTIONS BY BORINSKI, DERBOLAV, FLITNER, KERN, RANG, RITZEL, TH. WILHELM. 1976. iv, 356 p.

Volume 3: CONTRIBUTIONS BY EDDING, ENGLERT, KREITMAIR, LANGEVELD, LENNERT, LOEBNER, LOCHNER, REBLE, SCHULTZE. 1978. Forthcoming.

Price, Kingsley. EDUCATION AND PHILOSOPHICAL THOUGHT. 2d ed. Boston: Allyn and Bacon, 1967. xiv, 605 p.

This study is a literate exposition of principal educational theories by Plato, Quintilian, Augustine, Aquinas, Comenius, Locke, Rousseau, Kant, Herbart, Mill, and Dewey with brief selections of their writings. Each is introduced by an encompassing essay and then the common elements of these theories are compared for their insights into goal objectives, human nature, training programs, and the philosophy of education.

Protestant Christianity

Fuller, Edmund, ed. THE CHRISTIAN IDEA OF EDUCATION. Papers and discussions by William G. Pollard et al. 1957. Reprint. Hamden, Conn.: Archon Books, 1975. xv, 265 p.

Horne, Herman H. THE DEMOCRATIC PHILOSOPHY OF EDUCATION. 1932. New York: Macmillan, 1960. xxiii, 547 p.

Opposed to the pragmatism of his time and its implied materialism, Horne endeavored to unite his Christian outlook with a return to basic ideals and values as the prerequisite for education in a democracy. This classic is also an important commentary of, and ought to be studied in conjunction with, Dewey's DEMOCRACY AND EDUCATION.

Schuessler, Roland. PAEDAGOGISCHE DENKSTRUKTUREN UND CHRISTLICHE SCHULERZIEHUNG. [Pedagogical thought-structures and Christian education]. Hildesheim, W. Ger.: Gerstenberg, 1973. 515 p.

Schuessler attempts to erect what he calls the normative structures of religious education particularly on the foundations of Protestant Christianity. From the premises of this philosophy of education, he then suggests a solution to the general problematic of Christian education in this age.

Reid, Louis Arnoud. PHILOSOPHY AND EDUCATION: AN INTRODUCTION. Salem, N.H.: Heineman Educational Books, 1962. 244 p.; New York: Random House, 1965. xv, 203 p.

Reid surveys the nature of philosophy, philosophical assumptions, values, theory and practice, freedom and the self, and the professional preparation of teaching personnel. Chapter 1 explains philosophical methods analytically. [Cf. Broudy (1967), cited in chapter 13, pp. 221, 256].

Reitman, Sandford W. FOUNDATIONS OF EDUCATION FOR PROSPECTIVE TEACHERS. Boston: Allyn and Bacon, 1977. 471 p.

After examining the perspectives and the underlying meaning of education in society, Reitman submits to scrutiny the purposes, models, agencies, values, and goals of education in this transitional age. The concluding sections aim to show how these educational purposes can be realized.

Riestra, Miguel A. FUNDAMENTOS FILOSOFICOS DE LA EDUCACION. 4th ed. San Juan: Editorial Universitaria, Universidad de Puerto Rico, 1976. 317 p.

Rubio, Latorre Rafael. EDUCACION Y EDUCADOR EL PENSAMIENTO DE UNAMUNO. Salamanca, Spain: Edicion Instituto Pontificio San Pio X, 1974. 156 p.

Schweyen, Renate. GUARINO VERONESE: PHILOSOPHIE UND HUMANIST. Munich: Fink, 1973. 268 p.

Shermis, Sherwin Samuel. PHILOSOPHIC FOUNDATIONS OF EDUCATION. New York: American Book, 1967. ix, 292 p.

The author examines the assumptions of educational philosophy through the traditional philosophical categories of metaphysics, epistemology, axiology, and social philosophy. Since World War

II, Shermis finds growing interest in idealism and linguistic analysis as the two major trends in contemporary educational philosophy.

Smith, Philip G. PHILOSOPHY OF EDUCATION: INTRODUCTORY STUDIES. New York: Harper and Row, 1965. x, 276 p.

Each chapter treats a specific question: what is philosophy? what is education? what is knowledge? what is science? what are structures of knowledge? what is value? what is man? and what is democracy? Smith distinguishes, in chapter 3, the ways of linking philosophy to education. Philosophy, he states, "analyzes the total discipline into philosophy and education, philosophy in education, philosophy for education, and philosophy of education." Smith shows how educational theory does shape and influence school practice. Additional readings are suggested at the end of each chapter. [See Broudy (1967), cited in chapter 13, pp. 209, 260].

Taylor, Albert J. AN INTRODUCTION TO THE PHILOSOPHY OF EDUCATION. Dubuque, Iowa: Kendall/Hunt Publishing, 1975. viii, 194 p.

Thompson, Keith. EDUCATION AND PHILOSOPHY: A PRACTICAL APPROACH. Oxford: Blackwell; New York: Halsted Press Division, 1972. x, 169 p.

Ulich, Robert. FUNDAMENTALS OF DEMOCRATIC EDUCATION: AN INTRODUCTION TO EDUCATIONAL PHILOSOPHY. 1940. Reprint. Westport, Conn.: Greenwood Press, 1970. x, 362

Voudoures, Konstantinos Ioannou. PHILOSOPHIA TES PAIDEIAS. [Philosophy of education]. Athens: n.p., 1975. 110 p.

Wegener, Frank Corliss. THE ORGANIC PHILOSOPHY OF EDUCATION. Dubuque, Iowa: Wm. C. Brown, 1957. Reprint. Westport, Conn.: Greenwood Press, 1974. xx, 472 p.

Weisskopf, Traugott. IMMANUEL KANT UND DIE PAEDAGOGIK. Zurich: EVZ-Verlag Abt.-Editio Academica, 1970. xix, 704 p.

Willmann, Otto

Hamann, Bruno. DIE GRUNDLAGEN DER PAEDAGOGIK. [The foundations of education]. Freiburg, W. Ger.: Verlag Herder, 1965. x, 238 p.

The author systematically investigates Willmann's understanding of the philosophical, sociological, and religious foundations of education. Hamann demonstrates how Willmann establishes the philo-

sophy of education as a full-fledged science. Critical to
Willmann's system is his conception of wisdom as the inspiriting of a
human person through liberal and moral education.

Moritz, Franz. ENTSTEHUNG UND ENTWICKLUNG DES GUETERBEGRIFFES
IN DER PAEDAGOGIK OTTO WILLMANNS. [The origin and development of
Otto Willmann's concept of values in education]. Munich: Ludwig-
Maximilians-Universitaet, 1960. vi, 321 p.

Willmann ranks values vertically, in the order of their importance,
from the material to the intellectual, moral, and spiritual-religious.
This vertical hierarchy is complemented by a horizontal ordering
that embraces both the personal-individual and the social values
of life and education. Values are transcendental when they
perfect men and unite men with God.

Pfeffer, Fritz. DIE PAEDAGOGISCHE IDEE OTTO WILLMANNS IN DER
ENTWICKLUNG. [The development of Otto Willmann's concept of education].
Freiburg, W. Ger.: Verlag Herder, 1962. xi, 219 p.

Otto Willmann establishes the philosophy of education as the
science of educational purposes and values that concentrates its
study on the nature of man and reality, on the nature and being
of cultural and intellectual transmission of ideals and excellences.
Willmann was the pioneer investigator into the sociological foundations of education.

Willmann, Otto. DIDAKTIK ALS BILDUNGSLEHRE: NACH IHREN
BEZIEHUNGEN ZUR SOZIALFORSCHUNG UND ZUR GESCHICHTE DER
BILDUNG. [The science of education: relationships to the sociological and
historical aspects of liberal education]. 6th ed. Freiburg, W. Ger.: Verlag
Herder, 1957. xxxvi, 677 p.

This latest edition in German has a review of Willmann's life and
career (1839-1920) written by F.X. Eggersdorfer. Part 1 is a
unique synopsis of the historical types of education. The remaining four parts examine, in order, the motives and aims of education, the content of education, the process of education, and the
system of education. A concluding section summarizes the philosophy of education from the viewpoint of Christian ethics.

_____. KLEINE PAEDAGOGISCHE SCHRIFTEN. [Essays in education].
Arranged and edited by Joseph Antz and Eugen Schoelen. Paderborn, W. Ger.:
F. Schoeningh, 1959. 232 p.

The essays are grouped around three important areas in the philosophy of education: the foundations of education, the instructional
content and educative form, the history and philosophy of intellectual and moral education. Notes and observations explain key
ideas in the texts.

_____. THE SCIENCE OF EDUCATION IN ITS SOCIOLOGICAL AND HIS-TORICAL ASPECTS. Translated from 5th German edition by Felix M. Kirsch. 2d ed. Latrobe, Pa.: Archabbey Press, 1930. vol. 1: xvi, 358; vol. 2: xxiii, 493 p.

> Willmann constructs the science of education as a process that is discernible in both (1) the systems of education which represent the collective efforts of human society and (2) the personal acquiring of an education which represents the efforts of the individual. The work concludes with a profoundly reasoned synthesis of education in its relation to the sum total and full circle of life's responsibilities.

Woods, Ronald George, and Barrow, Robin St. C. AN INTRODUCTION TO PHILOSOPHY OF EDUCATION. London: Methuen; distributed by Harper and Row, 1975. 200 p.

Xochellis, Panagiotis (Panos). PAEDAGOGISCHE GRUNDBEGRIFFE: EINE EINFUEHRUNG IN DIE PAEDAGOGIK. [Fundamental ideas in education: an introduction to education]. 4th ed. Munich: Ehrenwirth, 1973. 148 p.

CRITICAL ISSUES

Agazzi, Aldo. I PROBLEMI DELL'EDUCAZIONE E DELLA PEDAGOGIA. Milan: Vita e Pensiero, 1975. 275 p.

Allen, Dwight William, and Hecht, Jeffrey C. CONTROVERSIES IN EDUCA-TION. Philadelphia: W.B. Saunders, 1974. xxvi, 549 p.

Allison, Clinton B., ed. WITHOUT CONSENSUS: ISSUES IN AMERICAN EDUCATION. Boston: Allyn and Bacon, 1973. 394 p.

Bandman, Bertram. THE PLACE OF REASON IN EDUCATION. Columbus: Ohio State University Press, 1967. 200 p.

> Bandman states the arguments for believing that the problems and issues of education are explicable chiefly through rational argument, whether moral or metaphysical or both.

Barrow, Robin St. Clair. RADICAL EDUCATION: A CRITIQUE OF FREE-SCHOOLING AND DESCHOOLING. New York: John Wiley and Sons, 1978. 207 p.

> Critically analyzes the thought of Rousseau, A.S. Neil, Paul Goodman, Everett Reimer, Ivan Illich, Neil Postman, and Charles Weingartner in regard to such key concepts as nature, reality, knowledge, and their radical perceptions of them.

Bell, Bernard Iddings. THE CRISIS IN EDUCATION: A CHALLENGE TO AMERICAN COMPLACENCY. 1949. New York: McGraw-Hill, 1961. ix, 237 p.

Despite his writing a generation ago, Bell's observations and recommendations are still very timely.

Berlin, Sir Isaiah. RUSSIAN THINKERS. New York: Viking Press, 1978. 336 p.

The eleven essays, of which an important one is "The Hedgehog and the Fox," seek to still a gnawing question: are men of the twentieth century so insecure with diverse and free philosophies of life that they prefer the sometimes enslaving determinism of a uniquely controlled and all-embracing mode of living?

Brackenbury, Robert Leo. GETTING DOWN TO CASES: A PROBLEM APPROACH TO EDUCATIONAL PHILOSOPHIZING. New York: G.P. Putnam's Sons, 1959. 222 p.

Brauner, Charles J., and Burns, Hobert W. PROBLEMS IN EDUCATION AND PHILOSOPHY. Englewood Cliffs, N.J.: Prentice-Hall, 1965. 165 p.

Broudy, Harry S., et al. PHILOSOPHY OF EDUCATION: AN ORGANIZATION OF TOPICS AND SELECTED SOURCES. Urbana: University of Illinois Press, 1967. xii, 287 p. Paperbound.

The preface and first two chapters raise issues that have implications for the entire field of educational philosophy: the reality of such a thing as the philosophy of education, the differences in quality of courses in philosophy of education, the competence of those who teach such courses, their value in teacher preparation, the schemata for a professional curriculum and the organization of topics and materials, the problems and assumptions of classification, defining the philosophy of education as making explicit the relevance of philosophy to the problems of education, and the extent of necessary training in general philosophy.

Brumbaugh, Robert S., and Lawrence, Nathaniel M. PHILOSOPHICAL THEMES IN MODERN EDUCATION. Boston: Houghton Mifflin, 1973. x, 294 p. Paperbound.

These essays complement the authors' previous study, PHILOSOPHERS ON EDUCATION (1963), and are divided into two categories: (1) "Theories of Learning and Knowledge" (Hippias, Augustine, Descartes, Locke, and Hume) and (2) "Theories of Human Nature and Personality" (Freud, Neill, Skinner, Piaget, and Bruner-Erikson-Jones).

Cave, Donald, ed. PROBLEMS IN EDUCATION: A PHILOSOPHICAL

APPROACH. Stanmore, N.S.W.: Cassell Australia, 1976. xiii, 183 p.

Cirigliano, Gustavo F. TEMAS DE FILOSOFIA DE LA EDUCACION. Maracaibo, Venezuela: Departamento de Ciencias Pedagogicas, Escuela de Educacion, Facultad de Humanidades y Educacion, Universidad del Zulia, 1965. 123 p.

Clifford, Geraldine Joncich. THE SHAPE OF AMERICAN EDUCATION. Englewood Cliffs, N.J.: Prentice-Hall, 1975. 272 p.

> Clifford exposes the myths and the existing habits of mind and behavior which grip both the defenders and the attackers of contemporary American education. She gives an understanding of education as a social institution and as an American achievement.

Corallo, Gino. L'EDUCAZIONE: PROBLEMI DI PEDAGOGIA. Turin, Italy: Societa Editrice Internazionale, 1961. 511 p.

Counts, George Sylvester. THE CHALLENGE OF SOVIET EDUCATION. 1957. Westport, Conn.: Greenwood Press, 1975. xi, 330 p.

Craig, Robert P., ed. ISSUES IN PHILOSOPHY AND EDUCATION. New York: MSS Information, 1974. 128 p.

> The selections are written by Rogers, Skinner, Broudy, Craig, Scudder, Hook, Strike, Neff, and others.

Derbolav, Josef. FRAGE UND ANSPRUCH. PAEDAGOG. STUDIEN UND ANALYSEN. [Inquiry and response. Educational essays and analyses]. Wuppertal, W. Ger.; Ratingen, W. Ger.; and Dusseldorf, W. Ger.: Henn, 1970. 447 p.

Dottrens, Robert. LA CRISE DE L'EDUCATION ET SES REMEDES. Neuchatel: Delachaux and Niestle, 1971. 173 p.

Doyle, James F., ed. EDUCATIONAL JUDGMENTS: PAPERS IN THE PHILOSOPHY OF EDUCATION. London and Boston: Routledge and Kegan Paul, 1973. x, 265 p. Paperbound ed., 1975. 276 p.

> The reader enjoys a fine opportunity to philosophize with distinguished contemporary thinkers as they comment on each other's positions. Who can resist a professional discussion with Doyle, Frankena, Gewirth, Kaufman, Pincoffs, Baier, Broudy, Price, Peters, Feinberg, Olafson, Melden, Scheffler, and Edel? The dialogs will raise the level of the reader's competence.

Dropkin, Stan; Full, Harold; and Schwarcz, Ernest. CONTEMPORARY AMERI-

CAN EDUCATION: AN ANTHOLOGY OF ISSUES, PROBLEMS,
CHALLENGES. 2d ed. New York: Macmillan, 1970. xi, 563 p.

Dunkel, Harold Baker. HERBART AND EDUCATION. New York: Random
House, 1969. 146 p. Bibliog. Paperbound.

Dunkel summarizes, with criticism useful to the beginner,
Herbart's pedagogy as an integral part of his total philosophic system, his ethical theory as revealing the aims of education, and
his psychology as both specifying the means to ethical goals and
justifying the educational program.

Eacker, Jay N. PROBLEMS OF PHILOSOPHY AND PSYCHOLOGY. Chicago:
Nelson-Hall, 1975. 201 p.

The problems discussed in this introductory text have far-reaching
ramifications in educational philosophy: mind-body problem, metaphysics, reification, explanation, causality, theory, laws and principles, anthropomorphism, purpose, freedom, knowledge, induction,
and the fact-value dilemma.

Ehlers, Henry, et al., eds. CRUCIAL ISSUES IN EDUCATION. 6th ed.
New York: Holt, Rinehart and Winston, 1977. xiii, 305 p.

The claims of outstanding educators are juxtaposed with reference
to reason in education, equalizing educational opportunity, providing new and varied ways for learning, emphasizing values, and
related issues. About seventy-five authors with opposing points of
view provide a unique forum within which to engage in critical
philosophical thinking about education.

Elzer, Hans-Michael. PHILOSOPHISCHE VERGEWISSERUNG: FRAGEN ZUR
PAEDAGOGIK UND IHRER THEORIE. [Philosophical verification: questions
pertinent to educational theory]. Ratingen, W. Ger.; Kastellaun, W. Ger.;
and Dusseldorf, W. Ger.: Henn, 1974. 246 p.

These thirteen essays, written between 1949 and 1966, are critical
discussions over present disagreements about the content, the conditions, the validity, and the political relevance of education and
its claims. Any attempt to answer these questions involves educational theory.

Ewers, Michael. BILDUNGSKRITIK UND BIOLOGIEDIDAKTIK. [Educational
criticism and biological instruction]. Frankfort on the Main, W. Ger.:
Athenaeum-Fischer-Taschenbuecher, 1974. 128 p.

Feinberg, Walter, and Rosemont, Henry. WORK, TECHNOLOGY, AND
EDUCATION: DISSENTING ESSAYS IN THE INTELLECTUAL FOUNDATIONS
OF AMERICAN EDUCATION. Urbana: University of Illinois Press, 1975.
222 p.

Full, Harold, ed. CONTROVERSY IN AMERICAN EDUCATION: AN AN-THOLOGY OF CRUCIAL ISSUES. 2d ed. New York: Macmillan, 1972. xv, 422 p.

Full has edited fifty-three essays.

Goodlad, John I. FACING THE FUTURE: ISSUES IN EDUCATION AND SCHOOLING. Introduction by Ralph W. Tyler. Papers selected by Judith S. Golub. New York: McGraw-Hill, 1976. 274 p.

Topics include curriculum reform, setting goals, restructuring teacher education, computers and the schools, desegregating inte-grated schools, educational alternatives, and other questions dis-cussed by Goodlad since his SCHOOL, CURRICULUM, AND THE INDIVIDUAL.

Harris, Alan Edward. THINKING ABOUT EDUCATION. London: Heinemann Educational, 1970. ix, 118 p.

Heitger, Marian, in collaboration with Heinz-Juergen Ipfling. PAEDAGOG-ISCHE GRUNDPROBLEME IN TRANZENDENTALKRITISCHER SICHT. [Funda-mental educational problems in their transcendental-critical aspect]. Bad Heilbrunn/Obb, W. Ger.: Klinkhardt, 1969. 132 p.

Kolesnik, Walter B. HUMANISM AND/OR BEHAVIORISM IN EDUCATION. Boston: Allyn and Bacon, 1975. 170 p.

Major topics include common criticisms of education, the basic principles and assumptions of humanism and behaviorism, the application of humanism and behaviorism as a means of correcting the criticisms of education.

Kroll, Arthur M., ed. ISSUES IN AMERICAN EDUCATION. New York: Oxford University Press, 1970. 208 p.

Lambruschini, Raffaello. DELLA EDUCAZIONE. Edited by Mario Casotti. 14th ed. Brescia, Italy: La Scuola, 1968. xxxviii, 336 p.

Langford, Glenn, and O'Connor, Daniel John, eds. NEW ESSAYS IN THE PHILOSOPHY OF EDUCATION. London: Routledge and Kegan Paul, 1973. xi, 266 p.

Essays by Langford, Smart, O'Connor, Hirst, Daveney, Baier, Peters, Hare, Hudson, Collinson, Ormell, and Nidditch are reflec-tions over the concepts of education, indoctrination, educational theory, and moral education. The discussions are controversial and pointed toward issues of current interest.

Lucas, Christopher J., ed. CHALLENGE AND CHOICE IN CONTEMPORARY EDUCATION: SIX MAJOR IDEOLOGICAL PERSPECTIVES. New York:

Macmillan, 1976. viii, 455 p.

McClellan, James E. PHILOSOPHY OF EDUCATION. Englewood Cliffs, N.J.: Prentice-Hall, 1976. xiii, 176 p.

> The issues raised concern the criteria for a definition of education, the concepts and acts of teaching, and the dilemma between the morality of teaching and the teaching of morality. The concluding essay "For Further Reading" should be noted for its bibliographic commentary. The author suggests reading this work in conjunction with Plato's MENO. He treats philosophy of education as a branch of general philosophy closely related to epistemology.

_____. TOWARD AN EFFECTIVE CRITIQUE OF AMERICAN EDUCATION. Philadelphia: J.B. Lippincott, 1968. x, 324 p.

> The last chapter ought to be read in the light of what has since occurred in educational theory and practice. The observations on what Conant, Brameld, Barzun, Skinner, and Goodman deem significant for education are worth careful review.

Maerz, Fritz. STUDIEN ZUR PERSONORIENTIERTEN PAEDAGOGIK. [Studies for a person-oriented education]. Wuppertal, W. Ger.; Ratingen, W. Ger.; and Kastellaun, W. Ger.: Henn, 1971. 94 p.

> The essays discuss the phenomenon of belief as intrinsic to liberal education. Topics cover the fundamental concept of education, the person and his function, the scope of education, the relevance of what is learned, an interpretation of Augustine's DE MAGISTRO, the problem of responsibility or competence, and present criticisms of a person-oriented theory of education.

Marantz, Haim. "A Note on Educational Reductionism." EDUCATIONAL THEORY 25, no. 3 (1975): 330-31.

May, Philip R. WHICH WAY TO EDUCATE? Chicago: Moody Press, 1975. 159 p.

Meiklejohn, Alexander. EDUCATION BETWEEN TWO WORLDS. 1942. Reprint. Freeport, N.Y.: Books for Libraries Press, 1972. x, 303 p.

Mialaret, Gaston, et al. EDUCATION NOUVELLE ET MONDE MODERNE. 2d ed. Paris: Presses Universitaires de France, 1969. 176 p.

Mosley, Frances S. A STUDENT'S GUIDE TO PROBLEMS IN EDUCATION, WITH SPECIAL EMPHASIS ON THE HISTORICAL-PHILOSOPHICAL FOUNDATIONS OF EDUCATION. Dubuque, Iowa: Kendall/Hunt Publishing, 1974. ix, 213 p.

Noll, James William, and Kelly, Sam P., eds. FOUNDATIONS OF EDUCA-
TION IN AMERICA. New York: Harper and Row, 1970. xiii, 519 p.

> This anthology includes almost one hundred primary documents that
> have been influential in shaping some aspect of American educa-
> tion. Each of the four sections is preceded by a helpful commen-
> tary, a discussion of educational issues, and an index of themes.
> It is a convenient sourcebook.

O'Connor, Daniel John. AN INTRODUCTION TO THE PHILOSOPHY OF
EDUCATION. 1957. 5th impression. London: Routledge and Kegan Paul,
1966. vii, 148 p.

> Philosophical issues are analyzed in regard to specific educational
> problems. The ends of education and the value judgments to be
> made about them are discussed in chapter 3. Metaphysical,
> valuational, and empirical hypotheses relate directly to educa-
> tional theory but not necessarily to educational practice.

Pai, Young, and Myers, Joseph T., eds. PHILOSOPHIC PROBLEMS AND
EDUCATION. Philadelphia: J.B. Lippincott, 1967. xii, 467 p.

Park, Joe, ed. SELECTED READINGS IN THE PHILOSOPHY OF EDUCATION.
New York: Macmillan, 1958. vi, 440 p.

> Selections are grouped in six sections with introductions and bio-
> graphical sketches: "The Place of Philosophy in the Study of Edu-
> cation" (Finney, Brubacher, Kircher), "The Pragmatic Philosophy
> of Education" (James, Dewey, Bode, Childs, Kilpatrick, Counts,
> Brameld), "Idealism" (Horne, Greene, Butler), "Realism" (Breed,
> Whitehead, Wild, Adler, Hutchins), "The Catholic Philosophy of
> Education" (Pope Pius XI, Cunningham, Maritain), and "The Phi-
> losophy of Education in Some Protestant and Jewish Thought"
> (Butler, Greene, Mueller, Chipkin, Williams).

_____. SELECTED READINGS IN THE PHILOSOPHY OF EDUCATION. 3d
ed. New York: Macmillan, 1968. ix, 433 p. Bibliog.

> Park introduces and classifies the essays under the following head-
> ings: "The Place of Philosophy in the Study of Education" (Ducasse,
> Levison, Kircher), "Pragmatism and Education" (James, Dewey,
> Kilpatrick, McMurray, Brameld), "Idealism" (Horne, Greene,
> Butler), "Realism" (Whitehead, Broudy, Hutchins), "Religious
> Thought and the Philosophy of Education" (Pope Paul VI,
> Cunningham, Jahsmann, Ben-Horin), "Existentialism" (Morris,
> Kneller, Baker), and "Philosophical Analysis" (Newsome,
> Montefiore, Komisar and Coombs). The bibliography is annotated (pp.
> 393-418).

_____. SELECTED READINGS IN THE PHILOSOPHY OF EDUCATION. 4th ed. New York: Macmillan, 1974. xii, 367 p. Bibliog.

Selections, collected into four parts, have their own introductions: "The Place of Philosophy in the Study of Education" (Levision, Newsome, Kircher), "The Language of Education" (Scheffler, Urmson, Green, Strike, Komisar and Coombs), "Analyzing and Synthesizing Philosophical Positions" (Nagel, Weldon, Baker, Frankena, Whitehead, Dewey), and "Some Normative Issues in Education" (Means, Komisar, Stein, Neff, Park, the Sacred Ecumenical Council, Jahsmann, Hardie, Hutchins, Coffey, Baldwin). The bibliography is well annotated (pp. 335-57).

Peden, Creighton, and Chipman, Donald, eds. PHILOSOPHICAL REFLECTIONS ON EDUCATION AND SOCIETY. Washington, D.C.: University Press of America, 1978. 310 p. Paperbound.

Twenty-two members of the Southeast Philosophy of Education Society offer essays on issues dealing with the philosophy of education. It is a fine example of what other regional groups ought to publish in regard to their thinking and findings in educational philosophy and related issues.

Peters, Richard Stanley. AUTHORITY, RESPONSIBILITY AND EDUCATION. 3d ed. New York: Paul S. Eriksson; London: Allen and Unwin, 1973. 160 p. Paperbound.

The book is divided into three parts according to three basic issues introduced for discussion from the analytic philosophy of education: the changing face of authority; Freud, Marx, and responsibility; and education and moral education--must an educator have an aim? Peters concludes that values are more germane to ways of proceeding in education than goals or aims. Note his observation that mechanistic-biological models of all human behavior ignore the essentially rational and characteristically human powers of man.

Petrelli, Rodolfo. CONTESTAZIONE E SPERANZA. UNA NUOVA TEORIA DELL'EDUCAZIONE. Turin, Italy: P. Gribaudi, 1973. 132 p.

Pleines, Juergen-Eckhardt. BILDUNG. [Liberal education]. Heidelberg: Quelle and Meyer, 1971. 122 p. Bibliog.

Relates the philosophy of liberal education to anthropology in such a way as to highlight their historical antecedents. The author proceeds to project the meaning of liberal education against the widely held belief that practicality and liberal education are in opposition to each other. His bibliography is extensive (pp. 114-22).

Schofield, Harry. THE PHILOSOPHY OF EDUCATION: AN INTRODUCTION. London: Allen and Unwin; New York: Barnes and Noble, 1972. xvi, 288 p. Paperbound.

This basic book is a gradual introduction to the techniques of linguistic analysis and concept analysis in a way that reveals the usefulness of these two techniques even for the beginner in the modern approach to philosophy of education. Since it assumes no previous training in philosophy, the text is enriched by extensive explanatory notes and background from the history of philosophy, literature, psychology, sociology, and other disciplines.

Seckinger, Donald S. A PROBLEMS APPROACH TO FOUNDATIONS OF EDUCATION. New York: John Wiley and Sons, 1976. 220 p.

This comprehensive, interdisciplinary overview intends to stimulate thought and action on the problems of cultural change, social class and mobility, racism, sexism, religious diversity, the freedoms to teach and to learn, and the restoration of community in school and society.

Shields, James J. THE CRISIS IN EDUCATION IS OUTSIDE THE CLASSROOM. Bloomington, Ill.: Phi Delta Kappa Educational Foundation, 1973. 49 p.

Speck, Josef, ed. PROBLEMGESCHICHTE DER NEUEREN PAEDAGOGIK. [The problematic history of the newer education]. 3 vols. Stuttgart, Berlin, Cologne, Mainz: Kohlhammer, 1976.

Volume 1: WISSENSCHAFT, SCHULE, GESELLSCHAFT. [Science, school, society]. 231 p.

Volume 2: DIE PAEDAGOGIK UND IHRE NACHBARDISZIPLINEN. [Education and its related disciplines]. 199 p.

Volume 3: AUSGEWAEHLTE GRUNBEGRIFFE DER PAEDAGOGIK. [Selected fundamental ideas in education]. 211 p.

Wilbanks, Jan J. "Educational Reductionism." EDUCATIONAL THEORY 24, no. 1 (1974): 73-84.

Wilbanks tries to set forth, as clearly and straightforwardly as possible, the problem of educational reductionism in reference to the exact nature of the logical or conceptual relationships between educational and moral discourse.

_____. "Response to Haim Marantz." EDUCATIONAL THEORY 27, no. 2 (1977): 150-52.

Marantz is accused of failing to distinguish the concept version from the statement version of the problem of educational reductionism. For, to say that normative educational concepts can be defined in terms of moral concepts is not to claim that normative

educational concepts do not exist. Marantz does not seem to no-
tice that this question opens new ground or that Wilbanks has
made a worthwhile effort.

Xochellis, Panagiotis (Panos). PAEDAGOGIK ODER ERZIEHUNGSWISSEN-
SCHAFT?: DIE WISSENSCHAFTSTHEORETISCHE PROBLEMATIK DER GEGEN-
WAERT PAEDAGOGIK. [Instruction or science of education?: A philosophical
dilemma in education today]. Munich: Goldmann, 1973. 77 p.

CRITIQUES

Archambault, Reginald D., ed. DEWEY ON EDUCATION: APPRAISALS.
New York: Random House, 1966. 235 p. Paperbound.

This balanced gathering of appraisals by such critics of Dewey's
philosophy of education as Kilpatrick, Cremin, Handlin, Phenix,
Lilge, Meiklejohn, Scheffler, Hardie, Hook, Archambault, M.I.
Berger, Lynd, and Bruner is intended to help the student see the
lasting value of many aspects of Dewey's thought. The hope is
for a possible reconstruction of his educational philosophy in the
light of real contemporary problems.

Baatz, Charles Albert. A CRITICAL ANALYSIS OF WILLMANN'S SOCIAL
PHILOSOPHY OF EDUCATION. Ann Arbor, Mich.: University Microfilms,
1966. v, 345 p. Bibliog. Paperbound.

Since one may not deny the validity of theological wisdom in
philosophy and education without renouncing the contributions of
the other sciences to the social philosophy of education, Willmann
insists the social ethos of education must spring directly from the
natural and supernatural significance of man and society. This
position is evaluated from the educational and theological viewpoints contained in the documents of Vatican Council II. The
selected bibliography (pp. 331-45) is the only substantial listing
available in English of writings by and about Otto Willmann.

Barrow, Robin. PLATO AND EDUCATION. London: Routledge and Kegan
Paul, 1976. vi, 83 p.

Students' introduction to Plato's educational thought presents Plato's
approach to key questions and arguments in both education and
philosophy. There are some reflections on contemporary philosophical thinking in education with an analysis of Plato's value in
today's world. The work is no substitute for direct study of the
Platonic dialogs together with the help of classical commentators.

Barzun, Jacques. THE TYRANNY OF IDEALISM IN EDUCATION. New York:
Woodrow Wilson Foundation, 1959. 14 p.

Brameld, Theodore. PHILOSOPHIES OF EDUCATION IN CULTURAL PERSPEC-
TIVE. New York: Holt, Rinehart and Winston, 1960. xvii, 446 p.

Brameld investigates perennialism, essentialism, and progressivism
within cultural contexts. Realism and idealism are also involved
in the discussions concerning learning, curriculum design, and the
function of school in society. Brameld regards himself as a reconstructionist.

_____. "Reconstructionism as Radical Philosophy of Education: A Reappraisal."
EDUCATIONAL FORUM 42, no. 1 (1977): 67-76.

The ideas of reconstructionism are products of experimental naturalism and dialectical materialism, either of which can contribute to
the other. Some theorists find rather uncomfortable Brameld's
insistence on learning from Marxists about consensual validation,
defensible partiality, and the place of mythologizing in education, and social self-realization. Whatever convergence these
means may achieve, reconstructionism recognizes, in dialectical
fashion, that all conceptual universalities require countervailing
pluralities.

Brubacher, John Seiler. MODERN PHILOSOPHIES OF EDUCATION. 4th ed.
New York: McGraw-Hill, 1969. 393 p.

Butler, James Donald. FOUR PHILOSOPHIES AND THEIR PRACTICES IN EDU-
CATION AND RELIGION. 3d ed. New York: Harper and Row, 1968.
528 p. Bibliog.

The introduction contrasts philosophy, its problems, history, and
types, with the approaches of other fields and then concludes with
a most useful six-page glossary of philosophical terms. The other
parts are given to a systematic exposition and synopsis of naturalism, idealism, realism, pragmatism, existentialism, and language
analysis with a concluding essay on building a philosophy of education. The sources are listed in the bibliography according to
philosophical schools.

Cahn, Steven Mark, ed. NEW STUDIES IN THE PHILOSOPHY OF JOHN
DEWEY. Hanover, N.H.: University Press of New England, 1977. 213 p.

The special essays study Dewey's social philosophy (Frankel), metaphysics (Rorty), theory of the aesthetic practice (Kadish), epistemology (Margoli), the truth about ethics (Rachels), the school and
society (Olafson). All are oriented toward the relevance of John
Dewey's thought to contemporary education.

Campbell, Harry M. JOHN DEWEY. New York: Twayne Publishers, 1971.
161 p.

Campbell tries to give the general reader a reasonable and fair introduction to Dewey's philosophy but also feels obligated to call attention to its serious limitations. He believes few converts have been made since the death of John Dewey.

Cassirer, Ernst. THE QUESTION OF JEAN-JACQUES ROUSSEAU. Translated and edited with an introduction and notes by Peter Gay. Bloomington: Indiana University Press, 1963. vi, 129 p.

Childs, John Lawrence. AMERICAN PRAGMATISM AND EDUCATION, AN INTERPRETATION AND CRITICISM. New York: Holt, Rinehart and Winston, 1956. 373 p.

In the tradition of Dewey and Peirce, Childs develops the meaning of the experimental method and the theory of experimental inquiry.

_____. AN ASSESSMENT OF THE EXPERIMENTALIST EDUCATIONAL THEORY. Columbus: Ohio State University, 1958. 33 p.

Classen, Johannes, ed. ANTIAUTORITAERE ERZIEHUNG IN DER WISSEN-SCHAFTLICHEN DISKUSSION. [A critical analysis of anti-authoritarian education]. Heidelberg, W. Ger.: Quelle and Meyer, 1973. 295 p.

This anthology of about twenty essays presents controversies, viewpoints, and criticisms of education conceived as being antiauthoritarian. These readings would be otherwise difficult to locate.

Coombs, Philip H. THE WORLD EDUCATIONAL CRISIS. New York: Oxford University Press, 1968. x, 241 p.

The first aim is to assemble the root facts about an unfolding world crisis in education, to make explicit the tendencies in these facts, and to suggest some strategy for dealing with them. The second aim is to present a method for looking at an educational system and its interacting elements to indicate whether the enterprise is going well or badly. The assumptions call for deep analysis.

Gerner, Berthold, ed. MARTIN BUBER: PAEDAGOGISCHE INTERPRETA-TIONEN ZU SEINEM WERK. [Martin Buber: educational interpretations of his work]. Munich: Ehrenwirth, 1974. 131 p.

Gutek, Gerald Lee. PESTALOZZI AND EDUCATION. New York: Random House, 1968. 178 p. Paperbound.

The author offers a sympathetic critique of the Swiss educator's ideas on natural education, his axiological conception of the educated man, and his basic humanitarianism. Gutek sees in the Pestalozzian philosophy of education a love message in which men are simply invited to love one another.

Gutzke, Manford George. JOHN DEWEY'S THOUGHT AND ITS IMPLICA-
TIONS FOR CHRISTIAN EDUCATION. New York: Columbia University
Press, 1956. xv, 270 p.

> Gutzke's thesis, that the "scientific method is applicable in the
> field of religious phenomena," is maintainable only if Dewey's
> philosophy is known to assume a religion of science and nature
> instead of the Christian religion that believes in a transcendent
> God.

Haefner, George Edward. A CRITICAL ESTIMATE OF THE EDUCATIONAL
THEORIES AND PRACTICES OF A. BRONSON ALCOTT. Westport, Conn.:
Greenwood Press, 1970. vii, 130 p.

> Amos Bronson Alcott (1799-1888) anticipated Dewey's child-centered
> school. His informal conversational technique and application of
> Pestalozzian educational innovations made his schools very popular
> and stimulating.

Hamm-Bruecher, Hildegard. BILDUNG IST KEIN LUXUS. [Education is not an
extravagance]. Munich: List, 1976. 214 p.

> This writer is alarmed at the tendency in recent years to suborn
> education to purely political purposes. Her criticism, of the ten-
> dency and its consequences, is directed specifically toward educa-
> tional developments in Japan, Peru, China, Canada, Norway,
> and the USSR.

Hammel, Walter. KRISE UND BILDUNG. [Crisis and liberal education].
Ratingen by Dusseldorf, W. Ger.: Henn, 1967. 137 p.

> Hammel explores the phenomenon of crisis as a maturing factor in
> intellectual and moral education. The various critical situations
> in German schools and society have many implications for other
> peoples as well.

Hartong, Konrad. OTTO WILLMANN UND SEINE STELLUNG IN DER
GESCHICHTE DER PAEDAGOGISCHEN THEORIE. [Otto Willmann and his
place in the history of educational theory]. Ann Arbor, Mich., and London:
University Microfilms, 1955. vii, 214 p.

> Hartong credits Willmann for his contributions in determining the
> philosophy of education as a science but believes that Willmann's
> synthesis is merely the beginning to an actual paedagogia perennis.

Hutchins, Robert Maynard. THE CONFLICT IN EDUCATION IN A DEMO-
CRATIC SOCIETY. New York: Harper and Row, 1953. Reprint. Westport,
Conn.: Greenwood Press, 1972. 112 p.

Hutchins restates the case for liberal education against the pretensions of the progressivists. In the current debate over liberal versus illiberal education, the arguments of Hutchins have an undeniable cogency and force.

Lawrence, Nathaniel M., and Brumbaugh, Robert S., eds. PHILOSOPHERS ON EDUCATION: SIX ESSAYS ON THE FOUNDATIONS OF WESTERN THOUGHT. Boston: Houghton Mifflin, 1963. x, 211 p.

The essays underscore the great importance of Plato, Aristotle, Rousseau, Kant, Dewey, and Whitehead to the adequate formulation of any future philosophy of education.

Lesnoff-Caravaglia, Gari. EDUCATION AS EXISTENTIAL POSSIBILITY. New York: Philosophical Library, 1972. 108 p.

The existentialist notions of Nicola Abbagnano are placed in contrast to the thought of Jean Paul Sartre and Martin Heidegger. Abhorring the philosophy of nihilism, the author finds in Abbagnano a positive faith in man and in his real potentialities for a hopeful future.

Loewisch, Dieter-Juergen. ERZIEHUNG UND KRITISCHE THEORIE: KRITISCHE PAEDAGOGIK ZWISCHEN THEORETISCH ANSPRUCH UND GESELLSCHAFTLICHE REALITAET. [Education and critical theory: the promise of critical education and sociological reality]. Munich: Koesel, 1974. 119 p.

The writer attempts to bring together the thought of Horkheimer, Adorno, Marcuse, and Bloch with the critical philosophy of Lessing and Kant. His purpose is to formulate a useful and timely critical philosophy of education in the face of currently disintegrating sociological structure.

Mason, Robert Emmett. CONTEMPORARY EDUCATIONAL THEORY. New York: David McKay, 1972. ix, 288 p.

Mason reviews almost two centuries of Western educational theory.

Mathias, Theophane A., ed. NOT WITHOUT A COMPASS (MEANING AND RELEVANCE OF CHRISTIAN EDUCATION IN INDIA TO-DAY). Delhi: Jesuit Educational Association of India, 1971. ix, 218 p.

Noteworthy are the essays about the meaning and relevance of Christian education, education for social revolution, the secular-apostolic dilemma, the declaration-statement of objectives, and a non-Christian's understanding of what Christian education can offer today. The philosophic vision is an open-ended humanism and appreciation for the person of action ever available for greater service in the cause of justice.

Moore, T.W. EDUCATIONAL THEORY: AN INTRODUCTION. London and Boston: Routledge and Kegan Paul, 1976. 112 p.

> The author emphasizes with clarity and exactness the importance of educational aims in the mind of the teacher and how these may be translated into actuality by the choice of proper methods. Moore shows by his review and critique of the educational thinking of Plato, Rousseau, James Hill, and Dewey, how the teacher can locate the point of balance between theory and practice.

Morgenbesser, Sidney, ed. DEWEY AND HIS CRITICS: ESSAYS FROM THE JOURNAL OF PHILOSOPHY. Indianapolis: Hackett Publishing, 1977. 760 p.

> The articles by Dewey and some thirty others are selected for their concern with realism, theory of knowledge, metaphysics and aesthetics, mind, meaning, and logic, ethics and social philosophy, and a general orientation toward Dewey himself.

Morris, Van Cleve, and Pai, Young. PHILOSOPHY AND THE AMERICAN SCHOOL: AN INTRODUCTION TO THE PHILOSOPHY OF EDUCATION. 2d ed. Boston: Houghton Mifflin, 1976. xiii, 476 p.

> The authors present an experimentalist view of how all philosophy deals essentially with what is real (metaphysics), what is true (epistemology), and what is good (axiology), and then they explore how idealism, realism, neo-Thomism, experimentalism, and existentialism treat these questions. The models of education, such as behavior engineering, self-actualization, and cultural pluralism, are respectively estimated for their value in American education. The reader is advised to compare interpretations from several other sources. The work presents the philosophy of experimentalism but the exposition of differing philosophic theories of education requires more reading. In responding to what is real, true, and good, the authors conceive an educational philosophy of action.

Muehlbauer, Reinhold. DER BEGRIFF "BILDUNG" IN DER GEGENWARTS-PAEDAGOGIK. [The concept of LIBERAL EDUCATION in contemporary education]. St. Ottilien, W. Ger.: Eos-Verlag, 1965. xxiii, 328 p.

Mueller, Herman. A CRITICAL ANALYSIS OF THE JEWISH EDUCATIONAL PHILOSOPHY IN RELATIONSHIP TO THE EPISTLES OF ST. PAUL. Siegburg, W. Ger.: Steyler Verlag, 1967. 80 p.

> The Jewish ideal of education was the righteous man who endeavored to imitate the just God. Man is just if true to his being as the image of God. For Paul also, knowledge and practice, life and religion all belonged together in a life given to divine justice. The only non-Jewish element in Paul's educational philosophy is the appropriation of justice by faith in Jesus Christ, the Son of God.

Nyberg, David, ed. THE PHILOSOPHY OF OPEN EDUCATION. London: Routledge and Kegan Paul, 1975. 228 p.

The essays, classified under six general headings, deal with the problems of definition, knowledge, socialization, freedom, cultural perspective, unique meanings and metaphors. The critical analyses represent the thinking of Hill, Tunnell, Petrie, Gowin, Morgan, Simmons, Arnstine, Strike, Waks, Egan, Vandenberg, and Peters.

Okafor, Festus Chukwudi. AFRICA AT THE CROSSROADS. New York: Vantage Press, 1974. 186 p.

Okafor studies the philosophical dimensions of African education from the vantage point of Christian ecumenical humanism. Recommends that African thought and institutions assimilate the positive achievements of the world in order to enhance the refinement of Africans, individually and socially. Okafor urges Africans to avoid the excesses of Lockean liberalism, totalitarian communism, or any form of materialism because these philosophies will only lead Africa from its true destiny.

The book was reviewed by Sylayman S. Nyang (AMERICAN EDUCATIONAL RESEARCH JOURNAL 12, no. 4 [1975]: 526-28).

Ozmon, Howard. DIALOGUE IN THE PHILOSOPHY OF EDUCATION. Columbus, Ohio: Charles E. Merrill, 1972. xiv, 123 p.

Peters, Richard Stanley, ed. JOHN DEWEY RECONSIDERED. London: Routledge and Kegan Paul, 1977. 136 p.

These public lectures given at the University of London range from Dewey's general philosophy of man and society to his theories of knowledge and interest, his understanding of democracy and education, and his philosophy of education. The contributors are distinguished: Anthony Quinton, Jerome Bruner, Alan R. White, Martin Hollis, Anthony Flew, and R.S. Peters.

Petrullo, Salvatore, and Virgilio, P., eds. PAGINE CRITICHE DELLA PEDAGOGIA CONTEMPORANEA. Sicily: C. Tringale, 1975. 403 p.

Rich, John Martin, ed. INNOVATIONS IN EDUCATION: REFORMERS AND THEIR CRITICS. 2d ed. Boston: Allyn and Bacon, 1978. 400 p. Paperbound.

These articles reflect the philosophical undercurrents of reforms in competency-based teacher education, career education, values and moral education, bilingual education, mainstreaming, open classrooms, and the return to basics. It is useful in showing the impact of educational philosophy on educational praxis.

Rosen, F. Bruce. PHILOSOPHIC SYSTEMS AND EDUCATION. Columbus, Ohio: Charles E. Merrill, 1968. x, 116 p.

Rusk, Robert R. THE PHILOSOPHICAL BASES OF EDUCATION. Rev. and enl. ed. Boston: Houghton Mifflin, 1956. viii, 176 p.

> Rusk contrasts the philosophies of materialism, realism, naturalism, pragmatism, instrumentalism, and experimentalism together with his own espousal of idealism.

Scheffler, Israel. FOUR PRAGMATISTS: A CRITICAL INTRODUCTION TO PEIRCE, JAMES, MEAD, AND DEWEY. New York: Humanities Press, 1974. 269 p.

> This balanced yet critical evaluation of pragmatism presents, rather fairly, the relevant philosophical texts and their criticism. The actual issues for discussion are limited chiefly to the problems of epistemology, the mind-body situation, and methodology. Scheffler thinks pragmatism does not really appreciate the autonomy of theory. Here the reader has a fine example of Scheffler's genius for scrutinizing the various levels of meaning in a text.

Seth, Kirti Devi. IDEALISTIC TRENDS IN INDIAN PHILOSOPHIES OF EDU-CATION. Allahabad, India: Education Department, University of Allahabad, 1966. xv, 510 p.

Thompson, Craig R. "The Humanism of More Reappraised." THOUGHT 52, no. 206 (1977): 231-48.

> Thompson considers the irenic and ecumenical character of scholar-ship, under the aegis of Saint Thomas More, to be a triumph of genuine humanism. The analysis and history of the concept of humanism given here should be read by everyone for its clear distinctions and depth of analysis.

Weber, Christian O. BASIC PHILOSOPHIES OF EDUCATION. New York: Holt, Rinehart and Winston, 1960. xii, 333 p.

> After the introductory chapters on religion, politics, and philo-sophy of education, Weber gives a full treatment of essentialism and traditionalism, idealism, realism, pragmatism, and instrumen-talism.

White, H.R. FOUNDATIONS OF EDUCATION: HISTORICAL, SOCIOLOGI-CAL, PHILOSOPHICAL. New York: David McKay, 1968. xii, 92 p.

> White explains philosophical method and content in education to-gether with summary treatments of idealism, realism, pragmatism, fascism, communism, and democracy.

Wilds, Elmer Harrison, and Lottich, Kenneth V. THE FOUNDATIONS OF
MODERN EDUCATION. 4th ed. New York: Holt, Rinehart and Winston,
1970. xv, 590 p.

> In addition to its morphology, FOUNDATIONS provides a multiple
> approach to the study of individual movements or philosophies.
> It presents the evolution of educational theory and it attempts not
> only to relate the history of education with corresponding social
> movements but also to illuminate significant contemporary accom-
> plishments with their adjacent problems. Each chapter is followed
> by complete references.

Wingo, Glenn Max. PHILOSOPHIES OF EDUCATION: AN INTRODUCTION.
Lexington, Mass.: D.C. Heath, 1974. 367 p.

Wittiz, Hans. VERGLEICHENDE PAEDAGOGIK. [Comparative education].
Darmstadt, W. Ger.: Wissenschaftliche Buchgesellschaft, 1973. viii, 228 p.

> Wittig makes the direct object of his comparative education the
> plurality of significant educational philosophies. He presents them
> critically to harmonize their differences and to create a brand new
> understanding of education and pedagogical autonomy.

Wynne, John Peter. PHILOSOPHIES OF EDUCATION FROM THE STAND-
POINT OF THE PHILOSOPHY OF EXPERIMENTALISM. 1947. Reprint.
Westport, Conn.: Greenwood Press, 1970. xiv, 427 p.; Farmville, Va.:
Longwood College Foundation, 1971. xxiv, 390 p.

Xochellis, Panagiotis (Panos). ERZIEHUNG AM WENDEPUNKT? GRUND-
STRUKTUREN DES PAEDAGOGISCHES BEZUGES IN HEUTIGER SICHT. [Edu-
cation in crisis? A study of its foundations today]. Munich: Ehrenwirth,
1974. 173 p.

> Aiming for a clearer structuring of modern pedagogical phenomena,
> the author first examines the anthropological dimensions of educa-
> tion. This is followed by a further clarification of moral and in-
> tellectual education from a historical, empirical, and pheno-
> menological-hermeneutic viewpoint. The work then concludes with
> a sociological and critical analysis of contemporary education.

ANTHOLOGIES AND READINGS

Bernier, Normand R., and Williams, Jack E., eds. EDUCATION FOR LIBERA-
TION: READINGS FROM AN IDEOLOGICAL PERSPECTIVE. Englewood Cliffs,
N.J.: Prentice-Hall, 1973. ix, 310 p.

Burns, Hobert Warren, and Brauner, Charles J., eds. PHILOSOPHY OF EDU-
CATION: ESSAYS AND COMMENTARIES. Foreword by Robert H. Beck.

New York: Ronald Press, 1962. 422 p.

Callahan, Joseph F., and Clark, Leonard H., comps. FOUNDATIONS OF EDUCATION: PLANNING FOR COMPETENCE. New York: Macmillan, 1977. x, 283 p. Paperbound.

> Chapters 3 and 4, authored by Leo Charles Daley, are learning modules complete with rationale, behavioral objectives, and tests. The text presents the philosophical development of education according to the approaches of idealism, realism, experimentalism, pragmatism, logical analysis, existentialism, communism, and scholasticism.

Carron, Malcolm Theodore, and Cavanaugh, Alfred D., eds. READINGS IN THE PHILOSOPHY OF EDUCATION. 3d ed. Detroit: University of Detroit Press, 1963. 423 p.

Denton, David E., ed. EXISTENTIALISM AND PHENOMENOLOGY IN EDUCATION: COLLECTED ESSAYS. New York: Teachers College Press, 1974. 223 p. Paperbound, 1978.

> Among the educators represented are Maxine Greene, Leroy Troutner, J. Gordon Chamberlin, Clinton Collins, and Donald Vandenberg who provide a historical framework for discussion of recent developments, educational issues, and their philosophical origins and solutions.

Dupuis, Adrian Maurice, ed. READINGS IN THE PHILOSOPHY OF EDUCATION: NATURE, AIMS, AND POLICY. Urbana: University of Illinois Press, 1970. xiii, 344 p.

> Twelve articles pertain to epistemology, logic-semantic-language, and philosophy of science; thirteen articles relate directly to metaphysics, the philosophy of man and society; the final sixteen articles encompass value theory, ethics, aesthetics, and religion. Inserted at the end of each of the three sections is a listing of sources selected for further reading. This text provides an acquaintance with key ideas and important thinkers.

Martin, Jane Roland, ed. READINGS IN THE PHILOSOPHY OF EDUCATION: A STUDY OF CURRICULUM. Boston: Allyn and Bacon, 1970. viii, 301 p.

Ponton, Lionel, and Rioux, Jean, eds. PHILOSOPHIE DE L'EDUCATION. Selected texts. Quebec, Canada: Les Presses de L'Universite Laval, 1968. 196 p.

Rich, John Martin, ed. READINGS IN THE PHILOSOPHY OF EDUCATION. 2d ed. Belmont, Calif.: Wadsworth Publishing, 1972. ix, 382 p.

Rodgers, Edwin R. THE THINGS WE BELIEVE: A STATEMENT OF PHILOSOPHY AND A LIST FOR A JUNIOR HIGH SCHOOL. St. Petersburg, Fla.: Johnny Reads, 1968. 23 p.

Rombach, Heinrich, ed. WOERTERBUCH DER PAEDAGOGIK. [Concepts and terms in education]. Freiburg im Breisgau, W. Ger.; Basel, Switz.; Vienna, Austria: Herder, 1977. 3 vols.

> Important concepts are defined and explained within the appropriate contexts of their philosophical and educational origin and significance.

> Volume 1: ABENDSCHULEN BIS GENETISCHE METHODE. 1977. xv, 365 p.

> Volume 2: GEOGRAPHIEUNTERRICHT BIS POLITISCHE BILDUNG. 1977. 362 p.

> Volume 3: POLITISCHE OEKONOMIE BIS ZWEITER BILDUNG-SWEG. 1977. 380 p.

Scheffler, Israel, ed. PHILOSOPHY AND EDUCATION: MODERN READINGS. 2d ed. Boston: Allyn and Bacon, 1966. xi, 387 p.

> Scheffler illustrates and applies newer philosophical approaches to education: the philosophical activity of rational reflection, critical analysis of arguments and assumptions, systematic clarification of fundamental ideas for improved educational understanding. In

Schlosser, Courtney D., ed. THE PERSON IN EDUCATION: A HUMAN-ISTIC APPROACH. New York: Macmillan, 1976. 413 p.

> The readings in part 1 discuss the historical, philosophical, psychological, and sociological foundations of humanism. Those in part 2 deal with the educational implications of humanism.

Smith, Philip G., ed. READINGS IN THE PHILOSOPHY OF EDUCATION: THEORIES OF VALUE AND PROBLEMS OF EDUCATION. Urbana: University of Illinois Press, 1970. 232 p.

> The essays encompass the nature of value theory and its relevance for education, educational objectives and the conduct of schooling, and moral education. The work as a whole is limited in focus and the writers selected do not represent the larger body of literature on theories of value and problems of education. This was done deliberately to intensify the reader's thought within a more narrow range of study.

Stone, James C., and Schneider, Frederick W., eds. READINGS IN THE FOUNDATIONS OF EDUCATION. 2d ed. Commitment to Teaching Series, vol. 2. New York: Thomas Y. Crowell, 1971. 651 p.

The essays in section 2 comment on the goals of education and those in section 8 pertain to idealism (Zeigler), realism (Broudy), the philosophy of Catholic education (Driscoll), John Dewey (Sullivan), existentialism (Bowers), philosophies and aims of education (Parker et al.). The other fifty-seven articles are of general interest in educational foundations.

Strain, John Paul, ed. MODERN PHILOSOPHIES OF EDUCATION. New York: Random House, 1971. xi, 555 p.

Vandenberg, Donald, ed. READINGS IN THE PHILOSOPHY OF EDUCATION: THEORY OF KNOWLEDGE AND PROBLEMS OF EDUCATION. Urbana, Chicago, and London: University of Illinois Press, 1969. x, 302 p.

The materials are ordered in a fourfold division, each with its own introduction by the editor. The divisions are: the nature and aim of education, policy and the organization of instruction, curriculum selection and organization, teaching and learning. The editor tried to select primarily for quality and depth of treatment.

Wojtyla, Karol (Pope Paul II). THE ACTING PERSON. Edited by Anna-Teresa Tymieniecka and translated from Polish by Andrzej Potocki. Hingham, Mass.: D. Reidel Publishing Co., 1979. xxiii, 367 p.

The ideal of personal-social freedom, enjoyed uniquely by the person in action and participating with others, contains within itself extraordinary possibilities for a theory or humane philosophy of education. The phenomenological approach used here so effectively to highlight the freedom of the acting person can also bring into full view an educational philosophy based foursquare on the principles of human participation and efficacy.

Chapter 4
AIMS AND IDEALS—THE FINAL CAUSE OF EDUCATION

Inasmuch as an educator praises the value and usefulness of the philosophy of education, he speaks of final causes. When he speaks of the purposes or ends of education as solutions to human problems, he also speaks of final causes. For a final cause is the ultimate ground of value; it points to reasonableness; it indicates order and intelligibility; and it offers the reason for education being desired or intended.

A 1: THE PROBLEM OF KNOWING—EPISTEMOLOGY

Bloom, Benjamin Samuel, ed. TAXONOMY OF EDUCATIONAL OBJECTIVES. New York: Longmans, Green, 1956. 207 p.

> To what degree do specific learning outcomes and processes in human cognition point to a unique functional and structural unity in man? Bloom raises the question of man's unique subject-object relations. The suppositions here need critical evaluation.

Dearden, R.F.; Hirst, P.H.; Peters, R.S., eds. EDUCATION AND THE DEVELOPMENT OF REASON. London: Routledge and Kegan Paul, 1972. xiv, 536 p. Also available in 3 vols., 1975.

> Volume 1: A CRITIQUE OF CURRENT EDUCATIONAL AIMS. 166 p.
>
> Volume 2: REASON. 258 p.
>
> Volume 3: EDUCATION AND REASON. 148 p.
>
> The writers represented in this work are among the leading British philosophers concerned with education and its metaphysical foundations.

Heidegger, Martin. DISCOURSE ON THINKING. Translated by John M. Anderson and E. Hans Freund. New York: Harper and Row, 1969. 93 p.

Hyman, Herbert H., et al. THE ENDURING EFFECTS OF EDUCATION. Chicago: University of Chicago Press, 1975. 313 p.

"Education produces large, pervasive, and enduring effects on knowledge and receptivity to knowledge" (p. 109). It is the beginning to a more thorough investigation into all the factors that influence persons in search of an education.

Peters, Richard S., ed. THE CONCEPT OF EDUCATION. London: Routledge and Kegan Paul; New York: Humanities Press, 1967. viii, 223 p.

_____. EDUCATION AS INITIATION. London: Evans Brothers, 1964. 48 p.

_____. "Must An Educator Have An Aim?" In his AUTHORITY, RESPONSIBILITY AND EDUCATION, pp. 122-31. 3d ed. London: Allen and Unwin; New York: Paul S. Eriksson, 1973. Reprinted in READINGS IN THE PHILOSOPHY OF EDUCATION: NATURE, AIMS, AND POLICY, edited by Adrian Dupuis, pp. 83-95. Urbana: University of Illinois Press, 1970; and in CURRICULUM AND EVALUATION, edited by Arno A. Bellack and Herbert M. Kliebard, pp. 123-38. Berkeley, Calif.: McCutchan Publishing, 1977.

In Peters's view, disputes about educational aims are really disputes about principles of procedure. The truth is that a quality of life is embedded in the activities which constitute education and culture and these are passed on by example, explanation, and values.

Scheffler, Israel. THE CONDITIONS OF KNOWLEDGE: AN INTRODUCTION TO EPISTEMOLOGY AND EDUCATION. Chicago: Scott, Foresman, 1965. 117 p.

Defining the philosophy of education by way of propositional knowledge, Scheffler relates theories of knowledge to teaching, knowledge and truth, belief and skill. He emphasizes educational goals and tasks, the life of intellect and rationality, and teaching as an initiation into the rational life.

Toulmin, Stephen. HUMAN UNDERSTANDING. Princeton, N.J.: Princeton University Press, 1972.

White, Mary Alice, and Duker, Jan. EDUCATION: A CONCEPTUAL AND EMPIRICAL APPROACH. New York: Holt, Rinehart and Winston, 1973. 371 p.

The text is designed to help the student in thinking analytically about different models of education and their goals, about what qualifies as acceptable evidence for the claims of various approaches to education, and about contemporary issues in education. Seven readings for each of the three sections have been reprinted to illustrate the conceptual and empirical analyses. The line of research is narrow and limited.

A 2: THE PROBLEM OF BEING—METAPHYSICS

Bowyer, Carlton H. PHILOSOPHICAL PERSPECTIVES FOR EDUCATION. Glenview, Ill.: Scott, Foresman, 1970. viii, 402 p.

Bremer, John. A MATRIX FOR MODERN EDUCATION. Toronto, Canada: McClelland and Stewart, 1975. 207 p.

Brown, Leslie Melville, ed. AIMS OF EDUCATION. New York: Teachers College Press, 1970. 183 p. Paperbound.

> The more than thirty excerpts, including the work of Plato, Dewey, and Hook, are pointed toward educational aims and their theoretical assumptions. The anthology helps clarify the diverse approaches to aims, aim theories, and education by indicating their relationships to basic assumptions and philosophical theories.

Brumbaugh, Robert S., and Lawrence, Nathaniel M. "Aristotle's Philosophy of Education." EDUCATIONAL THEORY 9 (January 1959): 1-15.

> The authors present the Aristotelian system of causes, explain the nature of human knowing, and derive from Aristotle's premises a realist philosophy of education.

Buber, Martin. BETWEEN MAN AND MAN. Translated by Ronald Gregory Smith. Introduction by Maurice Friedman. 1947. Afterword by Buber "The History of the Dialogical Principle." New York: Macmillan, 1965. xxi, 229 p.

> Chapter 4 contains a statement of educational aims. The philosophy of personalism, while not always orthodox, is nonetheless hebraic and religious.

Frankena, William K. "Educational Values and Goals: Some Dispositions to be Fostered." MONIST 52, no. 1 (1968): 1-10. Reprinted in CURRICULUM AND EVALUATION, edited by Arno A. Bellack and Herbert M. Kliebard, pp. 131-38. Berkeley, Calif.: McCutchan Publishing, 1977.

> What dispositions is education to foster? Giving the philosophical reply that such dispositions are those required either for the moral life, the life of right action, or for the good life, Frankena further explores his answer in terms of Dewey's thought, analytic philosophy, and existentialism which, apart from Thomism and Marxism, he feels are the main currents in western philosophy today.

Gilbert, Roger. LES IDEES ACTUELLES EN PEGAGOGIE. Paris: Le Centurion, 1973. 301 p.

Greenbaum, William. "America in Search of a New Ideal: An Essay on the

Rise of Pluralism." HARVARD EDUCATIONAL REVIEW 44, no. 3 (1974): 411-40.

> The decline of Protestant domination has left America without an ideal to direct the socialization process. The need, therefore, is great for developing a new and universal ideal which will take pluralism seriously.

Jeffreys, Montagu Vaughan Castelman. EDUCATION: ITS NATURE AND PURPOSE. London: Allen and Unwin; New York: Barnes and Noble, 1971. xii, 124 p. Paperbound.

> Jeffreys gives a short introduction to the theory and methods of education in reference to the important personal and social problems all individuals must face who engage in the process of schooling, whether students or teachers.

Lauwerys, Joseph Albert, ed. IDEALS AND IDEOLOGIES. London: Evans Brothers, 1969. 127 p.

Leif, Jean. INSPIRATIONS ET TENDANCES NOUVELLES DE L'EDUCATION. Paris: Delagrave, 1967. 119 p.

Menck, Peter. DIE ERZIEHUNG DER JUGEND ZUR EHRE GOTTES UND ZUM NUTZEN DES NAECHSTEN. BEGRUENDUNG UND INTENTIONEN DER PAEDAGOGIK AUGUST HERMANN FRANCKES. [The education of youth to the love of God and neighbor. The foundation and aims of education of August Hermann Francke]. Wuppertal, W. Ger.; Ratingen, W. Ger.; and Dusseldorf, W. Ger.: Henn, 1969. 145 p.

Monahan, Bryan W. MYSTERY, MAGIC, MUSIC AND METAPHYSICS. Sydney, Australia: Tidal Publications, 1971. 219 p.

Morris, Ben. OBJECTIVES AND PERSPECTIVES IN EDUCATION: STUDIES IN EDUCATIONAL THEORY (1955-1970). London and Boston: Routledge and Kegan Paul, 1972. x, 272 p.

O'Neill, William F. SELECTED EDUCATIONAL HERESIES. Glenview, Ill.: Scott, Foresman, 1969. 373 p.

> Enjoy what the author believes to be some unorthodox views concerning the nature and purposes of contemporary education.

Troeger, Walter. ERZIEHUNGSZIELE. [Educational aims]. Munich: Ehrenwirth, 1974. 236 p.

Whitehead, Alfred North. THE AIMS OF EDUCATION AND OTHER ESSAYS. New York: Macmillan, 1929. vii, 247 p. Reprint. London: Williams,

1950; New York: New American Library of Literature, 1961; New York: Free Press, 1967.

Wilson, John. IDEALS: A GUIDE TO MORAL AND METAPHYSICAL OUT-LOOKS. New York: Morehouse-Barlow Co., 1974. 95 p.

A 3: HUMAN NATURE AND UNITY

Ackoff, Russell Lincoln, and Emery, Fred E. ON PURPOSEFUL SYSTEMS. Chicago and New York: Aldine-Atherton, 1972. xiii, 288 p.

> The nature and order of science can shed light on the ideal-seeking tendencies of personal and social human behavior. The notion of system, however, may break down when too narrowly applied to free and intelligent activities of man.

Bailey, Stephen K. THE PURPOSES OF EDUCATION. Bloomington, Ind.: Phi Delta Kappa, 1976. 142 p.

Goodlad, John I. "On the Cultivation and Corruption of Education." EDUCATIONAL FORUM 42 (March 1978): 267-78.

> Goodlad finds that the aims of education and the purpose or goals of schooling are not necessarily the same, nor is preparation of the individual for society always identical to personal development. Value lies not in the attainment of answers but in the quest for them; hence, the educational system will be invigorated if it is guided only loosely by ends and more sharply by concern for quality of education.

Novak, Michael. "One Species, Many Cultures." AMERICAN SCHOLAR 43, no. 1 (1973-74): 113-21.

> Culture has three main locations: the actual ways of ordinary people, the relatively few artists, scholars, and critical persons in whom is alive a genuinely high culture, and the host of professionals who though highly educated are not necessarily in tune with the best traditions of the past. Americans need a high culture, a public and popular humanities, in which they unselfishly respect the moral analogies between their lives and those of others.

Saint-Hilaire, Philippe B. EDUCATION AND THE AIM OF HUMAN LIFE. 3d ed. Pondicherry, India: Sri Aurobindo International Centre of Education, 1967. 167 p.

Schrag, Francis. "Development as the Aim of Education: A Response to Kohlberg and Mayer." HARVARD EDUCATIONAL REVIEW 43, no. 2 (1973): 309-11.

Schrag criticizes Kohlberg and Mayer for (1) their use of the open question argument and developmental-philosophic strategy and, possibly, ignoring that there is more for the development of children than cognitive stages; and (2) their constructing a philosophical joining of Dewey and Kant despite Dewey's antagonism to Kantian ethics and the basic incompatibility of the two approaches. An acceptable educational synthesis ought to be grounded in both philosophy and the empirical sciences.

Thelen, Herbert Arnold. EDUCATION AND THE HUMAN QUEST: FOUR DESIGNS FOR EDUCATION. Chicago: University of Chicago Press, 1972. vii, 228 p.

A 4: HUMAN INTELLECTIVE POWERS

Bauer, Norman J. "Curriculum and the Purposes of Education." KAPPA DELTA PI RECORD 15, no. 1 (1977): 46-47.

"Acquiring clear and accurate conceptual images of philosophies of education and the views of mankind which these philosophies generate is a central challenge for curriculum leadership in the years of collectivization which lie immediately ahead."

Brown, Stuart C., ed. PHILOSOPHERS DISCUSS EDUCATION. Totowa, N.J.: Rowman and Littlefield, 1975. ix, 260 p.

The symposia on the philosophy of education include topics on autonomy as an educational ideal (Dearden, Telfer, Hare), education and the development of the understanding (Elliott, Langford, Hirst), quality and equality in education (Cooper, O'Hagan, Atkinson), the neutral teacher (Warnock, Norman, Montefiore), and academic freedom (Brown, Griffiths, Peters).

Dearden, R.F.; Hirst, P.H.; Peters, R.S., eds. EDUCATION AND THE DEVELOPMENT OF REASON. 3 vols. London: Routledge and Kegan Paul, 1975.

Volume 2: REASON. 258 p.

Volume 3: EDUCATION AND REASON. 148 p.

Gagne, Robert M. "The Implications of Instructional Aims for Learning." In DEFINING EDUCATIONAL OBJECTIVES, edited by C.M. Lindvall, pp. 37-46. Pittsburgh: University of Pittsburgh Press, 1964. Reprinted in CURRICULUM AND EVALUATION, edited by Arno A. Bellack and Herbert M. Kliebard, pp. 111-22. Berkeley, Calif.: McCutchan Publishing, 1977.

The following categories of objectives must be distinguished, if the differential sets of conditions are to bring about optimal learning: problem solving and strategy using, principles, concepts, associations, chains, identifications, and responses. These are ordered from the more complex to the simple. The learning of the more complex requires the prelearning of the simpler forms of learning behavior.

Kollmann, Roland. BILDUNG, BILDUNGSIDEAL, WELTANSCHAUUNG. [Intellectual education, cultural ideal, philosophy of life]. Ratingen, W. Ger.; Kastellaun, W. Ger.; and Dusseldorf, W. Ger.: Henn, 1972. xvi, 336 p.

The ideals and philosophy of cultural education are examined from the theoretical positions of Eduard Spranger and Max Frischeisen-Koehler.

Scheffler, Israel. "Philosophical Models of Teaching." HARVARD EDUCATIONAL REVIEW 35, no. 2 (1965): 131-43.

This critique of learning, according to the theory of impression (Locke), insight (Plato and St. Augustine), and rule (Kant), is also a synthesis of these three models of teaching. Scheffler suggests new criteria for assessing the purposes of education.

Torbert, William. LEARNING FROM EXPERIENCE: TOWARD CONSCIOUSNESS. New York: Columbia University Press, 1972. xviii, 248 p.

Weisse, Edward B., et al. THE SYMMETRICAL TEACHER: AN INTRODUCTION TO AMERICAN EDUCATION. Dubuque, Iowa: Kendall/Hunt Publishing, 1976. xviii, 185 p.

A 5: HUMAN AFFECTIVE POWERS

Chynes, Manfred. SENTICS: THE TOUCH OF EMOTIONS. New York: Anchor Press, Doubleday, 1977. 288 p.

Grossman, Mordecai. THE PHILOSOPHY OF HELVETIUS, WITH SPECIAL EMPHASIS ON THE EDUCATIONAL IMPLICATIONS OF SENSATIONALISM. New York: Bureau of Publications, Teachers College, Columbia University, 1926. Reprint. New York: AMS Press, 1972. 181 p.

The ideas of Helvetius (1715-71) gave some shape to the school of utilitarianism in education. All mental powers are assumed to be forms of sensation responsive only to pleasure or pain. Education and society must give the greatest possible pleasure to the greatest number of citizens. To this end, the environment must be very much like Walden Two.

Heinen, Klaus. DAS PROBLEM DER ZIELSETZUNG IN DER PAEDAGOGIK WILHELM FLITNERS. [The problem of aims in Flitner's theory of education]. Bern, Switz., and Frankfort on the Main, W. Ger.: Lang, 1973. v, 306 p.

In this critical interpretation of Flitner's thought, Heinen discovers the answer to the problem of aims in what Flitner calls the emancipatory possibilities. Heinen intends his approach to be a model for all research into the thought of Flitner.

Kohlberg, Lawrence, and Mayer, Rochelle. "Development as the Aim of Education." HARVARD EDUCATIONAL REVIEW 42, no. 4 (1972): 449-96. Bibliog.

The authors maintain that only educational progressivism, most clearly identified with the work of John Dewey, can provide an adequate understanding of the process of education. They note progressivism's cognitive-developmental psychology, INTERACTIONIST EPISTEMOLOGY, and its philosophically examined ethics.

_____. "A Reply to Schrag." HARVARD EDUCATIONAL REVIEW 43, no. 2 (1973): 312-14.

The reply meets Schrag's criticism directly: (1) "The established fact that there is a cognitive-structural strand to all universal forms of development" in man does not lead them to claim that development is only cognitive, nor is it only Piagetian; (2) Dewey and Kant shared a conception of nonrelativistic ethical principles and of ethical justification.

A 6: HUMAN AESTHETIC POWERS

Fleming, William. ARTS AND IDEAS. Reprint. New York: Holt, Rinehart and Winston, 1968. 580 p.

Guggenheimer, Richard. SIGHT AND INSIGHT. Reprint. Port Washington, N.Y.: Kennikat Press, 1968. 246 p.

Hartshorne, Charles. THE PHILOSOPHY AND PSYCHOLOGY OF SENSATION. Reprint. Port Washington, N.Y.: Kennikat Press, 1968. 288 p.

Prall, David Wight. AESTHETIC JUDGMENT. Reprint. New York: Apollo Editions, 1967. 378 p. Paperbound.

Scruton, Roger. ART AND IMAGINATION: A STUDY IN THE PHILOSOPHY OF THE MIND. London: Methuen; New York: Harper and Row, 1974. 256 p. Paperbound.

A 7: THE PROBLEM OF VALUES—ETHICS

Bantock, Geoffrey Herman. EDUCATION AND VALUES: ESSAYS IN THE

THEORY OF EDUCATION. London: Faber and Faber, 1965; New York: Humanities Press, 1966. 182 p.

Beck, Clive M.; Crittenden, Brian S.; and Sullivan, Edmund V., eds. MORAL EDUCATION: INTERDISCIPLINARY APPROACHES. Toronto, Canada: University of Toronto Press, 1971. x, 402 p.

Belo, Michael, et al. APPROACHES TO VALUES AND EDUCATION. Dubuque, Iowa: Wm. C. Brown, 1966. xiii, 322 p.

Combs, Arthur W., et al. HUMANISTIC EDUCATION: OBJECTIVES AND ASSESSMENT. A report of the ASCD Working Group on humanistic education. Washington, D.C.: Association for Supervision and Curriculum Development, 1978. xiii, 56 p.

Humanistic education is a commitment to education and practice in which all facets of the teaching-learning process give major emphasis to the freedom, value, worth, dignity, and integrity of persons. A checklist of one hundred items is intended for observation, goals setting, and the support of humanistic endeavors.

Frankl, Viktor Emil. MAN'S SEARCH FOR MEANING: AN INTRODUCTION TO LOGOTHERAPY. 1962. Newly rev. and enl. ed. of FROM DEATH-CAMP TO EXISTENTIALISM. Translated by Ilse Lasch. Preface by Gordon W. Allport. Boston: Beacon Press, 1970. 150 p. New York: Washington Square Press, 1966. xv, 222 p. Also with introduction by Leslie D. Weatherhead. London: Hodder and Stoughton, 1964. xii, 137 p.

Frankl believes every human being must find a system of values that will make his life meaningful. The acceptance of life, sometimes even suffering, enables the individual to attain the purpose of life through self-transcendence.

Hare, R.M. ESSAYS ON THE MORAL CONCEPTS. Berkeley and Los Angeles: University of California Press, 1972. 109 p.

Kanz, Heinrich. DER HUMANE REALISMUS JUSTUS MOESERS. [The humane realism of Justus Moeser]. Wuppertal, W. Ger.; Ratingen, W. Ger.; and Kastellaun, W. Ger.: Henn, 1971. 302 p. Bibliog.

Justus Moeser (1720-94), a contemporary of Goethe, Kant, von Humboldt, and Herder, exercised a decisive influence on German thought by combining the ideals of justice, liberty, and humanity with the educational aims of a new humanism. Kanz presents his thinking in moral and intellectual education and brings out its special relevance today. The bibliography is very extensive (pp. 271-83).

Krikorian, Yervant Hovannes. THE PURSUIT OF IDEALS. Springfield, Ill.:

Charles C Thomas, 1970. 113 p.

Mill, John Stuart. JOHN STUART MILL ON EDUCATION. Edited with an introduction and notes by Francis W. Garforth. New York: Teachers College Press, 1971. xiii, 236 p.

Ozmon, Howard, ed. CONTEMPORARY CRITICS OF EDUCATION. Danville, Ill.: Interstate Printers and Publishers, 1970. 223 p.

> This text contains essays by Adler, Barzun, Bestor, Bruner, Conant, Goodman, A. Huxley, Hutchins, Koerner, Maritain, Montagu, Montessori, Neill, Rafferty, Rickover, Russell, Skinner, and Whitehead.

Parker, J. Cecil, et al. "Philosophies and Aims of Education." In CURRI-CULUM IN AMERICA, by J. Cecil Parker, T. Bentley Edwards, and William H. Stegeman, pp. 43-46. New York: Thomas Y. Crowell, 1962. Reprinted in READINGS IN THE FOUNDATIONS OF EDUCATION, edited by James C. Stone and Frederick W. Schneider, pp. 511-13. 2d ed. New York: Thomas Y. Crowell, 1971.

> The solution to the philosophic conflict seems to be found in developing a curriculum for decision making, wherein students learn through critical thinking to make decisions compatible with Democratic society's many conflicting philosophies such as realism, pragmatism, and idealism.

Riesman, David; Gusfield, Joseph; and Gamson, Zelda. ACADEMIC VALUES AND MASS EDUCATION. Garden City, N.Y.: Doubleday, 1970. xxii, 332 p.

Splete, Allen P. "Values and the Survival of the Liberal Arts College." LIBERAL EDUCATION 63, no. 1 (1977): 118-25.

> Inspired by the life of the Japanese educator Makiguchi, Splete looks at the central purpose of collegiate education as the creation of values which were defined at the Danforth Foundation Workshop of 1975 as "the determiners in persons and groups that influence choice and behavior. Values cause persons to believe that a particular alternative is preferable to another. . ." (p. 118).

A 8: THE PROBLEM OF THOUGHT AND LANGUAGE— PHILOSOPHICAL ANALYSIS

Broudy, Harry S. "The Philosophical Foundations of Educational Objectives." EDUCATIONAL THEORY 20, no. 1 (1970): 3-21. Reprinted in CURRICULUM AND EVALUATION, edited by Arno A. Bellack and Herbert M. Kliebard, pp. 91-110. Berkeley, Calif.: McCutchan Publishing, 1977.

Broudy believes philosophy contributes to objectives by providing value hierarchies or schemata. Analytic philosophy clarifies ideas and tests their adequacy. He argues that both are necessary to the professional philosopher of education for precise and internally consistent educational scholarship and insight.

Ferre, Frederick. LANGUAGE, LOGIC, AND GOD. New York: Harper and Row, 1961; Westport, Conn.: Greenwood Press, 1977. viii, 184 p.

Geertz, Clifford. THE INTERPRETATION OF CULTURES. New York: Basic Books, 1973. 470 p.

Geertz tries to encounter humanity by penetrating specific structures of signification, symbol systems, and social orders in an effort to discover a common meaning and language for the social sciences. Men complete themselves variously in different cultures: "Becoming human is becoming individual and we become individual under the guidance of cultural patterns, historically created systems of meaning in terms of which we give form, order, point, and direction to our lives" (p. 52).

Hirst, Paul Heywood, and Peters, Richard Stanley. THE LOGIC OF EDUCATION. London: Routledge and Kegan Paul, 1970; New York: Humanities Press, 1971. x, 147 p.

The authors believe that the cognitive domain of learning is uppermost.

Hollins, T.H.B., ed. AIMS IN EDUCATION: THE PHILOSOPHIC APPROACH. Manchester, Engl.: Manchester University Press, 1964. 135 p.

A wide range of educational purposes, from education to indoctrination, are discussed against the backdrop of logical and linguistic analysis. Peters also evaluates the concept of mental health.

Ihde, Don. SENSE AND SIGNIFICANCE. Pittsburgh: Duquesne University Press; New York: Humanities Press, 1973. 183 p.

Pei, Mario. VOICES OF MAN: THE MEANING AND FUNCTION OF LANGUAGE. London: Allen and Unwin, 1962; New York: Humanities Press, 1964. 138 p.

Polanyi, Michael, and Prosch, Harry. MEANING. Chicago: University of Chicago Press, 1975. 246 p.

Soltis, Jonas F. SEEING, KNOWING, AND BELIEVING. London: Allen and Unwin; Reading, Mass.: Addison-Wesley, 1966. 156 p.

Weaver, Richard M. "A Responsible Rhetoric." INTERCOLLEGIATE REVIEW 12, no. 2 (1976-77): 81-87.

> In the language of philosophy, Weaver sees four basic ways of thinking about reality or interpreting experience: being, cause, relationship, authority. These four norms can be applied to determine the credibility of any writer, speaker, or thinker. Every student in the philosophy of education is urged to test the probative value of these basic ways of thinking in the critical evaluation of any educational philosophy.

White, Alan R. MODAL THINKING. Ithaca, N.Y.: Cornell University Press, 1975. 190 p.

Whitehead, Alfred North. SYMBOLISM: ITS MEANING AND EFFECT. 1927. New York: Capricorn, 1959. 88 p. Paperbound.

Wilson, John. LANGUAGE AND THE PURSUIT OF TRUTH. Cambridge: Cambridge University Press, 1967. 105 p.

Zabeeh, Farhang, et al. READINGS IN SEMANTICS. Urbana: University of Illinois Press, 1974. 853 p.

A TR: THE PROBLEM OF GOD—THEOLOGY AND RELIGION

Ben-Horin, Meir. COMMON FAITH--UNCOMMON PEOPLE: ESSAYS IN RECONSTRUCTIONIST JUDAISM. New York: Reconstructionist Press, 1970. 245 p.

> The author is utterly opposed to an excessive antirationalistic treatment or interpretation of revelation and the faith-and-reason understanding of Judaism, Jewish education, and Zionism. This work represents but a segment of Hebraic thinking on the subject of religion and education. It is a voice echoed by many other religious philosophers of education.

Casotti, Mario. IL PENSIERO PEDAGOGICO DI PADRE GEMELLI. Milan: Editrice Vita e Pensiero, 1961. 108 p.

Ferre, Frederick. LANGUAGE, LOGIC, AND GOD. New York: Harper and Row, 1961. Reprint. Westport, Conn.: Greenwood Press, 1977. viii, 184 p.

Fuller, Edmund, ed. THE CHRISTIAN IDEA OF EDUCATION: PAPERS AND DISCUSSIONS BY WILLIAM G. POLLARD AND OTHERS. New Haven, Conn.: Yale University Press, 1957. Reprint. Hamden, Conn.: Archon Books, 1975. xv, 265 p.

This symposium volume contains lectures on education by John Courtney Murray, Jacques Maritain, Reinhold Niebuhr, and others.

Greenbaum, William. "America in Search of a New Ideal: An Essay on the Rise of Pluralism." HARVARD EDUCATIONAL REVIEW 44, no. 3 (1974): 411-40.

> Greenbaum examines these questions: is it true that Protestant domination has declined in America? what are the alternatives to the basic Judeo-Christian outlook?

Hoye, William J. ACTUALITAS OMNIUM ACTUUM: MAN'S BEATIFIC VISION OF GOD AS APPREHENDED BY THOMAS AQUINAS. Meisenheim am Glan, W. Ger.: Hain, 1975. 363 p.

> Since every person is called to share God's life for all eternity, education has the specific goal of helping men toward the unending enjoyment of the Divine Presence.

Jaeger, Werner. EARLY CHRISTIANITY AND GREEK PAIDEIA. Oxford: Oxford University Press, 1961. 154 p.

Jahsmann, Allan Hart. WHAT'S LUTHERAN IN EDUCATION? St. Louis, Mo.: Concordia Publishing, 1960. x, 185 p.

> Jahsmann outlines, from revelation and theology, a religious philosophy of education for schools of the Missouri Synod within the Lutheran Church. Since human beings belong to God, their education must prepare for everlasting life with God.

Kasch, Wilhelm Friedrich, ed. OEKUMENISCHE BIBLIOGRAPHIE. [Ecumenical bibliography in religious education]. Paderborn, W. Ger.: F. Schoeningh, 1976. xxiii, 348 p.

> This bibliography offers an important entry to differing Christian outlooks on the philosophy of religious education. The problem of Christian education, in its aims and curriculum, has preoccupied German educators for several centuries and their writings have always been important in this field.

Morgan, John H. IN SEARCH OF MEANING: FROM FREUD TO TEILHARD DE CHARDIN. Washington, D.C.: University Press of America, 1977. 128 p. Bibliog., biographies. Paperbound.

> This study probes the nature of man's quest for life's meaning through the critical analysis of classic statements by Freud, Sartre, Michael Novak, Alan Watts, Abraham Joshua Heschel, Karl Barth, Dietrich Bonhoeffer, and Teilhard De Chardin.

Pilch, Judah, and Ben-Horin, Meir, eds. JUDAISM AND THE JEWISH

SCHOOL: SELECTED ESSAYS ON THE DIRECTION AND PURPOSE OF JEWISH EDUCATION. New York: Bloch Publishing, 1966. xii, 336 p.

> The role of the Hebrew language and religion shapes the philosophy and the curriculum of Judaic education. Background studies facilitate understanding the purpose and reasons for the Jewish school and its fundamental directions.

Stoops, John A. RELIGIOUS VALUES IN EDUCATION. Danville, Ill.: Interstate Printers and Publishers, 1967. 161 p.

Zeigler, Earle F. "Idealism in Education." In READINGS IN THE FOUNDATIONS OF EDUCATION, edited by James C. Stone and Frederick W. Schneider, pp. 469-79. 2d ed. New York: Thomas Y. Crowell, 1971.

> Idealists value society or civilization as a purposeful, spiritual means of individual personality developments. The educational process, in terms of society, school, aims, and objectives, and the individual, requires a continual adjustment of the human being to God that is manifested in the intellectual, emotional, and volitional environment of man (Horne).

A NS: THE PROBLEM OF THE COSMOS—PHYSICAL AND MATHEMATICAL SCIENCES

Ackoff, Russell Lincoln, and Emery, Fred E. ON PURPOSEFUL SYSTEMS. Chicago and New York: Aldine-Atherton, 1972. xiii, 288 p.

> Functional concepts of human behavior can be used to illuminate the meaning of concepts of formal science, which are often taken as indefinable. Concepts of science form a system and their wide range, both functional and structural, are compatible. Discussions center on human behavior, the process of pursuing purposes, interactions (feeling, signs, models, cooperation) of purposeful systems, social and ideal-seeking systems.

Bell, Terrel Howard. A PHILOSOPHY OF EDUCATION FOR THE SPACE AGE: A GUIDE TO PRACTICAL THINKING ABOUT THE AIMS AND PURPOSES OF EDUCATION TODAY. New York: Exposition Press, 1962. 62 p.

Bronowski, Jacob. SCIENCE AND HUMAN VALUES. Rev. ed. Harmondsworth, Engl.: Penguin Books, 1964. 94 p.

Haeussler, Peter, and Lauterbach, Roland. ZIELE NATURWISSENSCHAFTLICHEN UNTERRICHTS. [Aims of the natural science curricula]. Weinheim, W. Ger. and Basel, Switz.: Beltz, 1976. 170 p.

> The authors report research projects and symposia at the Christian Albrechts University at Kiel where the philosophy of science educa-

tion and its outcomes are of major interest. Not all will agree
with the solutions reached there.

Lecomte du Nouey, Pierre. HUMAN DESTINY. New York: Longmans,
Green; New York: New American Library, 1947. xix, 289 p.

The author outlines a theory of "telefinalism" which opposes the
mechanistic metaphysics of some realists with evidence that some
intelligence outside the realm of chance is discernible in the universe. Man is clearly destined for union with God.

_____. THE ROAD TO REASON. Translated and edited by Mary LeComte
du Nouey. New York: Longmans, Green, 1948. 254 p.

Levi, Isaac. GAMBLING WITH TRUTH: AN ESSAY ON INDUCTION AND
THE AIMS OF SCIENCE. Cambridge: M.I.T. Press, 1974. 251 p.

Piaget, Jean. BIOLOGY AND KNOWLEDGE: AN ESSAY ON THE RELATIONS
BETWEEN ORGANIC REGULATIONS AND COGNITIVE PROCESSES. Trans-
lated from French by Beatrix Walsh. Edinburgh: Edinburgh University Press;
Chicago: University of Chicago Press, 1971. xii, 384 p.

Rogers, Joseph A. "A Compass Rose for Educators." EDUCATIONAL FORUM
42 (January 1978): 145-50.

Hypothesizing that man lives in a cosmos rather than a chaos, the
Greeks had, in their use of pattern, rooted their sturdy sense of
self-worth in the universe itself and thus gained entree to the
realm of excellence. Modern educators are urged by Rogers to
reorient themselves once again by this compass rose.

A HS: THE PROBLEM OF HUMAN SOCIETY—HUMAN AND
   SOCIAL SCIENCES

Berger, Peter L. "'Sincerity' and 'Authenticity' in Modern Society." PUBLIC
INTEREST 31 (Spring 1973): 81-90.

After reviewing the intellectual drama depicted in Lionel Trilling's
SINCERITY AND AUTHENTICITY, Berger attempts a sociological
amplification on the presupposition that most of the time ideas are
grounded in social experience. The reflections on the political
events of 1972 still offer a challenge to the thinker in education.

Brameld, Theodore. EDUCATION AS POWER. New York: Holt, Rinehart
and Winston, 1965. xi, 146 p.

Brameld looks to long-range educational goals to convert the global
community into a humane and fulfilling society. The path to

social action and reform is reconstructionism.

_____. EDUCATION FOR THE EMERGING AGE: NEWER ENDS AND STRONGER MEANS. 1961. Foreword by Robert Ulich and new post-scripts by the author. New York: Harper and Row, 1965. 244 p.

[Cf. Broudy (1967), cited in Chapter 13, p. 234, for comment on Chapter 15, "Shall the Schools Indoctrinate?"].

Brembeck, Cole S., and Thompson, Timothy, eds. NEW STRATEGIES FOR EDUCATIONAL DEVELOPMENT. Lexington, Mass.: D.C. Heath, 1973. 170 p.

This collection of seventeen papers defines nonformal education and mounts a search for nonformal education with its own specific goals and organization.

Brose, Karl. PHILOSOPHIE UND ERZIEHUNG. [Philosophy and education]. Bern, Switz., and Frankfort on the Main, W. Ger.: Lang, 1976. 111 p.

From the philosophy of Kant, Dilthey, and the critical understand-ing of society, Brose draws important implications for education in the future. He examines traditional education in its idealistic-spiritual and ontotheological aspects, critical education from the viewpoint of Adorno and the Frankfort School of critical theory, and education for the future in terms of a free society.

Brown, Stuart C., ed. PHILOSOPHERS DISCUSS EDUCATION. Totowa, N.J.: Rowman and Littlefield, 1975. ix, 260 p.

Elliott, Langford, and Hirst discuss education as the development of understanding.

Carlson, Robert A. THE QUEST FOR CONFORMITY: AMERICANIZATION THROUGH EDUCATION. New York: John Wiley and Sons, 1975. 188 p.

The author interprets Americanization as the total effort to bring all, especially nonconformists, to accept the mores and doctrinal norms of authentic Democratic living.

Fisher, Bernice. INDUSTRIAL EDUCATION: AMERICAN IDEALS AND INSTI-TUTIONS. Madison: University of Wisconsin Press, 1967. xiii, 267 p.

Harrington, Jack. AIMS OF EDUCATION: EARLY TWENTIETH CENTURY. New York: MSS Information, 1974. 297 p.

Heintel, Peter. POLITISCHE BILDUNG ALS PRINZIP ALLER BILDUNG. [Polit-ical education as the principle for all education]. Vienna and Munich: Jugend and Volk, 1977. 156 p.

Heintel sees political education as a kind of linear adaptation or accommodation and as a mediator of ideological identity particularly for certain interest groups. Education, therefore, is directed not merely toward the removal of ignorance or the accumulation of knowledge, but toward the assimilation of ideals for political or ideological reasons. The work is a challenge to anyone who wishes to understand the dynamics of educational and cultural transmission for political ends.

Lauwerys, Joseph Albert, ed. IDEALS AND IDEOLOGIES. London: Evans Brothers, 1969. 127 p.

Lee, Gordon C. EDUCATION AND DEMOCRATIC IDEALS. New York: Harcourt, Brace and World, 1965. x, 181 p.

The classical, Christian, experimentalist traditions in modern education are clarified and placed in proper perspective in regard to tomorrow's schools. Lee provides the general philosophical backgrounds of modern educational thought.

Litt, Theodor. DAS BILDUNGSIDEAL DER DEUTSCHEN CLASSIK UND DIE MODERNE ARBEITWELT. [The German classical ideal of education and the modern world of work]. 6th ed. Bochum, W. Ger.: Kamp, 1967. 152 p.

Lukes, Steven. INDIVIDUALISM. Oxford: Blackwell, 1973; New York: Harper and Row, 1974. x, 172 p.

McBride, William. "Social Theory Sub Specie Aeternitatis: A New Perspective." YALE LAW JOURNAL 81 (April 1972): 980-1003.

Rosenow, Eliyahu. "Methods of Research and the Aims of Education." EDUCATIONAL THEORY 26, no. 3 (1976): 279-88.

Central to the controversy concerning positivism in German sociology is the thinking of Popper and Adorno. Adorno rejects the positivistic assumptions of modern sociological research. Whoever does not respond to Adorno's challenge falls into Popper's materialism. If men are genuinely aware of their own significance, then they may exercise a prudent right in setting their own educational aims.

Smith, Vincent Edward. THE SCHOOL EXAMINED: ITS AIM AND CONTENT. Milwaukee, Wis.: Bruce Publishing, 1960. 300 p.

The philosophy of the school is presented in classic philosophical style and invites comparison with the thought of Illich and Dewey.

Starr, Paul. "The Edge of Social Science." HARVARD EDUCATIONAL REVIEW 44, no. 4 (1974): 393-415.

Starr locates the distinctiveness of social science in its questions and aims rather than its methods. Of itself, social science does not constitute a complete education of society nor can it expel moral concerns because in practice moral convictions and objective understanding are necessary complements of each other. This essay on social science is equally pertinent to education.

Tillery, Dale, and Kildegaard, Ted. EDUCATIONAL GOALS, ATTITUDES, AND BEHAVIOR: A COMPARATIVE STUDY OF HIGH SCHOOL SENIORS. Cambridge, Mass.: Ballinger Publishing, 1973. 288 p.

The authors compare the aspirations of high school youth within the literature of empirical research. The research points to the power of such variables as home, school, peers, race, and sex in affecting the educational aspirations of serious youth.

Villemain, Francis T. "The Significance of the Democratic Ethic for Cultural Alternatives and American Civilization." EDUCATIONAL THEORY 26, no. 1 (1976): 40-52.

What realistic and ethically sound posture should we assume in our relationships with other cultures? It must be clear and unmistakable to all that democracy is not negotiable. Our freedoms, our values, and the procedures known to be essentially Democratic cannot be the subject of barter, trade, or compromise. In this reality lies the chief hope for achieving a global distribution of high human accomplishment.

Whitehead, Alfred North. REFLECTIONS ON MAN AND NATURE. Selected, with prologue, and edited by Ruth Nanda Nashen. New York: Harper and Row, 1961. xiv, 177 p.

A AC: THE PROBLEM OF ART AND CULTURE—HUMANE ARTS AND LETTERS

Broudy, Harry S. "Humanism in Education." JOURNAL OF AESTHETIC EDUCATION 7 (April 1973): 67-77.

Hospers, John. MEANING AND TRUTH IN THE ARTS. Chapel Hill: University of North Carolina Press, 1967. 252 p.

Matejka, Ladislav, and Titunik, Irwin R., eds. SEMIOTICS OF ART: PRAGUE SCHOOL CONTRIBUTIONS. Cambridge: M.I.T. Press, 1976. 298 p.

O'Brien, Thomas. PHILOSOPHY OF POETRY. New York: Vantage Press, 1967. 126 p.

Oikonomou, Georgios N. HAI PAIDAGOGIKAI IDEAI TO SOPHOKLEOUS.

[The educational ideals of Sophocles].   Introduction by John L. Kitsara.
Athens: [n.p.], 1973.   84 p.

Read, Sir Herbert Edward.   THE REDEMPTION OF THE ROBOT: MY ENCOUN-
TER WITH EDUCATION THROUGH ART.   London: Faber and Faber, 1970.
xiv, 271 p.

Chapter 5

CURRICULUM: DESIGN AND CONTENT—THE MATERIAL AND INSTRUMENTAL CAUSES OF EDUCATION

Inasmuch as an educator uses subject matter to aid in the refinement and transformation of a person, he speaks of instrumental and also material causes. As instrumental cause, each study in the curriculum provides facts and content for the guided experiences of formal and informal instruction. As material cause, the subject matter becomes matter to be learned and to be made productive in the learner at the three degrees of abstraction. At every abstractive level, the knower comprehends, analyzes, synthesizes, and ultimately develops the power to philosophize. This also occurs within the moral and affective domains of human behavior. The collective experiences of such learning provide a content to be mastered, values to be assessed, a matrix from which to create a philosophy of life, a refinement or education that adorns the whole person, totally, and in all capacities.

B 1: THE PROBLEM ON KNOWING—EPISTEMOLOGY

Brent, Allen. PHILOSOPHICAL FOUNDATIONS FOR THE CURRICULUM. London: Allen and Unwin, 1978. 240 p.

The author looks at the work of Plato and its consequences in the ideas of J.H. Newman, Freire, and Hirst. Relying somewhat on the work of Chomsky, Brent presents his own objective foundation for curriculum judgments and the art of making truth judgments.

Brown, Richard, ed. KNOWLEDGE, EDUCATION, AND CULTURAL CHANGE. London: Tavistock Publications, 1973. Distributed by Harper and Row; Barnes and Noble. xii, 410 p.

Dicker, Georges. DEWEY'S THEORY OF KNOWING. Philadelphia: Temple University Press, 1976. 72 p.

This full-length account of Dewey's epistemology provides a sympathetic interpretative study and defense of what Dewey believes to be the nature of knowledge.

Diorio, Joseph A. "Knowledge, Truth and Power in the Curriculum." EDU-CATIONAL THEORY 27, no. 2 (1977): 103-10.

> Diorio is uncomfortable with a curriculum that is a vehicle for the social control of individuals and where the elements included can make a difference in the direction of such control. An independent ethical assessment of knowledge elements in the curriculum really requires equally independent epistemological criteria for the identification of legitimate knowledge.

Hirst, Paul Heywood. KNOWLEDGE AND THE CURRICULUM. London and Boston: Routledge and Kegan Paul, 1974. 208 p. Paperbound.

> This collection of philosophical papers is considered to be a very substantial work on the kind of rational principles that should determine the fashioning of school curricula. It will help clarify the fundamental thinking of teacher-educators and of all those preoccupied with developing rationally justified courses of study and curricula.

Jones, Howard Mumford. REFLECTIONS ON LEARNING. 1958. Reprint. Freeport, N.Y.: Books for Libraries Press, 1969. 97 p.

Rescher, Nicholas. DIALECTICS: A CONTROVERSY-ORIENTED APPROACH TO THE THEORY OF KNOWLEDGE. Albany: State University of New York Press, 1977. xiv, 128 p.

Wilson, John. PHILOSOPHY AND PRACTICAL EDUCATION. London: Routledge and Kegan Paul, 1977. 144 p.

> Wilson examines the practical importance of a philosophy of education. The emphasis is on the critical and dialectical significance of educational philosophy and on the necessity for clear conceptual thinking. This is a good introduction for the beginning teacher or student of education to the discussions about the meaning of education, the concepts of discipline and authority, and the content of the curriculum.

B 2: THE PROBLEM OF BEING—METAPHYSICS

Bellack, Arno A., and Kliebard, Herbert M., eds. READINGS IN EDUCATIONAL RESEARCH: CURRICULUM AND EVALUATION. Berkeley, Calif.: McCutchan Publishing, 1977. xv, 666 p.

> These readings present viewpoints not only of self-styled curriculum specialists, but also of other educators and philosophers who address themselves to fundamental curriculum questions. In regard to curriculum purposes, the articles by Broudy, Gagne, Peters, Frankena, Hirst, and Wirth raise significant philosophical issues.

Bennett, John B. "Liberal Education--Why?" LIBERAL EDUCATION 63, no. 1 (1977): 67-79.

> In reassessing the rationales for liberal education, Bennett takes up, one at a time, the arguments based on vocational and economic utility, the contribution to society, the enhancement of self-knowledge, and its value simply as such.

Blueher, Hans. DIE HUMANISTISCHE BILDUNGSMACHT. [The humanizing power of education]. Edited by Helmwart Hierdeis. Heidenhem/B, W. Ger.: Suedmarkverlag Fritsch, 1976. 165 p.

> The last word of this famous historian, author, philosopher, and therapist was in defense of humanistic education. His naturalism and shocking impiety have drawn criticism from many educational writers. He remains quite controversial.

Cenacchi, Giuseppe. IL LAVORO NEL PENSIERO DI TOMMASO D'AQUINO. Rome: Coletti Editore, 1977. 200 p.

Durkheim, Emile. THE EVOLUTION OF EDUCATIONAL THOUGHT. Introduction by Maurice Halbwachs. Translator's introduction by Peter Collins. London: Routledge and Kegan Paul, 1977. 384 p.

> These lectures of 1902, among the last to be translated, cover eight hundred years of educational development in Europe and deal chiefly with the kind of theoretical training teachers ought to have. They focus on the curriculum as well as on the formation and development of secondary education in France.

Guttchen, Robert S., and Bandman, Bertram, eds. PHILOSOPHICAL ESSAYS ON CURRICULUM. Philadelphia: J.B. Lippincott, 1969. x, 388 p.

> The essays review, from a philosophical foundation, the course of studies in the formal sciences, the physical and natural sciences, history and the social sciences, literature and the arts, and philosophy itself. The question of what values to teach still remains to the authors an open one.

Milligan, Nancy Gertrude. RELATIONSHIP OF THE PROFESSED PHILOSOPHY TO THE SUGGESTED EDUCATIONAL EXPERIENCES: A STUDY IN CURRENT ELEMENTARY SCHOOL CURRICULUM MAKING. New York: Bureau of Publications, Teachers College, Columbia University, 1937. Reprint. New York: AMS Press, 1972. vi, 198 p.

Patty, William Lovell. A STUDY OF MECHANISM IN EDUCATION: AN EXAMINATION OF THE CURRICULUM-MAKING DEVICES OF FRANKLIN BOBBITT, W.W. CHARTERS, AND C.C. PETERS FROM THE POINT OF VIEW OF RELATIVISTIC PRAGMATISM. New York: Bureau of Publications, Teachers College, Columbia University, 1938. Reprint. New York: AMS Press, 1972. v, 183 p.

Phenix, Philip H. REALMS OF MEANING: A PHILOSOPHY OF THE CUR-
RICULUM FOR GENERAL EDUCATION. New York: McGraw-Hill, 1964.
xvi, 391 p.

> The philosophy of the curriculum embraces symbolics, empirics,
> aesthetics, synnoetics, ethics, synoptics. The author's comprehen-
> sion of learning is broadly humane.

Pinar, William, ed. CURRICULUM THEORIZING: THE RECONCEPTUALISTS.
Berkeley, Calif.: McCutchan Publishing, 1975. xiv, 452 p.

Short, Edmund C., and Marconnit, George D., eds. CONTEMPORARY
THOUGHT ON PUBLIC SCHOOL CURRICULUM. Dubuque, Iowa: Wm. C.
Brown, 1968. xxvii, 369 p.

Tyler, Ralph W.; Gagne, Robert M.; and Scriven, Michael. PERSPECTIVES
OF CURRICULUM EVALUATION. Chicago: Rand McNally, 1967. 102 p.

> The articles of Stake, Tyler, Gagne, and Scriven are followed
> with a synopsis by Ahmann. Evaluation is a secondary and relative
> activity in the development of curricula but essential for the dis-
> covering of principles and the testing of assumptions.

Venable, Tom C. PHILOSOPHICAL FOUNDATIONS OF THE CURRICULUM.
Chicago: Rand McNally, 1967. 119 p.

Von Wright, G.H. WHAT IS HUMANISM? Monograph of the Department of
Philosophy. Lawrence: University of Kansas, 1977. 25 p.

B 3: HUMAN NATURE AND UNITY

Burns, Richard W. NEW APPROACHES TO BEHAVIORAL OBJECTIVES.
Dubuque, Iowa: Wm. C. Brown, 1972. viii, 118 p.

> By learning to create and express objectives properly, the reader
> can extend his ability to plan and communicate a program of
> studies. All domains of behavior are well explained with examples
> taken from various curricula.

Clark, D. Cecil. USING INSTRUCTIONAL OBJECTIVES IN TEACHING.
Glenview, Ill.: Scott, Foresman, 1972. vi, 167 p.

> The book, written primarily for teachers, curriculum designers, and
> administrators, is inherently tied to curriculum organization as a
> whole. Gives practice in the art of sequencing study, not by sub-
> ject matter, but by instructional objectives.

Crary, Ryland Wesley. HUMANIZING THE SCHOOL: CURRICULUM DEVEL-

OPMENT AND THEORY. New York: Alfred A. Knopf, 1969. xi, 481 p.

Geiger, Louis G. "On the Liberal Arts and Employability: Educational Mis-understanding and Intellectual Snobbery." LIBERAL EDUCATION 63, no. 3 (1977): 491-95.

> A liberal education is one that can enrich any occupation and truly approaches the utopian ideal of democracy. There is no such thing as being liberally overeducated for any job.

Hackett, Marie G. SUCCESS IN THE CLASSROOM: AN APPROACH TO INSTRUCTION. New York: Holt, Rinehart and Winston, 1971. 109 p.

> General goals, intellectual skills, performance objectives, criterion-referenced assessment, components of the learning process, and evaluation are identified and discussed as interrelated factors of the curriculum.

Hamachek, Don E. ENCOUNTERS WITH THE SELF. 2d ed. New York: Holt, Rinehart and Winston, 1978. xvii, 284 p.

> This work, about self-help, explains how the self grows, changes, and expresses its personality in intellectual, affective, and moral behavior. The entire work is directed toward helping the student respond positively to the Socratic dictum: "Know thyself."

Havighurst, Robert J. DEVELOPMENTAL TASKS AND EDUCATION. 3d ed. New York: David McKay, 1972. vii, 119 p.

> The accent of this work is on learning tasks from infancy to middle age and late maturity. Developmental tasks are defined as those that arise at a very early or later period in the life of the indi-vidual. The successful achievement of which leads to happiness and to success with subsequent tasks.

Klausmeier, Herbert J., and Ripple, Richard E. LEARNING AND HUMAN ABILITIES: EDUCATIONAL PSYCHOLOGY. 3d ed. New York: Harper and Row, 1971. xxii, 810 p.

> The authors describe a system that permits the educator to organize his knowledge about learning, abilities, and educational practices effectively. The nature of learning and human abilities, educa-tional and instructional objectives, and the achieving of learning outcomes are related to changing the young person into a thinking, doing, feeling adult of magnificent abilities.

McAshan, H.H. THE GOALS APPROACH TO PERFORMANCE OBJECTIVES. Philadelphia: W.B. Saunders, 1974. v, 306 p.

> The text is primarily designed to benefit students through better planned, implemented and evaluated instructional programs. It

offers techniques of ordering any institution's course materials and curricula to attainable goals and objectives.

Mann, John. LEARNING TO BE: THE EDUCATION OF HUMAN POTENTIAL. London: Collier-Macmillan; New York: Free Press, 1972. xii, 269 p.

Mann emphasizes the personal growth of the individual as the heart of the educational experience. He wishes to describe educational potentialities and alternatives in which the goal is to teach the student how to understand, direct, and develop himself. The author gives details of the processes for educating human potential and strategies for changing human behavior.

Payne, David A., ed. CURRICULUM EVALUATION: COMMENTARIES ON PURPOSE, PROCESS, PRODUCT. Lexington, Mass.: D.C. Heath, 1974. vii, 357 p.

The authors are chosen for their appeal to curriculum workers and educational evaluators. Educational goals and curriculum objectives, curriculum design and plan, and curriculum evaluations are the main concerns of the majority of authors. Curriculum and evaluation methodology, training, and theory constitute future needs and directions in this field.

B 4: HUMAN INTELLECTIVE POWERS

Acland, Sir Richard. A MOVE TO THE INTEGRATED CURRICULUM. Exeter, Engl.: Institute of Education, English University of Exeter, 1967. 16 p.

Bailey, Stephen K. "Education for Practical Wisdom." LIBERAL EDUCATION 63, no. 2 (1977): 133-40.

Bailey asks educators to concentrate more strongly on liberal arts education by reviewing, rethinking, and restating the specific aspects of the pursuit of new knowledge, the existential implications of existing curricula content, and the freeing of academic structures and procedures.

Bauer, Norman J. "Curriculum and the Purposes of Education." KAPPA DELTA PI RECORD 15, no. 2 (1977): 46-47.

Bauer believes curriculum is a natural outcome of educational aims.

Berger, Peter L.; Berger, Brigitte; and Kellner, Hansfried. THE HOMELESS MIND: MODERNIZATION AND CONSCIOUSNESS. New York: Random House, Vintage Books, 1973. xii, 258 p.

Describes in stark contrasts the dangers of modern technological reality to civilization and the life of the mind.

Block, James H., and Anderson, Lorin W. MASTERY LEARNING IN CLASS-ROOM INSTRUCTION. New York: Macmillan, 1975. v, 88 p.

> There are three preconditions for mastery learning: formulate a set of course instructional objectives, divide the course into a sequence of smaller and manageable teaching-learning units, then develop a set of alternative instructional materials or "correctives" keyed to objectives and testing.

Boehme, Guenter. DIE PHILOSOPHISCHEN GRUNDLAGEN DES BILDUNGS-BEGRIFFS: EINE PROPAEDEUTIK. [The philosophical foundations of intellectual education: a propaeduetic]. Saarbrucken, W. Ger.: Universitaets-und Schulbuchverl; Kastellaun, W. Ger.: Henn, 1976. 221 p.

Booth, Wayne C., ed. THE KNOWLEDGE MOST WORTH HAVING. Chicago: University of Chicago Press, 1967. xi, 212 p.

> The essays discuss the knowledge a person must have, the contemporary woman, Platonic education, role of the liberal arts college within a university, and other themes.

Bourdieu, Pierre, and Passeron, Jean-Claude. LES ETUDIANTS ET LEUR ETUDES. Paris and The Hague: Mouton, 1964. 149 p.

> This volume contains the data and findings used to support the conclusions in the authors' LES HERITIERS. These were derived chiefly from studies with philosophy and sociology students.

_____. LES HERITIERS: LES ETUDIANTS ET LA CULTURE. Paris: Les Editions de Minuit, 1964. 179 p.

> Bourdieu, director of the Centre de Sociologie Europeenne, scrutinizes rather critically the central values of the French educational system despite a humanistic quality not found in other European systems. He finds the values and ideals entrenched in the schooling system somewhat unfair and discriminatory.

Chatterjee, Kalyan Kumar. IN PRAISE OF LEARNING: JOHN COLET AND LITERARY HUMANISM IN EDUCATION. New Delhi, India: Affiliated East-West Press, 1974. vii, 121 p.

Diaz, May. "Thoughts From Santa Cruz: The Question of Form and Substance in a Liberal Education." LIBERAL EDUCATION 63, no. 2 (1977): 301-8.

> "A liberal education rests not only upon changes in character structure and acquisition of a range of thought styles and problem solving methods, but ultimately upon being able to share and transmit what was learned" (p. 307).

Hawkins, Hugh. BETWEEN HARVARD AND AMERICA: THE EDUCATIONAL

Curriculum: Design and Content

LEADERSHIP OF CHARLES W. ELIOT. New York: Oxford University Press, 1972. xi, 404 p.

> Hawkins examines how Eliot used the elective system, religion within an intellectual community, scholarship and research, and the accessibility of a college career in a democracy to elevate the quality of American educational institutions. He relates Eliot's thought to modern questions of which an important one is the place of the university in American society.

Hirst, Paul Heywood. "Liberal Education and the Nature of Knowledge." In PHILOSOPHICAL ANALYSIS AND EDUCATION, edited by Reginald D. Archambault, pp. 113-38. London: Routledge and Kegan Paul; New York: Humanities Press, 1972. Reprinted in CURRICULUM AND EVALUATION, edited by Arno A. Bellack and Herbert M. Kliebard, pp. 139-60. Berkeley, Calif.: McCutchan Publishing, 1977. Also in his KNOWLEDGE AND THE CURRICULUM, pp. 30-53. London: Routledge and Kegan Paul, 1974.

> Figuratively, a liberal education is comparable to the various forms of knowledge seen as voices in a conversation, a conversation to which each form contributes in a distinctive way.

Hook, Sidney; Kurtz, Paul; and Todorovich, Miro, eds. THE PHILOSOPHY OF THE CURRICULUM: THE NEED FOR GENERAL EDUCATION. Buffalo, N.Y.: Prometheus Books, 1975. xii, 281 p.

Huber, Curtis E. "The Dynamics of Change: A Core Humanities Program." LIBERAL EDUCATION 63, no. 2 (1977): 159-70.

> On the assumption that modern liberal education must address the problem of change in order to be worthy of its claims to value, Huber proposes four sequences of study, each with its own pair of courses, with respect to the themes of (1) the dynamics of change, (2) human responsibility, (3) word and world, and (4) limits to growth. The goal is unity of form and content. The essay includes a listing of the most serious dangers inherent in various integrated studies programs (p. 170).

Jaspers, Karl. THE IDEA OF THE UNIVERSITY. Edited by Karl W. Deutsch. Preface by Robert Ulich. Translated by H.A.T. Reiche and H.F. Vanderschmidt. Boston: Beacon Press, 1959. xxi, 135 p.; London: P. Owen, 1960. 149 p.

Levit, Martin, ed. CURRICULUM. Urbana: University of Illinois Press, 1971. xvi, 396 p.

> The work offers readings in the philosophy of education with some insights into the nature and problem of the curriculum.

Mashruwala, Kischorial Ghanshyamlal. TOWARDS NEW EDUCATIONAL PATTERN. Ahmedabad, India: Navajivan Publishing House, 1971. vii, 88 p.

PAEDAGOGICA EUROPAEA/THE EUROPEAN YEARBOOK OF EDUCATIONAL/
RESEARCH REVUE ANNUELLE DES ETUDES ET RECHERCHES PEDAGOGIQUES
EUROPEENES/EUROPAISCHES JAHRBUCH FUER PAEDAGOGISCHE FORSCHUNG.
Hertogenbosch, Netherlands: Malmberg; Braunschweig, W. Ger.: Westermann.
Vol. 6: 1970-71. THE CHANGING SCHOOL CURRICULUM IN EUROPE.
1971. 268 p.

> The following articles invite further study for the philosophy of
> education: limitations on the use of objectives (Stenhouse), the
> application of principles and methods drawn from the experimental
> sciences to the process of deciding learning goals (Haller), inte-
> grating the curriculum, a case study in the humanities (Bolam),
> elites and the content of education (Halls), the International Asso-
> ciation for the Advancement of Educational Research, a note on
> the Warsaw Conference 1969 (D'Aeth).

Phillips, John L. THE ORIGINS OF INTELLECT: PIAGET'S THEORY. San
Francisco: W.H. Freeman, 1969. xviii, 149 p.

> Phillips clarifies the sensorimotor, concrete operations, and formal
> operations periods of human cognitive development. The educa-
> tional implications in the epilogue, derived from Piagetian theory,
> are stated as principles of action, sequence and integration of struc-
> tures, structure and transfer, optimal discrepancy, and motivation.

Poznar, Walter. "The Survival of the Humanities." LIBERAL EDUCATION 63,
no. 1 (1977): 19-25.

> Give primacy, says the author, to a kind of teaching that is at
> once grounded in the variety of human experience and also the
> highest expression of the spiritual life of an institution. The task
> of the humanities is to remove everything that impedes individual
> growth, to expose ideas and human experience to open scrutiny in
> a spirit of respect and understanding.

Sullivan, Edmund V. PIAGET AND THE SCHOOL CURRICULUM--A CRITICAL
APPRAISAL. Toronto, Canada: Ontario Institute For Studies in Education,
1967. vii, 38.

> Piaget's stage observations show considerable promise for intellectual
> assessment; uncritical extrapolation of his observations and metatheo-
> retical considerations offers no educational advantage; the
> Piagetian-type probing is an excellent model for evaluating the out-
> comes of certain teaching sequences; the weakest elements of Piaget's
> theories are being used to support the mystique of discovery learning.

B 5: HUMAN AFFECTIVE POWERS

Antrobus, John S., ed. COGNITION AND AFFECT. Boston: Little, Brown,
1970. vii, 210 p.

Curriculum: Design and Content

Studies by Antrobus, Sternberg, Tomkins. Singer, Neiser, and
Rosenberg concern perception, fantasy, affect, affective-cognitive
consistency, and cognitive styles. Brought into the discussion are
also attitudes, imagery, internal monologue, and dreaming.

Baker, Eva L., and Popham, W. James. EXPANDING DIMENSIONS OF IN-
STRUCTIONAL OBJECTIVES. Englewood Cliffs, N.J.: Prentice-Hall, 1973.
vii, 129 p.

Humanizing educational objectives are formulated for social and
personal development goals. Defensible goals are established
through needs assessment and the preferences of representative
groups. But most difficult of all is identifying affective and non-
cognitive objectives. The programs outlined are self-instructional.

Berman, Louise M., and Roderick, Jessie A. CURRICULUM: TEACHING THE
WHAT, HOW, AND WHY OF LIVING. Columbus, Ohio: Charles E. Merrill,
1977. xv, 267 p.

The work places stress on decisions, involvement, and human con-
tacts. Schools and teachers are expected to construct their curricular experiences so that persons can face up to their own humanness.

Borton, Terry. REACH, TOUCH AND TEACH: STUDENT CONCERNS AND
PROCESS EDUCATION. New York: McGraw-Hill, 1970. ix, 218 p.

Borton provokes the reader into thinking about the curriculum from
the aspect of affective needs and the emotional concomitants of
learning. He presents numerous examples of affective techniques in
reaching the student through the instrumentality of subject matter.

Brown, George Isaac. HUMAN TEACHING FOR HUMAN LEARNING: AN
INTRODUCTION TO CONFLUENT LEARNING. New York: Viking Books,
1971. xvii, 298 p.

Affective techniques are applied to the curriculum and examples
given for their classroom application. Brown stands with those who
would make education and living more human. If we are to choose
creative change, Brown expects us to work with feeling and with
intellect. That means fostering freedom with responsibility, innovation without destruction, concern for preserving American freedom.

Castillo, Gloria A. LEFT-HANDED TEACHING: LESSONS IN AFFECTIVE
EDUCATION. 2d ed. New York: Holt, Rinehart and Winston, 1978. 256 p.

Castillo presents a plan for the systematic development of the whole
child. To her, confluent education is the discovery of the connectedness of things; it is the Gestalt when cognition, affect, readi-
ness/awareness, and responsibility are totally integrated. Her plan
includes twelve units of about one hundred forty lessons.

Fantini, Mario D., and Weinstein, Gerald. TOWARD A CONTACT CUR-
RICULUM. New York: Anti-Defamation League of B'nai B'rith, [1967]. 55 p.

Fethe, Charles. "Curriculum Theory: A Proposal for Unity." EDUCATIONAL
THEORY 27, no. 2 (1977): 96-102.

> Fethe finds the model for unity in Dewey's concept of rational be-
> havior, especially as presented in HUMAN NATURE AND CON-
> DUCT. In this model, intellectual discipline is conceived not as
> a static body of knowledge but as a social experience that produces
> and conveys knowledge through social interaction. The momentum
> of this dialectical process produces conflicts in thought and behavior
> and the impulse to break beyond this habit of regularity in re-
> sponse to more innovative challenges.

Hall, Gene E., and Jones, Howard L. COMPETENCY-BASED EDUCATION:
A PROCESS FOR THE IMPROVEMENT OF EDUCATION. Englewood Cliffs,
N.J.: Prentice-Hall, 1976. viii, 376 p.

> The conceptual framework for this study is the personalization of
> instruction. The cognitive, the affective, and the behavioral are
> manifested in each chapter. The authors, steeped in the humanist
> tradition, try to practice teaching as a highly personal and human
> act.

Jones, Richard Matthew. FANTASY AND FEELING IN EDUCATION. New
York: New York University Press, 1968; Harper and Row, 1970. xi, 276 p.
Paperbound.

> The Education Development Center's curriculum program, "Man: A
> Course of Study," is assessed rather sharply for neglecting the emo-
> tional and affective side of learning. Jones thinks the curriculum
> ought to develop the learner's imagination and foster the fantasy
> and feeling that is the accompaniment of genuine creative thinking.

_____. THE NEW PSYCHOLOGY OF DREAMING. New York: Grune and
Stratton, 1970. xvii, 221 p.

Lyon, Harold C. LEARNING TO FEEL--FEELING TO LEARN: HUMANISTIC
EDUCATION FOR THE WHOLE MAN. Columbus, Ohio: Charles E. Merrill,
1971. xxii, 321 p.

Shibles, Warren. EMOTION: THE METHOD OF PHILOSOPHICAL THERAPY.
Whitewater, Wis.: Language Press, 1974. iv, 492 p. Bibliogs.

> Shibles provides a rather complete clarification of the concept of
> emotion in the light of contemporary philosophical psychology. He
> averts not to the curriculum as such, yet his treatment relates
> directly to the direct and indirect affective power of learning con-
> tent.

Stewart, Don. INSTRUCTION AS A HUMANIZING SCIENCE. 3 vols. Fountain Valley, Calif.: Slate Services, 1975-76. 1,216 p.

> Volume 1: THE CHANGING ROLE OF THE EDUCATOR: THE INSTRUCTIONEER, 1975. 320 p.

> Volume 2: BEHAVIORAL LEARNING SYSTEMS APPROACH TO INSTRUCTION: ANALYSIS AND SYNTHESIS, 1975. Pp. 321-834.

> Volume 3: CREATING AN EMPHASIS ON LEARNING: QUALITY CONTROL, PRODUCTIVITY, AND ACCOUNTABILITY, 1976. Pp. 835-1,216.

> Volume 3 has much to say about the affective power of instruction and the curriculum in humanizing the learner.

Thayer, Louis, ed. AFFECTIVE EDUCATION: STRATEGIES FOR EXPERIENTIAL LEARNING. La Jolla, Calif.: University Associates, 1976. 230 p.

> Thayer shares ideas and strategies in establishing more humanistic learning environments.

Weinstein, Gerald, and Fantini, Mario D., eds. TOWARD HUMANISTIC EDUCATION: A CURRICULUM OF AFFECT. Foreword by Edmund J. Meade, Jr. New York: Praeger Publishers, 1970. xi, 228 p.

B 6: HUMAN AESTHETIC POWERS

Axelrod, Joseph. THE UNIVERSITY TEACHER AS ARTIST: TOWARD AN AESTHETICS OF TEACHING WITH EMPHASIS ON THE HUMANITIES. San Francisco: Jossey-Bass, 1973. 246 p.

> Compared to the didactic teacher who will stress skill or information mastery, the evocative professor teaches either "what he knows" or "what he is" or the student-person in search of a genuine education. Such an instructor is more likely, as several hundred class sessions testify, to be the model, the evocative teacher-artist who is also the expert in the helping relationships.

Bedford, Mitchell. EXISTENTIALISM AND CREATIVITY. New York: Philosophical Library, 1972. 376 p.

Gilson, Etienne. PAINTING AND REALITY. Cleveland: World Publishing, 1967. 515 p.

Mackinlay, E. THE SHARED EXPERIENCE. London: Methuen, 1970. 144 p.

> Mackinlay shows how the aesthetic senses are developed through creative writing and sensitive self-expression.

Schwartz, Sheila, ed. TEACHING THE HUMANITIES: SELECTED READINGS. New York: Macmillan, 1970. ix, 421 p.

> The humanities are discussed in terms of their values for the con-temporary scene, elementary and secondary school, teacher educa-tion, and the disadvantaged. The articles, over fifty of them, have been selected with great insight into the current situation on the humanities.

Steveni, M. ART AND EDUCATION. London: Batsford, 1968. 40 p.

B 7: THE PROBLEM OF VALUES—ETHICS

Barrow, Robin. COMMON SENSE AND THE CURRICULUM. London: Allen and Unwin; Hamden, Conn.: Shoe String Press (Linnet Books), 1976. 169 p.

> In order to clear up any possibility of misunderstanding his utili-tarianism in ethics that "an activity is worthwhile insofar as it promotes pleasure and/or diminishes pain in general," Barrow has written his philosophy of the curriculum. He believes it meets his first criterion of acceptability that there is nothing immoral about it.

Beck, Clive M., et al., eds. MORAL EDUCATION: INTERDISCIPLINARY APPROACHES. Toronto, Canada: University of Toronto Press, 1971. x, 402 p.

Gustafson, James M., et al. MORAL EDUCATION. Introduction and edited by Nancy F. and Theodore R. Sizer. Cambridge, Mass.: Harvard University Press, 1970. 136 p.

Johann, Robert O., ed. FREEDOM AND VALUE. New York: Fordham University Press, 1976. 186 p.

Johnson, Mauritz. "Definitions and Models in Curriculum Theory." In CUR-RICULUM AND EVALUATION, edited by Arno A. Bellack and Herbert M. Kliebard, pp. 3-19. Berkeley, Calif.: McCutchan Publishing, 1977. Reprinted from EDUCATIONAL THEORY 17, no. 1 (1967): 127-40.

> Where curriculum theory has been confused with valuative positions, the alleged curriculum is either prescriptive or suggested; where it has been confused with the curriculum-development system or the instructional system, it has not yielded learning outcomes. Johnson provides his own schema for convenience and clarity.

Phenix, Philip H. EDUCATION AND THE COMMON GOOD: A MORAL PHILOSOPHY OF THE CURRICULUM. New York: Harper and Row, 1961. 271 p.

> Education must be concerned with values of an objective and univer-

sal worth that lead to the choice of the good life. Intrinsic to
the moral life is excellence that gives intelligence (thought and
communication), creativity (beauty, manners, work, recreation),
conscience (nature, health, sex, family life, class, race, political
and world responsibility), and reverence (as applied to religion)
their unique moral significance.

Walhout, Donald. THE GOOD AND THE REALM OF VALUES. Notre Dame,
Ind.: University of Notre Dame Press, 1978. xii, 259 p.

B 8: THE PROBLEM OF THOUGHT AND LANGUAGE—
PHILOSOPHICAL ANALYSIS

Black, Max. MARGINS OF PRECISION: ESSAYS IN LOGIC AND LAN-
GUAGE. Ithaca, N.Y.: Cornell University Press, 1971. 277 p.

Cassirer, Ernst. THE LOGIC OF THE HUMANITIES. Translated by Clarence
Smith Howe. New Haven: Yale University Press, 1961. 217 p.

Chomsky, Noam. SYNTACTIC STRUCTURES. The Hague: Mouton, 1971.
117 p.

Marras, Ausonio. INTENTIONALITY, MIND AND LANGUAGE. Urbana:
University of Illinois Press, 1972. 527 p.

Murray, John Courtney. "The Catholic University in a Pluralist Society."
St. Louis University Address delivered 15 November 1955, at the Founder's
Day Commemoration. Also published as "Unity of Truth." COMMONWEAL 63
(13 January 1956): 381-82, and in CATHOLIC MIND 57 (May-June 1959):
253-60.

Rose, Gregory A. GROUNDS FOR GRAMMAR. Washington, D.C.: Catholic
University of America Press, 1976. 120 p.

Williamson, William Bedford. LANGUAGE AND CONCEPTS IN CHRISTIAN
EDUCATION. Philadelphia: Westminster Press, 1970. 173 p.

B TR: THE PROBLEM OF GOD—THEOLOGY AND RELIGION

Johann, Horst-Theodor, ed. ERZIEHUNG UND BILDUNG IN DER HEIDNISCHEN
UND CHRISTLICHEN ANTIKE. [Education in the classical and Christian era].
Darmstadt, W. Ger.: Wissenschaftliche Buchgesellschaft, 1976. 597 p.

Of the twenty-two essays written from 1927 to 1969, three discuss
liberal education and paideia, fifteen are chiefly historical studies

of education in ancient times, and four concern the impact of Christianity.

McLean, George F. TRACES OF GOD IN A SECULAR CULTURE. Staten Island, N.Y.: Alba House, 1973. 407 p.

McShane, Philip. THE SHAPING OF THE FOUNDATIONS: BEING AT HOME IN THE TRANSCENDENTAL METHOD. Washington, D.C.: University Press of America, 1976. 212 p. Paperbound.

A close colleague of Bernard Lonergan, McShane draws on the transcendental method in approaching modern science, literature, and music to reveal the reciprocal relationship of religious and secular studies. While the perspective is critical to an understanding of how contemporary theology can develop, McShane's contribution to a reorientation of contemporary humanism has very important consequences for the reworking of a modern philosophy of education.

Murray, John Courtney. "Christian Humanism in America." SOCIAL ORDER 3 (May-June 1953): 233-44.

_____, ed. RELIGIOUS LIBERTY: AN END AND A BEGINNING. New York: Macmillan; London: Collier-Macmillan, 1966. 192 p.

This ecumenical discussion on the Vatican II DECLARATION ON RELIGIOUS FREEDOM ought to command the interest of anyone who wishes to argue the issue of religious freedom in some depth. The notes by Murray himself are an invaluable asset of this publication.

Steensma, Geraldine. TO THOSE WHO TEACH . . . KEYS FOR DECISION-MAKING. Signal Mountain, Tenn.: Signal/Publishing/Consulting, 1971. xi, 96 p.

In seeking to present a wisdom beyond ourselves for educational problems, Steensma begins with Scripture: what it says about man, his origin, his task, and his relationships. From these insights, the author formulates the eight keys for decision making.

B NS: THE PROBLEM OF THE COSMOS—PHYSICAL AND MATHEMATICAL SCIENCES

Cantore, Enrico. ATOMIC ORDER: AN INTRODUCTION TO THE PHILOSOPHY OF MICROPHYSICS. Cambridge: M.I.T. Press, 1969. 334 p.

Laszlo, Ervin. THE SYSTEMS VIEW OF THE WORLD: THE NATURAL PHILOSO-

PHY OF THE NEW DEVELOPMENTS IN THE SCIENCES. New York: George Braziller, 1972. 131 p.

_____, ed. THE WORLD SYSTEM: MODELS, NORMS, APPLICATIONS. New York: George Braziller, 1973. 215 p.

Newmark, Joseph, and Lake, Frances. MATHEMATICS AS A SECOND LAN-GUAGE. Reading, Mass.: Addison-Wesley Publishing, 1974. 477 p.

Wallace, William A. CAUSALITY AND SCIENTIFIC EXPLANATION. 2 vols. Ann Arbor: University of Michigan Press, 1972-74.

> Volume 1: MEDIEVAL AND EARLY CLASSICAL SCIENCE, 1972. xi, 228 p.

> Volume 2: CLASSICAL AND CONTEMPORARY SCIENCE, 1974. xi, 422 p.

B HS: THE PROBLEM OF HUMAN SOCIETY—HUMAN AND SOCIAL SCIENCES

Bauer, Hans. DAS ENDE DES DEUTSCHEN GYMNASIUMS. [The demise of the German gymnasium]. Freiburg/B, W. Ger.; Basel, Switz.; and Vienna: Herder, 1973. 142 p.

> Bauer disagrees with present educational reforms in West Germany. He quarrels with the educational philosophy that has led to a mis-alliance between the academic and political worlds and forecasts the end of classical secondary and university traditions. He finds the curriculum suitable only for Pavlov's dog!

Cheit, Earl F. THE USEFUL ARTS AND THE LIBERAL TRADITION. McGraw-Hill, 1975. 166 p.

> Cheit offers models for integrating the useful and the liberal arts particularly in agriculture, engineering, business administration, and forestry. The process must center on value education so that the liberal and the technical may be blended in the educated person.

Davis, O.L., ed. PERSPECTIVES ON CURRICULUM DEVELOPMENT. 1776-1976. Washington, D.C.: Association for Supervision and Curriculum Develop-ment, 1976. vii, 272 p.

> The purpose of the ASCD 1976 yearbook is to celebrate the con-ception, birth, and growth of the idea of free public education and of a suitable curriculum for all in the schools of the United States.

Doll, Ronald C. CURRICULUM IMPROVEMENT: DECISION MAKING AND PROCESS. 3d ed. Boston: Allyn and Bacon, 1974. xv, 389 p.

The bases for decision making are historical, philosophical, psychological, social, and curricular. Curriculum improvements require a process for change, leadership, initiative, communication, and strategies. They must flow from design models, evaluation, and common sense in assessing the value of old and new ideas.

Eggleston, John. THE SOCIOLOGY OF THE CURRICULUM. London and Boston: Routledge and Kegan Paul, 1977. ix, 171 p.

The analysis of schooling makes the curriculum the central focus: its knowledge content and its determination by historical, ideological, and political influences.

Jencks, Christopher, ed. RATIONALITY, EDUCATION AND THE SOCIAL ORGANIZATION OF KNOWLEDGE. London: Routledge and Kegan Paul, 1977. 104 p.

Major educational themes are discussed from the viewpoint of reflexive sociology: the nature of rationality, commonsense beliefs about education, the nature of literary study as education, and the place of science in education. The contributors are David Walsh, Paul Filmer, Michael Young, and Nell Keddie.

Kohl, Herbert R. ON TEACHING. New York: Schocken Books, 1976. 185 p.

The book is about the specifics of teaching, developing curriculum material, and educational politics. The appendix contains a report by Joe Nathan that describes all the research supporting educational change.

McDermott, John J. THE CULTURE OF EXPERIENCE: PHILOSOPHICAL ESSAYS IN THE AMERICAN GRAIN. New York: New York University Press, 1976. 237 p.

Magill, Samuel H. "The Aims of Liberal Education in the Post-Modern World." LIBERAL EDUCATION 63, no. 3 (1977): 435-42.

Magill feels the important objectives of modern liberal education should be to (1) aid the development of an understanding and perspective about the world adequate for post-modern life; (2) develop a sense of vocation for self and life in general; and (3) empower persons with basic communication, analytic interpersonal, recreational, and citizenship skills.

Schwenk, Bernhard. UNTERRICHT ZWISCHEN AUFKLAERUNG UND INDOKTRI-NATION: STUDIEN ZUR BEGRIFF DER DIDAKTIK. [The curriculum between enlightenment and indoctrination: studies on the meaning of education]. Foreword by Herwig Blankertz. Frankfort on the Main, W. Ger.: Athenaeum-Fischer-Taschenbuch-Verlag, 1974. 181 p.

These reflections on a sociological theory of education center on the function of the curriculum according to the philosophical assumptions of the Prussian principia regulativa, Tuiskon Ziller, Otto Willmann, and Erich Weniger. Appended to the discussion is the 1931 correspondence between Eduard Spranger and Erich Weniger.

Selden, Steven. "Conservative Ideology and Curriculum." EDUCATIONAL THEORY 27, no. 3 (1977): 205-22.

A survey of the common school revival, the language and concepts used in twentieth-century school planning, and the impact of naturalism leading to eugenics, force Selden to conclude that too many individuals have been sacrificed on the altar of conservative ideology. He proposes a kind of Democratic ideology which guarantees the equality of all and decisions based on fact not assumption.

B AC: THE PROBLEM OF ART AND CULTURE—HUMANE ARTS AND LETTERS

Aagaard-Mogenson, Lars, ed. CULTURE AND ART. Atlantic Highlands, N.J.: Humanities Press, 1976. 211 p.

Arnold, Matthew. MATTHEW ARNOLD. Edited with an introduction by James Gribble. London: Collier-Macmillan; New York: Macmillan, 1967. 182 p.

Bird, Otto A. CULTURES IN CONFLICT: AN ESSAY IN THE PHILOSOPHY OF THE HUMANITIES. Notre Dame, Ind.: University of Notre Dame Press, 1976. 232 p.

Derisi, Octavio N. ESENCIA Y AMBITO DE LA CULTURA. Buenos Aires: Coleccion Esquemos, 1975. 72 p.

Gilson, Etienne. FORMS AND SUBSTANCES IN THE ARTS. Translated from French by Salvator Attanasio. New York: Charles Scribner's Sons, 1966. 282 p.

Jacobson, Jerry I. PERSPECTIVISM IN ART. New York: Philosophical Library, 1973. 177 p.

Makkreel, Rudolf A. DILTHEY: PHILOSOPHER OF THE HUMAN STUDIES. Princeton: Princeton University Press, 1975. 456 p.

Snow, C.P. THE TWO CULTURES AND SECOND LOOK. New York: Cambridge University Press, 1964. 108 p.

Van Buren, Paul. THE EDGES OF LANGUAGE. New York: Macmillan, 1972. 178 p.

Wirth, Arthur G. EDUCATION IN THE TECHNOLOGICAL SOCIETY: THE VOCATIONAL-LIBERAL STUDIES CONTROVERSY IN THE EARLY TWENTIETH CENTURY. Scranton, Pa.: Intext Educational Publishers, 1972. xi, 259 p.

Chapter 6

PERSONAL AGENCIES OF TEACHING AND LEARNING—
THE EFFICIENT CAUSALITY OF EDUCATION

Inasmuch as persons act of and upon themselves and accept the formative
influence of teachers, learners are the primary efficient causes of their education. The primacy lies in the inbred and willed self-activity of the person;
for education does not occur without the initiative and coaction of the learner.
Yet, to acquire an education likewise demands the cooperation of others: parents, teachers, schools, God, various formal and informal educational agencies.
Works, therefore, that concentrate on self-actualization through the educative
action of self and other persons acting individually in the helping relationship
are mentioned in this chapter.

C 1: THE PROBLEM OF KNOWING—EPISTEMOLOGY

Bhattacharya, Srinibas. "Review of Research on Theory of Teaching." Baroda,
India: Centre of Advanced Study in Education, M.S. University of Baroda,
1973. vi, 81 p.

Bollnow, Otto Friedrich. PHILOSOPHIE DER ERKENNTNIS: DAS VORVER-
STAENDNIS UND DIE ERFAHRUNG DES NEUEN. [Philosophy of knowing;
the prehension and experience of the new]. Stuttgart, W. Ger.: W.
Kohlhammer, 1970. 100 p.

Browne, M. Neil; Haas, Paul F.; Keeley, Stuart. "Measuring Critical Thinking
Skills in College." EDUCATIONAL FORUM 42, no. 2 (1978): 219-26.

> In an attempt to render performance objectives quite explicit, the
> authors have devised an evaluative instrument known as the "Criti-
> cal Thinking Rubric." The major goal is to assess how well stu-
> dents can analyze a controversy and then create a reasonable re-
> sponse.

Cassirer, Ernst. THE PROBLEM OF KNOWLEDGE: PHILOSOPHY, SCIENCE,

AND HISTORY SINCE HEGEL. Translated by William H. Woglom and Charles
W. Hendel. New Haven: Yale University Press, 1966. xviii, 334 p.

Chomsky, Noam. "The Case Against B.F. Skinner." NEW YORK REVIEW OF
BOOKS, 30 December 1971, pp. 18-24.

_____. LANGUAGE AND MIND. Enl. ed. New York: Harcourt Brace
Jovanovich, 1972. xii, 194 p.

This book contains the widely discussed arguments for a rationalist
understanding of man, for the existence of innate factors in the
acquisition of language, as well as the rules and procedures for
inquiry in the human cognitive domain.

Dewey, John, and Bentley, Arthur F. KNOWING AND THE KNOWN.
1949. Reprint. Westport, Conn.: Greenwood Press, 1975. xiii, 334 p.

Gage, N.L. THE SCIENTIFIC BASIS OF THE ART OF TEACHING. New
York: Teachers College Press, 1978. 128 p. Paperbound.

This practitioner and theorist of educational research finds that the
discoveries about teaching promise no millenium but do yield useful
knowledge.

Kluge, Norbert, ed. DAS PAEDAGOGISCHE VERHAELTNIS. [The helping
relationship]. Darmstadt, W. Ger.: Wissenschaftliche Buchgesellschaft, 1973.
xxxi, 510 p.

The philosophical thrust of the twenty works cited here is fundamentally existential in the tradition of Dilthey, Nohl, Buber, Peter
Petersen, and their followers. The stress centers not only on trust
and pedagogical tact but on such profound concepts as the educative act, the teachable moment, the pedagogical situation, and the
teaching-helping relationship. Here the gateway to the philosophy
of education is psychology and the teaching-learning dialectic.

Mischel, Theodore, ed. COGNITIVE DEVELOPMENT AND EPISTEMOLOGY.
New York: Academic Press, 1971. xv, 423 p.

Piaget, Jean. GENETIC EPISTEMOLOGY. Translated from French by Eleanor
Duckworth. New York: Columbia University Press, 1970; W.W. Norton,
1971. 84 p. Paperbound.

_____. INTRODUCTION A L'EPISTEMOLOGIE GENETIQUE. 2d ed. Paris:
Presses Universitaires de France, 1973.

_____. THE PRINCIPLES OF GENETIC EPISTEMOLOGY. Translated from
French by Wolfe Mays. London: Routledge and Kegan Paul; New York:
Basic Books, 1972. v, 98 p.

Searles, John E. A SYSTEM FOR INSTRUCTION. Scranton, Pa.: International Textbook, 1967. xiv, 170 p.

"In this book, a chapter is journalistic because much needs reporting; a chapter is encyclopedic because definitions must be established; a chapter is philosophic because a sense of order and logic is needed; a chapter is sociological-psychological because an objective analysis of the human must be attempted; a chapter is avuncular because advice is necessary; a chapter (or several) is technical because technique reflecting artistry and thought is necessary" (p. vii).

Snook, Ivan A. "Teaching Pupils to Think." STUDIES IN PHILOSOPHY AND EDUCATION 8, no. 2 (1973): 146-62.

C 2: THE PROBLEM OF BEING—METAPHYSICS

Bausola, Adriano. NATURA E PROGETTO DELL'UOMO. Milan: Vita e Pensiero (Universita Cattolica), 1977. 300 p.

Bronowski, Jacob. THE IDENTITY OF MAN. Rev. ed. Garden City, N.Y.: Doubleday, 1971; Natural History Press for American Museum of Natural History, 1972. xii, 153 p.

Bronowski scrutinizes man's scientific and artistic imagination for special clues to what actually constitutes the essential characteristics of human nature.

Combs, Arthur W., et al. THE PROFESSIONAL EDUCATION OF TEACHERS: A HUMANISTIC APPROACH TO TEACHER PREPARATION. 2d ed. Boston: Allyn and Bacon, 1974. xiii, 187 p.

The revision has addressed itself to the following questions: what makes a good teacher? what do these concepts mean for student teachers? what do they mean for program developers? how does an institution go about solving these problems?

Denton, David E. EXISTENTIAL REFLECTIONS ON TEACHING. North Quincy, Mass.: Christopher Publishing House, 1972. 92 p.

Fetz, Reto Luzius. ONTOLOGIE DER INNERLICHKEIT: REDITIO COMPLETA UND PROCESSIO INTERIOR DEI THOMAS VON AQUIN. Freiburg, Switz.: Universitatsverlag, 1975. 199 p.

Greene, Maxine. TEACHER AS STRANGER: EDUCATIONAL PHILOSOPHY FOR THE MODERN AGE. Belmont, Calif.: Wadsworth Publishing Co., 1973. 308 p. Paperbound.

This introduction to the existentialist view of education makes an appeal to the understanding of the teaching profession.

Hamachek, Don E. HUMAN DYNAMICS IN PSYCHOLOGY AND EDUCATION: SELECTED READINGS. 3d ed. Boston: Allyn and Bacon, 1977. x, 344 p.

The fourteen chapters are divided into five groups of essays toward understanding: (1) learning and cognitive processes, (2) the nature of instruction, (3) forces that influence growth and development, (4) maladaptive behavior and developing positive classroom management, and (5) what happens within oneself. The fifty-four selections reflect the idea that there is no best way to learn or teach or behave or understand oneself.

Harper, Ralph. THE EXISTENTIAL EXPERIENCE. Baltimore: Johns Hopkins Press, 1972. 162 p.

Hartnett, Anthony, and Naish, Michael. THEORY, VALUES AND THE CLASSROOM TEACHER. London: Heinemann Educational, 1976. xx, 204 p.

Hughes, James Monroe, and Schultz, Frederick Marshall. EDUCATION IN AMERICA. 4th ed. New York: Harper and Row, 1976. 500 p.

The overview of American education provides introductory chapters on the teacher's philosophy, the educational ideas influential in America, and the aims discoverable in American education. The readings, suggested at the end of each part of the text, are carefully annotated.

Johnstone, Henry W. THE PROBLEM OF THE SELF. University Park: Pennsylvania State University Press, 1970. 156 p.

Lauwerys, Joseph Albert. THE ENTERPRISE OF EDUCATION. London: Ampersand Books, 1963. 78 p.

Lloyd, D.I., ed. PHILOSOPHY AND THE TEACHER. London and Boston: Routledge and Kegan Paul, 1976. viii, 137 p.

This introductory work for nonspecialists includes contributions from Lloyd, Berenson, Cleife, Degenhardt, Higginbotham, and Wringe on a broad scope of topics from the role of the teacher to such educational issues as indoctrination and the teacher's philosophical commitment. Its chief values are the exposure to the latest and more troublesome educational problems and the help it gives the reader to learn to think for himself philosophically.

Macmillan, Charles James Barr, and Nelson, Thomas W. CONCEPTS OF TEACHING: PHILOSOPHICAL ESSAYS. Chicago: Rand McNally, 1968. viii, 154 p.

Maslow, Abraham H. TOWARD A PSYCHOLOGY OF BEING. 2d ed.
Princeton, N.J.: D. Van Nostrand, 1968. xvi, 240 p. Bibliog. Paperbound.

This new edition contains minor revisions, an expanded bibliography,
and a new appendix: "Is a Normative Social Psychology Possible?"
Part 5 on "Values" and part 6 on "Future Tasks" reflect Maslow's
views of the changing conception of man's capacities, potentialities, and goals. He states unequivocally that, when the philosophy
of man changes, then everything changes: the philosophy of education, the philosophy of psychotherapy and of personal growth, and
the theory of how to help men become what they deeply need to
become.

May, Rollo. EXISTENTIAL PSYCHOLOGY. 2d ed. New York: Random
House, 1969. ix, 117 p.

Monefeldt, Fannie A. Simonpietri. LO INDIVIDUAL Y SUS RELACIONES
INTERNAS EN ALFRED NORTH WHITEHEAD. Pamplona, Spain: Ediciones
Universidad de Navarra, S.A., 1977. 145 p.

Puettmann, Josef. DAS PRINZIP DER GANZHEIT IN DER PAEDAGOGIK.
[The principle of wholeness in education]. Munich: Ehrenwirth, 1967. 149 p.

Rotman, Brian. JEAN PIAGET: PSYCHOLOGIST OF THE REAL. Ithaca,
N.Y.: Cornell University Press, 1978. 200 p. Bibliog.

Snook, Ivan A., ed. CONCEPTS OF INDOCTRINATION: PHILOSOPHICAL
ESSAYS. London and Boston: Routledge and Kegan Paul, 1972. xiv, 210 p.

The writers, in this important collection of articles about indoctrination, define the term and relate the concept to its implications
in ethics, epistemology, metaphysics, and education. The articles
are by Gatchel, Wilson, Green, Kilpatrick, Flew, Atkinson,
Moore, White, Crittenden, Snook, and others.

Soderquist, Harold O. THE PERSON AND EDUCATION. Columbus, Ohio:
Charles E. Merrill, 1964. 200 p. [Cf. Broudy (1967), cited in chapter 13,
p. 132].

Wilson, John. EDUCATIONAL THEORY AND THE PREPARATION OF TEACHERS.
Windsor, Engl.: National Foundation for Educational Research in England and
Wales, 1975. 182 p.

C 3: HUMAN NATURE AND UNITY

Aristotle. DE ANIMA. Edited by Paul Siwek. 3d ed. 3 vols. in one.
Rome: Aedes Universitatis Gregorianae, 1957.

The Greek text and Latin translations are parallel on opposite pages.

_____. DE ANIMA. Edited by W.D. Ross. Oxford: Clarendon Press, 1963. ix, 110 p.

Aune, Bruce. REASON AND ACTION. Boston: D. Reidel, 1977. 206 p.

Bloom, Benjamin Samuel. STABILITY AND CHANGE IN HUMAN CHARAC-TERISTICS. New York: John Wiley and Sons, 1964. xiv, 237 p.

The teaching-learning objectives in the cognitive domain actually subsume a theory of human nature that calls for further analysis and verification by the educational philosopher.

Donno, Olindo del. LA PEDAGOGIA DI SAN GIOVANNI BOSCO: STUDIO. 2d ed. Lecce, Italy: Edition Milella, 1965. 240 p.

Ghougassian, Joseph P. ALLPORT'S ONTOPSYCHOLOGY OF THE PERSON. New York: Philosophical Library, 1972. 314 p.

Jourard, Sidney M. DISCLOSING MAN TO HIMSELF. Princeton, N.J.: D. Van Nostrand, 1968. xiii, 245 p.

_____. THE TRANSPARENT SELF. Rev. ed. New York: Van Nostrand Reinhold, 1971. xiv, 250 p.

Kron, Friedrich W. THEORIE DES ERZIEHERISCHEN VERHAELTNISSES. [The theory of helping relationships]. Bad Heilbrunn/Obb, W. Ger.: Klinkhardt, 1971. 174 p.

Manheimer, Ronald J. KIERKEGAARD AS EDUCATOR. Berkeley and Los Angeles: University of California Press, 1977. 270 p.

Manheimer underscores the fact that Kierkegaard understood education to be central to his work. The specific issues concern education as self-transformation, the effect of theories of human development on intentions to educate, and Kierkegaard's approach to Socrates and the process of sharing that brings about self-realization.

Meissner, Erich. THE BOY AND HIS NEEDS. London: Macdonald, 1956. 176 p.

Menezes, Vicente Porto de. EDUCACAO E PERSONALIDADE. Belo Horizonte, Brazil: Promocao da Familia Ed., 1968. 94 p.

Milholland, Frank, and Forisha, Bill E. FROM SKINNER TO ROGERS: CON-
TRASTING APPROACHES TO EDUCATION. Lincoln, Nebr.: Professional
Educators Publications, 1972. 128 p.

Natalis, Ernest. CARREFOURS PSYCHO-PEDAGOGIQUES. Brussels, Belgium:
C. Dessart, 1970. 272 p.

O'Connell, Robert J. ST. AUGUSTINE'S EARLY THEORY OF MAN. Cambridge, Mass.: Belknap Press of Harvard University Press, 1968. xxii, 301 p.

> O'Connell leans rather strongly toward Plotinus as the way to under-
> stand Augustine. The reader should compare this work with other
> authoritative commentaries and analyses.

Reitman, Sandford W. "The Reconstructionism of Harold Rugg." EDUCATIONAL
THEORY 22, no. 1 (1972): 47-57.

> Rugg is credited with intuiting the essential problem of our time--
> helping people find meaningful personal identity in a world which
> has become meaningless.

Roth, Robert J., ed. PERSON AND COMMUNITY: A PHILOSOPHICAL
EXPLORATION. New York: Fordham University Press, 1975. x, 175 p.

> Noteworthy are the essays on psyche and self with implications of
> Freud's theory of the unconscious, a Deweyan perspective of person
> and technology, a Whiteheadian critique of Skinner, and especially
> the contributions by Lonergan, Lauer, W. Norris Clark, and McCool.
> The last four clarify the issues involved in the problematic of pro-
> cess and the dynamics of development.

Vesey, Godfrey. PERSONAL IDENTITY: A PHILOSOPHICAL ANALYSIS.
New York: Cornell University Press, 1977. 128 p.

C 4: HUMAN INTELLECTIVE POWERS

Aquila, Richard E. INTENTIONALITY: A STUDY OF MENTAL ACTS. University Park: Pennsylvania State University Press, 1977. xi, 168 p.

Bandman, Bertram, and Guttchen, Robert S., eds. PHILOSOPHICAL ESSAYS
ON TEACHING. Philadelphia: J.B. Lippincott, 1969. x, 326 p.

> This anthology of essays deals directly with the issues of teaching,
> learning, and intellection.

Bolton, Neil. CONCEPT FORMATION. Elmsford, N.Y.: Pergamon Press,
1977. 108 p.

An introductory analysis of the reciprocal relationship between the subject and his environment and of the dialectic between attention and intention, and logicomathematical and physical experience, this work brings together cohesively three approaches to the study of thought: the philosophical analysis of the nature of concepts, the developmental studies in concept formation, and the experimental work on variables affecting concept attainment and individual differences in cognitive style.

Bruner, Jerome Seymour. BEYOND THE INFORMATION GIVEN: STUDIES IN THE PSYCHOLOGY OF KNOWING. Selected, edited, and introduced by Jeremy M. Anglin. New York: W.W. Norton, 1973.

Anglin observes the influence of Darwin's natural selection, Freud's psychoanalysis, and the development of behaviorism under Thorndike, Watson, Guthrie, Hull, Spence, and Skinner in overemphasizing man's similarity with other animals. Bruner's views of man, in contrast, show man to be a thinker and creator with a rationality and dignity unique to the human person.

Campbell, Keith. BODY AND MIND. Garden City, N.Y.: Doubleday, 1970. 160 p. Paperbound.

Campbell provides a short but adequate exposition of recent trends in the philosophy of the mind. He includes suggested readings on the body-mind problem.

Casin, Renee. SAINT THOMAS D'AQUIN: OU, L'INTELLIGENCE DE LA FOI. QUATRE POINTS CHAUDS. Montsurs, France: Editions Resiac, 1973. 137 p.

Culler, Arthur Dwight. THE IMPERIAL INTELLECT, A STUDY OF CARDINAL NEWMAN'S EDUCATIONAL IDEAL. New Haven: Yale University Press, 1958. xiii, 327 p.

Dale, Edgar. BUILDING A LEARNING ENVIRONMENT. Bloomington, Ind.: Phi Delta Kappa Educational Foundation, 1972. vii, 132 p.

Green, Thomas F. THE ACTIVITIES OF TEACHING. New York: McGraw-Hill, 1971. xiv, 234 p.

Green gives a very fruitful and philosophical analysis of complex educational concepts. He concludes that it is the grounds, rather than the content, of belief that distinguishes indoctrination from instruction.

Guzie, Tad W. THE ANALOGY OF LEARNING: AN ESSAY TOWARD A THOMISTIC PSYCHOLOGY OF LEARNING. New York: Sheed and Ward, 1960. 241 p.

The reader should refer especially to pages 1-25 and 225-36 for a full and excellent bibliography on Thomistic educational theory.

_____. "St. Thomas and Learning Theory: A Bibliographical Study." NEW SCHOLASTICISM 34 (1960): 275-96.

"Three further articles on the subject of learning appeared in the first two decades of the century; one of these, by Willmann, is the only satisfactory encyclopedic treatment of St. Thomas' teaching that is to be found" (p. 282).

Hofstadter, Richard. ANTI-INTELLECTUALISM IN AMERICAN LIFE. New York: Alfred A. Knopf, 1963; Vintage Books, 1964. xiii, 434 p. Paperbound.

This book treats the historical reasons for what Hofstadter assumes to be the distrust of the intellect by average Americans. An intellectual, to Hofstadter, is one who examines, ponders, wonders, theorizes, criticizes, imagines and therefore enjoys the critical, creative, and contemplative life of the mind.

Hullfish, H. Gordon, and Smith, Philip G. REFLECTIVE THINKING: THE METHOD OF EDUCATION. New York: Dodd, Mead, 1961. x, 273 p.

Largely dependent on the value theory of Clarence Irving Lewis and on reflective inquiry as described by Dewey, the authors try to connect the theory of thinking with educational method and practice. The chapters concerned with the art of teaching and the problem of education clarify the meaning of reflective thinking in the classroom.

Katz, M.S. "Two Views of 'Teaching People to Think.'" EDUCATIONAL THEORY 26, no. 2 (1976): 158-64.

After comparing the Deweyan inquiry model with the discipline model, Katz notes that some spontaneous modes of thinking are not necessarily significant for education, that thinking can be improved through superior formal instruction, and that developing the higher-order skills of inductive problem solving or deductive theoretical reasoning is no easy task.

Klauder, Francis J. THE WONDER OF PHILOSOPHY: A REVIEW OF PHILOSOPHERS AND PHILOSOPHIC THOUGHT. New York: Philosophical Library, 1973. 75 p.

_____. THE WONDER OF THE REAL: A SKETCH IN BASIC PHILOSOPHY. North Quincy, Mass.: Christopher Publishing House, 1973. 114 p.

Kuiken, Don. "Immediacy in Self-Representation and the Development of Abstract Thought." JOURNAL OF HUMANISTIC PSYCHOLOGY 16, no. 3 (1976): 29-50.

Lange, John. THE COGNITIVITY PARADOX. Princeton: Princeton University Press, 1971. 117 p.

Laska, John A., and Goldstein, Stanley L. FOUNDATIONS OF TEACHING METHOD. Dubuque, Iowa: Wm. C. Brown, 1973. x, 121 p.

> Greek and Roman writers on education were acquainted with three different basic teaching methods; telling-showing, exercise-imitation, and discovery-restructuring. To these, Rousseau added the student interest method while Thorndike and Skinner contributed reinforcement as a method of teaching.

Mayer, Frederick. THE GREAT TEACHERS. New York: Citadel Press, 1967. 384 p.

Moreau, Joseph. DE LA CONNAISSANCE SELON S. THOMAS D'AQUIN. Paris: Editions Beauchesne, 1976. 132 p.

Morrish, Ivor. DISCIPLINES OF EDUCATION. London: Allen and Unwin, 1967. 336 p.

> W. Kenneth Richmond, in his THE LITERATURE OF EDUCATION: A CRITICAL BIBLIOGRAPHY (Metheun, 1972) likes the chapters on Plato, Rousseau, and Dewey.

Pai, Young. TEACHING, LEARNING, AND THE MIND. Boston: Houghton Mifflin, 1973. 226 p. Paperbound.

> Pai gives a thorough analysis of how the mind is conceived by behaviorists, materialists, analytic philosophers, and others before restating, in more modern dress, the tenets of experimentalism. [Cf. Broudy (1967), cited in chapter 13, pp. 102, 153].

Patterson, C.H. FOUNDATIONS FOR A THEORY OF INSTRUCTION AND EDUCATIONAL PSYCHOLOGY. New York: Harper and Row, 1977. xiii, 346 p.

> The materials do not constitute theories but systems or approaches toward instruction. These center around the philosophical and psychological conceptions of Montessori, Piaget, Bruner, Skinner, and Carl Rogers.

Penta, Gerard C. "Discipline: A Theoretical Perspective." EDUCATIONAL THEORY 27, no. 2 (1977): 137-40.

> Penta considers what seems to be unrelated uses of the term "discipline" and formulates six useful postulates. For example, the author believes what is learned is intelligent behavior and is itself the discipline. The postulates point to an underlying philosophy of education.

Piaget, Jean. THE CHILD'S CONCEPTION OF PHYSICAL CAUSALITY. New York: Harcourt Brace, 1927. Reprint. Totowa, N.J.: Littlefield, Adams, 1972. viii, 309 p. Paperbound.

Piaget, Jean, and Garcia, R. UNDERSTANDING CAUSALITY. Translated by Donald Miles and Marguerite Miles. New York: W.W. Norton, 1978. 192 p.

> This summary of about one hundred studies at the International Center for Genetic Epistemology is divided into two parts; the first treats of the general relationship between causality and operations, and the second deals with the relationship between geometry and dynamics in modern physics. These results shed light on the stages in the development of understanding causality.

Scholz, Guenter. CONVERSIO MENTIS ALS BILDUNGSPRINZIP. [Intellectual transformation as a principle of liberal education]. Vienna: Verlag Notring, 1972. 225 p.

> The key ideas of this work are derived from the SOLILOQUIA and CONFESSIONES of St. Aurelius Augustine.

Taylor, Harold. ESSAYS IN TEACHING. 1950. Freeport, N.Y.: Books for Libraries Press, 1971. ix, 239 p.

Tornatore, Lydia. EDUCAZIONE E CONOSCENZA. Turin, Italy: Loescher, 1974. 337 p.

Travers, John. LEARNING: ANALYSIS AND APPLICATION. 2d ed. New York: David McKay, 1972. xiii, 321 p. Bibliog.

> Travers believes successful teaching-learning interaction depends upon a teacher who knows who and what he is and acts according to this knowledge. Chapters in this work emphasize motor, cognitive, problem-solving types of learning, affective and emotional behavior, and a general philosophy of teaching. The sixteen-page bibliography is very helpful.

Vandenberg, Donald, ed. TEACHING AND LEARNING. Urbana: University of Illinois Press, 1969. 297 p.

Wadsworth, Barry J. PIAGET'S THEORY OF COGNITIVE DEVELOPMENT: AN INTRODUCTION FOR STUDENTS OF PSYCHOLOGY AND EDUCATION. New York: David McKay, 1971. 160 p.

C 5: HUMAN AFFECTIVE POWERS

Arendt, Hannah. WILLING. Edited by Mary McCarthy. Vol. 2: THE LIFE OF THE MIND. New York: Harcourt Brace Jovanovich, 1978. 272 p.

The experience of philosophers of every age as well as personal encounter with internal conflicts, wherein individuals can actually oppose themselves, has led some thinkers to postulate a will. This faculty for telling right from wrong, dealing directly with the problem of good and evil, is an essential but difficult to understand activity in the life of the mind. The appendix has a collection of excerpts from Arendt's lectures on judging.

Benjamin, Alfred. THE HELPING INTERVIEW. 2d ed. Boston: Houghton Mifflin, 1969. xviii, 167 p.

The author examines, on the practical level, the external and internal conditions of the helping interview, stages, attitudes and behavior, questioning and records, communication, responses and leads, and leave-taking. The reading list is supplemented by Benjamin's comments.

Berman, Louise M., and Roderick, Jessie A., eds. FEELING, VALUING, AND THE ART OF GROWING: INSIGHTS INTO THE AFFECTIVE. Washington, D.C.: Association for Supervision and Curriculum Development, 1977. viii, 308 p. Bibliog.

Part 1 includes insights into human development and social foundations (Yamamoto, Webb). In part 2 are essays by experts from various fields (Phenix, L'Engle, Beittel, Fair, Patterson, Simpson). The discussions in part 3 consider schooling and the feeling, valuing, growing nature of the human person (Roderick, Hedges and Martinello, Berman). The bibliography is limited to works that have a curricular orientation (pp. 279-85).

Bloom, Benjamin Samuel. HUMAN CHARACTERISTICS AND SCHOOL LEARNING. New York: McGraw-Hill, 1976. xiii, 284 p.

The research relates empirical data to assumptions about human nature. The theory of school learning examined here attempts to explain the interaction of cognitive and affective talent with the strength of the educational process. What are the profound psychological and philosophical reasons for the need of men to identify with one another?

Broudy, Harry S. "Didactics, Heuristics, and Philetics." EDUCATIONAL THEORY 22, no. 3 (1972): 251-61.

Colman, John E. THE MASTER TEACHERS AND THE ART OF TEACHING. New York: Pitman Publishing, 1967. 180 p.

Over twenty methods are described to underscore the undeniable fact that teaching is nothing less than the vibrant contact of one person with another person. Vibrancy, to Colman, means interactive resonance for the good of both teacher and learner.

Curran, Charles Arthur. COUNSELING-LEARNING: A WHOLE-PERSON MODEL FOR EDUCATION. New York: Grune and Stratton, 1972. xiv, 258 p.

Daniels, LeRoi, and Parkinson, Shirley. "Role X'ing and Moral Education--Some Conceptual Speculation." EDUCATIONAL THEORY 26, no. 4 (1976): 329-36.

> The authors examine the idea that the rational handling of moral issues may require the ability to enter imaginatively into the feelings, thoughts, attitudes, or role of another person. This raises the further issue of role playing and the pedagogy of receptions. Confrontation with reality seems necessary.

Delp, Paul S. THE GENTLE WAY. New York: Philosophical Library, 1977. xviii, 171 p.

Fromm, Erich. THE ART OF LOVING. 1956. Planned and edited by Ruth Nanda Anshen. New York: Harper and Row, 1962. 146 p.; Bantam Books, 1963. 146 p.

_____. FEAR OF FREEDOM. 1942. London: Routledge and Kegan Paul, 1960. 257 p. Also DIE FURCHT VOR DER FREIHEIT. New ed. Frankfort on the Main, W. Ger.: Europaische Verlags-Anstalt, 1966. 292 p.

Fukuzawa, Yukichi. AN ENCOURAGEMENT OF LEARNING. Translated and introduced by David A. Dilworth and Umeyo Hirano. Tokyo: Sophia University, 1969. xv, 128 p.

Kluge, Norbert. PAEDAGOGISCHE VERHAELTNIS UND ERZIEHUNGSWIRK-LICHKEIT. [The helping relationship and educational reality]. Essen, W. Ger.: Neue-Deutsche-Schule-Verlagsgesellschaft, 1972. 144 p.

> In regard to human helping relationships, Kluge tries to overcome the discrepancy between pedagogical theory and actual practices. He relies on empirical methods and the phenomenological approach in general to illuminate the actual conditions of human relationships in the educative process. He cites very pertinent sources (pp. 137-44).

Kron, Friedrich W. DAS ERZIEHERISCHE VERHAELTNIS. [The helping relationship]. Bad Heilbrunn/Obb., W. Ger.: J. Klinkhardt, 1970. 127 p.

May, Rollo. LOVE AND WILL. New York: W.W. Norton, 1969. 352 p.

Menke, Anton. DAS GEGENSTANDS-VERSTAENDNIS PERSONALER PAEDA-GOGIK. [The existential encounter in the education of the person]. Wiesbaden, W. Ger.: F. Steiner, 1964. vi, 116 p.

The discussion centers on educative value (Bildungsgut) as systematically elaborated from the thought of Martin Buber and Romano Guardini. Willmann's contributions shed light on the issues discussed here.

Miller, John P. HUMANIZING THE CLASSROOM: MODELS OF TEACHING IN AFFECTIVE EDUCATION. New York: Praeger Publishers, 1976. vii, 183 p.

Miller has grouped models into four families: developmental (ego, adolescent, psychosocial, and moral), self-concept (values clarification, identity, role playing, classroom and self-directed), sensitivity and group orientation (communications, consideration, transactional, and human relations), consciousness-expansion (mediation, synectics, confluent, and psychosynthesis).

Mischel, Theodore, ed. UNDERSTANDING OTHER PERSONS. Oxford: Blackwell; Totowa, N.J.: Rowman and Littlefield, 1974. 259 p.

Peters, Richard Stanley. REASON AND COMPASSION. London and Boston: Routledge and Kegan Paul, 1973. 128 p.

This volume contains the Lindsay Memorial Lectures delivered to the University of Keele during February and March of 1971 and the Swarthmore Lecture addressed to the Society of Friends in 1972. Peters is concerned with the implications of reason and compassion for moral education.

Repusseau, Jean. HOMO DOCENS: L'ACTION PEDAGOGIQUE ET LA FORMATION DES MAITRES. Paris: A. Colin, 1972. 206 p.

Ringness, Thomas A. THE AFFECTIVE DOMAIN OF EDUCATION. Boston: Little, Brown, 1975. xiii, 184 p.

"The fact that attitudes and values are learned presents us with our greatest hopes for the future" (p. xii). Whether the theory be behaviorist or humanistic or one that falls in between, Ringness urges learner and teacher to use whatever is helpful in rendering educative interaction effective.

Rogers, Carl. FREEDOM TO LEARN: A VIEW OF WHAT EDUCATION MIGHT BECOME. Columbus, Ohio: Charles E. Merrill, 1969. x, 358 p.

Scheflen, Albert E. COMMUNICATIONAL STRUCTURE: ANALYSIS OF A PSYCHOTHERAPY TRANSACTION. Bloomington: Indiana University Press, 1973. xiv, 378 p.

C 6. HUMAN AESTHETIC POWERS

Arnstine, Donald. "Learning, Aesthetics, and Schooling: The Popular Arts as Textbook on America." EDUCATIONAL THEORY 27, no. 4 (1977): 261-273.

> Through a conceptual analysis of experience that is aesthetic in quality, Arnstine looks to the contributions of art in learning and to the more appropriate use of the arts in schooling.

Berlyne, D.E. STUDIES IN THE NEW EXPERIMENTAL AESTHETICS: TOWARD AN OBJECTIVE PSYCHOLOGY OF AESTHETIC APPRECIATION. Washington, D.C.: Hemisphere Publishing, 1974. 350 p.

Gombrich, E.H.; Hochberg, Julian; and Black, Max. ART, PERCEPTION, AND REALITY. Baltimore: Johns Hopkins Press, 1972. 132 p.

Jeffreys, Montagu Vaughan Castelman. THE MINISTRY OF TEACHING: SEVEN ESSAYS ON EDUCATION. London: Pitman Publishing, 1967. vi, 72 p.

Kreitler, Hans, and Kreitler, Shumalith. PSYCHOLOGY OF THE ARTS. Durham, N.C.: Duke University Press, 1972. 514 p.

Prall, David Wight. AESTHETIC ANALYSIS. New York: Thomas Y. Crowell, 1936. Reprint. New York: Apollo Editions, 1968. 211 p. Paperbound.

Reimer, Bennett. A PHILOSOPHY OF MUSIC EDUCATION. Englewood Cliffs, N.J.: Prentice-Hall, 1970. 173 p.

Reimer, Bennett, et al. TOWARD AN AESTHETIC EDUCATION. Washington, D.C.: Music Educators National Conference, 1971. 190 p.

Thalberg, Irving. PERCEPTION, EMOTION, AND ACTION: A COMPONENT APPROACH. New Haven: Yale University Press, 1977. 142 p.

C 7: THE PROBLEM OF VALUES—ETHICS

Boyle, John P. "Faith and Christian Ethics in Rahner and Lonergan." THOUGHT 50, no. 198 (1975): 247-65.

> Boyle summarizes the moral doctrines of both writers to highlight the role of faith in Christian morals and give a theological under- standing of the influence of faith or conversion on moral perception, judgment, and action. If asked what is specific to a Christian ethic, Lonergan and Rahner might point to "the transformed hori- zon and the transvalued values of the converted subject who has

accepted in faith the grace of God's self-communication"
(p. 265).

Craig, Robert P. "Form, Content and Justice in Moral Reasoning." EDUCA-
TIONAL THEORY 26, no. 2 (1976): 154-57.

> After reviewing the formalism of R.M. Hare and Lawrence
> Kohlberg, Craig insists that both form and content must be con-
> sidered in the development of moral reasoning for an individual
> must rely on substantive principles and precepts for the basis of
> his arguments and actions.

_____. "Response to David Swanger." EDUCATIONAL THEORY 27, no. 2
(1977): 148-49.

> Craig disagrees with Swanger that decisions become moral only
> "when a concern for right and wrong is involved." Craig adds
> the note of intentionality as prerequisite. Form and content are
> so integral to each other that any separation is unintelligible to
> Craig.

Dewey, John. EXPERIENCE AND EDUCATION. New York: Macmillan,
1916. Reprint. New York: Collier-Macmillan, 1963. xvi, 116 p.

> Dewey warns against simplistic either/or thinking because he is
> optimistic that one can usually find an acceptable middle ground
> between extremes. For this reason, he believes it is possible to
> reach a compromise between traditional and progressive education.
> [See also Broudy (1967), cited in chapter 13, p. 234]

Doran, Robert M. "Aesthetics and the Opposites." THOUGHT 72, no. 205
(1977): 117-33.

> Soul is aesthesis. Soul making, as the recovery of the aesthetic
> dimension, is the post-therapeutic basis of morals and prayer.
> Lonergan's opening of a distinct level of consciousness that has to
> do with value, dialectics, and foundations as something distinct
> from, including, but more than and sublating meaning and truth is
> really an opening upon aesthetic consciousness as distinct from,
> including, but more than and sublating cognitional consciousness.
> "Ethics is radically aesthetics; and the existential subject, concerned
> with character as his or her issue, is the aesthetic subject. Soul,
> beyond intelligence and reasonableness, is the key to character"
> (p. 131).

Gnagey, William J. MAINTAINING DISCIPLINE IN CLASSROOM INSTRUC-
TION. New York: Macmillan, 1975. viii, 50 p.

> According to Gnagey there are five elements of discipline: school
> must be a good place; students must know the school rules; (within
> reason) students should agree with the rules; students should partici-

pate in rule making; and students should know the consequences
of rule breaking.

Hall, Robert William. PLATO AND THE INDIVIDUAL. The Hague: Martinus
Nijhoff, 1963. v, 224.

> Plato's concern for the individual is exhibited in his strong empha-
> sis on the moral tendance of the soul, the rejection of a utilitarian
> ethic, the belief in the soul's personal immortality, the concept
> of freedom based not on appetite but reason, the insistence that
> man's good lies in the justice of the soul, and the fundamental
> equality of men endowed with the same capacity to acquire the
> same kind of justice. Platonic and modern individualism are
> placed in stark contrast to each other in this book.

Hare, R.M. APPLICATIONS OF MORAL PHILOSOPHY. Berkeley and Los
Angeles: University of California Press, 1972. 112 p.

Irwin, Terence. PLATO'S MORAL THEORY. Oxford: Oxford University
Press, 1977. xviii, 376 p.

Lepley, Ray. DEPENDABILITY IN PHILOSOPHY OF EDUCATION. New York:
Bureau of Publications, Teachers College, Columbia University, 1931. Reprint.
New York: AMS Press, 1972. v, 96 p.

McGrath, Michael. FROMM: ETHICS AND EDUCATION. Lexington:
College of Education, University of Kentucky, 1969. 55 p.

Pedersen, Eigil; Faucher, Therese Annette; and Eaton, William W. "A New
Perspective on the Effects of First-Grade Teachers on Children's Subsequent
Adult Status." HARVARD EDUCATIONAL REVIEW 48, no. 1 (1978): 1-31.

> The findings of the authors differ from the conclusions of Coleman,
> Campbell, Hobson, McPartland, Mood, Weinfeld, and York (1966)
> and from those of Jencks, Smith, Acland, Bane, Cohen, Gintis,
> Heyns, and Michelson (1972) who seriously question the effects of
> schooling on one's adult status. This research underscores the
> likelihood that teachers' best efforts may have positive long-range
> results.

Roberts, T.A. THE CONCEPT OF BENEVOLENCE. London: MacMillan;
New York: Humanities Press, 1973. 119 p.

Sichel, Betty A. "Can Kohlberg Respond to Critics?" EDUCATIONAL THEORY
26 (Fall 1976): 337-47, 394.

> According to Sichel, Kohlberg cannot meet the requirements of a
> moral cognitive development theory or the needs of moral education

unless (1) he faces the issue of habit and reason and (2) relates the affective and the cognitive, the passions and reason, the emotions and the rational. No theorist or practitioner can afford to ignore these problems.

Smith, Philip G. "Knowledge and Values." EDUCATIONAL THEORY 26, no. 1 (1976): 29-39.

In his analysis of the relation of human knowing to human valuing, Smith examines eight problems: the relation of knowing to doing, the role of valuing in doing, modes of valuing, forms of evaluation, evaluations, justifying standards, the moral viewpoint, and contributory moral value.

Stoff, Sheldon P., and Schwartzberg, Herbert, eds. THE HUMAN ENCOUNTER: READINGS IN EDUCATION. 2d ed. New York: Harper and Row, 1973. 463 p. Also paperbound.

The topics in this book are related to educational issues and philosophies: freedom for the individual, spiritual viewpoints, open and traditional educational thought.

Sullivan, Edmund V. MORAL LEARNING: SOME FINDINGS, ISSUES, AND QUESTIONS. New York: Paulist Press, 1975. v, 123 p.

Tapp, June L., and Kohlberg, Lawrence. "Developing Senses of Law and Legal Justice." JOURNAL OF SOCIAL ISSUES 27, no. 2. (1971): 65-91.

Building on Kohlberg's reduced model of three inclusive stages of moral development--preconventional, conventional, postconventional --and on the relationship between moral and legal socialization and its meaning for education, the authors feel too many authorities have failed to appreciate the universality and the dynamic of either moral or legal reasoning. To stimulate principled perspectives, educators and societies' agents must understand more entirely the process of developing and crystallizing legal values.

Wagner, Paul A. "Indoctrination in Moral Education: A Recurrent Dilemma." KAPPA DELTA PI RECORD 15, no. 2 (1977): 57-59.

Wagner thinks that Lawrence Kohlberg and Matthew Lipman are themselves not free of indoctrination when they encourage children to make decisions in accord with a specific notion of morality. Wagner agrees with Aristotle that it makes all the difference whether habits of one kind or another are formed in youth. The question still remains how to diminish the role of indoctrinated behavior as one matures morally.

Wilson, John, et al. AN INTRODUCTION TO MORAL EDUCATION. Harmondsworth, Engl.: Penguin Books, 1968. 480 p.

C 8: THE PROBLEM OF THOUGHT AND LANGUAGE—
PHILOSOPHICAL ANALYSIS

Ashley, Benedict M. THE ARTS OF LEARNING AND COMMUNICATION:
A HANDBOOK OF THE LIBERAL ARTS. Dubuque, Iowa: Priory Press, 1958.
ix, 622 p.

>The first part covers the four kinds of proof and logic: demonstra-
tive logic, dialectical logic, rhetoric, and poetics; the second
part presents the philosophy of fine art; the third part distinguishes
the sciences of numbers, magnitudes, pure and applied mathematics;
the fourth is given to the study of discourse in its grammatical,
poetic, rhetorical, dialectical, and scientific forms.

Belth, Marc. THE NEW WORLD OF EDUCATION: A PHILOSOPHICAL
ANALYSIS OF CONCEPTS OF TEACHING. Boston: Allyn and Bacon, 1970.
xviii, 217 p.

Ennis, Robert H. LOGIC IN TEACHING. Englewood Cliffs, N.J.: Prentice-
Hall, 1969. 520 p.

Peters, Richard Stanley. EDUCATION AND THE EDUCATION OF TEACHERS.
London: Routledge and Kegan Paul, 1977. 208 p.

>This collection of ten papers written by England's leading analytic
philosopher explores concepts and issues fundamental to the development of education wherever man is found. It serves as an excellent introduction to the student who wishes to grapple with the
thought of a modern thinker expert in the analytic style. The work
is scholarly and challenging. The first section clarifies the concept of education and some problems that face the teacher while
section 2 is more interested in the role of educational theory in
the education of teachers. [Cf. Broudy (1967), pp. 14, 131;
Broudy-Smith (1969), pp. 16, 38].

Scheffler, Israel. REASON AND TEACHING. Indianapolis: Bobbs-Merrill;
London: Routledge and Kegan Paul, 1973. xi, 203 p.

>Writing in an analytical spirit, Scheffler treats philosophy of educa-
tion and the new activism, philosophy and the curriculum, and
also philosophical models of teaching. He sees a direct link between the study of philosophy and the school experiences of teaching, learning, and maturing.

Smith, Frank. COMPREHENSION AND LEARNING: A CONCEPTUAL FRAME-
WORK FOR TEACHERS. New York: Holt, Rinehart and Winston, 1975.
v, 275 p.

>While covering the conventional range of educational psychology
topics, the book has utility in general courses on cognitive psy-

chology, psycholinguistics, and applied linguistics since it attempts to provide a plain-language theoretical integration not otherwise available.

C TR: THE PROBLEM OF GOD—THEOLOGY AND RELIGION

Anthon, Peter. PERSON UND VERANTWORTUNG: EMIL BRUNNERS DIA-LEKTISCHE THEOLOGIE IN PAEDAGOGISCHER SICHT. [Person and responsibility: Emil Brunner's dialectical theology from an educational viewpoint]. Zurich, Switz.: Juris, 1974. xi, 181 p.

Buber, Martin. I AND THOU. A new translation with a prologue "I and You" and notes by Walter Kaufmann. New York: Charles Scribner's Sons, 1970. 185 p.

This unique existential approach to communication between persons sees man's relation with God as the basis for true humanity and God entering into relationship with man in creative, revealing, and redeeming acts. This understanding of divine and human encounter gives a more spiritual interpretation to the engagement of teacher and learner in the educational experience.

Frankl, Viltor Emil. THE UNCONSCIOUS GOD: PSYCHOTHERAPY AND THEOLOGY. New York: Simon and Schuster, 1975. 163 p. Bibliog.

There is, in fact, a religious sense deeply rooted in each and every man's unconscious depths that may break through unexpectedly under a variety of circumstances. This sense of religion may be defined as man's search for ultimate meaning. The bibliography deals not only with the relationship between religion and psychiatry but with publications that cover logotherapeutic teachings and practices.

Kirkpatrick, Frank G. "Process or Agent: Models for Self and God." THOUGHT 58, no. 188 (1973): 33-60. Appendix.

The agent model of the human self does more than the process model to sustain adequately the notion of God as a relating, acting, personal other. The assumption is made that man's conception of God is based on an understanding of ourselves. The appendix contains a critique of the process model of God as living person.

Lonergan, Bernard J.F. GRACE AND FREEDOM: OPERATIVE GRACE IN THE THOUGHT OF ST. THOMAS AQUINAS. Edited by J. Patout Burns with an introduction by Frederick E. Crowe. London: Darton, Longman and Todd; New York: Herder and Herder, 1971. xi, 187 p.

The key position in St. Thomas that reconciles human instrumentality with human freedom is cooperation: "In habitual grace divine operation infuses the habit, to become cooperation when the habit leads to free acts; in actual grace divine operation effects the will of the end to become cooperation when this will of the end leads to an efficacious choice of means..." In this explanation, metaphysics and psychology, divine providence and human instrumentality, grace and nature are meshed in synthesis.

Mol, Hans J. IDENTITY AND THE SACRED. New York: Macmillan, 1977. 326 p.

Schmidt, Heinz. RELIGIONSPAEDAGOGISCHE REKONSTRUKTIONEN. [Reconstructions of religious education]. Stuttgart, W. Ger.: Calwer Verlag, 1977. 228 p.

> The philosophy of religious education must explore the dialectic between Christian tradition and modern experience, the broad outlines of a dialectic approach to the problems of religious education, the actual intent of Christ's good news, and the transmission of Christian belief. Schmidt tries to find an answer to the problem of how youth can arrive at a state of belief.

Stinnette, Charles Roy. LEARNING IN THEOLOGICAL PERSPECTIVE. New York: Association Press, 1965. 96 p.

C NS: THE PROBLEM OF THE COSMOS—PHYSICAL AND MATHEMATICAL SCIENCES

Brown, Harold I. PERCEPTION, THEORY, AND COMMITMENT: THE NEW PHILOSOPHY OF SCIENCE. Chicago: Precedent Publishing, 1977. 203 p.

Cantore, Enrico. SCIENTIFIC MAN: THE HUMANISTIC SIGNIFICANCE OF SCIENCE. New York: ISH Publications, 1977. xviii, 487 p.

Clayton, Alfred Stafford. EMERGENT MIND AND EDUCATION: A STUDY OF GEORGE H. MEAD'S BIO-SOCIAL BEHAVIORISM FROM AN EDUCATIONAL POINT OF VIEW. 1943. Reprint. New York: AMS Press, 1972. xiii, 180 p.

Dewey, John. EXPERIENCE AND NATURE. 1925, 1929. 2d ed. La Salle, Ill.: Open Court Publishing, 1965. 360 p.

Paci, Enzo. THE FUNCTION OF THE SCIENCES AND THE MEANING OF MAN. Translated from Italian by Paul Piccone and James E. Hansen. Evanston, Ill.: Northwestern University Press, 1972. 475 p.

Penfield, Wilder. "The Mind and the Highest Brain-Mechanism." AMERICAN SCHOLAR 43, no. 2 (1974): 237-46.

> Penfield finds it impossible to explain the mind on the sole basis of brain neuronal action. The evidence forces him to admit that the mind develops and matures independently throughout an individual's life and that the mind is not only an agency which operates the brain but also a reality in itself capable of independent understanding.

Quine, W.V. THE ROOTS OF REFERENCE. La Salle, Ill.: Open Court Publishing, 1974. xii, 151 p.

> This book was reviewed by James E. McClellan and Thomas S. Costello in EDUCATIONAL THEORY 26, no. 3 (1976): 310-18. The reviewers feel that, in the course of moving from logic to children and learning, Quine has made a mess of things. They assert, however, that any research required to test Quine's thesis "would move educational thought out of the backwater of behaviorism and back into the mainstream of science."

Robinson, James T. THE NATURE OF SCIENCE AND SCIENCE TEACHING. Belmont, Calif.: Wadsworth Publishing, 1968. 149 p.

> Robinson's effort is to construct a conception of the structure of scientific knowledge critical for instruction and curriculum development. F. Michael Connelly sees Robinson as one of the few "to undertake an inquiry into this genuinely problematic situation."

C HS: THE PROBLEM OF HUMAN SOCIETY—HUMAN AND SOCIAL SCIENCES

Bernstein, Basil B. THEORETICAL STUDIES TOWARD A SOCIOLOGY OF LANGUAGE. CLASS, CODES AND CONTROL. Vol 1. London: Routledge and Kegan Paul, 1972. 238 p.

> Language is distinguished as a social institution and human relationship and may be based, in part, upon a range of very closely shared identifications (the code is said to be restricted) or upon a form of social living that does not necessarily presuppose shared identifications (the code is then called elaborated). A significant essay, "On the Classification and Framing of Educational Knowledge," refers to framing as the degree of control teacher and pupil possess over the knowledge mutually exchanged in the pedagogical relationship.

Charmion, Claude. SCIENCES HUMAINES ET PEDAGOGIE. Paris: Le Centurion, 1974. 343 p.

Cicourel, Aaron Victor. COGNITIVE SOCIOLOGY: LANGUAGE AND MEANING IN SOCIAL INTERACTION. Harmondsworth, Engl.: Penguin Books; New York: Free Press, 1974. 191 p.

Good, Thomas L., and Brophy, Jere E. LOOKING IN CLASSROOMS. 2d ed. New York: Harper and Row, 1978. xii, 433 p.

> The first purpose of the book is to develop ways of looking at and describing what actually goes on in classrooms. The second is to make concrete suggestions about the positive influences teachers can have on the interests, learning, and social development of their students. Exercises and practice examples are relevant to personal and sociological problems.

Nyberg, David. TOUGH AND TENDER LEARNING. Palo Alto, Calif.: National Press Books, 1971. vi, 186 p.

Reichart, Sandford. CHANGE AND THE TEACHER: THE PHILOSOPHY OF A SOCIAL PHENOMENON. New York: Thomas Y. Crowell, 1969. vii, 151 p.

Steinberg, Stephen. THE ACADEMIC MELTING POT: CATHOLICS AND JEWS IN AMERICAN HIGHER EDUCATION. Report prepared for the Carnegie Commission on Higher Education. New York: McGraw-Hill, 1974. xx, 183 p.

> A sociologist directly attacks the myths of Jewish intellectualism and Catholic anti-intellectualism. If related to some of the notions held by Andrew Greeley, the academic atmosphere may be cleared up enough for joint contributions by Jews and Catholics in the philosophy of education.

White, J.P. "Indoctrination." In THE CONCEPT OF EDUCATION, edited by Richard S. Peters, pp. 177-91. London: Routledge and Kegan Paul, 1967.

> White clarifies the concept of indoctrination as it is exemplified in the teaching of political history, religion, and morality.

C AC: THE PROBLEM OF ART AND CULTURE—HUMANE ARTS AND LETTERS

Berleant, Arnold. THE AESTHETIC FIELD: A PHENOMENOLOGY OF AES-THETIC EXPERIENCE. Springfield, Ill.: Charles C Thomas, 1970. 199 p.

Chomsky, Noam. REFLECTIONS ON LANGUAGE. New York: Pantheon Books, 1975. 269 p.

> Chomsky's reflections are a restatement of his arguments for the restoration of human reason and its study as an innate cognitive power clearly evidenced by human language, creativity, freedom,

and dignity. He also outlines a future program for the human
sciences firmly based in a humanistic rationalism.

Gardner, Howard. THE ARTS AND HUMAN DEVELOPMENT. New York:
Wiley-Interscience, 1973. 395 p.

Gordon, Haim. "Can Literature Clarify Existential Encounters?" EDUCA-
TIONAL FORUM 42, no. 2 (1978): 189-202.

> The author feels that the reading of literature, particularly under
> the guidance of a true educator, may help one clarify existential
> encounters. The art of listening to and reading literature illumines
> human existence.

Howes, Frank. MAN, MIND AND MUSIC. 1948. Reprint. Freeport, N.Y.:
Books for Libraries Press, 1970. 184 p.

Landor, R.A. THE EDUCATION OF EVERY CHILD: ON THE TEACHING
AND LEARNING OF LIBERAL ARTS. Berea, Ohio: Liberal Arts Publishing,
1974. 150 p.

McMullen, Roy. ART, AFFLUENCE AND ALIENATION: THE FINE ARTS
TODAY. New York: Frederick A. Praeger, 1968. 272 p.

Read, Sir Herbert Edward. EDUCATION THROUGH ART. 3d ed. New York:
Pantheon Books, 1974. xxii, 328 p.

Rogers, A. Robert. THE HUMANITIES: A SELECTIVE GUIDE TO INFORMA-
TION SOURCES. Littleton, Colo.: Libraries Unlimited, 1974. 400 p.

Slattery, Sister May Francis. HAZARD, FORM, AND VALUE. Detroit: Wayne
State University Press, 1971. 127 p.

> The author gives a vigorous new insight into aesthetic theory and
> the meaning of value in art. After approaching affective hazard
> from the angles of temporal, spatial, numerical, hierarchical, and
> natural differentiation, she turns to the nature of form and its unity,
> organicity, and complexity. The discussion of value is philosophical
> and does have educational implications.

Chapter 7

FORMAL AND INFORMAL SOCIETAL AGENCIES OF EDUCATION—THE SECONDARY EFFICIENT CAUSE OF EDUCATION

Since, for every person, educative values are at once individual and social, individuals actuate their capacities not only by way of self-activity but through cooperation, institution, role, and task. These follow a pattern fixed by a role to be fulfilled or a task to be performed within such institutional frameworks as "the family and manners (mores), society and education, the state and the law, the economy and technology, the church or sect" (Bernard Lonergan). The ideal basis for these agencies is community and so education must be by nature communitarian; the educative effort by which the person receives and actuates the intellectual and moral form conferred by society is matched by a complementary educative action by which the society, in assimilating a cultured and civilized member, rejuvenates itself. The individual and society are, therefore, reciprocal intersubjective agencies of education; the individual person primary and society secondary to the coactivity of persons who choose to be educated or to educate themselves.

D 1: THE PROBLEM OF KNOWING—EPISTEMOLOGY

Berger, Peter L., and Luckmann, Thomas. THE SOCIAL RECONSTRUCTION OF REALITY: A TREATISE IN THE SOCIOLOGY OF KNOWLEDGE. New York: Doubleday, 1966. Reprint. Garden City, N.Y.: Doubleday, 1967. vii, 203 p.

Breed, Frederick S. "Education and Human Society: A Realistic View." In FORTY-FIRST YEARBOOK OF THE NATIONAL SOCIETY FOR THE STUDY OF EDUCATION, part 1, edited by Nelson B. Henry, pp. 87-138. Chicago: University of Chicago Press, 1942.

> Realists are distinguishable for their insistence on the principle of independence; becoming is an event that happens to realities known to exist prior to and independently of the act of knowing. They assert that the test of truth is conformity with something not of one's own creation, that the content objectives of a good curriculum are but selections of values thus attested.

Dewey, John. CONTEXT AND THOUGHT. Berkeley: University of California Press, 1931. Reprint. New York: Johnson Reprint, 1969. 224 p.

Dougherty, Jude P. "Dewey and the Value of Religion." NEW SCHOLASTI-CISM 51, no. 3 (1977): 303-27.

> Dewey's concept of knowledge and his metaphysical commitments are ultimately responsible for his failure as a philosopher of religion. The key to Dewey's mature inquiry is his conviction that religion is mistaken in its claims to knowledge.

Mazzeo, Joseph Anthony. "Interpretation, Humanistic Culture, and Cultural Change." THOUGHT 51, no. 200 (1976): 65-81.

> Peaceful cultural change, cultural evolution rather than cultural revolution, validates itself through interpretative acts for only interpretation can mediate between the past and the present laden with the future. Cultural innovations, independently generated, may be conceived as the cultural equivalent of biological analogies.

Phillips, Denis Charles. "The Piagetian Child and the Scientist: Problems of Assimilation and Accommodation." EDUCATIONAL THEORY 28, no. 1 (1978): 3-15.

> The link made between the external world and the intellectual structures of humans may be (1) necessitated by a particular network configuration, and/or (2) explained by social factors, and/or (3) forged by rival accommodations that are, at the time they are made, all functionally equivalent. Not all adults seem to accommodate to recalcitrant experience in the same way.

Selden, Steven. "Curricular Metaphors: From Scientism to Symbolism." EDUCATIONAL THEORY 25, no. 3 (1975): 243-62.

> Metaphors tacitly adopted by educators have led to a scientific view of person restricted to nineteenth-century mechanistic models of the physical and social sciences. Besides the positive harm of such models, they have also prevented the asking of potentially fruitful questions.

Suchodolski, Bogdan. ERZIEHUNG UND KOMMUNIKATION. [Education and communication]. Edited by Werner Faber. Paderborn, W. Ger.: F. Schoeningh, 1976. 104 p.

> These six essays review educational humanism from the Renaissance to Karl Marx, authority and legalization of education, foundations of a philosophy of educational communication, the family and educational communication, educational communication through media (claims and limitations), and learning through directive and non-directive experiences of the schools.

Toffler, Alvin. FUTURE SHOCK. New York: Random House, 1970; Bantam Books, 1971. 505 p.; London: Bodley Head, 1970. 504 p.

The premises and conclusions of this widely discussed best seller must be challenged by the philosopher of education. The accelerating rate of change in our society does produce a kind of "future shock" that needs to be understood if future generations are to cope successfully with change. To gain perspective, follow the examination of this pregnant idea with a review of critical studies.

Van Kaam, Adrian. EXISTENTIAL FOUNDATIONS OF PSYCHOLOGY. Garden City, N.Y.: Doubleday, 1969. 396 p.

Van Kaam attempts to assimilate man's evolving existential view of reality into scientific psychology. By rooting his frame of reference in the existential image of man, Van Kaam constructs an existential anthropological psychology that can integrate empirical, clinical, and theoretical psychologies within an open theory of personality. He notes that assimilation is a two-way process in which both the assimilating field and the assimilated aspect are so progressively transformed that the prefix "existential" should be eventually dropped the moment the assimilation is complete.

Williams, Raymond. THE COUNTRY AND THE CITY. New York: Oxford University Press, 1973. 335 p.

Williams contends that contemporary students have no real connection with either the country or the urban image because they are lost in a world of abstractions. Humanization will require the rediscovery of community, revitalization of communication skills among real persons, reliving the experiences of a human being in a world with other human beings.

D 2: THE PROBLEM OF BEING—METAPHYSICS

Conrad, David R. EDUCATION FOR TRANSFORMATION: IMPLICATIONS OF LEWIS MUMFORD'S ECOHUMANISM. Palm Springs, Calif.: ETC Publications, 1976. 230 p.

Cox, Harvey. THE SECULAR CITY: SECULARIZATION AND URBANIZATION IN THEOLOGICAL PERSPECTIVE. New York: Crowell-Collier and Macmillan, 1965. 276 p. Paperbound.

Traditional religion is thought to be losing the struggle with urban civilization and its consequent secularism. Americans must find new and alternate means to preserve and transmit the treasury of faith.

Crockenberg, Vincent, and LaBrecque, Richard, eds. CULTURE AS EDUCATION. Dubuque, Iowa: Kendall/Hunt Publishing, 1977. 304 p. Paperbound.

This collection of readings is organized around the theme that the
values and norms embedded in the web of American culture itself,
in its dominant nonschooling institutions are the chief educative
forces in society. Educational reconstruction must therefore focus
broadly on the dynamics of American culture rather than narrowly
on the schools.

Fromm, Erich. THE DOGMA OF CHRIST, AND OTHER ESSAYS ON RELIGION,
PSYCHOLOGY, AND CULTURE. London: Routledge and Kegan Paul, 1963.
151 p.; New York: Holt, Rinehart and Winston, 1963. 212 p.

_____. MARX'S CONCEPT OF MAN. With a translation from Marx's eco-
nomic and philosophical manuscripts by T.B. Bottomore. New York: F. Ungar
Publishing, 1961. xii, 260 p. Also republished with an afterword by Erich
Fromm. New York: F. Ungar Publishing, 1966. xii, 263 p.

Hentig, Hartmut von. CUERNAVACA ODER ALTERNATIVEN ZUR SCHULE?
[Cuernavaca or alternatives to school?]. 2d ed. Stuttgart, W. Ger.: Klett;
Munich: Koesel, 1972. 139 p.

In response to the radical criticism of Ivan Illich and his deschooling human society, Hentig suggests his own theory of deschooling
the school. He presents a plan that has been worked out at the
Bielefeld University.

Hitchcock, James. "The Evolution of the American Catholic Left." AMERICAN
SCHOLAR 43, no. 1 (1973-74): 66-84.

The effects of the Catholic Left on the general climate of American opinion are probably unmeasurable. Departing from the liberalism of John Courtney Murray, the Berrigans and others have gone
almost full circle toward his thinking in making American Catholicism more pluralistic.

Hurn, Christopher J. "Recent Trends in the Sociology of Education." HARVARD
EDUCATIONAL REVIEW 46, no. 1 (1976): 105-14.

In reviewing the books of Esland, Dale, Esland-Dale-Dadler,
Hargreaves, Seaman-Esland-Cosin, McPherson-Swift-Berstein,
and one edited by Flude and Ahier, Hurn concludes that
the new sociology of education is profoundly relativistic and
rejects the traditional model of schooling in a most fundamental way.

Kirk, Russell. THE CONSERVATIVE MIND. 5th rev. ed. South Bend,
Ind.: Gateway Editions, 1977. 480 p.

In response to what he believes to be the liberal domination of
American intellectual life, Kirk marshals the evidence in favor
of the conservative tradition which he feels Americans can ignore

only at the peril of losing the qualities that have made America
a free and orderly society.

Kramer, Frank R. "New Light from Old Lamps." LIBERAL EDUCATION 63,
no. 1 (1977): 44-58.

Kramer demonstrates how Greek classical premises, such as the inter-
connectedness and interdependence of all things, limits, organic
growth, and the goodness of man and human society, can serve as
conceptual substrata for viewing contemporary problems in perspective. The two pages of suggested readings will provoke even other
possibilities.

Kunert, Hubertus. DEUTSCHE REFORMPAEDAGOGIK UND FASCHISMUS.
[German educational reform and fascism]. Hanover, Darmstadt, Dortmund, and
Berlin: Schroedel, 1973. 156 p.

The author ties together the cultural criticism of Lagarde and
Langbehn in the late nineteenth century with German fascism. He
offers an assessment of this intellectual incubation period with the
hope of finding the answer to the question of how Germany allowed
fascism to take over both school and society as it did.

Louisell, David W. "Does the Constitution Require a Purely Secular Society?"
CATHOLIC UNIVERSITY LAW REVIEW 26, no. 1 (1976): 17-72.

People of religious conviction today often seem quite timid about
asserting their legitimate role in the formulation of their country's
public philosophy. The court no longer guarantees neutrality but
is actually throwing its weight toward a purely secular society.

Ozmon, Howard. UTOPIAS AND EDUCATION. Minneapolis: Burgess Publishing, 1969. xiii, 155 p.

This representative selection of utopian writers concentrates specifi-
cally on education and its philosophic assumptions: Plato, More,
Campanella, Andreae, Gott, Owen Butler, Bellamy, Morris, Cram,
Wells, Huxley, and Skinner.

Phillips, Denis Charles, and Kelly, Mavis E. "Hierarchical Theories of Development in Education and Psychology." HARVARD EDUCATIONAL REVIEW 45,
no. 3 (1975): 351-75.

After reviewing the works of Piaget and Inhelder, Kohlberg, Jensen,
Erikson, and Gagne, the authors claim it is far from clear whether
the theories of these thinkers are empirically or conceptually
grounded. They believe a good many of the assumptions currently
accepted in developmental psychology are questionable.

Richter, Peyton E., and Fogg, Walter L., eds. PHILOSOPHY LOOKS TO

THE FUTURE: CONFRONTATION, COMMITMENT, AND UTOPIA. 2d ed. Rockleigh, N.J.: Allyn and Bacon, Holbrook Press, 1978. 600 p. Appendix. Paperbound.

> The readings engage the student in confronting the human condition, human nature, moral choice, authority, religious experience, and the future. The appendix is a guide to constructing a utopia.

Roth, Robert J. "John Dewey: Social Philosopher and Educator." In THE PHILOSOPHER AS EDUCATOR. Proceedings of the American Catholic Philosophical Association, edited by George F. McLean, pp. 115-22. Washington, D.C.: Catholic University of America, 1973.

> Roth presents the philosophical context in which Dewey developed his theory of education, the characteristic changes of American society calling for reconstruction in educational theory, the meaning of Dewey's proposed reconstruction, and the more significant features of Dewey's thinking today.

Sachs, Wolfgang. SCHULZWANG UND SOZIALE KONTROLLE: ARGUMENTE FUER EINE ENTSCHULUNG DES LERNENS. [Compulsory education and social control: arguments for the deschooling of learning]. Frankfort on the Main, Berlin, and Munich: Diesterweg, 1976. 174 p.

> The author has changed the original title of his doctoral dissertation "Belehrung und Soziale Kontrolle" [Instruction and social control] to COMPULSORY EDUCATION AND SOCIAL CONTROL.

Schmidt, Heiner, et al., eds. ADIEU: AUSWAHL-DIENST. [Adieu: a select information-service]. Appears annually. Duisburg, W. Ger.: Verlag fuer Paedagogische Dokumentation, 1976. 376 p.

> "Adieu 76" refers on 376 pages to 5,432 educational sources published in 1976. By cataloging all that has appeared in ERZIEHUNGS-WISSENSCHAFTLICHEN DOKUMENTATION (ED) and PAEDAGOG-ISCHEN JAHRESBERICHTES (PJ), this source brings the reader into direct contact with more than 180,000 citations in the literature of education and psychology between the years of 1945 and 1975.

Schultz, Frederick Marshall. SOCIAL-PHILOSOPHICAL FOUNDATIONS OF EDUCATION. Dubuque, Iowa: Kendall/Hunt Publishing, 1974. ix, 182 p.

Sharp, Rachel, and Green, Anthony. EDUCATION AND SOCIAL CONTROL: A STUDY IN PROGRESSIVE PRIMARY EDUCATION. London; Boston: Routledge and Kegan Paul, 1975. xi, 256 p.

> Among the substantive issues of importance are the teachers' philosophy of education, their set beliefs and practices, their helping learners to discover themselves. These raise further questions over educational perspectives, the nature and function of the school, and philosophy of education as such.

Steinberg, Ira S. EDUCATIONAL MYTHS AND REALITIES: PHILOSOPHICAL ESSAYS ON EDUCATION, POLITICS, AND THE SCIENCE OF BEHAVIOR. Reading, Mass.: Addison-Wesley Publishing, 1968. xi, 240 p.

Stoops, John A. THE EDUCATION OF INNER MAN: ESSAYS ON RELIGIOUS AND ACADEMIC IDEALISM. Danville, Ill.: Interstate Printers and Publishers, 1969. 177 p.

Sylvester, Richard S., and Marc'hadour, Germain, eds. ESSENTIAL ARTICLES FOR THE STUDY OF THOMAS MORE. Hamden, Conn.: Archon Books, 1977. xxiii, 676 p.

> Of the forty-seven contributions, nine center on the UTOPIA and approximately nine others on More's humanist outlook and mode of action.

Tanner, Fritz. ERZIEHUNG HEUTE ZUR GESELLSCHAFT VON MORGEN. [Education today for society tomorrow]. Munich and Basel, Switz.: E. Reinhardt, 1973. 246 p.

Tollkoetter, Bernhard. ARBEIT, BILDUNG, GESELLSCHAFT. [Work, education, society]. Wuppertal, W. Ger.; Ratingen, W. Ger.; and Dusseldorf, W. Ger.: Henn, 1970. 214 p. Bibliog.

> The point of the research into the Marxian and Pestalozzian ideas of work, education, and society is to elaborate both a philosophical and an educational anthropology. The author intends to enrich the general discussions over the theoretical foundations of education with insights from work experience. The bibliography (pp. 203-14) is helpful for further study of these ideas.

Voegelin, Eric. FROM ENLIGHTENMENT TO REVOLUTION. Edited by John H. Hallowell. Durham, N.C.: Duke University Press, 1975. ix, 307 p.

> Voegelin perceives progressivism, utilitarianism, and Marxism as diverse rejections of the spiritual understanding of man. The willingness of modern man to secure himself only in the mundane and thereby to forego his spiritual inheritance is symptomatic of a very serious and terminal spiritual disease.

Walgrave, Jan Henricus. PERSON AND SOCIETY: A CHRISTIAN VIEW. Pittsburgh: Duquesne University Press, 1965. 182 p.

White, Leslie A. THE SCIENCE OF CULTURE: A STUDY OF MAN AND CIVILIZATION. New York: Farrar, Straus and Giroux, 1969. xi, 444 p.

> White opposes cultural determinism in which culture appears to be autonomous and self-sufficient and human behavior is viewed as the outcome of cultural stimuli. This is an assumption of behavior-

ism. White would rather regard the study of man and civilization as being preoccupied not with the individual or independent culture exclusively but with the transactions of persons among themselves and with their cultural traditions.

D 3: HUMAN NATURE AND UNITY

Bowers, C.A. "Existentialism and Educational Theory." EDUCATIONAL THEORY 15, no. 3 (1965): 222-29. Reprinted in READINGS IN THE FOUNDATIONS OF EDUCATION, edited by James C. Stone and Frederick W. Schneider, pp. 502-10. 2d ed. New York: Thomas Y. Crowell, 1971.

> The existentialist, in reaction against the submergence of the individual in a system whether philosophical, religious, political, or technological, seeks through an introspective examination of his own experience to know what gives meaning to his existence, what is the nature of freedom and its impact on life, what forces man to become alienated from himself and his environment. Discovery of self and freedom to be no longer swayed by the premises of his own culture are important purposes in education. The real test of the curriculum is its ability to develop strong feelings toward one's surroundings so that, in the process of understanding them and one's sense of identity, a greater commitment is given to values that enhance the well being of others.

D'Souza, Austin Anthony. THE HUMAN FACTOR IN EDUCATION. Foreword by E.B. Castle. Bombay, India: Orient Longmans, 1969. xiv, 282 p.

Dupre, Louis. "Secularism and the Crisis of Our Culture: A Hermeneutic Perspective." THOUGHT 51, no. 202 (1976): 271-81.

> In a secularist society, where men live in a fragmented universe without support and without soul and tolerate only ephemeral ideas and transient values, the preliminary condition for regaining transcendence in our lives is the rediscovery of inwardness. Only thus can authentic religion be attained.

Fehl, Noah Edward. A GUIDE TO THE STUDY OF PLATO'S REPUBLIC AND THE SOCRATIC DIALOGUES. Rev. ed. Hong Kong: Chung Chi College, 1962. 114 p.

Frankl, Viktor Emil. THE PLURALISM OF SCIENCES AND THE UNITY OF MAN. New York: International Center for Integrative Studies, 1966. 17 p.

> The existentialist approach insists on the total unity of man. Man is in his entirety and must be so considered.

_____. PSYCHOTHERAPY AND EXISTENTIALISM. SELECTED PAPERS ON LOGOTHERAPY. With contributions by James C. Crumbaugh, Hans O. Gerz, and Leonard T. Maholick. New York: Washington Square Press, 1967. xii, 242 p. Bibliog.

The opening chapters are important for examining the philosophical foundations of logotherapy, existential dynamics, self-actualization, the nature of man, and the quest for meaning. The bibliography introduces the reader to a wide range of critical assessments of Frankl's thought.

Gopalakrishnaiah, V. A COMPARATIVE STUDY OF J.G. FICHTE AND J.H. NEWMAN. Waltair, India: Andhra University Press, 1973. 78 p.

Hill, Brian V. EDUCATION AND THE ENDANGERED INDIVIDUAL: A CRITIQUE OF TEN MODERN THINKERS. Foreword by Philip H. Phenix. New York: Teachers College Press, 1974. xiv, 322 p.

That the individual should be valued as an end in himself is not commonly held by the "prodigal sons of Hegel" (Kierkegaard, Nietzsche, and Marx), "scientific world-viewers" (Dewey and Whitehead), "social scientists at odds" (Nunn and Mannheim), and "modern religious thinkers" (Buber, Maritain, and Niebuhr). The disparity of views and modes of discourse makes a contemporary consensus rather difficult to achieve.

Hopkins, Levi Thomas. THE EMERGING SELF AND HOME. 1954. Reprint. Westport, Conn.: Greenwood Press, 1970. ix, 366 p.

Krolikowski, Walter P., and Reuland, Timothy J. "Autonomy and Education: In Response to Vincent Crockenberg." EDUCATIONAL THEORY 27, no. 3 (1977): 233-40.

Dissatisfied with the contradictions and problems of Crockenberg's understanding of autonomy, the authors have recourse to the Aristotelian concept of architectonics as a way of describing the relationships among individuals and between individuals and communities.

May, Rollo. MAN'S SEARCH FOR HIMSELF. New York: New American Library, 1967. 239 p.

Ollman, Bertell. ALIENATION: MARX'S CONCEPTION OF MAN IN CAPITALIST SOCIETY. Cambridge: Cambridge University Press, 1971. xvi, 325 p.

Roesel, Manfred. PAEDAGOGISCHE DIMENSIONEN DER DIALEKTIK VON INDIVIDUUM UND GESELLSCHAFT. [Educational dimensions of the dialectic between the individual and society]. Essen, W. Ger.: Neue Deutsche Schule Verlagsgesellschaft, 1972. 86 p.

Roth, Heinrich. PAEDAGOGISCHE ANTHROPOLOGIE. [Educational anthropology]. 2 vols. Hanover, Berlin, Darmstadt, and Dortmund: Schroedel, 1968-71.

> Volume 1: BILDSAMKEIT UND BESTIMMUNG. [Education: flexible and determinate]. 2d ed. 1968.

> Volume 2: ENTWICKLUNG UND ERZIEHUNG. [Human development and education]. 1971. 656 p.

> Roth explores the concept of development in terms of its consequences for an educational philosophy of development. He delineates the significance of developmental stages for the domains of intellectual, social, and ethical education.

Roth, Robert J. "Person and Technology: A Deweyan Perspective." In his PERSON AND COMMUNITY: A PHILOSOPHICAL EXPLORATION, pp. 87-102. New York: Fordham University Press, 1975.

> Roth maintains Dewey has developed a full-blown social and political theory applicable to many aspects of modern life and technology. Dewey's hope was based on the future commitment of all man to mutual development as human beings within a humane society.

D4: HUMAN INTELLECTIVE POWERS

Berkson, Isaac Baer. THE IDEAL AND THE COMMUNITY: A PHILOSOPHY OF EDUCATION. 1958. Reprint. Westport, Conn.: Greenwood Press, 1970. xii, 302 p.

Dewey, John. INTEREST AND EFFORT IN EDUCATION. New York: Houghton Mifflin, 1913. Reprint. Preface by James E. Wheeler. Carbondale: Southern Illinois University Press, 1975. 120 p.

> This is an important study on the scientific theory of learning. It gives a clear exposition of Dewey's thinking in educational philosophy and of how he would like his thinking to be carried out in practical schooling.

Fehl, Noah Edward. THE IDEA OF A UNIVERSITY IN EAST AND WEST. 2d ed. Hong Kong: Chung Chi College, 1965. xiv, 278 p.

> A synthesis between eastern and western educational thought and culture seems possible to the author at the university level. The most likely basis for the kind of philosophical unity that will be required is the university fully committed to the ideals of Christianity and to the realization of John Henry Newman's ideas of liberal education for ladies and gentlemen.

Fiedler, Ralph. DIE KLASSISCHE DEUTSCHE BILDUNGSIDEE: IHRE SOZIO-
LOGISCHEN WURZELN UND PAEDAGOGISCHEN FOLGEN. [The classical
German concept of liberal education: its sociological origins and educational
consequences]. Weinheim, W. Ger.: Beltz, 1973. viii, 189 p.

Hutchins, Robert Maynard. THE LEARNING SOCIETY. New York: Frederick
A. Praeger, 1968. xi, 142 p.

Lenzen, Dieter, ed. DIE STRUKTUR DER ERZIEHUNG UND DES UNTERRICHTS.
Kronberg, W. Ger.: Athenaeum-Verlag, 1976. 262 p.

> Thirteen international authorities in education discuss the problem
> of structuralism in education: J.S. Bruner, W. Edelstein, W.
> Flitner, H. Geissler, H.M. Kliebard, G. Kutscha, D. Lenzen,
> H. Paschen, G. Petersen, P.H. Phenix, J. Piaget, K. Sauer,
> and M. Wagenschein.

Maritain, Jacques. DISTINGUISH TO UNITE or THE DEGREES OF KNOWL-
EDGE. Translated from 4th French ed. under supervision of Gerald B. Phelan.
New York: Charles Scribner's Sons, 1959. xix, 476.

> The first part of this classic examines the degrees of rational knowl-
> edge in terms of philosophy and experimental science, critical
> realism, knowledge of sensible nature, and metaphysical knowledge.
> The second part is given to an understanding of mystical experience
> and philosophy, Augustinian wisdom, St. John of the Cross as prac-
> titioner of contemplation. The Thomistic realism here espoused
> preserves the value of the knowledge of things and opens the way
> to an exploration of the world of reflection.

_____. TRUE HUMANISM. Translated by M.R. Adamson. Freeport, N.Y.:
Books for Libraries Press; Westport, Conn.: Greenwood Press, 1970. xvii,
304 p.

Neufeld, Evelyn M. THE PHILOSOPHY OF JEAN PIAGET AND ITS EDUCA-
TIONAL IMPLICATIONS. Morristown, N.J.: General Learning Press, 1976.
xiv, 52 p.

Parsons, Talcott, et al. THE AMERICAN UNIVERSITY. Cambridge, Mass.:
Harvard University Press, 1973. 463 p.

> If the university is the guardian of intellectual culture, then gradu-
> ate professors must equally preserve this rationality through the other
> functions of socialization, professional training, and the education
> of generalists. But must these be the values of undergraduate study
> as well? Many may find the Parsonian insistence on the purely
> cognitive side of college education too much in the face of alter-
> nate patterns of human growth at the undergraduate level.

Peters, Richard Stanley. "Education and the Educated Man." PROCEEDINGS OF THE PHILOSOPHY OF EDUCATION SOCIETY OF GREAT BRITAIN 4 (1970): 5-20.

Riordan, Timothy M. "Karl Jaspers: An Existentialist Looks at University Education." EDUCATIONAL THEORY 26, no. 1 (1976): 113-20.

> Riordan examines the existentialism of Karl Jaspers, his idea of a university, and implications for the future. If intellectual insight is the purpose of the university, then the pragmatism that lulls the mind to sleep is its enemy. The university is no place for the unphilosophical spirit.

D 5: HUMAN AFFECTIVE POWERS

Dewey, John. DEMOCRACY AND EDUCATION: AN INTRODUCTION TO THE PHILOSOPHY OF EDUCATION. New York: Macmillan, 1916. Reprint. New York: Free Press; London: Collier-Macmillan, 1966. vi, 378 p. Paperbound.

> The growth of a true democracy originates with the schools where all learn to work together toward a common good and develop social and cultural dispositions necessary for a free life in common. When education is conceived as the process of forming dispositions, intellectual and emotional, toward nature and fellow men, then philosophy may be defined as the general theory of education and the school becomes the means for a free people to reconstruct society. The metaphysics of experience and education are mutually interwoven and inseparable.

_____. THE EDUCATIONAL SITUATION. Chicago: University of Chicago Press, 1902. 104 p.

Frankl, Viktor Emil. MAN'S SEARCH FOR MEANING: AN INTRODUCTION TO LOGOTHERAPY. 1962. Newly rev. and enl. ed. of FROM DEATH-CAMP TO EXISTENTIALISM. Translated by Ilse Lasch with a preface by Gordon W. Allport. Boston: Beacon Press, 1970. 150 p.

Hart, Joseph Kinmont. EDUCATION IN THE HUMAN COMMUNITY. Introduction by H. Gordon Hullfish. 1951. Reprint. Westport, Conn.: Greenwood Press, 1971. xiii, 172 p.

Hemmings, Ray. CHILDREN'S FREEDOM: A.S. NEILL AND THE EVOLUTION OF THE SUMMERHILL IDEA. New York: Schocken Books, 1973. xiii, 218 p.

_____. FIFTY YEARS OF FREEDOM: A STUDY OF THE DEVELOPMENT OF THE IDEAS OF A.S. NEAL. London: Allen and Unwin, 1972. xiii, 218 p.

Hickey, Howard W., et al., eds. THE ROLE OF THE SCHOOL IN COMMU-
NITY EDUCATION. Midland, Mich.: Pendell Publishing, 1969. 136 p.

Hickey regards the community school as a social imperative and
gives students a basic reference for the study of philosophy, objectives, and activities in pilot programs within community education.

Hopkins, Richard L. "Freedom and Education: The Philosophy of Summerhill."
EDUCATIONAL THEORY 26, no. 2 (1976): 188-213.

In contrast to Rousseau, Pestalozzi, Montessori, Dewey, Kilpatrick,
and existentialism, Hopkins concludes that the philosophy of the
anarchists seems closest to that of Neill. Both seem to concentrate
on eliminating control by others over an individual's life and development. No one is really good enough to tell children anything.

Kagan, Jerome, and Lang, Cynthia. PSYCHOLOGY AND EDUCATION: AN
INTRODUCTION. New York: Harcourt Brace Jovanovich, 1978. 626 p.

Part 1 compares the educational goals of six different cultures
(Sparta, Athens, Rome, Tanzania, China, and Israel) with those of
contemporary American education. After surveying the major changes
in American values since 1800, the authors examine the role of the
school in socializing personality and teaching values. The remaining eleven chapters are chiefly oriented toward the psychological
study of education.

Lapassade, Georges, and Scherer, Rene. LE CORPS INTERDIT: ESSAIS SUR
L'EDUCATION NEGATIVE. Preface by Daniel Zimmermann. Paris: Editions
E.S.F., 1976. 141 p.

Lickona, Thomas; Geis, Gilbert; Kohlberg, Lawrence, eds. MORAL DEVELOP-
MENT AND BEHAVIOR: THEORY, RESEARCH AND SOCIAL ISSUES. New
York: Holt, Rinehart and Winston, 1976. xiv, 430 p.

Murray, John Courtney. THE PROBLEM OF RELIGIOUS FREEDOM. Westminster,
Md.: Newman Press, 1965. 112 p.

Murray presents two views of the problem, examines the tradition,
then addresses himself to the heart of the issues. The work is an excellent summation and clarification of the debate on religious freedom.

Peters, Richard Stanley. PSYCHOLOGY AND ETHICAL DEVELOPMENT: A
COLLECTION OF ARTICLES ON PSYCHOLOGICAL THEORIES, ETHICAL DE-
VELOPMENT AND HUMAN UNDERSTANDING. London: Allen and Unwin,
1974. 480 p.

_____, ed. NATURE AND CONDUCT. New York: St. Martin's Press, 1975.
xv, 315 p.

Pritzkau, Hilo T. ON EDUCATION FOR THE AUTHENTIC. Scranton, Pa.:
International Textbook, 1970. ix, 148 p.

Skinner, B[urrhus]. F[rederic]. ABOUT BEHAVIORISM. New York: Alfred A.
Knopf, 1974. viii, 256 p.

_____. BEYOND FREEDOM AND DIGNITY. New York: Alfred A. Knopf,
1971. 225 p.; New York: Bantam, Vintage, 1972. 215 p.

> Skinner raises a controversy over the value of a carefully controlled
> society in which individuals are programmed and conditioned in the
> Skinnerian concept of behavior modification. He rejects the ideals
> of personal freedom and human dignity for a kind of laboratory-
> controlled existence to which he himself will not submit.

D 6: HUMAN AESTHETIC POWERS

Cunningham, Francis J. "Plato: Archaic or Modern Man?" THOUGHT 50,
no. 199 (1975): 400-17.

> Despite his being subject to cultural and social conditioning by
> forces of which he may or may not have been conscious, Plato
> did articulate in his philosophy a kind of creativity that   modern
> thinkers can support and this openness to creativity marks him as
> a modern man.

Greene, Maxine. LANDSCAPES OF LEARNING. New York: Teachers College
Press, 1978. 288 p. Paperbound.

> The essays are grouped into four sections: intellectual and moral
> components of emancipatory education, social issues and their impli-
> cations for approaches to pedagogy, artistic-aesthetic considerations
> in the making of a curriculum, and the cultural significance of
> women's predicaments today. The author's philosophy is largely
> existential, humanist, and phenomenological.

Kokemohr, Rainer. ZUKUNFT ALS BILDUNGSPROBLEM. [The future as an
educational problem]. Ratingen, W. Ger.; Kastellaun, W. Ger.; and Dusseldorf,
W. Ger.: Henn, 1973. 184 p.

> In the educational reflections of the young Nietzsche, Kokemohr
> finds a distinction between education and "education" conceived
> negatively; the former term conveys the notion of self-identity and
> the latter conventionality. The first part of this work studies
> Nietzsche's criticism of education in its historical meaning. The
> second delineates authentic education as being anticipatory of self-
> development and self-fulfillment.

D7: THE PROBLEM OF VALUES—ETHICS

Bandman, Bertram. "Some Legal, Moral and Intellectual Rights of Children."
EDUCATIONAL THEORY 27, no. 3 (1977): 169-78.

> The order of argument involves the role of rights in philosophy and
> education, the attribution of rights to children, and pertinent re-
> cent Supreme Court cases. If rights imply freedom, correlative
> duties, and justice, then children must have these rights.

Barrow, Robin. MORAL PHILOSOPHY FOR EDUCATION. London: Allen and
Unwin; Hamden, Conn.: Shoe String Press, Linnet Books, 1975. 214 p.
Paperbound.

> Barrow takes students' concerns with moral issues as the basis for
> an introduction to the philosophy of education. By having them
> focus their attention on the concepts of freedom, equality, and
> happiness, students are invited to work out a reasonable, utilitarian
> ethical theory. Testing their formulation against the ideas of Kant,
> and the theories of other philosophers, students then consider the
> moral implications of the limits of freedom for children, the justifi-
> cation of the emphasis on creativity, and the provision of equal
> education.

_____. PLATO, UTILITARIANISM AND EDUCATION. London and Boston:
Routledge and Kegan Paul, 1975. ix, 203 p.

> Refuting Russell, Popper, and Crossman as the misinterpreters of
> Plato, Robin then fashions Plato into a kind of utilitarian who be-
> lieves happiness is the ultimate good. Readers are advised to re-
> view utilitarianism and to check for themselves whether Plato is
> being used to support an alien philosophy. The value of this work
> will have to be assessed with greatest care.

Berlin, Sir Isaiah. FOUR ESSAYS ON LIBERTY. Oxford and New York:
Oxford University Press, 1969. xiii, 213 p. Paperbound.

Bethel, Dayle M. MAKIGUCHI THE VALUE CREATOR. New York: John
Weatherhill, 1973. 174 p.

> Founder of a new religion, Soka Gakkai, Tsunesaburo Makiguchi
> (1871-1944) followed the thought of John Dewey in teaching that
> the pursuit and creation of values is the ultimate purpose of life
> and schooling.

Braun, Walter. EMANZIPATION ALS PAEDAGOGISCHES PROBLEM: ANTHRO-
POLOG. VORAUSSETZUNGEN UND PAEDAG. MOEGLICHKEITEN. [Individual
freedom as an educational problem]. Saarbrucken, W. Ger.: Universitaets-
und Schulbuchverl.; Kastellaun, W. Ger.: Henn, 1977. 121 p. Bibliog.

Brown, Stuart C., ed. PHILOSOPHERS DISCUSS EDUCATION. Totowa, N.J.: Rowman and Littlefield, 1975. ix, 260 p.

> This book includes topics on autonomy as an educational ideal (Dearden, Telfer, and Hare) and on academic freedom (Brown, Griffiths, and Peters).

Chapin, Lloyd W. "Augustine's Challenge to Liberal Education." LIBERAL EDUCATION 63, no. 1 (1977): 5-18.

> The challenge to liberal education is man's self-centeredness which can be transformed by the working of such external powers as the action of God, parental influence, teacher-philosophers, writings such as those of St. Paul, and final commitment to Christianity. These educative agencies are complemented by the individual's capacities and urges to love and understand and these are the sources of human greatness.

Chomsky, Noam. PROBLEMS OF KNOWLEDGE AND FREEDOM. The Russell Lectures. New York: Pantheon Books, 1971; Vintage Books, 1972. xi, 111 p. Paperbound.

Craig, Robert P. "Lawrence Kohlberg and Moral Development: Some Reflections." EDUCATIONAL THEORY 24, no. 2 (1974): 121-29.

> Craig disagrees with Kohlberg by finding no logical reason for claiming that a higher stage is necessarily a better one! (See Swanger, cited in chapter 7.)

Crittenden, Brian C. FORM AND CONTENT IN MORAL EDUCATION. Monograph Series, no. 12. Toronto, Canada: Ontario Institute for Studies in Education, 1972. 102 p.

Ellison, Craig W., ed. MODIFYING MAN: IMPLICATIONS AND ETHICS. Washington, D.C.: University Press of America, 1977. 375 p. Paperbound.

> This evangelically oriented book deals with human engineering issues and contains the major papers and responses of the International Conference on Human Engineering and the Future of Man held at Wheaton College in July 1975. The original papers presented are by Callahan, MacKay, Sinsheimer, Valenstein, London, and Hatfield; the responses are from Allen, Spencer, Herrmann, Othius, Anderson, Ramm, Wilson, Feinberg, Clement, Verhey, Bufford, Scanzoni, and Henry.

Facione, P., et al. VALUES AND SOCIETY: AN INTRODUCTION TO ETHICS AND SOCIAL PHILOSOPHY. Englewood Cliffs, N.J.: Prentice-Hall, 1978. viii, 294 p.

Field, Frank L. FREEDOM AND CONTROL IN EDUCATION AND SOCIETY.
New York: Thomas Y. Crowell, 1970. xiii, 196 p. Paperbound.

> Chapter 2, "On the Absence of an Integrating Philosophy for the
> Process of Education," truly challenges the reader to mine whatever
> resources are available for structuring a new theory of man. After
> describing the current conceptual bases for educational practice,
> Field proposes a basic strategy for integrating these principles into
> educational policy. How the transfer of controls from outside to
> inside is accomplished within education is, for Field, a key variable
> distinguishing democracy from totalitarianism.

Franklin, Benjamin. AUTOBIOGRAPHY. 1868. Reprint. Edited from his
manuscript with notes and an introduction by John Bigelow. Philadelphia:
J.B. Lippincott, 1974. 409 p.

> Franklin singles out thirteen fundamental moral virtues and explains
> how these virtues contribute to the "good life" on earth. Temper-
> ance, silence, order, resolution, frugality, industry, sincerity,
> justice, moderation, cleanliness, tranquility, charity, and humility
> have each a special contribution toward making one a better and
> happier person. He suggests a day-by-day inventory of progress.
> It is also available in microfilm.

Freire, Paulo. EDUCATION, THE PRACTICE OF FREEDOM. London: Writers
and Readers Publishing Cooperative, 1976. xiv, 162 p.

Fromm, Erich. ESCAPE FROM FREEDOM. New York: Rinehart, 1960.
ix, 305 p.; Avon Books, 1965. 333 p.

> Modern man enjoys an independence and rationality born of the
> freedom to exercise individuality. Can man follow the consequences
> of this personal freedom in the face of a growing totalitarianism?

Gustafson, James M. CAN ETHICS BE CHRISTIAN? Chicago and London:
University of Chicago Press, 1975. xi, 191 p.

> The seven chapters treat the moral dimensions of experience, the
> moral self and the influence of Christian faith, the reasons of
> mind and heart which Christian faith offers for being moral, the
> theological interpretation of circumstances, religious beliefs and
> the determination of conduct, and the inference from the Christian
> experience of the reality of God that religion does indeed qualify
> morality. For example, nonviolent resistence to evil is a Christian
> moral act justified only by religious reasons.

Heilbroner, Robert L. AN INQUIRY INTO THE HUMAN PROSPECT. New
York: W.W. Norton, 1974. 150 p.

> Heilbroner's pessimistic thesis on the future of mankind, in the opin-
> ion of Joseph Anthony Mazzeo, has been often attacked without

being refuted. "If the trends we now discern continue we
are headed for great social upheavals in the world" (Joseph
Anthony Mazzeo, "Interpretation, Humanistic Culture, and Cultural
Change." THOUGHT 51 [March 1976]: 70).

Martindale, Don Albert. SOCIOLOGICAL THEORY AND THE PROBLEM OF
VALUES. Columbus, Ohio: Charles E. Merrill, 1974. x, 246 p.

Osborne, Thomas J. "1776 and the New Radicalism." THOUGHT 48, no.
188 (1973): 19-32.

> Jefferson's dictum that all men were created equal and endowed
> with the same inalienable rights has become America's "standard
> maxim." After primacy is given to this principle, then the right
> to revolution can be viewed in its proper perspective. This,
> today's revolutionaries have failed to do, according to Osborne.

Staffelbach, Elmer Hubert. MORAL CRISIS IN AMERICA. New York: Pagent
Press, 1964. 276 p.

Swanger, David. "A Response to Robert Craig." EDUCATIONAL THEORY 25,
no. 2 (1975): 203-5.

> This article provides some reflections on Craig's disagreement with
> Kohlberg's theory of moral development. (See Craig, cited in
> chapter 7.)

D 8: THE PROBLEM OF THOUGHT AND LANGUAGE—
PHILOSOPHICAL ANALYSIS

Duncan, Otis Dudley. "Path Analysis: Sociological Examples." AMERICAN
JOURNAL OF SOCIOLOGY 72, no. 1 (1966): 1-16.

> Duncan believes linear models are conveniently developed by path
> coefficients that focus on the problem of interpretation but do not
> constitute a method for discovering causes. Path analysis is in-
> valuable for rendering interpretations explicit, self-consistent, and
> susceptible to further modification and even rejection by subsequent
> research.

Emerson, Thomas. THE SYSTEM OF FREEDOM OF EXPRESSION. New York:
Random House, 1970. 754 p.

> "The values sought by society in protecting the right to freedom of
> expression may be grouped into four broad categories. Maintenance
> of a system of free expression is necessary (1) as a method of
> assuring individual self-fulfillment, (2) as a means of attaining the
> truth, (3) as a method of securing participation by the members of
> the society in social, including political, decision-making, and

(4) as a means of maintaining the balance between stability and change in society" (p. 3).

Percy, Walter. THE MESSAGE IN THE BOTTLE. New York: Farrar, Straus and Giroux, 1975. x, 335 p.

The refutations of Carnap and Skinner have to be ranked with the best of Cassirer, Langer, and Chomsky. Percy sees in man a visible difference, namely, that only man has a capacity for symbolic language. These profound essays discuss the major psycholinguistic issues from the mysteries of speech to the unique nature of man himself.

Peters, Richard Stanley. ETHICS AND EDUCATION. New ed. London: Allen and Unwin, 1970. 333 p. Also paperbound.

The study exemplifies the resourcefulness of critical thinking in the systematic analysis of education and its implied value judgments about human freedom, authority, equality, and democracy. Peters uses the analytic method, in establishing the ethical foundations of education, to reach a positive theory of justification for a new social philosophy of Democratic education. The student will find here much help in training his own critical powers as well.

Pratte, Richard. IDEOLOGY AND EDUCATION. New York: David McKay, 1977. viii, 305 p.

Presupposing at least an introductory course in philosophy or logic, Pratte applies conceptual, language, and argument analysis to ideology in an effort to question answers. He finds that ideology is a belief system (metaphysical, epistemological, moral) that enables an individual to marshal his thinking and actions around such agenda as schooling and cultural diversity. Schooling should produce students who will be capable of judging well and this purpose can be justified in terms of education. The arguments for encouraging free choices and decision making, by individuals and groups, are worth a thorough and critical review.

D TR: THE PROBLEM OF GOD—THEOLOGY AND RELIGION

Bechtle, Regina. "Karl Rahner's Supernatural Existential: A Personalist Approach." THOUGHT 58, no. 188 (1973): 61-77. Bibliog.

Given the fact that all men share in the ontological determination toward the vision of God which is the supernatural existential, there can be no purely natural action or existence. Once God chooses to create a being which is self-transcending spirit, God commits himself to the personal and social demands consequent upon this love relationship. Rahner's theme, in his doctrine of the supernatural existential, helps solve the nature-grace problem and remains a skillful and valuable starting point for contemporary man.

Berger, Peter L. THE SACRED CANOPY: ELEMENTS OF A SOCIOLOGICAL THEORY OF RELIGION. New York: Doubleday, 1967. 230 p.

This noted thinker and sociologist addresses himself to the question, "How can any religious view of the world be made plausible to people?" The assumptions, answers, and implications of this question have far-reaching significance for the philosopher of education.

Brickman, William W. THE JEWISH COMMUNITY IN AMERICA. New York: Burt Franklin, 1977. xxvii, 396.

This bibliographical guide lists materials pertinent to Hebrew thought in education, in religious life, thought, and affairs, and other fields of human activity.

Greeley, Andrew M., and Rossi, Peter H. THE EDUCATION OF CATHOLIC AMERICANS. Chicago: Aldine Publishing, 1966. xxii, 368 p. Garden City, N.Y.: Doubleday, 1968. 403 p. Paperbound.

In terms of the religious consequences of Catholic education on adult religious behavior, Greeley suggests that the impact of family and schools is most evident where the background and ambience is strongly religious.

Krahl, Helfried. DER SOZIALERZIEHERISCHE ASPEKT FRANZISKANISCHER GEISTIGKEIT: ERZIEHUNGSWISSENSCHAFT. [Theory of education and the sociological aspects of Franciscan spirituality]. Werl (Westfallen), W. Ger.: Dietrich-Coelde-Verlag, 1974. 115 p..

Krahl views, in perspective, the social and caritative thrust of Franciscan institutions and delineates its importance in a modern social theory of education. Franciscan spirituality calls for a radical social reconstruction in life and schools.

Lonergan, Bernard J.F. A SECOND COLLECTION. Edited by William F.J. Ryan, S.J., and Bernard J. Tyrrell, S.J. Philadelphia: Westminster Press, 1975. 302 p.

The nineteen essays by Lonergan analyze contemporary culture, the science on which it is based, and the historical world view which dominates its thinking. In a Catholic education, the proper place for a natural theology is within the theology which thematizes the religious experience of the converted Christian.

Murray, John Courtney, ed. FREEDOM AND MAN. New York: P.J. Kenedy and Sons, 1965. 217 p.

The essays by Kueng, Fransen, Lynch, Mooney, Johann, Callahan, Calvez, Malik, K. Rahner, and Murray map out the foundations of a Christian philosophy of freedom. The subject of this discussion is very much in the forefront today.

Oppolzer, Siegfried, and Lassahn, Rudolf, eds. ERZIEHUNGSWISSENSCHAFT 1971: ZWISCHEN HERKUNFT UND ZUKUNFT DER GESELLSCHAFT [Between the past and future of human society]. Wuppertal, W. Ger., and Ratingen, W. Ger.: Henn, 1971. 371 p.

> These twenty essays commemorate the work of Ernst Lichtenstein (1900-1971), a philosopher of education in the Lutheran tradition. A substantial bibliography of his work is included (pp. 365-71).

Stone, Ronald H. REALISM AND HOPE. Washington, D.C.: University Press of America, 1977. 216 p. Paperbound.

> Investigating the politics of religious thinkers and the value philosophy of political thinkers, this volume focuses on the problem of revolution and counterrevolution while applying hopeful realism to religion and politics. The thinking represents a revision of Niebuhr's Christian realism and reexamines the relevance of Karl Marx's thought within a framework of Christian realism. Stone attempts to offer a fresh approach to the concept of power.

_____. REINHOLD NIEBUHR. Nashville, Tenn.: Abingdon Press, 1972. 272 p.

> William Gangi, in his review for THOUGHT 48, no. 188 (1973), recommends reading this work as a "sequel or accompanying volume to Hofstadter's SOCIAL DARWINISM, Commager's AMERICAN MIND and Golden's RENDEZVOUS WITH DESTINY" (p. 151).

Van Dusen, Henry P. GOD IN EDUCATION. New York: Charles Scribner's Sons, 1951. 118 p.

> Van Dusen counters the method and traditions of Cartesian thought with a strong stance for faith and religion in the affairs of men. The transcendence of religious faith and belief in God is crucial to the proper education of man regardless of the legalism now found in the courts to the contrary.

Wieman, Henry Nelson. MAN'S ULTIMATE COMMITMENT. Carbondale: Southern Illinois University Press, 1974. 328 p. Paperbound.

> As a liberal expression of the Hebrew-Christian understanding of life, the book challenges current pessimistic views of man.

D NS: THE PROBLEM OF THE COSMOS—PHYSICAL AND MATHEMATICAL SCIENCES

Fehl, Noah Edward. SCIENCE AND CULTURE. Hong Kong: Chung Chi College, 1965. xv, 503 p.

Russell, Bertrand. A FREE MAN'S WORSHIP, AND OTHER ESSAYS. London: Allen and Unwin, 1976. 224 p.

> This reissue of MYSTICISM AND LOGIC (1917, 1957) draws attention to Russell's ideas on mysticism, mathematics, the place of science in a liberal education, and the notions of cause, knowledge, and scientific method.

D HS: THE PROBLEM OF HUMAN SOCIETY—HUMAN AND SOCIAL SCIENCES

Ackley, Charles Walton. THE MODERN MILITARY IN AMERICAN SOCIETY: A STUDY IN THE NATURE OF MILITARY POWER. Philadelphia: Westminster Press, 1972. 400 p.

> Ackley poses the problem of whether the military, influencing American thought and public schools, promotes the will to win, excessive fascination with the concrete, tendency toward structural hardness through fixed order, discipline, or rules, excess, reification, and the illusion of omnipotence. This is a comprehensive treatment of debatable issues.

Bantock, Geoffrey Herman. FREEDOM AND AUTHORITY IN EDUCATION. London: Faber and Faber, 1970. 212 p. Paperbound.

> Bantock gives a fundamental criticism of modern cultural and educational assumptions. Such critical thinking is greatly needed.

Berger, Peter L. PYRAMIDS OF SACRIFICE. New York: Basic Books, 1974, 1975. xiv, 242 p.

> Berger analyzes political ethics and the phenomenon of social change.

Bohnsack, Fritz. ERZIEHUNG ZUR DEMOKRATIE: JOHN DEWEY'S PAEDAGOGIK UND IHRE BEDEUTUNG FUER DIE REFORM UNSERER SCHULE. [Education for democracy: John Dewey's educational thought and its meaning for school reform]. Ravensburg, W. Ger.: Maier, 1976. 553 p.

> Bohnsack discusses, in terms relevant to the German school, Dewey's understanding of human growth and development, moral and social education, education for Democratic living, social efficiency, vocational aspects of education, and his philosophy of education particularly from the prospect of the experimental school.

Bourdieu, Pierre. "Cultural Reproduction and Social Reproduction." In KNOWLEDGE, EDUCATION, AND CULTURAL CHANGE, edited by Richard Brown. London: Tavistock Publications; New York: distributed by Harper and Row and Barnes and Noble, 1973.

> The evidence, so similar to that of Bernstein for England and that

of Bowles and Gintis for the United States, affirms the role of
education in reproducing the class structure and its inefficiency as
a tool for educational reform.

Brameld, Theodore. EDUCATION AS POWER. New York: Holt, Rinehart
and Winston, 1965. xi, 146 p.

_____. THE TEACHER AS WORLD CITIZEN: A SCENARIO OF THE 21ST
CENTURY. Palm Springs, Calif.: ETC Publications, 1976. xi, 83 p.

_____. THE USE OF EXPLOSIVE IDEAS IN EDUCATION: CULTURE, CLASS,
EVOLUTION. Pittsburgh: University of Pittsburgh Press, 1965. x, 248 p.

Almost in Hegelian and Marxist style, Brameld seeks to effect a
sociological synthesis of science, philosophy, and education.

Burnett, Jacquetta, et al. ANTHROPOLOGY AND EDUCATION: AN ANNO-
TATED BIBLIOGRAPHIC GUIDE. New Haven: HRAF Press for the Council on
Anthropology and Education, 1974. vii, 159 p.

For the purposes of selecting references, the distinctive feature of
education is defined as teaching or instruction, whether formal or
informal. The study branches into, but not inclusively, the fields
of psychological anthropology, linguistics, and comparative education.

Elias, John L. CONSCIENTIZATION AND DESCHOOLING: FREIRE'S AND
ILLICH'S PROPOSALS FOR RESHAPING SOCIETY. Philadelphia: Westminster
Press, 1976. 170 p.

Filler, Louis. PROGRESSIVISM AND MUCKRACKING. New York: R.R.
Bowker, 1976. 200 p.

This special bibliographic essay explores the literature of social
dissent. It identifies and comments on some fifteen hundred titles
with the intention of showing how the progressivism-muckraking
strain exposed and remedied economic and political ills. Offers
an opportunity for ·assumption-finding and evaluation.

Graham, Patrick. COMMUNITY AND CLASS IN AMERICAN EDUCATION,
1865-1918. New York: John Wiley and Sons, 1974. xi, 256 p.

Ianni, Francis A.J., and Storey, Edward, eds. CULTURAL RELEVANCE AND
EDUCATIONAL ISSUES: READINGS IN ANTHROPOLOGY AND EDUCATION.
Boston: Little, Brown, 1973. 533 p.

The editors view education as a social problem involving the development and transmission of culture. The issues are examined from
the double perspectives available through the anthropology of education and anthropology in education.

Itzkoff, Seymour W. CULTURAL PLURALISM AND AMERICAN EDUCATION. Scranton, Pa.: International Textbook, 1969. xiii, 202 p.

> In the effort to find new intellectual roots for a theory of cultural pluralism, Itzkoff examines the Democratic context of education, John Dewey and cultural pluralism, Ernst Cassier and the sources of cultural thought as well as the social and educational problems of equality, universality, and plurality in a democracy.

_____. "The Sources of Cultural Pluralism." EDUCATIONAL THEORY 26, no. 2 (1976): 231-33.

> Itzkoff holds that the failure of Horace Kallen to have an impact on social and educational problems was caused by Dewey's failure to account intellectually for pluralism and by the absorption of Kallen's thinking into the intellectual milieu of Dewey and progressivism. Hence Kallen's views lay fallow too long and faded from the scene.

Jencks, Christopher, et al. INEQUALITY: A REASSESSMENT OF THE EFFECT OF FAMILY AND SCHOOLING IN AMERICA. New York: Basic Books, 1972. xii, 399 p.

> The objective of this work is limited to showing that equalizing opportunity, especially educational opportunity, would not do much to reduce economic inequality or alleviate poverty. See also "Perspectives," HARVARD EDUCATIONAL REVIEW 43, no. 1 (1973): 37-164.

Kaplan, Michael H., and Warden, John W., eds. COMMUNITY EDUCATION PERSPECTIVES: SELECTIONS FROM THE COMMUNITY EDUCATION JOURNAL. Midland, Mich.: Pendell Publishing, 1978. 172 p.

> Thirty different authors offer their understanding of conceptual and historical interagency, community involvement, educational and curricular planning and implementation, community education coordinator and evaluation perspectives. The introductions identify emerging trends and include numerous references for further study.

Karier, Clarence J. MAN, SOCIETY, AND EDUCATION: A HISTORY OF AMERICAN EDUCATIONAL IDEAS. Glenview, Ill.: Scott, Foresman, 1967. xvii, 334.

> Karier examines the last one hundred years because they were influenced by Marx, Darwin, Freud, and Dewey. By this decade, American conceptions of man and society have been radically altered by developments in psychology, sociology, and anthropology, as well as astounding advances in human knowledge in the theoretical and technical sciences and by an increasing concern with human rights.

Kraushaar, Otto R. AMERICAN NON-PUBLIC SCHOOLS: PATTERNS OF DIVERSITY. Baltimore: Johns Hopkins University, 1972. 287 p.

Are private schools truly different? Kraushaar believes the data he has amassed give reason to think they are for their values and training. It is only a beginning to comparative studies that will eventually explore the same issues in public schooling.

Kremendahl, Hans. PLURALISMUSTHEORIE IN DEUTSCHLAND. [The theory of pluralism in Germany]. Dusseldorf, W. Ger.: Heggen Verlag, 1977. 494 p.

Kremendahl concentrates on the origin, criticism, and perspectives of German pluralismus. The study is particularly informative when conclusions are compared with actual American practices and the approaches used in the United States.

Lapati, Americo. "Education: Privilege, Claim or Right?" EDUCATIONAL THEORY 26, no. 1 (1976): 19-28.

This thoughtful analysis establishes the right of education for all citizens of a Democratic society. Delay in such recognition results from an unjust philosophical interpretation of rights as privileges or claims.

Levitas, Maurice. MARXIST PERSPECTIVES IN THE SOCIOLOGY OF EDUCA-TION. London: Routledge and Kegan Paul, 1974. 216 p.

This Marxist critique explores major theories derived from a rela-tivist position in sociology and is chiefly concerned with social mobility. It examines prevalent notions in the sociology of educa-tion and gives some understanding of the Marxist understanding of educational philosophy.

Rodham, Hillary. "Children Under the Law." HARVARD EDUCATIONAL REVIEW 43, no. 4 (1973): 487-514.

Rodham summarizes recent Supreme Court decisions which will extend more adult rights to children and recognize certain unique needs and interests of children as legally enforceable rights.

Schoen, Konrad. VERFASSUNG UND ERZIEHUNG. [Constitutional govern-ment and education]. Wuppertal, W. Ger.; Ratingen, W. Ger.; and Kastellaun, W. Ger.: Henn, 1971. 132 p. Bibliog.

As examples of his thesis, that government and education are intrin-sically related, Schoen cites the Republican-Democratic thinking of Montesquieu, the French revolution and its school politics, the authoritarian state under King William I, the governance of schools in the Weimar Republic. Schoen also averts to Gustav Radbruch and to his philosophy of education for good citizenship. The bibli-ography is on pages 127-32.

Simon, Brian, ed. THE RADICAL TRADITION IN EDUCATION IN BRITAIN. London: Lawrence and Wishart, 1972. 299 p.

> The writers include Godwin (concerning political justice), Paine (the age of reason, part one), Owen (a new view of society), Thompson (distribution of wealth), and Lovett (chartism--a new organization of the people).

Steinberg, Ira S. RALPH BARTON PERRY ON EDUCATION FOR DEMOCRACY. Columbus: Ohio State University Press, 1970. xv, 182 p.

D AC: THE PROBLEM OF ART AND CULTURE—HUMANE ARTS AND LETTERS

Coleman, James Samuel, et al. EQUALITY OF EDUCATIONAL OPPORTUNITY. 2 vols. Washington, D.C.: Government Printing Office, 1966. vi, 737 p. and vii, 548 p.

Engelmayer, Otto, ed. DIE ANTIAUTORITAETSDISKUSSION IN DER PAEDA-GOGIK. [The anti-authoritarian debate in education]. Neuburgweier (Karlsruhe), W. Ger.: G. Schindele, 1973. 242 p.

> Engelmayer discusses, in considerable detail, the question of anti-authoritarianism in modern education. The movement is traced to its Rousseauan, psychoanalytic, sociological, political, and critical origins. Every text cited is accompanied with commentary and an analysis.

Van Ness, Wilhelmina. "The Tragic Dilemma of Modern Art." AMERICAN SCHOLAR 43, no. 2 (1974): 288-302.

> One of the worst sins of the modern-contemporary culture is that it has become a system for transforming everything real into grist for an art, entertainment, news, and advertising mill. Modern art has so rationalized and degraded the image of human nature that, if it be allowed to career uninterruptedly along its present course, twentieth-century culture will only end in an ultimate lifeless entropy or unending nightmare.

Chapter 8

ORGANIZATION AND POLICY OF THE EDUCATIONAL SYSTEM—THE EFFICIENT CAUSES OF EDUCATION ACT IN CONCERT THROUGH THE INSTRUMENTALITY OF THE EDUCATIONAL SYSTEM

The aggregate of educational agencies devoted to the work of human refinement and conditioned on collective activity is rightly called the system of education. At the heart of this educative organism are the institutions that give collective instruction, often called the school system. While but a part of the entire educational system, the school is nevertheless the home of collective educational activity where persons in the process of actualizing themselves can also benefit from the teaching of other agents or agencies of education.

E 1: THE PROBLEM OF KNOWING—EPISTEMOLOGY

Ennis, Robert H. "Equality of Educational Opportunity." EDUCATIONAL THEORY 26, no. 1 (1976): 3-18.

> Most people favor equality of educational opportunity but find the implementation of this ideal difficult. The exploration of the concept helps locate the problem not in the concept of equality itself but in the common conception of education and the opportunity to benefit from education.

Gonzalez, Angel Alvarez. POLITICA EDUCATIVA Y ESCOLARIDAD OBLIGATORIA. Madrid: Editorial Gredos, 1975. 275 p.

Karabel, Jerome, and Halsey, A.H., eds. POWER AND IDEOLOGY IN EDUCATION. New York: Oxford University Press, 1977. 670 p. Also paperbound.

> This collection of readings embodies important contemporary developments in the sociology and practice of education. The editorial introductions provide very insightful sociological commentaries, particularly in regard to relativism and the weaknesses found in modern phenomenology and ethnomethodology.

Lee, Gordon C. EDUCATION AND DEMOCRATIC IDEALS. New York: Harcourt, Brace and World, 1965. x, 181 p.

McDermott, John E. INDETERMINACY IN EDUCATION: SOCIAL SCIENCE EDUCATIONAL POLICY AND THE SEARCH FOR STANDARDS. Berkeley, Calif.: McCutchan Publishing, 1976. xx, 336 p.

Ott, Ernst Hermann. GRUNDZUEGE DER HERMENEUTISCH-PRAGMATISCHEN PAEDAGOGIK IN DEUTSCHLAND. [Principles of hermeneutic-pragmatic education in Germany]. Goppingen, W. Ger.: Kuemmerle, 1971. 168 p.

> This monograph reviews the realistic thrust of German education in the years preceding Hitler's coming to power. Ott is primarily concerned with the school system, proposed curriculum reforms, philosophical presuppositions of the school, and the societal orientation of the entire educative process. At the heart of the discussions are educational aims and the changes that these seem to indicate are the most fruitful. The chief source of documentation are the issues of DIE ERZIEHUNG published from 1925 to 1933.

Pritchard, Keith W., and Buxton, Thomas H. CONCEPTS AND THEORIES IN SOCIOLOGY OF EDUCATION. Lincoln, Nebr.: Professional Educators Publications, 1978. 167 p. Paperbound.

> Pritchard gives a clear understanding of sociological concepts related to the educational process through such study units as the relationship of culture, social class stratification, role analysis, and social personality structure to education.

Tostberg, Robert E. "Observations on the Logical Bases of Educational Policy." EDUCATIONAL THEORY 25, no. 1 (1975): 74-82.

Yee, Albert H., ed. PERSPECTIVES ON MANAGEMENT SYSTEMS APPROACHES IN EDUCATION. Englewood Cliffs, N.J.: Educational Technology Publications, 1974.

> This book proposes institutional reform through management-by-objectives administration.

E 2: THE PROBLEM OF BEING—METAPHYSICS

Aristotle. POLITICS. New York: Oxford University Press, 1962. lxxvi, 411 p. Paperbound.

_____. THE POLITICS OF ARISTOTLE. Translated by Ernest Barker. Oxford: Clarendon Press, 1968. lxxvi, 411 p.

Bantock, Geoffrey Herman. CULTURE, INDUSTRIALIZATION AND EDUCATION. New York: Humanities Press, 1968. 96 p. Paperbound.

_____. EDUCATION IN AN INDUSTRIAL SOCIETY. 2d ed. London: Faber and Faber, 1973. xiii, 238 p. [Cf. Broudy (1967), cited in chapter 13, pp. 123, 187].

Blishen, Edward, ed. THE SCHOOL THAT I'D LIKE. Harmondsworth, Engl. and Baltimore: Penguin Books, 1969. 171 p.

Carlson, Robert A. THE QUEST FOR CONFORMITY: AMERICANIZATION THROUGH EDUCATION. New York: John Wiley and Sons, 1975. 188 p.

Castell, Alburey. PHILOSOPHY AND THE TEACHER'S WORLD. Eugene: Bureau of Educational Research, University of Oregon, 1967. 54 p.

Chanan, Gabriel, and Gilchrist, Linda. WHAT SCHOOL IS FOR. Introduction by Miriam Wasserman. New York: Praeger Publishers, 1974. xxii, 133 p.

> Assuming that American society is "a sort of federation of subcultures in various states of tolerance and tension" and that emphasing one subculture at the expense of others is chiefly responsible for the failure of our schools, the authors propose reforms in this subculture orientation to benefit the education of working-class students.

Counts, George S. DARE THE SCHOOL BUILD A NEW SOCIAL ORDER? 1932. New York: Arno Press, 1969. 56 p.

Cremin, Lawrence Arthur. THE TRANSFORMATION OF THE SCHOOL: PROGRESSIVISM IN AMERICAN EDUCATION, 1876-1957. New York: Alfred A. Knopf, 1961; Random House Vintage Books, 1964. 387 p. Paperbound.

Dearden, R.F. THE PHILOSOPHY OF PRIMARY EDUCATION. London: Routledge and Kegan Paul, 1969. 196 p.

Easthope, Gary. COMMUNITY, HIERARCHY AND OPEN EDUCATION. London: Routledge and Kegan Paul, 1975. 152 p.

> Easthope discusses modern educational reform in relationship to social theory. The empirical evidence about the reality of schools is presented in connection with the discussion about equality of educational opportunity and integrated curricula.

Fantini, Mario, and Weinstein, Gerald. MAKING URBAN SCHOOLS WORK: SOCIAL REALITIES AND THE URBAN SCHOOL. Foreword by Francis A.J. Ianni. New York: Holt, Rinehart and Winston, 1968. x, 62 p.

Ianni believes that the ideas developed here have meaning for all educational programs regardless of geographical setting and that the urban school is a model which gets social realities into the school and relates community and the school to each other.

Feinberg, Walter. REASON AND RHETORIC: THE INTELLECTUAL FOUNDATIONS OF TWENTIETH CENTURY LIBERAL EDUCATIONAL POLICY. New York: John Wiley and Sons, 1975. xiv, 287 p.

Liberal theorists are said to understand progress and technology in a way that really limits their conception of freedom and equality. Feinberg singles out for criticism the basic views of Dewey, Counts, Kilpatrick, Beard, and J.H. Robinson.

Fingerle, Karlheinz. FUNKTIONEN UND PROBLEME DER SCHULE. [School functions and problems]. Munich: Koesel, 1973. 199 p.

The author sees the theory of the school emerging from one's philosophy of education. Despite the impact of certain systematic and theoretical principles, the school and curriculum are affected by influences embedded in actual situational structures. These must be taken into account in any theory of the school.

Hacquard, Georges. VERS UNE ECOLE IDEALE. Paris: R. Laffont, 1971. 248 p.

Hostetler, John Andrew. "Education in Communitarian Societies." In EDUCATION AND CULTURAL PROCESSES: TOWARD AN ANTHROPOLOGY OF EDUCATION, edited by George Dearborn Spindler. New York: Holt, Rinehart and Winston, 1974.

Illich, Ivan. DESCHOOLING SOCIETY. New York: Random House and Harper and Row, 1971. xx, 116 p.

Justmann, Joseph. THEORIES OF SECONDARY EDUCATION IN THE UNITED STATES. New York: Bureau of Publications, Teachers College, Columbia University, 1940; AMS Press, 1972. viii, 481 p. Paperbound.

Katz, Michael B. CLASS, BUREAUCRACY AND SCHOOLS: THE ILLUSION OF EDUCATIONAL CHANGE IN AMERICA. New York: Praeger Publishers, 1971. 158 p.

Giving a historical framework for better understanding, Katz distinguishes in progressivism three traditions that pertain to child centeredness, social reform, and the elaboration of an educational science. He argues for a school reform that will depart from mid-nineteenth century structures and values.

_____, ed. SCHOOL REFORM: PAST AND PRESENT. Boston: Little, Brown, 1971. xi, 303 p.

> If the past and present in educational history are closely knit to each other, then Katz wants to use history as a means of making education somewhat independent of the past. The major purpose of his book is to "help develop the strength of will and clear judgment that come from an ability to confront both past and present as they actually exist" (p. xxv).

Kerr, Donna H. EDUCATIONAL POLICY: ANALYSIS, STRUCTURE, AND JUSTIFICATION. New York: David McKay, 1976. x, 214 p.

Lodge, George C. THE NEW AMERICAN IDEOLOGY. New York: Alfred A. Knopf, 1975. 350 p.

> The traditional ideology includes the ideas of property rights, competition, the limited state, scientific specialization, and individualism. This is being replaced by a new ideology that prefers to consider the rights of membership, community need, the state as planner, holism, and communitarianism. These operative social values infuse our understanding of the person in society, govern the guarantees of human rights, prescribe the function of state and government, condition the fields, the nature, and the structuring of knowledge or science.

McClellan, B. Edward. "Vocation, School, and Society: A Study of Late Nineteenth-Century Educational Thought." EDUCATIONAL THEORY 27, no. 3 (1977): 223-32.

> Nineteenth-century educators were never able to develop a world view that integrated the skill needs of a productive system with the moral values of personal equality and political cohesion, according to McClellan. They used an older social framework to contain a world of hierarchy, differentiation, and specialization.

Macklin, Michael. WHEN SCHOOLS ARE GONE: A PROJECTION OF THE THOUGHT OF IVAN ILLICH. St. Lucia: University of Queensland Press, 1976. 72 p.

Mathias, Theophane A., ed. EDUCATION AND SOCIAL CONCERN. Delhi: Jesuit Educational Association of India, 1968. xxi, 269 p.

> These position papers center around the school and society, the social bases of education, education for responsible participation in a Democratic society, and the function of moral and spiritual teaching in creating and fostering social consciousness.

May, Philip R. WHICH WAY TO SCHOOL? London: Lion Publishing, 1972. x, 148 p.

Pillsbury, Kent; Seckinger, Donald; and Lottich, Kenneth. SOCIAL ISSUES AND EDUCATION IN THE AMERICAN URBAN AND SUBURBAN SOCIETY. Chicago: Nelson Hall Publishers, 1977. 284 p.

An original and pragmatic discussion of social and educational philosophy on the role of school and teacher in American society. The central issues concern transmission, social order and reform, continued but gradual and peaceful social progress.

Pulliam, John D., and Bowman, Jim R. EDUCATIONAL FUTURISM--IN PURSUANCE OF SURVIVAL. Introduction by Daniel Selakovich. Norman: University of Oklahoma Press, 1974. 164 p.

The new movement known as "educational futurism" has many characteristic ideas developed by educational pioneers decades ago and may represent an updating of the social foundations of education.

Reimer, Everett. SCHOOL IS DEAD: ALTERNATIVES IN EDUCATION. Garden City, N.Y.: Doubleday, 1971. 216 p. Paperbound.

Reimer indicts the school system for blindly following tradition and not meeting the goals of a free society. His suggested alternatives call for radical reform.

Rich, John Martin. NEW DIRECTIONS IN EDUCATIONAL POLICY. Lincoln, Nebr.: Professional Educators Publications, 1978. 104 p. Paperbound.

Rich describes how a philosophy of education is transformed into educational policy, how such policy is formed and may be improved. His suggestions are intended to help all in the making and the executing of school policies, for this philosophical and political process affects not only teaching practices, but the lives of all concerned.

Roehrs, Hermann, ed. THEORIE DER SCHULE. VERSUCH EINER GRUNDLEGUNG. [Theory of the school: an inquiry into its foundations]. Frankfort on the Main, W. Ger.: Akademische Verlags-GESELLSCHAFT, 1968. xvi, 444 p.

Sexton, Patricia Cayo. THE AMERICAN SCHOOL: A SOCIOLOGICAL ANALYSIS. Englewood Cliffs, N.J.: Prentice-Hall, 1967. 122 p.

Shipman, M.D. EDUCATION AND MODERNISATION. London: Faber and Faber, 1971. 276 p.

_____. THE SOCIOLOGY OF THE SCHOOL. New York: Longmans, Green, 1968. 196 p.

Spindler, George Dearborn, ed. EDUCATION AND CULTURAL PROCESS: TOWARD AN ANTHROPOLOGY OF EDUCATION. New York: Holt, Rinehart and Winston, 1974. xii, 561 p.

_____. THE TRANSMISSION OF AMERICAN CULTURE. Cambridge, Mass.: Harvard University Press, 1959. 51 p.

E 3: HUMAN NATURE AND UNITY

Bernfeld, Siegfried. SISYPHUS: OR, THE LIMITS OF EDUCATION. Translated by Frederic Lilge. Foreword by Anna Freud. Preface by Peter Paret. Berkeley and Los Angeles: University of California Press, 1973. xxix, 120 p.

Gilbert, John P., et al. "Assessing Social Innovations: An Empirical Base for Policy." In EVALUATION AND EXPERIMENT: SOME CRITICAL ISSUES IN ASSESSING SOCIAL PROGRAMS, edited by Carl A. Bennett and Arthur A. Lumsdaine. New York: Academic Press, 1975.

Grambs, Jean Dresden. SCHOOLS, SCHOLARS AND SOCIETY. 2d ed. Englewood Cliffs, N.J.: Prentice-Hall, 1978. 288 p.

> Grambs probes society as an educator, its values, its schools, institutional tensions, and multilevel cultures. Private, parochial, and public schools and their functions are viewed from research in education, sociology, psychology, anthropology, and political science.

Hillson, Maurie, and Hyman, Ronald T., eds. CHANGE AND INNOVATION IN ELEMENTARY AND SECONDARY ORGANIZATION. 2d ed. New York: Holt, Rinehart and Winston, 1971. xi, 435 p.

> The orientation of the whole educative process seems to be in the direction of the individualization or personalization of instruction. The readings stress limitless possibilities for unhampered and continuous progress-oriented growth, collaborative education, and greater student involvement in decision-making with respect to content and educative processes.

Karier, Clarence J., et al. ROOTS OF CRISIS: AMERICAN EDUCATION IN THE TWENTIETH CENTURY. Chicago: Rand McNally, 1973. 243 p. Paperbound.

> These writers believe American society is not structured to enhance the dignity of man but rather fosters a dehumanizing quest for status, power, and wealth. They view American educational thought and practice rather critically on the assumption that this society is in fact racist, fundamentally materialistic, and institutionally structured to protect vested interests. The reader is expected to judge whether these essays in fact connect with and add meaning to our present world.

Purves, Alan C., and Levine, Daniel M., eds. EDUCATIONAL POLICY AND INTERNATIONAL ASSESSMENT: IMPLICATIONS OF THE IEA SURVEYS OF ACHIEVEMENT. Berkeley, Calif.: McCutchan Publishing, 1975. 184 p.

> Among the findings are stated the relative importance of school and nonschool variables, the usefulness of some assessments in and of themselves, and the unfortunate lack of incentive to synthesize the research critically in a form useful to policy makers.

Scheflen, Albert E., and Ashcraft, Norman. HUMAN TERRITORIES: HOW WE BEHAVE IN SPACE-TIME. Englewood Cliffs, N.J.: Prentice-Hall, 1976. xiv, 210 p.

Schultz, Stanley. THE CULTURE FACTORY: BOSTON PUBLIC SCHOOLS, 1789-1860. New York: Oxford University Press, 1973. xvi, 394 p.

Smith, Philip G. PHILOSOPHIC-MINDEDNESS IN EDUCATIONAL ADMINI-STRATION. Columbus: College of Education, Ohio State University, 1956. 129 p.

> Conceiving philosophy more as a practical than as a speculative discipline, Smith offers sound advice on the traits and attitudes that should mark the thinking of an effective administrator.

Spindler, George Dearborn, ed. EDUCATION AND CULTURE: ANTHROPO-LOGICAL APPROACHES. New York: Holt, Rinehart and Winston, 1963. xx, 571 p.

> This may be, in the judgment of Maurice P. Hunt, the best book on the use of anthropological insights in the study of educational problems. The readings include essays by Theodore Brameld, Jules Henry, Margaret Mead, and seven by George Spindler himself.

Zoepfl, Helmut, ed. BESINNUNG AUF DEN MENSCHEN IN DER PAEDA-GOGIK. [Reflections on man in education]. Essays in honor of Max Mueller on his seventieth birthday. Donauworth, W. Ger.: Auer, 1976. 104 p.

> Educational philosophy is very much concerned with the image of man, the concept of human freedom and responsibility, and the possibilities of human refinement in a pluralistic world. Does learning have any value today? What response should be made to Martin Buber's concept of freedom? These thoughts center on education, its outcomes, and the reformation of the schools.

E 4: HUMAN INTELLECTIVE POWERS

Belknap, Robert L., and Kuhns, Richard. TRADITION AND INNOVATION: GENERAL EDUCATION AND THE REINTEGRATION OF THE UNIVERSITY. Irvington, N.Y.: Columbia University Press, 1978. 130 p.

After introducing the Columbia report with a discussion of the aim-
less responses of American universities to the many crises since
World War II, the authors tackle the problems, explain Columbia's
solutions, and offer plans and projects that may profit other universities.

Blau, Peter Michael. THE ORGANIZATION OF ACADEMIC WORK. New
York: Wiley-Interscience, 1973. xvii, 310 p.

Bode, Boyd Henry. HOW WE LEARN. 1940. Westport, Conn.: Greenwood
Press, 1971. 308 p.

Brubacher, John Seiler. ON THE PHILOSOPHY OF HIGHER EDUCATION.
San Francisco: Jossey-Bass, 1977. xii, 143 p.

Dell, George W. "Robert M. Hutchins' Philosophy of General Education and
the College at the University of Chicago." JOURNAL OF GENERAL EDUCA-
TION 30, no. 1 (1978): 45-57.

Dell briefly records the evolution of Hutchins's philosophy of education in the decade from 1929 to 1939. The philosophic clash of
educational philosophies during Hutchins's tenure at the University
of Chicago accentuates his understanding of education as the cultivation of the intellect.

Dolce, Massimo. LA SCUOLA NEL NOSTRO TEMPO: PROBLEMI E
PROSPETTIVE. Preface by Vicenzo Monforte. Palermo, Italy: Herbita, 1975.
119 p.

Habermas, Jurgen. TOWARD A RATIONAL SOCIETY. Translated from German
by Jeremy J. Shapiro. London: Heinemann Educational; Boston: Beacon Press,
1971. ix, 132 p.

Jerome, Judson. CULTURE OUT OF ANARCHY: THE RECONSTRUCTION OF
HIGHER LEARNING IN AMERICA. New York: Herder and Herder, 1970.
xxii, 330 p.

Morris, Bertram. INSTITUTIONS OF INTELLIGENCE. Columbus: Ohio State
University Press, 1969. xii, 230 p.

Newman, Cardinal John Henry. THE IDEA OF A UNIVERSITY. Edited by
I.T. Kerr. Oxford: Oxford University Press, 1976. v, 684 p.

This modern critical edition is rich in notes, explanations, and
commentary. The appendix includes the original Fifth Discourse.
As to Newman's understanding of religion and knowledge, Kerr
concludes: "What gives the Discourses their peculiar rhetoric

is . . . the tension between the genuinely unconditional insistence on the absolute value of knowledge in itself and the equally firm conviction that knowledge is emphatically not the highest good."

E 5: HUMAN AFFECTIVE POWERS

Bruno, James E., ed. EMERGING ISSUES IN EDUCATION: POLICY IMPLI-CATIONS FOR THE SCHOOLS. Foreword by John Pincus. Lexington, Mass.: D.C. Heath, 1972. iv, 318 p.

This Rand Corporation research study, based on fourteen seminars, brings together various views on the critical issues in education and on their implications for the schools. Chief concerns include instructional efficiency and equal educational opportunity.

Comenius, John Amos. DIE ERNEUERUNG DER SCHULEN. [The reformation of schools]. Edited in Latin and German together with notes and extended commentary by Klaus Schaller. Bochum, W. Ger.: Kamp, 1967. 76 p.

Dewey, John. MORAL PRINCIPLES IN EDUCATION. With a new preface by Sidney Hook. 1909. Carbondale: Southern Illinois University Press, 1975. xvi, 60 p. Paperbound.

To Dewey, man is a natural being who is notable for his moral principles and for the obligation of establishing schools that assure the moral training of children. Dewey believes those ideas are moral which affect or prompt human conduct.

Forisha, Bill E., and Forisha, Barbara E. MORAL DEVELOPMENT AND EDU-CATION. Lincoln, Nebr.: Professional Educators Publications, 1978. 88 p. Paperbound.

What is the responsibility of the school system to develop good character or proper behavior by inculcating high moral standards and values? The authors describe what has been tried, and not only provide an analysis of current practices, but project what national solutions may be possible.

Goodenow, Ronald K. "Racial and Ethical Tolerance in John Dewey's Educational and Social Thought: The Depression Years." EDUCATIONAL THEORY 27, no. 1 (1977): 48-64.

Goodenow chides Dewey and his contemporaries for not preparing and urging the schools to deal with the life experiences of black and minority children. These educators may have contributed, in a paradoxical and tragic way, to the conflicts they wished to avoid and eventually eliminate by not undergirding institutional and social structures sufficently to eliminate educational disadvantage and racism.

Katz, Michael B. THE IRONY OF EARLY SCHOOL REFORM. Cambridge, Mass.: Harvard University Press, 1968. xii, 325 p.

Katz rejects the idea of progress in the expansion of educational opportunity because innovation and school changes are too often used by social, political, and industrial leaders to impose their own value system on the populace.

McClintock, Robert. MAN AND HIS CIRCUMSTANCES: ORTEGA AS EDUCATOR. New York: Teachers College Press, 1971. 648 p.

Treating Ortega Y. Gasset's life and thought as a whole within a European and Western context, McClintock explores and assesses his understanding of education as the state agency for creating a humane posterity.

May, Rollo. PSYCHOLOGY AND THE HUMAN DILEMMA. Princeton, N.J.: D. Van Nostrand, 1967. 221 p.

May shows that alienation begins with feelings of impotence that lead to apathy and finally to violence. His conclusion to the analysis of contemporary American culture and its effect on individuals is provocative and deserves consideration from the educational philosopher: if men choose to view themselves as objects, the danger is loss of identity and meaning; if men choose to be viewed as subjects, the way is then open to greater personal development and creativity. He gives important insights into the dilemma of freedom versus determinism.

Mosteller, Frederick, and Moynihan, Daniel P., eds. ON EQUALITY OF EDUCATIONAL OPPORTUNITY. New York: Random House, Vintage, 1972. xiv, 570 p.

The papers, derived from the Harvard Faculty Seminar on the Coleman report, reconsider its controversial findings. In addition to those of the editors themselves, contributions are made by Pettigrew, Beshers, and Coleman.

Myers, Henry S. FUNDAMENTALLY SPEAKING. San Francisco: Strawberry Hill Press; distributed by Stackpole Books, 1977. 127 p.

Novak, Michael. FURTHER REFLECTIONS ON ETHNICITY. Middletown, Pa.: Jednota Printery, 1977. vi, 85 p.

Schnacht, Richard. ALIENATION. Garden City, N.Y.: Doubleday, 1970. 360 p. Paperbound.

Schnacht shows the development of the concept of alienation from Hegel to the present.

Schwartz, Barry N., ed. AFFIRMATIVE EDUCATION. Englewood Cliffs, N.J.: Prentice-Hall, 1972. x, 180 p.

E 6: HUMAN AESTHETIC POWERS

Central Midwest Regional Education Laboratory. THE FIVE SENSE STORE: THE AESTHETIC EDUCATION PROGRAM. New York: Viking Press, 1973.

> These multimedia curriculum materials are designed for orienting the school toward the development of aesthetic powers and the mastering of a cultural content.

Dimondstein, Geraldine. EXPLORING THE ARTS WITH CHILDREN. New York: Macmillan, 1974. 320 p.

Gould, Samuel B. "Arts in Higher Education: Valid or Valueless?" MUSIC EDUCATORS JOURNAL 54, no. 5 (1968): 33-35, 89-91.

Mahoney, Margaret, and Moore, Isabel, eds. ARTS ON CAMPUS: THE NECESSITY FOR CHANGE. Greenwich, Conn.: New York Graphic Society, 1970. 143 p.

Roe, Paul F. CHORAL MUSIC EDUCATION. Englewood Cliffs, N.J.: Prentice-Hall, 1970. 400 p.

> Roe deals with the practical problems of planning and administering choral music activities.

E 7: THE PROBLEM OF VALUES—ETHICS

Buckley, William F. GOD AND MAN AT YALE. With a new introduction by the author. South Bend, Ind.: Gateway Editions, 1977. 300 p. Paperbound.

> Buckley's comments in his new introduction add a fresh interest and pungency to the description of his alma mater as "an institution that derives its moral and financial support from Christian individualists and then addresses itself to the task of persuading the sons of those supporters to be atheistic socialists." His case against liberalism and current college instruction still requires a hearing.

Butts, R. Freeman. "Public Education in a Pluralistic Society." EDUCATIONAL THEORY 27, no. 1 (1977): 3-11, 47.

> Butts faces three of the most fundamental problems that confront public education and American governmental institutions: the search for freedom, the search for equality, and the search for community. All are rooted in a fundamental moral commitment.

Cremin, Lawrence Arthur. PUBLIC EDUCATION. Foreword by Maxine Greene. New York: Basic Books, 1976. xi, 100 p.

_____, ed. THE REPUBLIC AND THE SCHOOL: HORACE MANN ON THE EDUCATION OF FREE MEN. 1957. Reprint. New York: Teachers College Press, 1975.

The excerpts and essays are based on the twelve annual reports and on the Horace Mann legacy.

Iyer, Raghavan. THE MORAL AND POLITICAL THOUGHT OF MAHATMA GANDHI. New York: Oxford University Press, 1978. xiii, 449 p.

Kohn, Melvin. CLASS AND CONFORMITY: A STUDY IN VALUES. Homewood, Ill.: Dorsey Press, 1969. xxiii, 315 p.

Lazerson, Marvin. ORIGINS OF THE URBAN SCHOOL: PUBLIC EDUCATION IN MASSACHUSETTS, 1870-1915. Cambridge, Mass.: Harvard University Press, 1971. xix, 278 p.

Lazerson and Tack are among the best histories of the centralization and professionalization of school systems (William Greenbaum, "Essay on the Rise of Pluralism," p. 423).

Means, Richard L. THE ETHICAL IMPERATIVE: THE CRISIS IN AMERICAN VALUES. Garden City, N.Y.: Doubleday, 1969. 277 p.

Mehan, Hugh. "Structuring School Structure." HARVARD EDUCATIONAL REVIEW 48, no. 1 (1978): 32-64.

Mehan enters the debate on the structuring of inequality in the schools by way of constitutive ethnography which, claims Mehan, offers rigorous methodology, exhaustive findings, suggestions for specific actions to change educational situations, and concrete motivation. The two-page list of references is itself an introduction to the debate.

Miller, Harry L. SOCIAL FOUNDATIONS OF EDUCATION. 3d ed. New York: Holt, Rinehart and Winston, 1978. vii, 407 p.

The chapters are grouped into two parts, social and economic influences in urban schools, and the schools and their communities. Important analyses concern the drive to equality, cultural values and language differences, the family, the struggle for the control of urban schools.

Murray, John Courtney. "School and Christian Freedom." NATIONAL CATHOLIC EDUCATIONAL ASSOCIATION PROCEEDINGS 48 (August 1951): 63-68.

Rawls, John. A THEORY OF JUSTICE. Cambridge, Mass.: Harvard University Press, 1971. 607 p. Also paperbound.

> This advanced treatise on the meaning of justice and ethical theory examines our system of criminal justice philosophically. This approach helps put into focus some important relationships that concern crime, justice and education and also stresses the philosophy of a society based on equality and justice.

Sanchez, Ramon. SCHOOLING AMERICAN SOCIETY: A DEMOCRATIC IDEOLOGY. Syracuse, N.Y.: Syracuse University Press, 1976. ix, 175 p.

> Assuming that "educational ideas are essentially political in nature," Sanchez regards the school in America as the means for maintaining a community of free and equal citizens. Since he believes there is no way out and up for slum children, he concludes that self-interest must be converted to common interest typified by the attitude "we all learn and move forward together." The thought of Plato and Rousseau is viewed within this ideological context.

Spring, Joel. A PRIMER OF LIBERTARIAN EDUCATION. Montreal: Black Rose Books, 1975. 157 p.

Strike, Kenneth A., and Egan, Kieran, eds. ETHICS AND EDUCATIONAL POLICY. London: Routledge and Kegan Paul, 1977. 220 p.

> This collection of essays by Peters, Schrag, Ennis, Magsino, Nyberg, and Broudy examine practical educational problems from a philosophical standpoint; the neutrality of universities, the nature of student academic freedom, the legal rights of children, the justice of compulsory education, free schools and personal liberty, the equality of education. They all shed some light on a basic dilemma: Should the philosophy of education concentrate much more on conceptual issues than on improving education for the young?

Troost, Cornelis J. RADICAL SCHOOL REFORM: CRITIQUE AND ALTERNATIVES. Foreword by Sidney Hook. Boston: Little, Brown and Co., 1973. xviii, 314 p. Paperbound.

> After a lively review of the radical reform movement, Troost concludes that unstructured education does not help produce moral development. He feels that moral education requires the preservation of certain traditional values.

Wilson, John. THE ASSESSMENT OF MORALITY. Windsor, Berks: National Foundation for Educational Research in England and Wales Publishing, 1973. x, 115 p.

Worsfold, Victor L. "A Philosophical Justification of Children's Rights." HARVARD EDUCATIONAL REVIEW 44, no. 1 (1974): 142-57.

The paternalistic views of children and social justice found in Hobbes, Locke, and Hume are discouraging in their implications. Adopting the proposal of Maurice Cranston that children's rights be practical, genuinely universal, and of paramount importance, Worsfold argues for children's rights under John Rawl's theory of justice.

E 8: THE PROBLEM OF THOUGHT AND LANGUAGE— PHILOSOPHICAL ANALYSIS

Archambault, Reginald D., ed. PHILOSOPHICAL ANALYSIS AND EDUCATION. 1965. London: Routledge and Kegan Paul; Atlantic Highland, N.J.: Humanities Press, 1972. 212 p. Paperbound.

The quadripartite division of essays covers the nature and function of educational theory, the context of educational discussion, the conceptions of reaching, and the essence of education. The essays are authored by leading British philosophers who concentrate on the meaning of schooling from the aspect of analytic philosophy. The opening chapter clarifies the relationship of modern philosophical thinking to present educational theory.

Wirsing, Marie E. TEACHING AND PHILOSOPHY: A SYNTHESIS. Boston: Houghton Mifflin, 1972. x, 226 p.

Wirsing believes that, since values are often in conflict, particularly when learners are exposed to contradictory principles or ideas, philosophy and teaching must be brought into closer relationship with each other. Identical actions can be attributed to different outlooks and may even originate from different assumptions. The dilemma of transmitting core values requires some harmony between philosophical theory and schoolroom practice.

E TR: THE PROBLEM OF GOD—THEOLOGY AND RELIGION

Froembgen, Maria Erika. NEUER MENSCH IN NEUER GEMEINSCHAFT. [Modern man in a renovated society]. Vallendar, W. Ger.: Schoenstatt-Verlag, 1973. 342 p.

This introduction to the development and goals of an international Schoenstatt--a model for a Christian utopian society--describes an educational and moral religious movement within the Roman Catholic Church. In 1914, Josef Kentenich (1885-1968) drew up the plans for the renovation of men in a society reconstructed according to Christian ideals and values. The movement has caught on internationally and is the exponent of a special kind of educational philosophy and program.

Hostetler, John Andrew. CHILDREN IN AMISH SOCIETY. Rev. ed. Baltimore: Johns Hopkins University Press, 1968. xviii, 369 p.

Hostetler, John Andrew, and Huntington, Gertrude Enders. CHILDREN IN SOCIETY: SOCIALIZATION AND COMMUNITY EDUCATION. New York: Holt, Rinehart and Winston, 1971. xiv, 119 p.

Janowsky, Oscar Isaiah, ed. THE EDUCATION OF AMERICAN JEWISH TEACHERS. Foreword by Abram Leon Sachar. Boston: Beacon Press, 1967. xvii, 352 p.

> The essays on backgrounds, curricula, and problems of Jewish teacher preparation delineate an underlying philosophy of education.

Mooney, Christopher F. RELIGION AND THE AMERICAN DREAM: THE SEARCH FOR FREEDOM UNDER GOD. Philadelphia: Westminster Press, 1977. 144 p.

> The genre is American civil religion. The final chapter is a stimulating reflection on religious pluralism and the search for meaning in Democratic America.

Murray, John Courtney. "The Catholic University in a Pluralistic Society." Address delivered 15 November 1955, at the Founder's Day Commemoration of the 137th anniversary of St. Louis University. CATHOLIC MIND 57 (May-June 1959): 253-60. Also published as "Unity of Truth." COMMONWEAL 63 (13 January 1956): 381-82.

> Murray explains the role of the Catholic university in a pluralist society as one commissioned with the ministry of clarification and work of discernment.

Schneider, Jan Heiner. SCHULE, KIRCHE, SEELSORGE. [School, church, ministry]. Dusseldorf, W. Ger.: Patmos-Verlag, 1976. 183 p.

> Seeing that the educational function of the churches is very much in transition, Schneider suggests new standards and criteria for the future role of the churches in education. The dominant purpose in his own philosophy is the humanization of the school.

E NS: THE PROBLEM OF THE COSMOS—PHYSICAL AND MATHEMATICAL SCIENCES

Bronowski, Jacob. ON BEING AN INTELLECTUAL. Published with "Engagement and Objectivity in Science," by Gerald Holton. Baltimore: Barton-Gillet for Smith College, 1968. 31 p.

Karier, Clarence J. SHAPING THE AMERICAN EDUCATIONAL STATE: 1900 TO THE PRESENT. New York: Free Press, 1975. 439 p.

Liberals and progressivists, who believe in the primacy of science, technology, and reason, are held responsible for the pervasive materialism, classism, and racism that is said to have penetrated and even altered the nature of American social and educational institutions. Many primary sources are made available for assessing the evidence and verifying Karier's own interpretations.

E HS: THE PROBLEM OF HUMAN SOCIETY—HUMAN AND SOCIAL SCIENCES

Arbib, Michael A. "Man-Machine Symbiosis and the Evaluation of Human Freedom." AMERICAN SCHOLAR 43, no. 1 (1973-74): 38-54.

Using John Rawls's A THEORY OF JUSTICE as a support for his thinking, Arbib describes the need for a thorough investigation into how Americans can steer between the Scylla of blind adoption of all technical innovations and the Charybdis of out-of-hand rejection of all technological aid. Technology will provide no magical solution to any societal problem, Arbib feels, unless it be governed by a highly refined sense of human justice.

Arons, Stephen. "The Separation of School and State: Pierce Reconsidered." HARVARD EDUCATIONAL REVIEW 46, no. 1 (1976): 76-104.

The case Pierce v. Society of Sisters (268 U.S. 510) ended in a decision guaranteeing private schools' rights to do business because the state may not "standardize" children. If parents have a right or educational choice where inculcation of values or beliefs are concerned, then the present scheme of compulsory attendance and school financing may be unconstitutional.

Bernstein, Basil B. CLASS, CODES AND CONTROL. 3 vols. London: Routledge and Kegan Paul, 1971-75.

Like Bowles and Gintis for the United States and Bourdieu for France, Bernstein sees the system of education as reproducing the class structure and not as a tool for educational reform.

Volume 1: THEORETICAL STUDIES TOWARD A SOCIOLOGY OF LANGUAGE. 2d ed. New York: Schocken Books, 1975. 266 p.

Volume 2: APPLIED STUDIES TOWARD A SOCIOLOGY OF LANGUAGE, 1973. 377 p.

Volume 3: A THEORY OF EDUCATIONAL TRANSMISSION, 1975. 167 p.

Bowers, C.A. PROGRESSIVE EDUCATION AND THE DEPRESSION: THE RADICAL YEARS. New York: Random House, 1969. xi, 269 p.

Bowles, Samuel, and Gintis, Herbert. SCHOOLING IN CAPITALIST AMERICA:

EDUCATIONAL REFORM AND THE CONTRADICTIONS OF ECONOMIC LIFE. New York: Basic Books, 1976. ix, 340 p.

Since education does not solve social inequalities, these Marxist thinkers do not see educational reform as important promoters of the Socialist revolution. Their strategies may bear comparison with the voucher plan of Jencks and Illich's deschooling society.

Carnoy, Martin. EDUCATION AS CULTURAL IMPERIALISM. New York: David McKay, 1974. 378 p.

Economic determinism, be it capitalistic or social, enables those in power to use education for maintaining their dominion over the others. To transform the system, institutions are necessary of the type sponsored by the free school movement. These and other assumptions made by Carnoy require very critical evaluation.

Chase, Jerome, and Bono, James D. THE LAST WORD. Boston: Branden Press, 1976. iv, 79 p.

The authors draw out some implications from the Vietnamese episode in America (1961-75).

Cleary, Robert Edward. POLITICAL EDUCATION IN THE AMERICAN DEMOCRACY. Scranton, Pa.: Intext Educational Publishers, 1971. xiv, 185 p.

Although his thrust is toward political education and the present ineffectiveness of schools, Cleary provides a strongly documented proof of certain perennial value conflicts in America.

Corwin, Ronald G. EDUCATION IN CRISIS: A SOCIOLOGICAL ANALYSIS OF SCHOOLS AND UNIVERSITIES IN TRANSITION. New York: John Wiley and Sons, 1974. xii, 380 p.

Cosin, B.R., ed. EDUCATION: STRUCTURE AND SOCIETY. Baltimore: Penguin Books, 1972. 303 p.

The readings range from Marx to Galbraith and contribute to the debate over the relationship of the educational system to the economy and to politics.

Entwistle, Harold. "Antonio Gramsci and the School as Hegemonic." EDUCATIONAL THEORY 28, no. 1 (1978): 23-33.

Asserting that the school is hegemonic, Gramsci understands that to substitute proletarian for bourgeois hegemony would require radical school reform. Yet, despite his Marxism, Gramsci prescribes curricula and teaching methods that are essentially conservative of the best traditions. How to resolve this seeming paradox is the point of this article.

Freire, Paulo. PEDAGOGY OF THE OPPRESSED. Translated by Myra Bergman Ramos. New York: Herder and Herder, 1970. 186 p.

Grant, Nigel. SOCIETY, SCHOOLS, AND PROGRESS IN EASTERN EUROPE. New York: Pergamon Press, 1969. xxvi, 363 p.

_____. SOVIET EDUCATION. Rev. ed. Baltimore: Penguin Books, 1968. 192 p.

Hauser, Robert Mason. SOCIOECONOMIC BACKGROUND AND EDUCATIONAL PERFORMANCE. Washington, D.C.: American Sociological Association, 1972. x, 166 p.

Hollander, Paul. SOVIET AND AMERICAN SOCIETY: A COMPARISON. New York: Oxford University Press, 1973. xx, 476 p.

Lowe, John; Grant, Nigel; and Williams, T. David, eds. EDUCATION AND NATION-BUILDING IN THE THIRD WORLD. Edinburgh: Scottish Academic Press; New York: Barnes and Noble, 1971. vii, 264 p.

Makarenko, Anton Semenovich. PROBLEMS OF SOVIET SCHOOL EDUCATION. Compiled by V. Aransky and A. Piskunov and translated from Russian by O. Shartse. Moscow: Progress Publishers, 1965. 153 p.

Messerli, Jonathan. HORACE MANN. New York: Alfred A. Knopf, 1972. xviii, 604, xxxvii p.

"Perspectives on Inequality." HARVARD EDUCATIONAL REVIEW 43, no. 1 (1973): 37-164.

> After the editor's introduction (pp. 37-50), Jackson, Rivlin, Edmonds et al., Michelson, Thurow, Clark, Duncan, and Coleman each respond to INEQUALITY: A REASSESSMENT OF THE EFFECT OF FAMILY AND SCHOOLING IN AMERICA by Jencks and his associates. The rejoinder by Christopher Jencks (pp. 138-64) concludes with rejecting both the conservative notion that income inequality is related to unequal abilities and unequal home environments and the liberal notion that equalizing educational opportunity will equalize people's incomes.

Spring, Joel. AMERICAN EDUCATION--AN INTRODUCTION TO SOCIAL AND POLITICAL ASPECTS. New York and London: Longman, 1978. vi, 234 p.

> In chapter 1, Spring regards the political, social, and economic purposes of schooling as the major reasons for the American support of public schools. Politically, the public schools promise the establishment of a Democratic community held together by a consensus

of political values. The social purposes of schooling look to a society free from crime, poverty, and other social ills. Finally, the school as a socializer and sorter for the economy prepares students for an existing labor market. Part 1 discusses "The School and the Social Structure" and Part 2 views "Power and Control in American Education."

E AC: THE PROBLEM OF ART AND CULTURE—HUMANE ARTS AND LETTERS

Albrecht, Milton C., et al. THE SOCIOLOGY OF ART AND LITERATURE: A READER. New York: Praeger Publishers, 1970. 751 p.

Arnold, Matthew. MATTHEW ARNOLD AND THE EDUCATION OF THE NEW ORDER. Introduction and notes by Peter Smith and Geoffrey Summerfield. London: Cambridge University Press, 1969. viii, 260 p.

Brembeck, Cole S., and Hill, Walker H., eds. CULTURAL CHALLENGES TO EDUCATION. Lexington, Mass.: D.C. Heath, 1973. 208 p.

This collection of writings, with an interdisciplinary approach, discusses the influence and uses of cultural values in learning and educational decision making. Values and cross-cultural differences influence school learning particularly where culture and education intersect each other.

Callahan, Daniel Michael. THE TYRANNY OF SURVIVAL AND OTHER PATHOLOGIES OF CIVILIZED LIFE. New York: Macmillan, 1973. xv, 284 p.

Glenn, Neal E., et al. SECONDARY SCHOOL MUSIC: PHILOSOPHY, THEORY, AND PRACTICE. Englewood Cliffs, N.J.: Prentice-Hall, 1970. 275 p.

Incardona, N., and Rubino, R. CRISI DELL'OCCIDENTE E FONDAZIONE DELLA CULTURA. Palermo, Italy: U. Manfredi, 1977. 279 p.

New York State Commission on Cultural Resources. ARTS AND THE SCHOOLS: PATTERNS FOR BETTER EDUCATION. Albany, N.Y.: 1972. 100 p.

Scholl, Sharon, and White, Sylvia. MUSIC AND THE CULTURE OF MAN. New York: Holt, Rinehart and Winston, 1970. 307 p.

Volpicelli, Luigi, and Morosov, Vaslii Stepanovich. A SCUOLA DA TOLSTOI. Rome: A. Armando, 1971. 314 p.

Chapter 9

THE PROCESS AND METHODS
OF EDUCATION—INSTRUMENTALITIES OF
PERSONAL AND SOCIETAL AGENCIES

The process and methods of education are directed toward (1) the orderly
assembling of educational and cultural values and (2) the assimilating of them
in a manner that gives the learner free and wise use of them. They constitute
an educational "framework for collaborative creativity" within which learners
develop themselves, and society assures itself not only the proper transmission
and continuity of culture, but its own survival. Process and methods are intended to effect a normative pattern of recurrent and related educative experiences
and personal operations likely to yield cumulative and progressive results for
both individual and society (Bernard Lonergan).

F 1: THE PROBLEM OF KNOWING—EPISTEMOLOGY

Arendt, Hannah. THINKING. Edited by Mary McCarthy. Vol. 1: THE
LIFE OF THE MIND. New York: Harcourt Brace Jovanovich, 1978. 258 p.

> Following Kant, this modern philosopher believes the need of
> reason is not inspired by the quest for truth but by the quest for
> meaning. Thinking springs from and accompanies life and most
> likely surpasses all the activities of the active life because con-
> templative thought is itself not only nonmaterial but the very quin-
> tessence of being alive.

Birley, Derek. PLANNING AND EDUCATION. London: Routledge and
Kegan Paul, 1972. 152 p.

Broudy, Harry S. THE REAL WORLD OF THE PUBLIC SCHOOLS. New York:
Harcourt Brace Jovanovich, 1972. 271 p.

> Fully within the finer traditions of classical realism, Broudy believes
> the schools should always be "the critics of the culture by inducting
> the young into the science, the literature, and philosophy of the
> culture" (p. 79), and by being introduced to the arts and humani-

ties where the teaching of values is paramount and where they may enrich their minds and perpetuate the cultural heritage. Broudy is forthright in his demand for "knowledge, truth as certified by those expert in its discovery, defense, preservation, and promulgation" (p. 230).

Brown, James F. "Culture, Truth and Hermeneutics." AMERICA 138, no. 3 (1978): 54–57.

Brown reviews the dialogue between Paul Ricoeur and Georg Gadamer at the 1977 annual meeting of the Society for Phenomenology and Existential Philosophy. Since culture is defined by its posture toward learning and its attempts to live by the truths it tries to explore, the problem of truth and interpretation is at the root of culture.

Dewey, John. HOW WE THINK: A RESTATEMENT OF THE RELATION OF REFLECTIVE THINKING TO THE EDUCATIVE PROCESS. Boston: D.C. Heath and Co., 1910. Rev. ed. Chicago: Henry Regnery, 1971. x, 301 p.

This important restatement requires close reading. Kolesnik suggests, as an easier introduction to Dewey's concept of problem solving, EXPERIENCE AND EDUCATION (1938) and, for advanced readers, LOGIC: THE THEORY OF INQUIRY (1938). The complete act of thought is explored for its place in teaching and learning.

Frick, Stephen. "Toward a Definition of Experience." LIBERAL EDUCATION 63, no. 3 (1977): 495–99.

"An experience, in the sense that is most significant for educators, is any activity which causes us to understand values whose validity we had judged previously on the basis of faith or prejudice" (p. 499).

Herron, Marshall D. "The Nature of Scientific Enquiry." SCHOOL REVIEW 79, no. 2 (1971): 171–212.

The first part directs attention to the problems of conceptual framework development; the second to the mastery of enquiry; and the third to the extent teachers of science actually grasp and express genuine scientific enquiry. Dewey, Einstein, Peirce, and Whewell give their own clarifications of what scientific enquiry means.

Jaspers, Karl. PHILOSOPHY IS FOR EVERYMAN: A SHORT COURSE IN PHILOSOPHICAL THINKING. Translated from the German by R.F.C. Hull and Grete Wels. London: Hutchinson, 1969. xviii, 125 p.

_____. PLATO, AUGUSTINE, KANT: DREI GRUENDER DES PHILOSO-PHIERENS. [Plato, Augustin, Kant: three masters of the philosophizing art]. Munich: Piper, 1967. 404 p.

Lonergan, Bernard J.F. METHOD IN THEOLOGY. New York: Herder and Herder, 1972. xii, 405 p.

To understand this work, one must have learned the four levels of conscious operations stated in Lonergan's INSIGHT: research-data (experience), interpretation-understanding, history-judgment, dialectic-decision. The book is concerned not with the objects that theologians or any other thinkers expound but with the operations that occur consciously in an invariant pattern: experiencing, understanding, judging, and deciding. Although the work is chiefly concerned with Catholic theology, the many implications for education ought to be examined.

Martin, Jane Roland. EXPLAINING, UNDERSTANDING, AND TEACHING. New York: McGraw-Hill, 1970. viii, 248 p.

Schaefer, Robert Joseph. THE SCHOOL AS A CENTER OF INQUIRY. Foreword by Arthur G. Wirth. New York: Harper and Row, 1967. x, 77 p.

Sforza, Giulio. LA FUNZIONE DIDACTICA: SPUNTI PER UN DISCORSO SUL METODO COME EPISTEME. Rome: Bulzoni, 1976. 196 p.

Soltis, Jonas F. "Philosophy of Education: A Fourth Dimension." TEACHERS COLLEGE RECORD 67 (April 1966): 524-31.

Vlastos, Gregory, ed. PHILOSOPHY OF SOCRATES. Garden City, N.Y.: Doubleday, 1971. 354 p. Paperbound.

F 2: THE PROBLEM OF BEING—METAPHYSICS

Bereiter, Carol Edward. MUST WE EDUCATE? Englewood Cliffs, N.J.: Prentice-Hall, 1973. 146 p. Also paperbound.

Some readers may be very unhappy with an author who does not distinguish philosophy from despotism and whose claim to the acquaintance with the former is at best to be held questionable. Nyberg's comments appear in EDUCATIONAL THEORY 26, no. 2 (1976): 214-22.

Berlin, Sir Isaiah. THE HEDGEHOG AND THE FOX. 1953. New York: Simon and Schuster, 1970. 86 p.

Hedgehogs grasp the universe of reality in a single vision in the manner of Plato, Dante, or Hegel. The foxes, such as Aristotle, Shakespeare, or Goethe experience life simultaneously and variously at all levels of existence.

Brameld, Theodore. EDUCATION FOR THE EMERGING AGE: NEWER ENDS AND STRONGER MEANS. 1961. New York: Harper and Row, 1965. 244 p.

In this edition, Brameld has rewritten the postscript.

Bruner, Jerome Seymour. THE PROCESS OF EDUCATION. Cambridge, Mass.: Harvard University Press, 1960; New York: Vintage, 1963. 93 p.

The main themes of this book concern structure, learning readiness, intuitive and analytic thinking, and motives for learning. The final chapter includes learning aids for vicarious experiences. [See Broudy (1967), cited in chapter 13, p. 145].

Daley, Leo Charles. "Philosophical Development of Education: General Background" and "Philosophical Development of Education: Major Approaches." In FOUNDATIONS OF EDUCATION: PLANNING FOR COMPETENCE, by Joseph F. Callahan and Leonard H. Clark, pp. 63-98. New York: Macmillan, 1977.

Suggested readings are listed after each chapter. (See annotation under Callahan and Clark.)

Geiger, George R. JOHN DEWEY IN PERSPECTIVE. New York: Oxford University Press, 1958. vii, 248 p.

Geiger feels that Dewey's contribution is the outline of method, a method designed to replace the end-means dualism with a transactional approach and directed to enlist the power of science to solve human problems.

Joseph, Ellis A. THE PREDECISIONAL PROCESS IN EDUCATIONAL ADMINISTRATION: A PHILOSOPHICAL ANALYSIS. Homewood, Ill.: ETC Publications, 1975. 106 p.

Mollenhauer, Klaus. THEORIEN ZUM ERZIEHUNGSPROZESS: ZUR EINFUEHRUNG IN ERZIEHUNGSWISSENSCHAFTLICHE FRAGESSTELLUNGEN. [Theories of educational process: an introduction to educational issues]. Munich: Juventa Verlag, 1972. 200 p.

This is the first of fourteen volumes on fundamental issues in education.

Ornstein, Allan C., and Hedley, W. Eugene, eds. ANALYSES OF CONTEMPORARY EDUCATION. New York: Thomas Y. Crowell, 1973. xi, 320 p.

The nine selections constitute an interdisciplinary approach in education: the practice of teaching (Holt, Goodman, Silberman), the teaching profession (Conant), philosophy (Dewey, Whitehead), psychology (Erikson, Rogers), and curriculum (Bruner).

Rescher, Nicholas. METHODOLOGICAL PRAGMATISM. New York: New York University Press, 1977. xv, 311 p.

Salines, Michel, ed. PEDAGOGIE ET EDUCATION. EVOLUTION DES IDEES ET DES PRATIQUES CONTEMPORAINES. Selection of texts with commentary. Paris: La Haye, Mouton, 1972. 477 p.

Spencer, Herbert. HERBERT SPENCER ON EDUCATION. Edited with introduction and notes by Andreas M. Kazamias. New York: Teachers College Press, Columbia University, 1966. viii, 228 p.

Stachowiak, Herbert, ed. WERTE, ZIELE UND METHODEN DER BILDUNGS-PLANUNG. [Values, goals, and methods of educational design]. Paderborn, W. Ger.: F. Schoeningh, 1977. 333 p.

> This book contains sixteen discussions, held in Bad Lippspringe in October 1974. The discussions move from utopian ideals to ad hoc pragmatism in an effort to discover a central and objective core of intellectual experiences essential to the philosophy of teacher education. They cover the latest developments in educational philosophy.

F 3: HUMAN NATURE AND UNITY

Bourdieu, Pierre. OUTLINE OF A THEORY OF PRACTICE. Translated by Richard Nice. Cambridge: At the University Press, 1977. viii, 248 p.

> This international authority in social anthropology has begun to receive notice from professional educators and theorists in education.

Brembeck, Cole S., et al., eds. NEW STRATEGIES FOR EDUCATIONAL DEVELOPMENT. Lexington, Mass.: D.C. Heath, 1973. 170 p.

Drews, Ursula, ed. DIDAKTISCHE PRINZIPIEN: STANDPUNKTE, DISKUSSION-PROBLEME, LOESUNGSVORSCHLAEGE. [Educational principles: viewpoints, problems of discussion, suggested solutions]. Berlin: Volk und Wissen Volk-seigner Verlag, 1976. 272 p.

Gutek, Gerald Lee. PHILOSOPHICAL ALTERNATIVES IN EDUCATION. Columbus, Ohio: Charles E. Merrill, 1974. vii, 277 p.

> Gutek considers the bearing of systematic philosophy on classroom instruction and its significance for the teacher.

F 4: HUMAN INTELLECTIVE POWERS

Bourdieu, Pierre, and Passeron, Jean-Claude. LA REPRODUCTION: ELEMENTS POUR UNE THEORIE DU SYSTEME D'ENSEIGNEMENT. Paris: Editions de Minuit., 1970. 279 p.

Bruner, Jerome Seymour. TOWARD A THEORY OF INSTRUCTION. Cambridge, Mass.: Belknap Press of Harvard University, 1966. x, 176 p.

Hilbert, Betsy S. "The Skills of Humanistic Education." EDUCATIONAL FORUM 42, no. 2 (1978): 211-17.

> Hilbert feels there are skills to helping people learn to learn, to helping people learn to design their own learning programs. Learning to teach in humanistic ways is the job of turning elegant theory into people-centered practices.

Leeper, Robert R., ed. HUMANIZING EDUCATION: THE PERSON IN THE PROCESS. Washington, D.C.: Association for Supervision and Curriculum Development, 1967. 124 p.

Peretti, Marcello. TEORIA E STORIA DEL METODO EDUCATIVO. Brescia, Italy: La Scuola, 1973. 287 p.

Scurati, Cesare. STRUTTURALISMO E SCUOLA. Brescia, Italy: La Scuola, 1973. 393 p.

Szilak, Dennis. "Strings: A Critique of Systematic Education." HARVARD EDUCATIONAL REVIEW 46, no. 1 (1976): 54-75.

> Systematic education and problem-solving education are necessary complements; the renewal of creative teaching methods can be enriched by the best of systematic education. Similarly, if the promoters of systematic education are the loyal witnesses of the world that has just been made, then the forces of preservation cannot do without challenges from the unaccountable and the unknown.

Vico, Giovanni Battista. ON THE STUDY METHODS OF OUR TIME. Translated, with introduction and notes, by Elio Gianturo. Indianapolis: Bobbs-Merrill, 1965. xxxvii, 98 p.

F 5: HUMAN AFFECTIVE POWERS

Anderson, Terryl Joan. "Education and the Activities of Prizing." EDUCATIONAL THEORY 27, no. 4 (1977): 283-90.

> Anderson presents, within the context of the informal logic of

valuational discourse, an analysis of valuing activities that will further an understanding of recent developments in value education.

Bourdieu, Pierre, and Passeron, Jean-Claude. REPRODUCTION: IN EDUCA-TION, SOCIETY AND CULTURE. Translated by Richard Nice. Foreword by Tom Bottomore. Beverly Hills, Calif.: Sage Publications, 1977. xx, 254 p.

Carpenter, Finley. THE SKINNER PRIMER: BEHIND FREEDOM AND DIGNITY. London: Collier-Macmillan; New York: Free Press, 1974. xvi, 224 p.

Carpenter summarizes Skinner's thinking and tries to present the major objections and responses to his controversial denial of human freedom. The philosophy presumed by Skinnerian conditioning strategies has educational implications that require constant review and criticism.

DeLaney, William H. LEARN BY DOING: A PROJECTED EDUCATIONAL PHILOSOPHY IN THE THOUGHT OF BOOKER T. WASHINGTON. New York: Vantage Press, 1974. 250 p.

Hunter, Elizabeth. ENCOUNTER IN THE CLASSROOM: NEW WAYS OF TEACHING. New York: Holt, Rinehart and Winston, 1972. vii, 216 p.

The text is intended for undergraduate and graduate courses that focus upon the teaching process. It prescribes encounter and sensi-tivity group techniques for increasing personal and interpersonal effectiveness.

James, William. HABIT. 1890. Folcroft, Pa.: Folcroft Library Editons, 1974. 68 p.

Kestenbaum, Victor. THE PHENOMENOLOGICAL SENSE OF JOHN DEWEY: HABIT AND MEANING. Atlantic Highlands, N.J.: Humanities Press, 1977. 120 p.

Pestalozzi, Johann Heinrich. DIE ERZIEHUNG DES MENSCHEN. [The educa-tion of man]. Munich: Goldmann, 1970. 147 p.

_____. THE EDUCATION OF MAN: APHORISMS. Introduction by William Heard Kilpatrick. 1951. Reprint. New York: Greenwood Press, 1969. xii, 96 p.

F 6: HUMAN AESTHETIC POWERS

Carson, Janet. IT'S ART TIME: A HANDBOOK OF ART AWARENESS ACTIVITIES FOR TEACHERS. Columbus: Charles E. Merrill, 1975. xii, 242 p.

Chiari, Joseph. ART AND KNOWLEDGE. London: Elek; New York: Gordian Press, 1977. ix, 132 p.

Constable, Benjamin. ART, THE METAPHYSICS OF LOVE AND UNIVERSAL MYSTICAL SYMBOLISM. Albuquerque, N. Mex.: American Classical College Press, 1977. 23 leaves.

Dufrenne, Mikel. THE PHENOMENOLOGY OF AESTHETIC EXPERIENCE. Translated by Edward S. Casey et al. Evanston, Ill.: Northwestern University Press, 1973. lxvii, 578 p.

> "Aesthetic object" and "aesthetic perception" serve to define the movement of thought proceeding from a consideration of the aesthetic object to a theory concerning the perception of this object. These are inseparable. Finally, the work ends with an ontological and transcendental reflection on the reconciliation of subject and object.

Gaitskell, Charles D., et al. CHILDREN AND THEIR ART: METHODS FOR THE ELEMENTARY SCHOOL. 3d ed. New York: Harcourt Brace Jovanovich, 1975. xii, 547 p.

Klonsky, Ruth L. ART LESSONS THAT MIRROR THE CHILD'S WORLD. West Nyack, N.Y.: Parker Publishing, 1975. 270 p.

Lowenfeld, Victor, and Brittain, W. Lambert. CREATIVE AND MENTAL GROWTH. 6th ed. New York: Macmillan, 1975. xi, 430 p.

Moles, Abraham. INFORMATION THEORY AND ESTHETIC PERCEPTION. Translated from French by Joel E. Cohen. Urbana and London: University of Illinois Press, 1966. 317 p.

> In considering the communication to a human being from the aspect of art, Moles analyzes esthetic perception and actually outlines a program of research in the psychology of perception.

Popper, Frank. ART, ACTION AND PARTICIPATION. London: Studio Vista, 1975. 269 p.

Priestley, John Boynton. PARTICULAR PLEASURES--BEING A PERSONAL RECORD OF SOME VARIED ARTS AND MANY DIFFERENT ARTISTS. New York: Stein and Day, 1975. 192 p.

Sloan, John. GIST OF ART: PRINCIPLES AND PRACTICES EXPOUNDED IN THE CLASSROOM AND STUDIO. 3d rev. ed. New York: Dover Publications, 1977. li, 200 p.

Wayte, Nick; Cooper, David; and Eyre, David. A STUDY OF ASPECTS OF ART AND DESIGN EDUCATION. 2 vols. Manchester, Engl.: Polytechnic Institute of Advanced Studies, 1974–75.

Weiner, Egon. ART AND HUMAN EMOTIONS. Springfield, Ill.: Charles C Thomas, 1975. x, 90 p.

Wooff, Terence. DEVELOPMENTS IN ART TEACHING. London: Open Books, 1976. xii, 117 p.

F 7: THE PROBLEM OF VALUES—ETHICS

Bredemeier, Mary E., and Bredemeier, Harry C. SOCIAL FORCES IN EDUCATION. Sherman Oaks, Calif.: Alfred Publishing, 1978. x, 390 p.

> The joining of theory about the way things should be with descriptions of the way things are means three things: examine the pressures, forces, constraints, and opportunities that cause students to act as they do; understand similar factors that cause educators to behave as they do; reject deliberately the premise that no value judgment should intrude upon the analysis. The strategies for change recognize that evaluation for educational purposes must be in large measure evaluation of the practices used in educating.

Brickman, William W., and Lehrer, Stanley, eds. AUTOMATION, EDUCATION AND HUMAN VALUES. New York: School and Society Books, 1966; Thomas Y. Crowell, 1969. 415 p.

Callahan, Daniel Michael. CONFORMITY, DEVIATION, AND MORALE AMONG EDUCATORS IN SCHOOL SYSTEMS. Ann Arbor, Mich.: University Microfilms, 1969. viii, 143 p.

Chazan, Barry I., and Soltis, Jonas F., eds. MORAL EDUCATION. New York: Teachers College Press, 1973. 192 p. Paperbound.

> Assuming that some moral education occurs regardless of the inadequate communication between philosophers and educators, the authors seek the ways and the reasons for successful moral education and their underlying meanings.

Dewey, John. LIBERALISM AND SOCIAL ACTION. New York: Capricorn Books, 1963. 93 p.

Fellsches, Josef. MORALISCHE ERZIEHUNG ALS POLITISCHE BILDUNG. [Moral instruction as political and cultural education]. Heidelberg, W. Ger.: Quelle and Meyer, 1977. 240 p.

This work is an essay toward a critical theory of education in its moral and societal dimensions. It seeks to establish the theoretical underpinning for a critical understanding of moral education.

Fraenkel, Jack R. HOW TO TEACH ABOUT VALUES: AN ANALYTIC APPROACH. Englewood Cliffs, N.J.: Prentice-Hall, 1977. vi, 154 p.

Perry, William G. FORMS OF INTELLECTUAL AND ETHICAL DEVELOPMENT IN THE COLLEGE YEARS: A SCHEME. New York: Holt, Rinehart and Winston, 1970. vii, 256.

The address to values is expressive of contextualistic-pragmatic and existential traditions. The emphasis is on the interweaving of hierarchies of values with the hierarchies of thought, of metavaluing with metathinking. In this structural linking of valuing with thinking degrees of ethical objectivity are possible in which detachment, choice, and commitment may function at generalized levels.

Tanner, Laurel N. CLASSROOM DISCIPLINE FOR EFFECTIVE TEACHING AND LEARNING. New York: Holt, Rinehart and Winston, 1978. x, 214 p.

This practical guide deals with methods of teaching for the classroom teacher who wishes to understand the theory and applications of school discipline. The goal is self-direction in a Democratic society. Discipline is essential to such living.

Trotsky, Leon; Dewey, John; and Novack; George. THEIR MORALS AND OURS: MARXIST VERSUS LIBERAL VIEWS ON MORALITY. 5th ed. New York: Pathfinder Press, 1973. 80 p.

Marx is alleged to have said once in a heated debate: "Aber Sie vergessen, dass Ich kein Marxist bin!"

Wiener, Norbert. THE HUMAN USE OF HUMAN BEINGS: CYBERNETICS AND SOCIETY. Afterword by Walter A. Rosenblith. New York: Avon Books, 1970. 288 p.

Wilson, John. PRACTICAL METHODS OF MORAL EDUCATION. London: Heinemann Educational Group; New York: Crane, Russak, 1972. ix, 153 p.

F 8: THE PROBLEM OF THOUGHT AND LANGUAGE— PHILOSOPHICAL ANALYSIS

Ayer, Alfred Jules. PROBABILITY AND EVIDENCE. New York: Columbia University Press, 1972. x, 144 p.

Ayer centers his analysis on (1) Hume's formulation of the problem of induction and on the nature of probability and evidence;

(2) Harrod's intended refutation of Hume; and (3) the problem of conditionals. This inquiry demands advanced experience in analytical thought.

Black, Max. CAVEATS AND CRITIQUES: PHILOSOPHICAL ESSAYS IN LANGUAGE, LOGIC, AND ART. Ithaca, N.Y.: Cornell University Press, 1975. 274 p.

_____, ed. PHILOSOPHICAL ANALYSIS. 1950. Englewood Cliffs, N.J.: Prentice-Hall, 1963. 401 p.

Britton, James. LANGUAGE AND LEARNING. Coral Gables: University of Florida Press, 1970. 295 p.

Fornaca, Remo. SCELTE PEDAGOGISCHE E ISTANZE LOGICHE. Rome: A. Armando, 1974. 145 p.

Harman, Gilbert, ed. ON NOAM CHOMSKY: CRITICAL ESSAYS. Garden City, N.Y.: Doubleday, 1974. 384 p.

Of chief concern to the authors of the selections are the methodological issues and the relationship of Chomsky's linguistics to psychology, his theory of rationalism, and to the questions of grammar, meaning, and logical analysis.

Smith, Bunnie Othanel, and Ennis, Robert H., eds. LANGUAGE AND CONCEPTS IN EDUCATION. Chicago: Rand McNally, 1961. 221 p.

These theorists, expert in the use of the analytic method, test the meaning of such time worn shibboleths as learning by experience, meeting the needs of the child, neutral schools, equality of opportunity.

Soltis, Jonas F. AN INTRODUCTION TO THE ANALYSIS OF EDUCATIONAL CONCEPTS. 2d ed. Reading, Mass.: Addison-Wesley Publishing, 1978. xvi, 128 p. Bibliog. Paperbound.

The topics, selected from contemporary analytic writings, are simplified to acquaint the reader with analytic thinking about educational ideas in both its substantive and methodological dimensions. The thirteen-page bibliography provides sources for class discussions, papers, and other forms of practice, research, review, and involvement in philosophical analysis.

van Peursen, Cornelis A. PHENOMENOLOGY AND ANALYTICAL PHILOSOPHY. Pittsburgh: Duquesne University Press, 1972. 190 p.

F TR: THE PROBLEM OF GOD—THEOLOGY AND RELIGION

Rahner, Karl. A RAHNER READER. Edited by Gerald A. McCool. New York: Seabury Press, 1975. xxviii, 381 p.

> This selection of readings, with a finely balanced introduction to Rahner's guidance on important theological and philosophical questions, challenges the practice of not only faith but education. It covers Rahner's thought on philosophical anthropology, historical revelation, culture in relation to religion, mystery and symbol, the mystery of God's offering to communicate his own life to man, human freedom and ethical questions, ideology, and eschatology.

Taylor, George, and Saunders, John B. THE NEW LAW OF EDUCATION. 7th ed. London: Butterworth, 1971. xxi, 632 p.

Wieman, Henry Nelson. RELIGIOUS EXPERIENCE AND SCIENTIFIC METHOD. Carbondale: Southern Illinois University Press, 1971. 387 p.

F NS: THE PROBLEM OF THE COSMOS—PHYSICAL AND MATHEMATICAL SCIENCES

Salmon, Wesley C., et al. STATISTICAL EXPLANATION AND STATISTICAL RELEVANCE. Pittsburgh: University of Pittsburgh Press, 1971. 120 p.

Whitehead, Alfred North. PROCESS AND REALITY: AN ESSAY IN COSMOLOGY. 1929. New York: Free Press, 1969. xii, 429 p.

Young, Michael F.D., ed. KNOWLEDGE AND CONTROL: NEW DIRECTIONS FOR THE SOCIOLOGY OF EDUCATION. London: Collier-Macmillan, 1971. 289 p.

F HS: THE PROBLEM OF HUMAN SOCIETY—HUMAN AND SOCIAL SCIENCES

Bekker, John A. "Soviet Pedagogy: Philosophy and Methods." LIBERAL EDUCATION 45, no. 4 (1959): 481-93.

> Bekker explains that five principles of Communist educational philosophy, variously stressed according to needs and times, underlie virtually all of Soviet educational policies: materialism, collectivism, the Communist ethic, proletarian internationalism, and polytechnism.

Burns, James MacGregor. UNCOMMON SENSE. New York: Harper and Row, 1972. 196 p.

Writing in the area of social philosophy, Burns explores rather astutely the state of American culture. Very important is his clarification of the relationship of means to goals.

Corwin, Ronald G. REFORM AND ORGANIZATIONAL SURVIVAL: THE TEACHER CORPS AS AN INSTRUMENT OF EDUCATIONAL CHANGE. New York: Wiley-Interscience, 1973. xxv, 469 p.

Gramsci, Antonio. "The Organization of Education and Culture" and "In Search of the Educational Principle." In SELECTIONS FROM THE PRISON NOTEBOOKS OF ANTONIO GRAMSCI, edited by Quintin Hoare and Geoffrey Nowell Smith, pp. 24-43. New York: Lawrence and Wishart, 1971.

Kirp, David L., and Yudof, Mark G. EDUCATIONAL POLICY AND THE LAW. Berkeley, Calif.: McCutchan Publishing, 1974. 749 p.

Kirp highlights the interaction between legal decisions and educational practice. The text borrows liberally from social science sources both to assure greater understanding of educational problems that have become legal issues and to assess the effects of legal change.

Mehan, Hugh, and Wood, Houston. THE REALITY OF ETHNOMETHODOLOGY. New York: Wiley-Interscience, 1975. x, 259 p.

F AC: THE PROBLEM OF ART AND CULTURE—HUMANE ARTS AND LETTERS

Lockspeiser, Edward. MUSIC AND PAINTING: A STUDY IN COMPARATIVE IDEAS FROM TURNER TO SCHOENBERG. New York: Harper and Row, 1973. 197 p.

Martin, F. David, and Jacobus, Lee A. THE HUMANITIES THROUGH THE ARTS. New York: McGraw-Hill, 1975. 416 p.

Chapter 10
THE NATURE AND ETHOS OF EDUCATION—
THE FORMAL CAUSE OF EDUCATION

The nature and ethos of education refer to the essential and distinguishing character of human education. They embrace both the formal and material causes of education. In this meaning, education may be defined as the inner form enclosing a content--a personal elaboration or reception by the learner of an inner educative form conveyed by way of intellectual and moral didactic materials and techniques of formal and informal agencies. The writers listed in this section give some emphasis to the formality of education as such.

G 1: THE PROBLEM OF KNOWING—EPISTEMOLOGY

Chamberlin, John Gordon. TOWARD A PHENOMENOLOGY OF EDUCATION. Philadelphia: Westminster Press, 1969. 201 p.

Deats, Tom. "Educational Futures: What Do We Need To Know?" EDUCATIONAL THEORY 26, no. 1 (1976): 81-92.

Deats believes what people need to know today is how and why to expand and enrich the human stock of descriptions; ways of describing and explaining the reasons and purposes for knowledge, education, and people themselves.

Eames, S. Morris. PRAGMATIC NATURALISM: AN INTRODUCTION. Carbondale: Southern Illinois University Press, 1977. 256 p. Paperbound.

Eames reviews the ideas of Charles Sanders Peirce, William James, George Herbert Mead, and John Dewey as the founders of the pragmatic movement. Peirce abandoned the term pragmatism, Dewey favored the word naturalism, while Eames unites pragmatic with the term naturalism to indicate a method of philosophizing. A suggested order of readings is given at the end of each chapter. The topics of importance concern nature and human life, knowledge, value, and education.

Elvin, Lionel. THE PLACE OF COMMONSENSE IN EDUCATIONAL THOUGHT. London: Allen and Unwin, 1977. 165 p. Also paperbound.

> Elvin calls for the use and respect of informed experience and commonsense as a guide to action. It is important, for the educator or student faced with rival theories and alternate policy proposals, to maintain the ability to see problems not only in their many-sidedness, but in the light of general experience and several specializations. Elvin expects the reader to use commonsense in rethinking the place of liberal education, religion, and the classics and in scrutinizing the philosophical concepts of rights, values, and needs in modern education.

Gray, J. Glenn. THE PROMISE OF WISDOM. New York: J.B. Lippincott, 1968; New York: Harper and Row, 1972. 280 p. Paperbound.

> After discussing the definition of education in part 1, Gray seeks to answer what it means to be educated, why be educated, whom should we teach, what should we teach, and where is education headed. Thus, the process of building an adequate theory of education for a rapidly changing society also reveals the function of philosophy in meeting educational problems. [See Broudy-Smith (1969), cited in chapter 13, p. 6].

Hardie, Charles D. TRUTH AND FALLACY IN EDUCATIONAL THEORY. Preface by James E. McClellan and B. Paul Komisar. Cambridge: Cambridge University Press, 1942; New York: Teachers College, Bureau of Publications, 1962. xx, 156 p. Paperbound.

> Hardie applies linguistic and philosophic analysis to educational theory. A critique of Dewey may be found in chapter 3. Chapter 4 should be read for its analyses of the foundations essential to any philosophy of education.

Hodgkin, Robin A. RECONNAISSANCE ON AN EDUCATIONAL FRONTIER. London: Oxford University Press, 1970. xii, 108 p.

Hopper, Earl, ed. READINGS IN THE THEORY OF EDUCATIONAL SYSTEMS. London: Hutchinson, 1971. 336 p.

> The essays cover the important issues of typology for the classification of educational systems, the management of knowledge and critique of the use of typologies in educational sociology, systems of education and systems of thought, the political functions of the educational system, power and ideology in the transmission of knowledge, a crosscultural outline of education. Several questions pertain to stratification, education and mobility in industrial societies.

Judges, A.V., ed. EDUCATION AND THE PHILOSOPHIC MIND. London: George G. Harrap, 1957. 205 p.

Judges offers a group of challenging essays, by British authors, on Plato, Neo-Thomism, existentialism, pragmatism, behaviorism, logical positivism, scientific humanism, and dialectical materialism. Richmond finds the essays eminently readable.

Lippitz, Wilfried. DIALEKTISCHE BILDUNGSTHEORIE IN DIALEKTISCHER KRITIK. [Dialectic educational theory in dialectical criticism]. Bern, Switz.; Frankfort on the Main, W. Ger.; and Munich: Lang, 1976. 210 p.

The purpose of this work is a critical reconstruction of Joseph Derbolav's philosophy of education. It reviews Derbolav's chief educational and philosophical writings.

Lonergan, Bernard J.F. "Dimensions of Meaning." In COLLECTION: PAPERS BY BERNARD LONERGAN, edited by F.E. Crowe, pp. 252-67. New York: Herder and Herder, 1967.

_____. INSIGHT: A STUDY OF HUMAN UNDERSTANDING. 1957. Rev. ed. New York: Longmans, Green, 1961. xxx, 785 p.

In the language of Lonergan, the aim of this work is to (1) indicate what precisely is the nature of knowledge, (2) provide a discriminant or determinant of cognitive acts, (3) help the reader achieve a personal appropriation of the concrete, dynamic structure immanently and recurrently operative in his own cognitional activities, (4) assemble slowly (for ease of personal appropriation) the elements, alternatives, and implications of the knowledge structure, and (5) order the assembly of knowledge by concrete motives of pedagogical efficacy. This work is regarded by many authorities as a philosophy classic with profound implications for the philosophy of education.

Massa, Riccardo. LA SCIENZE PEDAGOGICA: EPISTEMOLOGIA E METODO EDUCATIVO. Florence, Italy: La Nuova Italia, 1975. vi, 216 p.

Nagai, Michio. EDUCATION AND INDOCTRINATION. Tokyo: University of Tokyo Press, 1976. 118 p.

This unrevised dissertation, presented in the Ohio State University College of Education a quarter of a century ago, analyzes the thought of Mannheim, Weber, Morris, and Dewey without benefit of the latest critical thinking. It gives a 1952 view of pragmatist epistemology and logical theory.

Nash, Paul. MODELS OF MAN: EXPLORATIONS IN THE WESTERN EDUCATIONAL TRADITION. New York: John Wiley and Sons, 1968. xiii, 470 p.

O'Connor, Daniel John. "The Nature of Educational Theory." PROCEEDINGS OF THE PHILOSOPHY OF EDUCATION SOCIETY OF GREAT BRITAIN 6 (January 1972): 97-109.

Peters, Richard Stanley, ed. THE CONCEPT OF EDUCATION. London: Routledge and Kegan Paul; New York: Humanities Press, 1967. xiii, 223 p.

Ruprecht, Horst. MODELLE GRUNDLEGENDER DIDAKTISCHER THEORIEN. [Models of fundamental educational theories]. 3d ed. Hanover, Dortmund, Darmstadt, and Berlin: Schroedel, 1976. 200 p.

Russell, Bertrand. MY PHILOSOPHICAL DEVELOPMENT. London: Allen and Unwin, 1975. 208 p.

Snook, Ivan A. INDOCTRINATION AND EDUCATION. London and Boston: Routledge and Kegan Paul, 1975. 128 p.

> This book is valuable for exposing the young educator to conceptual analysis in philosophy and education. The distinction between education and indoctrination is lucidly defined and consistently applied throughout the book.

Ulrich, Dieter. THEORIE UND METHODE DER ERZIEHUNGSWISSENSCHAFT: PROBLEME EINES SOZIALWISSENSCHAFTLICHES PAEDAGOGIK. [Theory and method in the science of education: problems of sociological education]. 2d ed. Weinheim, W. Ger. and Basel, Switz.: Beltz, 1974. 518 p.

Vandenberg, Donald, ed. THEORY OF KNOWLEDGE AND PROBLEMS OF EDUCATION. Urbana: University of Illinois Press, 1969. 302 p.

White, Nicholas P. PLATO ON KNOWLEDGE AND REALITY. Indianapolis: Hackett Publishing, 1976. 272 p.

> Writing a complete and unified account of Plato's epistemology, White argues that Plato developed and defended the conviction that realism is true and leaves no place for alternative conceptual schemes. White sees a continuous argument running through the MENO, PHAEDO, PHAEDRUS, CRATYLUS, THEAETETUS, and LETTER SEVEN.

Xochellis, Panagiotis (Panos), and Debl, Helmut, eds. DENKMODELLE FUER PAEDAGOGIK. [Intellectual models for education]. Munich: Ehrenwirth, 1975. 178 p.

> Because of their significance to the philosophy of education, the six essayists assess theories drawn from pedagogics (Xochellis), psychology (Debl), human biology (Engle and Vogel), theology (Feifel), philosophy (Muehlbauer), and sociology (Stieglitz).

G 2: THE PROBLEM OF BEING—METAPHYSICS

ARISTOTLE ON EDUCATION. Extracts from the ETHICS and POLITICS.

Translated from Greek and edited by John Burnet. Cambridge: Cambridge University Press, 1967. 141 p.

Boettcher, Hans. SOZIALPAEDAGOGIK IM UEBERBLICK. [Social philosophy of education in review]. Freiburg on the Main, W. Ger.; Basel, Switz.; Vienna: Herder; Gutersloh, W. Ger.: Gutersloher Verlagshaus Mohn, 1975. 271 p.

> Boettcher presents a systematic introduction to the problems and goals, the functions and methods of the sociological approach to the practice of education. His intent is to establish an agogic or systematic education in its sociological foundations.

Boettcher, Henry John. THREE PHILOSOPHIES OF EDUCATION. New York: Philosophical Library, 1967. xv, 248 p.

> Boettcher gives three basic assumptions underlying education: matter centered, idea centered, and God centered.

Braun, Edmund, ed. and trans. ARISTOTELES UND DIE PAIDEIA. Paderborn: F. Schoeningh, 1974. 258 p.

Cahn, Steven Mark, ed. THE PHILOSOPHICAL FOUNDATIONS OF EDUCATION. New York: Harper and Row, 1970. viii, 433 p. Paperbound.

> Cahn classifies educational philosophies as traditional (Plato, Aristotle, Locke, Rousseau, and Kant), as modern (Dewey, Whitehead, Russell, Maritain, and Hook), or as analytic (Cahn, Peters, Scheffler, Martin, and Ryle).

Classen, Johannes. METAPHYSIK DER BILDUNG NACH THOMAS VON AQUIN. [The metaphysics of education according to Thomas Aquinas]. Freiburg, W. Ger.: Herder, 1970. 303 p.

Cremin, Lawrence Arthur. THE GENIUS OF AMERICAN EDUCATION. New York: Random House, 1965. 116 p.

Debesse, Maurice, and Mialaret, Gaston. TRAITE DES SCIENCES PEDAGOGIQUES. Paris: Presses Universitaires de France, 1969.

Debl, Helmut, ed. DIE PAEDAGOGIK IM DIALOG MIT IHREN GRENZWISSENSCHAFTEN. [Education in dialogue with its bordering disciplines]. Munich: Ehrenwirth, 1971. 285 p.

> This book offers a complete analysis of education: its concept and aims; theoretical foundations; current movements; antinomies; its self-image. The twelve essays include discussions of research methodology, sociology, cultural anthropology, human genetics, theology, cybernetics, psychology, and philosophy.

Dewey, John. LECTURES IN THE PHILOSOPHY OF EDUCATION, 1899. Edited with introduction by Reginald D. Archambault. New York: Random House, 1966. xxxv, 366 p.

Donohue, John W. "Education and the Future: Opinions and Expectations." AMERICA 130 (26 January 1974): 46-49.

Drago, Pietro Crisiano. L'UNITA DELL'EDUCAZIONE. Assisi, Italy: La Bussola, 1968. 294 p.

Ellwein, Thomas. BILDUNGSTRADITION UND ZUKUNFTSORIENTIERTE AUS-BILDUNG. [Educational tradition and future-oriented culture]. Frankfort on the Main, W. Ger.: Heiderhoff, 1971. 23 p.

> Ellwein attempts to answer the question whether anyone today still needs education in its traditional interpretation. He finds a positive answer in a personal acknowledgment of the German tradition in liberal education.

Fink, Eugen. ERZIEHUNGSWISSENSCHAFT UND LEBENSLEHRE. [The science of education and life]. Freiburg, W. Ger.: Verlag Rombach, 1970. 240 p.

_____. METAPHYSIK DER ERZIEHUNG IM WELTVERSTAENDNIS VON PLATO UND ARISTOTELES. [The metaphysics of education within the world view of Plato and Aristotle]. Frankfort on the Main, W. Ger.: Klostermann, 1970. 327 p.

Gerner, Berthold. OTTO WILLMANN IM ALTER. BIOGRAPHISCH-SYSTEMATISCHE UNTERSUCHUNGEN UEBER LEBEN, WIRKEN UND PAEDA-GOGISCHES WERK 1900-20. Ratingen by Dusseldorf, W. Ger.: Henn, 1968. 439 p.

> Willmann's philosophical and educational thought is still very vital at many European and South American universities and teacher-training institutions. His later years in Prague, Salzburg, and Leitmeritz are conspicuous for his second edition of the GESCHICHTE DES IDEALISMUS and for his great contributions to Roloff's LEXIKON DER PAEDAGOGIK in five volumes (1913-17).

Goelz, Walter; Schmidhaeuser, Ulrich; Thies, Erich; and Zahn, Lothar, eds. WOZU HEUTE PHILOSOPHIE? [Whereto philosophy today?]. Bad Heilbrunn/Obb., W. Ger.: Klinkhardt, 1976. 169 p.

> The ten essays evaluate the position of philosophy in regard to the sciences and its relationship to the practical and educational problems of the day. The authors wish to locate the place and value of philosophy in the formation of teachers.

Guttchen, Robert S. "The Quest for Necessity." EDUCATIONAL THEORY 16, no. 2 (1966): 128-34.

Guttchen adverts to the special relationships of philosophy to educational theory and practice and finds the connection to be a necessary one only in some instances.

Hamm, Russell L. PHILOSOPHY AND EDUCATION: ALTERNATIVES IN THEORY AND PRACTICE. Danville, Ill.: Interstate Printers and Publishers, 1974. xvii, 330 p.

Hendricks, Wilfried, and Stuebig, Heinz, eds. ZWISCHEN THEORIE UND PRAXIS/MARBURGER KOLLOQUIUM ZUR DIDAKTIK (1976). [Between theory and practice/ the Marburg Colloquium on Education, 1976]. Kronberg/Ts., E. Ger.: Athenaeum-Verlag, 1977. x, 186 p.

The twelve discourses are concerned with the science of education, its status, and current developmental tendencies.

Izzo, Domenica. L'EDUCAZIONE COME SCIENZA. Florence, Italy: F. Le Monnier, 1974. 248 p.

Johnson, James A.; Collins, Harold W.; Dupuis, Victor L.; and Johansen, John H. INTRODUCTION TO THE FOUNDATIONS OF AMERICAN EDUCATION. 4th ed. Boston: Allyn and Bacon, 1979. xv, 480 p.

This introductory text has important chapters on the historical foundations of education (part 4), philosophical bases of education (part 5), and American education and the future (part 7).

Kazepides, Anastasios C. THE AUTONOMY OF EDUCATION. Athens, Greece: National Centre of Social Research, 1973. 107 p.

Kneller, George Frederick, ed. FOUNDATIONS OF EDUCATION. 3d ed. New York: John Wiley and Sons, 1971. ix, 674 p.

Langford, Glenn. "Education." PROCEEDINGS OF THE PHILOSOPHY OF EDUCATION SOCIETY OF GREAT BRITAIN 2 (January 1968): 31-41.

Laterza, Moacyr, and Rios, Terezinha Azeredo. FILOSOFIA DE EDUCACAO: FUNDAMENTOS. Sao Paulo, Brazil: Editora Herder, 1971.

Lawson, Douglas E., and Lean, Arthur E., eds. JOHN DEWEY AND THE WORLD VIEW. Carbondale: Southern Illinois University Press, 1966. 168 p. Paperbound.

This text provides a concise introduction to and a brief restatement of some of Dewey's major ideas. It is intended for readers not yet familiar with Dewey.

Leif, Joseph Jacques. LES DOCTRINES PEDAGOGIQUES PAR LES TEXTES. Paris: Delagrave, 1966. 336 p.

Lucas, Christopher J., ed. WHAT IS PHILOSOPHY OF EDUCATION? New York: Macmillan; London: Collier-Macmillan, 1969. vi, 313 p. Paperbound.

The essays are grouped in regard to the predicaments of contemporary philosophy, some historical perspectives, what is philosophy of education, educational philosophy and the teacher. The readings, chosen to illuminate the philosophical significance of education among teachers, are prefaced by an analysis of the five ways of teaching courses in educational philosophy: "great minds," "systems" or "schools of thought," "problems," "metaphilosophy," or "social foundations." The suggestions for further reading are stimulating.

Ludwig, Guenter. METAPHYSISCHE GRUNDFRAGEN DER ERZIEHUNGS-WISSENSCHAFT. [Metaphysical questions in education]. Wuppertal, W. Ger.; Ratingen, W. Ger.; and Dusseldorf, W. Ger.: Henn, 1970. 96 p.

The commentary begins with the opening line in Aristotle's META-PHYSICS that all men by nature have a desire to know. Ludwig then details the interpretation given to this passage and others by the great Jesuit philosopher Francis Suarez.

McBride, Alfred. CREATIVE TEACHING IN CHRISTIAN EDUCATION. Boston: Allyn and Bacon, 1978. 285 p. Paperbound.

McBride provides a two-year plan for formulating a community's educational philosophy, confronts the complexity of moral education in contemporary society, and reveals a diversified content and practical methodology for short- and long-term planning. It is a basic comprehensive guide to religious education.

McClellan, James E. "Educational Philosophy Resurrected." SCHOOL REVIEW 79, no. 2 (1971): 278-81.

The obligation of anyone concerned about educational philosophy is to maintain a deep and conscious commitment to the tradition of rational thought. In the event of such fidelity, the fortunate and resourceful teacher-philosopher will shed light on the dilemmas of education and enlighten his listeners. McClellan defines the philosophy of education as "an attempt to deal philosophically with the major problems and concepts of education."

Maritain, Jacques. ON THE USE OF PHILOSOPHY: THREE ESSAYS. 1961. New York: Atheneum Publishers, 1965. 71 p. Paperbound.

_____. POUR UNE PHILOSOPHIE DE L'EDUCATION. Rev. ed. Paris: Fayard, 1969. 199 p.

Mialaret, Gaston. INTRODUCTION A LA PEDAGOGIE. 4th ed. Paris: Presses Universitaires de France, 1973. 188 p.

Munk, Arthur W. A SYNOPTIC PHILOSOPHY OF EDUCATION. New York: Abingdon Press, 1965. 267 p.

> The discussion is oriented toward perspective, synthesis, and creativity.

Murray, John Courtney. "Reversing the Secularist Drift." THOUGHT 24, no. 92 (1949): 36-46.

Neff, Frederick C. PHILOSOPHY AND AMERICAN EDUCATION. New York: Center for Applied Research in Education, 1966. xii, 116 p.

Oelkers, Juergen. DIE VERMITTLUNG ZWISCHEN THEORIE UND PRAXIS IN DER PAEDAGOGIK. [Reconciling theory and practice in education]. Munich: Koesel, 1976. 187 p.

> The author first analyzes the relationship of theory and practice in modern societies with respect to the problem of education. Then he defines what theory and practice actually mean in education. Finally, he explores the concept of reconciling the two within the pedagogical framework of science and education.

Phenix, Philip H., ed. PHILOSOPHIES OF EDUCATION. New York: John Wiley and Sons, 1961. 137 p.

Pratte, Richard. CONTEMPORARY THEORIES OF EDUCATION. Scranton, Pa.: Intext Educational Publishers, 1971. xii, 338 p.

Rombach, Heinrich, ed. LEXIKON DER PAEDAGOGIK. [Dictionary of education]. New ed. in 4 vols. Freiburg, W. Ger.; Basel, Switz.; and Vienna: Herder, 1970-71.

> This magisterial work still reflects the genius of Otto Willmann and Ernst Roloff. In about three thousand articles, this very carefully edited encyclopedia covers the entire domain of educational philosophical theory and practice. It is a necessary source for any research into historical and contemporary European educational thought.

SANT' AGOSTINO EDUCATORE. SETTIMANA AGOSTINIANA, 2d, Pavia, Italy, 16-24 April 1970. Pavia, Italy: Industrie Lito-Tipografiche Mario Ponzio, 1971. 133 p.

Santelli, Luisa. PROBLEMI PEDAGOGICI IN HENRI BERGSON. Padoua: Liviana, 1974. vi, 106 p.

Scheffler, Israel, ed. PHILOSOPHY AND EDUCATION: MODERN READINGS. 2d ed. Boston: Allyn and Bacon, 1966. x, 387 p.

> Scheffler has grouped these representative essays according to the concepts of education, morals and education, intellect and skill, scientific method and education, educational content, and American education.

Suchodolski, Bogdan. PAEDAGOGIK AM SCHEIDEWEG: ESSENZ UND EXISTENZ. [Education at the crossroad: essence or existence]. Translated into German by Martin Donner. Vienna: Euopa Verlag, 1965. 119 p.

Tello, Belisario. FILOSOFIA PEGAGOGICA. Buenos Aires: Libreria Huemul, 1975. 213 p.

Vandenberg, Donald. BEING AND EDUCATION: AN ESSAY IN EXISTENTIAL PHENOMENOLOGY. Englewood Cliffs, N.J.: Prentice-Hall, 1971. 228 p. Also paperbound.

> This somewhat augmented collection of previously published articles centers interest around the existential and phenomenological concept of being. An important thesis is that growth in self-awareness is prerequisite to and an outcome of learning and knowing.

Wilson, John. EDUCATIONAL THEORY AND THE PREPARATION OF TEACHERS. Windsor: National Foundation for Educational Research in England and Wales, 1975. 182 p.

Wolff, Robert Paul. PHILOSOPHY: A MODERN ENCOUNTER. Englewood Cliffs, N.J.: Prentice-Hall, 1973. 327 p.

Woods, Ronald George, and Barrow, Robin St. Clair. AN INTRODUCTION TO PHILOSOPHY OF EDUCATION. London: Methuen; New York: Harper and Row, Barnes and Noble, 1975. 200 p.

G 3: HUMAN NATURE AND UNITY

Aristotle. DE ANIMA. Translated from Greek with notes by Robert Drew Hicks. 1907. New York: Arno Press, 1976. lxxxiii, 626 p.

> The texts are in both Greek and English.

Brumbaugh, Robert S. "Education and Reality: Two Revolutions." THOUGHT 48, no. 188 (1973): 5-18.

> Western educational thought has experienced only two great revolutions, each coinciding with a new recognition of an important

metaphysical principle. The Greeks discovered the power of reason and the importance of form by recognizing the principle of limitation. The moderns follow the principle of plenitude, which makes known that concrete individuals are not only more than mere type outlines in space and time, but operate in creative and interesting ways. Brumbaugh then describes a third possible revolution that may achieve a more realistic theory and practice of education.

Dickopp, Karl-Heinz. DIE KRISE DER ANTHROPOLOGISCHEN BEGRUENDUNG VON ERZIEHUNG. [The anthropological foundation of education in crisis]. Ratingen, W. Ger., and Kastellaun, W. Ger.: Henn, 1973. 108 p.

The fundamental inquiry into the foundations of education requires further investigation into the nature of man. The science of education, as an academic discipline, must concern itself with pedagogical anthropology and the philosophy of educating persons. The debate over human nature thus helps clarify the basic assumptions and aims of education in its theoretical as well as in its practical implications.

Doran, Robert M. SUBJECT AND PSYCHE: RICOEUR, JUNG AND THE SEARCH FOR FOUNDATIONS. Washington, D.C.: University Press of America, 1977. 314 p. Paperbound.

The power of Bernard Lonergan's method is clearly evident in the study of man's psyche. The efficacy of this method to generate categories for a science of the psyche also affects the science of education by offering alternate ways of studying human nature.

Drake, William E. INTELLECTUAL FOUNDATIONS OF MODERN EDUCATION. Columbus, Ohio: Charles E. Merrill, 1967. ix, 369.

Drake believes a warrantable theory of modern education must emphasize the nature of man, an interdisciplinary approach to the problem of meaning and value, and a concept of evolution that explains the progress of man toward a higher order of being.

_____. SOURCES FOR INTELLECTUAL FOUNDATIONS OF MODERN EDUCATION. Columbus, Ohio: Charles E. Merrill, 1967. vi, 408 p.

Selected readings are grouped according to man as symbol, art, science, empirical origin of ideas, romantic naturalism, scientific individualism, social reality, technology, professionalization of teaching, and critique of education in the United States.

Eggersdorfer, Franz Xaver. JUGENDBILDUNG. ALLGEMEINE THEORIE DES SCHULUNTERRICHTS. [The cultural education of youth: general theory of instruction]. 1928. 7th ed. Munich: Josef Koesel and Friedrich Pustet, 1961. ix, 459 p.

In the spirit of Otto Willmann, the author offers a philosophy of education in response to the following problems: the nature and aims of cultural education, educative values and their organization into the program of studies, the principles and foundations of the educative process, educational experiences together with their instructional forms and methods.

Fancelli, Manlio. EDUCAZIONE DELL'UOMO E FILOSOFIA DELLA CULTURA. Rome: Bulzoni, 1971. 217 p.

Groothoff, Hans Hermann. EINFUEHRUNG IN DIE ERZIEHUNGSWISSENSCHAFT. [Introduction to education]. With an essay on "Development and Education" by Linde Salber. Kastellaun, W. Ger.: Henn, 1975. 191 p.

Joly, Ralph Philip. THE HUMAN PERSON IN A PHILOSOPHY OF EDUCATION. The Hague: Mouton, 1965. 147 p.

Kant, Immanuel. EDUCATION. Translated by Annette Churton. Ann Arbor: University of Michigan Press, 1960. 121 p. Paperbound.

_____. THE EDUCATIONAL THEORY OF IMMANUEL KANT. Translated and edited with introduction by Edward Franklin Buchner. Philadelphia: J.B. Lippincott, 1904. Reprint. New York: AMS Press, 1971. 309 p.

This work is of very important historical interest. Kant actually influenced educational tradition much more through his philosophical speculations than through his pedagogical writing.

_____. REFLEXIONS SUR L'EDUCATION. Translated with introduction and notes by Alexis Philonenko. Paris: J. Vrin (Saint Amand, impr. C.-A. Bedu), 1966. 160 p.

_____. UEBER PAEDAGOGIK. [Education]. Edited by Otto Willmann. 3d ed. Leipzig, E. Ger.: Siegismund and Volkening, 1886. 128 p.

The original German text is accompanied by a fifty-seven page introduction and twelve pages of notes. Willmann ends his critical analysis of Kant's theory of education by referring to him as a model or paragon of self-education: "Ein Muster der Selbsterziehung."

McEvoy, J., ed. PHILOSOPHY AND TOTALITY. Belfast, Ireland: Department of Scholastic Philosophy, Queen's University, 1977. 147 p.

Maritain, Jacques. INTEGRAL HUMANISM: TEMPORAL AND SPIRITUAL PROBLEMS OF A NEW CHRISTENDOM. Translated from French by Joseph W. Evans. Notre Dame, Ind.: Notre Dame University Press, 1973. 308 p.

_____. TRUE HUMANISM. Translated from French by M.R. Adamson. 1941. Westport, Conn.: Greenwood Press, 1970. 304 p.

Molari, Alfredo. PEDAGOGIA DELLO SPIRITO. Cagliari, Italy: Editrice Sarda Fossataro, 1974. 394 p.

The contents include truth in education, educational psychology, educational teleology, and didactic methods.

Mourant, John Arthur. AUGUSTINE ON IMMORTALITY. Villanova, Pa.: Villanova University, 1969. 138 p.

Nash, Paul, et al., eds. THE EDUCATED MAN: STUDIES IN THE HISTORY OF EDUCATIONAL THOUGHT. New York: John Wiley and Sons, 1965. 421 p.

The philosophical visions of Plato, Isocrates, Zeno, Augustine, Aquinas, Erasmus, Comenius, Locke, Rousseau, Huxley, Marx, Dewey, Eliot, Buber, and Skinner are represented within an understanding of their ideas about education. Each interpretative essay is introduced by a biographical statement and followed by a very useful bibliographical note.

Phenix, Philip H. REALMS OF MEANING: A PHILOSOPHY OF THE CURRICULUM FOR GENERAL EDUCATION. New York: McGraw-Hill, 1964. xvi, 391 p.

Part 1 describes the search for meaning and human nature. The fundamental patterns of meaning are discussed in part 2: symbolics, empirics, aesthetics, synnoetics, ethics, synoptics. Part 3 presents a philosophy of the curriculum for general education.

Pleines, Juergen-Eckhardt. MENSCH UND ERZIEHUNG. [Man and education]. Kastellaun, W. Ger.: Henn, 1976. 323 p.

The eight studies, previously published between 1964 and 1975, together with two never before published concentrate on the relationship between philosophy and the science of education.

Poeggeler, Franz, ed. INNERLICHKEIT UND ERZIEHUNG. [Interiority and education]. Freiburg, W. Ger.: Herder, 1964. 356 p.

These essays concentrate on the mutual relationships that necessarily exist among education, philosophy, and theology in both the theoretical and practical aspects of human refinement.

Rich, John Martin. HUMANISTIC FOUNDATIONS OF EDUCATION. Worthington, Ohio: C.A. Jones Publishing, 1971. x, 342 p.

Ritzel, Wolfgang. DIE VIELHEIT DER PAEDAGOGISCHEN THEORIEN UND
DIE EINHEIT DER PAEDAGOGIK. [The plurality of pedagogical theories and
the unity of education]. Wuppertal, W. Ger.: Henn, 1968. 193 p.

Robb, James H. MAN AS INFINITE SPIRIT. Milwaukee, Wis.: Marquette
University Press, 1973. 57 p.

> Robb examines Maritain's conception of man and his specific excel-
> lence as a being of thought and love.

Roessner, Lutz. ERZIEHUNGSWISSENSCHAFT UND KRITISCHE PAEDAGOGIK.
[Education in its scientific and critical aspects]. Stuttgart, Berlin, Cologne,
and Mainz: Kohlhammer, 1974. 117 p.

Rosmini Serbati, Antonio. SULL'UNITA DELL'EDUCAZIONE. Edited by M.
Casotti. 5th ed. Brescia, Italy: La Scuola, 1968. xxi, 142 p.

Roth, Robert J. JOHN DEWEY AND SELF-REALIZATION. Englewood Cliffs,
N.J.: Prentice-Hall, 1962. 152 p.

> This scrutiny of Dewey's thinking finds a real possibility of the
> transcendent in the Deweyan conception of community and progress.
> This view is not generally shared by those who agree that Dewey's
> naturalism explicitly denies the transcendental.

Schadt, Armin L. A COUNTERFEIT REALITY: THE EDUCATION OF POST-
FAUSTIAN MAN. North Quincy, Mass.: Christopher Publishing House, 1975.
98 p.

Wrightsman, Lawrence S. ASSUMPTIONS ABOUT HUMAN NATURE: A SOCIAL-
PSYCHOLOGICAL APPROACH. Monterey, Calif.: Wadsworth Publishing,
Brooks/Cole Publishing, 1974. 298 p. Paperbound.

> This ten-year study indicates that the scientific study of psychology
> and sociology has promoted certain notable assumptions about human
> nature and overlooked others. The review of historically prominent
> speculations in Western civilization about human nature and the
> analysis of how they developed and may be changed offer unusual
> but rewarding approaches to the pivotal question of man in one's
> philosophy of education. The references are replete with challenges
> to reexamine one's own positions.

Zoepfl, Helmut. BILDUNG UND ERZIEHUNG ANGESICHT DER ENDLICH-
KEIT DES MENSCHEN. [Intellectual and moral education viewed from human
finality]. Donauworth, W. Ger.: Auer, 1967. 208 p.

G 4: HUMAN INTELLECTIVE POWERS

Ballauff, Theodor. PHILOSOPHISCHE BERGRUENDUNGEN DER PAEDAGOGIK. DIE FRAGE NACH URSPRUNG UND MASS DER BILDUNG. [Philosophical foundations of education: an inquiry into the source and nature of liberal education]. Berlin: Duncker und Humblot, 1966. 246 p.

Dearden, R.F.; Hirst, P.H.; Peters, R.S., eds. EDUCATION AND THE DEVELOPMENT OF REASON. 3 vols. London: Routledge and Kegan Paul, 1975. 166 p.; 258 p.; 148 p.

Dixon, Keith, ed. PHILOSOPHY OF EDUCATION AND THE CURRICULUM. Oxford; New York: Pergamon Press, 1972. 205 p.

Heydorn, Heinz Joachim. ZU EINER NEUFASSUNG DES BILDUNGSBEGRIFFS. [A new perspective on the concept of liberal education]. Frankfort on the Main, W. Ger.: Suhrkamp, 1972. 150 p.

Lichtenstein, Ernst, and Groothoff, Hans Hermann, eds. PAIDEIA. DIE GRUNGLAGEN D. EUROP. BILDUNGSDENKENS IM GRIECH.-ROM. ALTERTUM. [Paideia: the foundations of European educational thought in Classical Greece and Rome]. Hannover, Berlin, Darmstadt, Dortmund: Schroedel, 1970.

This series of books on education problems is published sporadically.

Livingstone, Sir Richard Winn. EDUCATION AND THE SPIRIT OF THE AGE. Bath, Engl.: Chivers, 1973. viii, 114 p.

Mommsen, Friedrich Jens. ERZIEHUNG, BILDUNG, RELIGION. [Refinement, education, religion]. Frankfort on the Main, Berlin, and Munich: Diesterweg, 1969. 120 p.

Mommsen considers education from both a professional and an evangelical standpoint.

Murray, John Courtney. "On the Future of Humanistic Education." In HUMANISTIC EDUCATION AND WESTERN CIVILIZATION, edited by Arthur A. Cohen in honor of the 65th birthday of Robert M. Hutchins, pp. 231-47. New York: Holt, Rinehart and Winston, 1964. Excerpted in CRITIC 22 (February, March 1964): 37-43.

Niblett, William Roy. EDUCATION AND THE MODERN MIND. London: Faber and Faber, 1967. 155 p.

Novak, Joseph D. A THEORY OF EDUCATION. Ithaca, N.Y.: Cornell University Press, 1977. 336 p.

Part 1 overviews the theory of education and its implications for schooling from the philosophical stance of Stephen Toulmin and Thomas Kuhn. The philosophical basis for education is explained in chapter 2 in terms of the problem of knowledge, human understanding, the use of knowledge, and cognitive learning. Later chapters include the theories of David Ausubel, Jean Piaget, and Robert Gagne in opposition to Skinnerian behaviorism.

Pinar, William, ed. CURRICULUM THEORIZING: THE RECONCEPTUALISTS. Berkeley, Calif.: McCutchan Publishing, 1975. xiv, 452 p.

This text introduces existentialism and phenomenology to the study of the curriculum in order to provide conceptual tools by which to understand the human experience of education. Having an intellectual heritage in the humanities, the postcritical reconceptualists address themselves to the reality of internal experience. The essays by Pinar, introducing the divisions of the text, ought to be studied by all interested in curricular studies.

Scholz, Guenter. CONVERSIO MENTIS ALS BILDUNGSPRINZIP. Vienna: Verl. Notring, 1972. 225 p.

The arguments are drawn from Saint Augustine's SOLILOQUIA and CONFESSIONES. These should be studied with Saint Augustine's DE MAGISTRO.

Shaffer, John B.F. HUMANISTIC PSYCHOLOGY. Englewood Cliffs, N.J.: Prentice-Hall, 1978. 224 p.

Ranging from rational approaches to the more mystical, Shaffer relates humanistic psychology to the socio-political movements of the last two decades and explores its philosophical background chiefly in existential-phenomenology. His humanistic theory of personality and approach to education actually move toward a science of being.

Shermis, Sherwin Samuel. "On Becoming an Intellectual Discipline." PHI DELTA KAPPAN 44 (November 1962): 84-86.

G 5: HUMAN AFFECTIVE POWERS

Augustine, Saint Aurelius. THE TEACHER. THE FREE CHOICE OF THE WILL. GRACE AND FREE WILL. Translated from Latin by Robert P. Russell. Washington, D.C.: Catholic University of America Press, 1968. vii, 331 p.

Deeb, Norman. CLOUD NINE: A SEMINAR ON EDUCATIONAL PHILOSOPHY. New York: Philosophical Library, 1975. xiv, 118 p.

Fromm, Erich. BEYOND THE CHAINS OF ILLUSION: MY ENCOUNTER WITH MARX AND FREUD. New York: Simon and Schuster, 1962. 182 p.; Pocket Books, 1963. 198 p.

Kurtz, Paul. EXUBERANCE: A PHILOSOPHY OF HAPPINESS. New York: Prometheus Books, 1977. 178 p.

Lombardi, Franco. SENSO DELLA PEDAGOGIA. 2d ed. rev. Rome: A. Armando, 1963. 245 p. Appendix: "Philosophy of March Education."

Piaget, Jean. THE SCIENCE OF EDUCATION AND THE PSYCHOLOGY OF THE CHILD. Translated from French by Derek Coltman. New York: Orion Press, 1970; Viking Press, 1971. 186 p.

Solomon, Robert C. THE PASSIONS: THE MYTH AND NATURE OF HUMAN EMOTION. New York: Doubleday Anchor Books, 1977. xxv, 448 p.

Stanage, Sherman M. "Meaning and Value: Human Action and Matrices of Relevance in Philosophies of Education." EDUCATIONAL THEORY 26, no. 1 (1976): 53-71.

> Schutz, Austin, Ortega y Gasset, and Collingwood have articulated different phenomenological and philosophical styles and views of human action in reference to the problem of relevance that are of the greatest significance to philosophies of education. This essay is directed toward continuing their work.

Wilson, John. EDUCATION IN RELIGION AND THE EMOTIONS. London: Heinemann Educational Group; New York: Humanities Press, 1971. xi, 268 p.

G 6: HUMAN AESTHETIC POWERS

Gilson, Etienne. THE ARTS OF THE BEAUTIFUL. New York: Charles Scribner's Sons, 1965. 189 p.

> For Gilson, the arts of the beautiful are those whose proper end is to produce things of beauty. Thus, he stresses the poietic arts, poietic being, and finally approaches the threshold of the metapoietic and the sacred.

Hardison, O.B., ed. THE QUEST FOR IMAGINATION: ESSAYS IN TWENTIETH CENTURY AESTHETIC CRITICISM. Cleveland and London: Press of Case Western Reserve University, 1971. xiv, 286 p.

> Twelve distinguished authors provide a cross section of an aesthetic tradition in order to find answers to such questions as the nature of literary experience, the form and function of works of literature,

the place of literature in culture, and its relation to politics and ethics. Each author states his position on his own terms.

Smith, Ralph Alexander, ed. AESTHETIC CONCEPTS AND EDUCATION. Urbana: University of Illinois Press, 1970. xv, 455 p.

Terzi, Carlo. FENELON. LA PERSONALITA E L'ATTUALITA DEL PENSIERO EDUCATIVO. Rome: Ciranna, 1971. vii, 157 p.

Vecchi, Giovanni. IL CONCETTO DI PEDAGOGIA IN HEGEL: DALLA EDUCAZIONE ESTETICA ALLA FORMAZIONE FILOSOFICA DELL'UOMO. Milan: Mursia, 1975. 202 p.

G7: THE PROBLEM OF VALUES—ETHICS

Aron, Israela Ettenberg. "Response to N.C. Bhattacharya." EDUCATIONAL THEORY 27, no. 2 (1977): 153-55.

Bhattacharya's critique does not hold because Dewey's valuation method is unnaturally made to fit philosophical traditions unacceptable to Dewey and assumptions have been made about the nature of moral philosophy which Dewey has explicitly denied.

Dalcourt, Gerard J. "The Pragmatist and Situationist Approach to Ethics." THOUGHT 51, no. 201 (1976): 135-46.

The moral theories of Dewey and Fletcher are the result not so much of the pragmatic method itself as of the different metaphysical stances which they adopt. Hence, moralists need a solid metaphysics from which to work and ought to make clear and explicit how their moral theories derive from their metaphysics.

Dewey, John. THE MORAL WRITINGS OF JOHN DEWEY. Edited with introduction and notes by James Gouinlock. New York: Hafner Press, 1976. lvi, 276 p.

Drinan, Robert F., ed. THE RIGHT TO BE EDUCATED. Foreword by Arthur J. Goldberg. Washington, D.C.: Corpus Books, 1968. xv, 271 p.

These studies commemorate the twentieth anniversary of the adoption by the United Nations of the universal declaration of human rights, 10 December 1948.

Granfield, Patrick. "Contemporary Prophecy: The Solzhenitsyn Case." THOUGHT 50, no. 198 (1955): 227-46.

Solzhenitsyn's crusade for truth, freedom, justice, and other human rights reveals him to be a contemporary prophet--a living witness

to the Christian message. He reminds the world of its spiritual
destiny, its responsibility to preserve human rights, and its need
to affirm the truth no matter how painful. This means fortitude and
self-denial: "The price of cowardice will only be evil; we shall
reap courage and victory only when we dare to make sacrifices"
(Solzhenitsyn in his Nobel lecture, p. 246).

Ho, Thomas C.K. A CRITICAL ANALYSIS OF THE PHILOSOPHICAL FOUN-
DATIONS OF VALUE THEORIES AS PRESENTED IN PHILOSOPHY OF EDUCA-
TION TEXTBOOKS PUBLISHED BETWEEN 1946 and 1962. Ann Arbor, Mich.:
University Microfilms, 1965. 251 p.

> The study deals with three fundamental problems: concept of value,
> sources of value, and kinds and hierarchy of value. Noteworthy
> is the fact that the mere use of the term "value" does not mean
> scholars are investigating the same subject matter.

Inlow, Gail M. VALUES IN TRANSITION: A HANDBOOK. New York:
John Wiley and Sons, 1972. 205 p. Bibliogs. Also paperbound.

> Inlow introduces the beginner to an examination of values and
> cultural change in regard to economics, politics, science, tech-
> nology, philosophy, the New Left, and the black community. The
> diversity of topics and opinion is reflected in the useful bibliog-
> raphies.

McLean, George F., ed. FREEDOM. Proceedings of the American Catholic
Philosophical Association, vol. 50. Washington, D.C.: Catholic University
of America, 1976. 247 p. Paperbound.

> This collection of essays contains philosophical reflections on the
> meaning and structure of freedom, the existential nature of freedom,
> the social realization of freedom, and special studies by Debra B.
> Bergoffen (Cartesian doubt), Jay Newman (Cardinal Newman),
> William J. Gavin (William James), and Mary B. Mahowald (femi-
> nism). Discussions advert to the thought of Heisenberg, Sartre,
> de Beauvoir, Jaspers, Bergson, Whitehead, Brownson, Newman,
> and James that have educational implications.

Phillips, Denis Charles. THEORIES, VALUES AND EDUCATION. Melbourne:
Melbourne University Press, 1971. ix, 84 p.

Smith, Philip G., ed. THEORIES OF VALUE AND PROBLEMS IN EDUCATION.
Urbana: University of Illinois Press, 1970. 232 p.

> The essays are by Aiken, Lewis, Taylor, Butler, Price, Beck,
> Frankena, Broudy, J.F. Smith, Clayton, Twain, Soltis, Scheffler,
> Peters, Piaget, Sleeper, and T.D. Perry.

Taylor, Harold. ON EDUCATION AND FREEDOM. Carbondale: Southern Illinois University Press, 1967. 320 p. Paperbound.

Taylor elaborates a philosophy of education and democracy in terms of human freedom.

G 8: THE PROBLEM OF THOUGHT AND LANGUAGE— PHILOSOPHICAL ANALYSIS

ARISTOTELES ARS RHETORICA. Edited by Rudolf Kassel. Berlin; New York: de Gruyter, 1976. xix, 259 p.

Text is in Greek, the preface and notes in Latin. This work may be compared with the Greek text edited by W.D. Ross, Clarendon Press, 1969.

Collins, K.T.; Downes, L.W.; Griffiths, S.R.; and Shaw, K.E. KEY WORDS IN EDUCATION. London: Longmans Group, 1973. 240 p.

Asserting that a profession cannot exist for long if its practice is not founded on a solid but dynamic theoretical structure, the authors help new readers find their way through the educational literature by defining terms and clarifying ideas. For them, education is very dependent for its growth and power on the established disciplines of philosophy, psychology, sociology, history, and mathematics.

D'Cruz, J.V., and Sheehan, P.J., eds. CONCEPTS IN EDUCATION: PHILOSOPHICAL STUDIES. Melbourne: Mercy Teachers' College, 1973. 96 p.

Denton, David E. THE LANGUAGE OF ORDINARY EXPERIENCE: A STUDY IN THE PHILOSOPHY OF EDUCATION. New York: Philosophical Library, 1970. 160 p.

Gilson, Etienne. LINGUISTIQUE ET PHILOSOPHIE: ESSAI SUR LES CONSTANTES PHILOSOPHIQUES DU LANGAGE. Paris: J. Vrin, 1969. 309 p.

Hospers, John. AN INTRODUCTION TO PHILOSOPHICAL ANALYSIS. 2d ed. London: Routledge and Kegan Paul; Englewood Cliffs, N.J.: Prentice-Hall, 1967. 629 p.

_____, ed. READING IN INTRODUCTORY PHILOSOPHICAL ANALYSIS. Englewood Cliffs, N.J.: Prentice-Hall, 1968. 387 p.

Scheffler, Israel. THE LANGUAGE OF EDUCATION. Springfield, Ill.: Charles C Thomas, 1960. x, 113 p. 9th Printing, 1974.

Philosophy of education ought to instruct the reader in the art of clarifying statements to prevent the confusion so often found in educational dialogue and writing. What may be more aptly called a logic of education offers models of procedure in the critical and systematic review of professional literature.

_____. "Toward an Analytic Philosophy of Education." HARVARD EDUCA-TIONAL REVIEW 24 (Fall 1954): 223-30.

Strawson, P.F. LOGICO-LINGUISTIC PAPERS. London: Methuen, 1971. viii, 251 p.

Ulich, Robert. PHILOSOPHY OF EDUCATION. New York: American Book, 1961. xiv, 286 p.

The first section treats of aims, the interpretation of man, ethics; the second examines religion, art, method, curriculum. In almost Hegelian fashion, Ulich would join humanism and religion in a kind of pantheistic or monistic philosophy of education. He suggests a schooling born of justice, love, and reverence for life.

G TR: THE PROBLEM OF GOD—THEOLOGY AND RELIGION

Abbott, Walter M., and Gallagher, Joseph, eds. THE DOCUMENTS OF VATICAN II. With notes and comments by Catholic, Protestant, and Orthodox authorities. New York: America Press, 1966. 792 p. Paperbound.

A fundamental concern of the council is the integration of Christian education into the whole pattern of human life since the church is intended to be in and for the world. These authoritative documents are crucial to any understanding of the present Catholic approach to modern life and thought. The index offers quick entry into all sixteen declarations and to those major themes of specific import to the philosophy of education.

Augustine, Saint Aurelius. CHRISTIAN INSTRUCTION. Translated from Latin by John J. Gavigan. 1947. Washington, D.C.: Catholic University of America Press, 1966.

The volume also contains ADMONITION AND GRACE translated by John Courtney Murray, CHRISTIAN COMBAT translated by Robert P. Russell, FAITH, HOPE, AND CHARITY translated by Bernard M. Peeples.

_____. CONCERNING THE CITY OF GOD AGAINST THE PAGANS. New translation by Henry Bettenson with introduction by David Knowles. Harmonds-worth, Engl.: Penguin Books, 1972. 1,097 p.

Black, Hubert P. RELIGIOUS AND PHILOSOPHICAL FOUNDATIONS OF EDUCATION. Cleveland, Tenn.: Pathway Press, 1967. 118 p.

Buber, Martin. KINGSHIP OF GOD. Translated by Richard Schiemann from 3d German ed. London: Allen and Unwin, 1967. 222 p.

> Although many thinkers in the Hebrew tradition find Buber's thinking somewhat unorthodox, this work is required study for a better understanding of the Judaic philosophy of education that believes in God as the creator and presence immanent in all reality.

Byrne, Herbert W. A CHRISTIAN APPROACH TO EDUCATION: EDUCATIONAL THEORY AND APPLICATION. Milford, Mich.: Mott Media, 1977. 372 p.

Cobb, John B., Jr. THE STRUCTURE OF CHRISTIAN EXISTENCE. Philadelphia: Westminster Press, 1967. 160 p.

Donlan, Thomas Cajetan. THEOLOGY AND EDUCATION. Dubuque, Iowa: Wm. C. Brown, 1952. 134 p.

> "No philosophy can make an adequate statement of Catholic education. . . . There is only a theology of Catholic education" (Footnote no. 5, p. 18).

Driscoll, Justin A. "A Philosophy of Catholic Education in a Time of Change." CATHOLIC SCHOOL JOURNAL 67, no. 9 (1967): 29-33. Reprinted in READINGS IN THE FOUNDATIONS OF EDUCATION, edited by James C. Stone and Frederick W. Schneider, pp. 485-94. 2d ed. New York: Thomas Y. Crowell, 1971.

> The author sketches, from the Declaration on Christian Education and other decrees of Vatican II, basic principles of Catholic education in terms of the individual and the community. Driscoll believes Catholic educators must take a stand on fundamentals, develop a positive plan for renewal, and remain steadfastly aware of the unchangeable in a changing world.

Eakin, Frank E. RELIGION AND WESTERN CULTURE: SELECTED ISSUES. Washington, D.C.: University Press of America, 1977. 342 p. Paperbound.

> Eakin reevaluates the liberating possibilities of the Judeo-Christian tradition by discussing what logically ensues from frequently held conceptions about biblical faith. His concern for misconceiving such faith has an indirect but still important bearing on any philosophy of education that may be drawn, in whole or in part, from the revelations of the Bible.

Esser, Wolfgang G. STUDIEN ZUR SAEKULARISIERUNG UND RELIGIOSITAET. [Studies in regard to secularization and religiousness]. Dusseldorf, W. Ger.: Patmos-Verlag, 1975. 200 p.

The author provides an intellectual background and analysis for the anthropological foundations of religious education. Probing philosophical, theological, and religious sources, Esser develops a theory of religious education that is existentially and sociologically oriented toward present needs and conditions.

Feifel, Erich, ed. HANDBUCH DER RELIGIONSPAEDAGOGIK. [Manual of religious education]. 3 vols. Gutersloh, W. Ger.: Gutersloher Verlagshaus Mohn; Zurich; Einsiedeln, Switz.; and Cologne: Benziger, 1973-75.

Volume 1: RELIGIOESE BILDUNG UND ERZIEHUNG. THEORIE UND FAKTOREN. 1973. 392 p.

Volume 1 explores intellectual and moral education in their reciprocal relationships as to both theory and practice. Religious education is viewed from the prospect of an emancipated humanity. [See DEUTSCHE BIBLIOGRAPHIE Heft 2/1974 p. 257]

Volume 2: DIDAKTIK DES RELIGIONSUNTERRICHTS. WISSENSCHAFTSTHEORIE. 1974. 397 p.

Volume 2 examines the philosophy of religious education in terms of fundamental principles, problems, goals, methods, models, and functions. It also discusses the theory and practice of the curriculum. [See DEUTSCHE BIBLIOGRAPHIE Heft 6/1974 p. 971]

Volume 3: RELIGIONSPAEDAGOGISCHE HANDLUNGSFELDER IN KIRCHLICHER VERANTWORTUNG. 1975. 482 p.

Volume 3 covers, in thirty-seven essays, the themes of intellectual and moral education as an obligation of the Church, the religious and educative values of the sacraments as service to God, spirituality, and responsibility.

Hoye, William J. ACTUALITAS OMNIUM ACTUUM: MAN'S BEATIFIC VISION OF GOD AS APPREHENDED BY THOMAS AQUINAS. Meisenheim am Glan: Hain, 1975. 363 p.

Moore, Donald J. MARTIN BUBER: PROPHET OF RELIGIOUS SECULARISM. Philadelphia: Jewish Publication Society of America, 1974. xxviii, 264.

In the words of Quentin Lauer, Martin Buber is not the prophet of religious secularism but of a kind of very religious religion which cannot be poured into any preconceived religious mold.

Murray, John Courtney. "The Christian Idea of Education." In THE CHRISTIAN IDEA OF EDUCATION: PAPERS AND DISCUSSION BY WILLIAM G. POLLARD AND OTHERS, edited by Edmund Fuller, pp. 152-63. New Haven: Yale University Press, 1957.

Phenix, Philip H. RELIGIOUS CONCERNS IN CONTEMPORARY EDUCATION: A STUDY OF RECIPROCAL RELATIONS. New York: Teachers College, Columbia University, 1959. ix, 108 p.

Phenix gives criteria for finding a way through the complex problems of interrelating church, state, and school. He conceives religion as "ultimate concern." This perspective makes it possible to grasp the underlying and governing principles of the educative process and ultimately to attain genuine spiritual inwardness and depth of understanding.

Santos, Miguel. MISTAGOGIA. Rio de Janeiro, Brazil: Companhia Editora Americana, 1972. 125 p.

Seung, T.K. CULTURAL THEMATICS: THE FORMATION OF THE FAUSTIAN ETHOS. New Haven: Yale University Press, 1976. 283 p.

Seung outlines "the genesis of the modern, Protestant, linear and scientific sensibility out of the Medieval, Catholic, hierarchical, and allegorical sensibility." This can be interpreted to mean the emergence of will, individuality, literal fact, and monism over intellectuality, community, allegory, and dualism, according to Paul Bove's review in THOUGHT 52, no. 204 (1977): 206-8.

Turner, Dean. COMMITMENT TO CARE: AN INTEGRATED PHILOSOPHY OF SCIENCE, EDUCATION, AND RELIGION. Old Greenwich, Conn.: Devin-Adair, 1978. xv, 415 p.

G NS: THE PROBLEM OF THE COSMOS—PHYSICAL AND MATHEMATICAL SCIENCES

Bertalanffy, Ludwig von. GENERAL SYSTEMS THEORY: FOUNDATIONS, DEVELOPMENT, APPLICATIONS. Rev. ed. New York: George Braziller, 1973. xxiv, 295 p.

_____. PERSPECTIVES ON GENERAL SYSTEMS THEORY. Edited by Edgar Taschdjian with foreword by Maria von Bertalanffy and Ervin Laszlo. New York: George Braziller, 1976. 183 p. Paperbound.

Sanguineti, Juan Jose. LA FILOSOFIA DE LA CIENCIA SEGUN SANTO TOMAS. Pamplona, Spain: Ediciones Universidad de Navarra, S.A., 1977. 371 p.

Whitehead, Alfred North. ADVENTURES OF IDEAS. 1933. New York: Free Press, 1967. x, 307 p. Paperbound.

Zeigler, Earle F. PHILOSOPHICAL FOUNDATIONS FOR PHYSICAL, HEALTH, AND RECREATION EDUCATION. Englewood Cliffs, N.J.: Prentice-Hall, 1964. xvii, 356 p.

G HS: THE PROBLEM OF HUMAN SOCIETY—HUMAN AND SOCIAL SCIENCES

Ash, Maurice, ed. WHO ARE THE PROGRESSIVES NOW? AN ACCOUNT OF AN EDUCATIONAL CONFRONTATION. London: Routledge and Kegan Paul, 1969. x, 253 p.

> These statements, extracts from the background papers prepared for the Darlington Colloquy held in April 1964, are included in the discussion on rural sociology.

Bigge, Morris L. POSITIVE RELATIVISM: AN EMERGENT EDUCATIONAL PHILOSOPHY. New York: Harper and Row, 1971. x, 182 p. Paperbound.

> Bigge enters the province of educational philosophy through the portal of psychology. Though many of the implications are drawn from the thought of Dewey, Bigge champions a kind of pragmatism of his own.

Boettiger, Helmut Hans Ludwig. ERZIEHUNG FUER EINE NEUE WIRTSCHAFTS-ORDNUNG. [Education for a new world economic order]. Wiesbaden, W. Ger.: Campaigner Publications Deutschland; Berlin: Freie Universitaet, 1976. 223 p.

> Boettiger explores the sociological foundations of education for a new social and economic order. He draws attention to the disparity between practical education and educational theory in its broader and universal compass. A possible solution may be found in education for a new world economic order.

Bowen, James, and Hobson, Peter R. THEORIES OF EDUCATION: STUDIES OF SIGNIFICANT INNOVATION IN WESTERN EDUCATIONAL THOUGHT. Sydney and New York: Wiley and Sons Australasia, 1974. ix, 448 p.

Dewey, John. DEWEY ON EDUCATION. Edited by Martin S. Dworkin. Classics in Education, no. 3. New York: Teachers College, Bureau of Publications, 1959. 134 p.

> This readily accessible edition contains Dewey's "My Pedagogic Creed" (pp. 19-32), "The School and Society" (pp. 33-90), "The Child and the Curriculum" (pp. 91-111), "Progressive Education and the Science of Education" (pp. 113-26), together with his introduction to Elsie Ripley Clapp's THE USE OF RESOURCES IN EDUCATION.

Kahn, Herman, and Bruce-Briggs, B. THINGS TO COME: THINKING ABOUT THE SEVENTIES AND EIGHTIES. New York: Macmillan, 1972. 262 p.

> The study of the future, developed in part by the Hudson Institute, analyzes both possibilities and probabilities of what may happen within the next two decades. Cultural revolution may occur with

the beginning of the second millenium though the likelihood favors a compromise culture fashioned from traditional, countercultural, and emerging values.

Kneller, George Frederick. EDUCATION AND ECONOMIC THOUGHT. New York: John Wiley and Sons, 1968. xiii, 139 p.

Mathewson, Robert Hendry. A STRATEGY FOR AMERICAN EDUCATION. Harper and Brothers, 1957. xv, 296 p.

Mathewson seeks to reconcile individual and social needs in a psycho-sociological theory and strategy of education. He conceives democracy as the educative society most favorable for the attainment of ultimate value, namely, the creative life of good and joyous persons.

Michel, Gerhard, and Schaller, Klaus, eds. PAEDAGOGIK UND POLITIK. [Education and politics]. Ratingen, W. Ger.; Kastellaun, W. Ger.; and Dusseldorf, W. Ger.: Henn, 1972. 91 p.

These seven lectures were given at a Comenius-Colloquium held in 1970 at the pedagogical institute of Ruhr University at Bochum. They survey the latest thinking about John Amos Comenius and his contributions today.

Niermann, Johannes. SOZIALISTISCHE PAEDAGOGIK IN DER DDR. [Socialistic education in the German Democratic Republic]. Heidelberg, W. Ger.: Quelle and Meyer, 1972. Bibliog. 112 p.

Niermann examines the foundations of socialistic educational theory, the object of education in respect to the other disciplines, and the sociological, political, and anthropological dimensions of the educative process with the intent of mounting a thoroughgoing criticism of the socialistic philosophy of education. The author includes a bibliography (pp. 107-12).

Ottaway, Andrew Kenneth Cosway. EDUCATION AND SOCIETY: AN INTRODUCTION TO THE SOCIOLOGY OF EDUCATION. Introduction by W.O. Lester Smith. 2d ed. rev. London: Routledge and Kegan Paul, 1966. 232 p. Paperbound.

Ottaway derives a sociology of education from the aims, methods, institutions, administration, and curricula of education with special consideration for the economic, political, religious, social, and cultural agents of the society through which these function. It is a work basic to the understanding of educational sociology.

Perkinson, Henry J. THE IMPERFECT PANACEA: AMERICAN FAITH IN EDUCATION, 1865-1976. 2d ed. New York: Random House, 1977. 257 p.

Pinilla, Antonio. "Cultural Crises and Educational Change." In CRISIS AND CHANGE IN TEACHER EDUCATION, pp. 17-18. Washington, D.C.: International Council for Teaching, 1971. Paperbound.

> Philosophical and historical evidence shows the functional dependence that exists between (1) political, legal, economic, social, military and educational action and organization, and (2) theological, philosophical, and scientific ideas. Pinilla observes rather profoundly that tension in the western world rises from the conflicting attitudes of pragmatism and a social philosophy inspired in the Christian values of love and generosity. In the Socialist world, inner contradictions exist between the ideals of social justice and the implications and shortcomings of totalitarianism.

Raman, Nayar R. PHILOSOPHICAL AND SOCIOLOGICAL BASES OF EDUCATION. 2d ed. Trivandrum: College Book House, 1971. ix, 229 p.

Warren, Donald R., et al. STANDARDS FOR ACADEMIC AND PROFESSIONAL INSTRUCTION. Ames: Iowa State University, 1978. 13 p. Reprinted from EDUCATIONAL STUDIES 8, no. 4 (1977-78): 329-42.

> The American Educational Studies Association Task Force on Academic Studies takes the position that the foundations of education have for their purpose the development of interpretive, normative, and critical perspectives on education, including the nonschooling enterprises.

G AC: THE PROBLEM OF ART AND CULTURE—HUMANE ARTS AND LETTERS

Beardsley, Monroe C. THE POSSIBILITY OF CRITICISM. Detroit: Wayne State University Press, 1970. 119 p.

Gilson, Etienne. THE ARTS OF THE BEAUTIFUL. New York: Charles Scribner's Sons, 1965. 189 p.

Gulbinas, Konstantin. DAS PAEDAGOGISCHE LEBENSWERK DER LITAUISCHEN DICHTERIN MARIJA PECKAUSKAITE. [The educational lifework of the Lithuanian poet Marja Peckauskeite]. Paderborn, Munich, and Wien: F. Schoeningh, 1971. 173 p.

> Gulbinas comments on the outstanding characteristics of this poet's educational philosophy and highlights the contributions of Marja Peckauskeite as educator and teacher as well as her insights into the perennial questions of education. The bibliography is on pp. 161-64.

Hook, Sidney. EDUCATION AND THE TAMING OF POWER. La Salle, Ill.: Open Court Publishing, 1973; London: Alcove Press, 1974. xiii, 310 p.

James of Rusholm, Sir Eric John Francis James, Baron. PLATO'S IDEAS ON ART AND EDUCATION. York, Engl.: William Sessions for the University of York, 1975. 21 p.

Nuttall, A.D. A COMMON SKY: PHILOSOPHY AND THE LITERARY IMAGI-NATION. Berkeley and Los Angeles: University of California Press, 1974. 298 p.

Nuttall records the debate between the soul and the body and between words and things over several centuries of literati, artists, and philosophers. This debate naturally originates from the rational personality of men who want not only to discover meaning, but to know the facts. The work is an intellectual feast, ordered in rather unusual fashion, stimulating and refreshing in its engagement with the worlds of mind, imagination, and being.

Pielow, Winfried. DICHTUNG UND DIDAKTIK. [Poetry and education]. 4th ed. Bochum, W. Ger.: F. Kamp, 1969. 146 p.

Tolstoi, Lev Nikolaevich. TOLSTOY ON EDUCATION. Translated from Russian by Leo Wiener. Introduction by Reginald D. Archambault. Chicago: University of Chicago Press, 1967. xviii, 360 p.

Chapter 11
PHILOSOPHY

If Donohue's description receives the reader's consent that the philosophy of education is "an effort to relate a generalized discussion of the aims, curricula, methods, and agencies of formal schooling to a philosophy of life and value,"[1] then educators had better become acquainted with some phases of educational philosophy and philosophers of education with the study of philosophy itself. The reason for this is given by Broudy: the philosophical literature is a store-house of the "concepts, distinctions, and arguments that have been strickingly useful and illuminating when applied to the description, analysis, clarification, interpretation, evaluation, and criticism of educational practices, problems and issues."[2] Philosophy contributes to education by deepening speculative interests and methods, by engendering deeper intellectual insight, by developing a total world view. It assists educators in formulating their problems and in delimiting the fields of inquiry. It supplies a systematic structure, it grounds diverse meaning and activities in fundamental principles, it promotes the unification of education within itself and with all the sciences. Philosophy transforms education into the pursuit of wisdom.

P 1: EPISTEMOLOGY—THE PHILOSOPHY OF KNOWING

Ahern, Denis M., et al. STUDIES IN EPISTEMOLOGY: ESSAYS. Oxford: Blackwell, 1975. 168 p.

Aristotle. POSTERIOR ANALYTICS. Translated from Greek with notes by Jonathan Barnes. Oxford: Clarendon Press, 1975. xix, 277 p.

---

1. John W. Donohue, ST. THOMAS AQUINAS AND EDUCATION (New York: Random House, 1968), p. 58.

2. Harry S. Broudy et al. PHILOSOPHY OF EDUCATION: AN ORGANIZATION OF TOPICS AND SELECTED SOURCES (Urbana: University of Illinois Press, 1967), p. 19.

Ayer, Alfred Jules. THE PROBLEM OF KNOWLEDGE. Harmondsworth, Engl.: Penguin Books; London: Macmillan, 1956. 258 p. Paperbound.

Benton, Ted. PHILOSOPHICAL FOUNDATIONS OF THE THREE SOCIOLOGIES. London: Routledge and Kegan Paul, 1977. 240 p.

> Benton evaluates critically empiricist and positivist theories of knowledge in respect to the philosophy of the social sciences. The book begins with the Kantian critique of empiricism, as a source of the antipositivist and antinaturalist approach to the social disciplines, and concludes to the possibility of a realist foundation of sociology. This text is valuable to all students interested in the philosophical validation of sociological principles.

Chomsky, Noam. CARTESIAN LINGUISTICS: A CHAPTER IN THE HISTORY OF RATIONALIST THOUGHT. New York: Harper and Row, 1966. xl, 119 p.

_____. CHOMSKY: SELECTED READINGS. Edited by J.P.B. Aloen and Paul Van Buren. London and New York: Oxford University Press, 1971. 166 p.

Copleston, Frederick Charles. "Philosophical Knowledge." In his PHILOSO-PHERS AND PHILOSOPHIES, pp. 1-16. London: Search Press; New York: Barnes and Noble, 1976.

> Bertrand Russell has remarked that philosophy is the no man's land between theology and science. While there does seem to be some uncertainty about the frontiers of this land of philosophy, Copleston does not hesitate to chart some of the terrain.

Cowan, Philip A. "Genetic Epistemology." In his PIAGET: WITH FEELING, pp. 373-99. New York: Holt, Rinehart and Winston, 1978.

> After considering Piaget's critique of rationalism, empiricism, and the Kantian tradition, Cowan explores the subject matter and methods of genetic epistemology together with Piaget's philosophical and psychological contributions.

Gadamer, Hans-Georg. PHILOSOPHICAL HERMENEUTICS. Translated and edited by David E. Linge. Berkeley and Los Angeles: University of California Press, 1977. 301 p. Also paperbound.

> After a valuable examination of the scope of hermeneutical reflec-tion, Gadamer looks at the philosophical foundations of the twen-tieth century from the aspects of phenomenology, existential phi-losophy, and philosophical hermeneutics.

Hare, R.M. ESSAYS ON PHILOSOPHIC METHOD. Berkeley and Los Angeles: University of California Press, 1972. 143 p.

Klauder, Francis J. THE WONDERS OF INTELLIGENCE: A STUDY OF HUMAN KNOWLEDGE. Quincy, Mass.: Christopher Publishing House, 1973. 154 p.

Lewis, Clarence Irving. AN ANALYSIS OF KNOWLEDGE AND VALUATION. 1946. La Salle, Ill.: Open Court, 1962. xxi, 568 p.

Polanyi, Michael. PERSONAL KNOWLEDGE: TOWARDS A POST-CRITICAL PHILOSOPHY. 2d ed. London: Routledge and Kegan Paul, 1962. 442 p.

Scientific knowledge is not all that objective. It can be harmonized with value judgments in a way to preserve in their respective excellencies both objective and subjective modes of knowledge.

Richardson, William J. HEIDEGGER: THROUGH PHENOMENOLOGY TO THOUGHT. 3d ed. The Hague: Martinus Nijhoff, 1974. xxix, 768 p.

This work is the definitive work acknowledged by Heidegger himself.

Russell, Bertrand. THE ART OF PHILOSOPHIZING AND OTHER ESSAYS. 1968. Totowa, N.J.: Littlefield, Adams, 1974. 119 p. Paperbound.

_____. AN INQUIRY INTO MEANING AND TRUTH. London: Allen and Unwin; New York: W.W. Norton, 1940. 352 p.

Schoepf, Alfred. AUGUSTINUS: EINF. IN SEIN PHILOSPHIERENS. Freiburg, Munich: Alber, 1970. 136 p.

Siegel, Harvey. "Piaget's Conception of Epistemology." EDUCATIONAL THEORY 28, no. 1 (1978): 16-22.

Siegel thinks Piaget has thoroughly obscured the clear and important distinction between the development-of-knowledge acquisition capacities and knowledge-claims appraisal which he prefers to designate as the proper subject matter of philosophical epistemology.

Steenberghen, Fernand van. EPISTEMOLOGY. Translated from French by Lawrence Moonan. New York: Fernhill House, 1971. 285 p.

Van Steenberghen has responded to the demands of modern critical philosophy by proving that Thomism is an organic system of philosophy, fully capable of meeting the most crucial requirements of modern thought. In his opinion, "Thomism is a strict philosophical system, well able to face up to the most brilliant systems of modern philosophy."

White, Alan R. TRUTH. Garden City, N.Y.: Doubleday, 1970. 150 p. Paperbound.

White seeks to clarify the notion of truth through an analysis of traditional and recent epistemological theories.

Wolff, Robert Paul. PHILOSOPHY: A MODERN ENCOUNTER. Englewood Cliffs, N.J.: Prentice-Hall, 1971. x, 613 p.

P 2: METAPHYSICS—THE PHILOSOPHY OF BEING

Adler, Mortimer J. PHILOSOPHER AT LARGE. New York: Macmillan, 1977. 329 p.

This intellectual autobiography describes Adler's surprise at finding that philosophy, as taught at Columbia University and elsewhere, had largely forgotten its own past and so had no idea that many of the problems it faced so agonizingly had already been answered. Then, to the astonishment of his peers and colleagues, Adler found missing answers in Aristotle and Saint Thomas Aquinas. Adler brings the philosopher of education into contact, and often sharp conflict, with powerful ideas that tend to unsettle one's complacencies. Yet, despite his admiration for deep, humane, fundamental principles of belief and action, Adler reveals little of his own.

Aquinas, St. Thomas, and Bonaventure, St. (John Fidenza). BONAVENTURE AND AQUINAS: ENDURING PHILOSOPHERS. Edited with introduction by Robert W. Shahan and Francis J. Kovach. Norman: University of Oklahoma Press, 1976. ix, 194 p.

Aristotle. METAPHYSICA. With critical notes by Werner Jaeger. 1957. Oxford: Clarendon Press, 1973. xxii, 312 p.

ARISTOTLE'S METAPHYSICS. Edited and translated from Greek by John Warrington. Introduction by Sir David Ross. Everyman's Library. London: Dent, 1970. xxvii, 388 p.

Bambrough, Renford, ed. NEW ESSAYS ON PLATO AND ARISTOTLE. London: Routledge and Kegan Paul; New York: Humanities Press, 1965. viii, 176 p.

_____. THE PHILOSOPHY OF ARISTOTLE. New York: New American Library, 1963. 432 p.

This is a new selection of texts with an introduction and commentary. The new translations are by A.E. Wardman and J.L. Creed.

Barral, Mary Rose. PROGRESSIVE NEUTRALISM: A PHILOSOPHICAL ASPECT OF AMERICAN EDUCATION. Louvain, Belgium: Editions Nauwelaerts, 1970. 140 p.

Barral defines neutralism as that doctrine which teaches there shall be no doctrines. She inquires into the philosophical presuppositions of neutralism, its implications, and its outcomes to discover that progressive neutralism leads only to decadence. This conclusion is forcefully enunciated to provoke "constructive discontent."

Berlin, Sir Isaiah. "The Hedgehog and the Fox." In his RUSSIAN THINKERS. New York: Viking Press, 1978.

Hedgehog thinkers (such as Dante, Plato, Lucretius, Pascal, Hegel, Dostoevsky, and Nietzsche) envision reality through a fundamental comprehensive conception. Foxes (such as Aristotle, Herodotus, Shakespeare, Erasmus, Montaigne, Goethe, Moliere, Pushkin, Balzac, and Joyce) understand reality at different, and sometimes simultaneously contradictory, levels or orders of reality. The essay concludes with an insightful study of Tolstoi.

Blewett, John, ed. JOHN DEWEY: HIS THOUGHT AND INFLUENCE. New York: Fordham University Press, 1960. xiv, 242 p.

This work contains a scholarly discussion by philosophers and theologians who find Dewey's naturalism basically unacceptable. The following are all discussed in terms of Dewey's thought: the genesis of his naturalism, democracy as religion, theory of knowledge, progressive education, the problem of technology, his ambivalent attitude toward history, process and experience, and his influence in China.

Bochenski, Innocentius M. CONTEMPORARY EUROPEAN PHILOSOPHY. Translated by Donald Nicholl and Karl A. Aschenbrenner from 2d rev. German ed. Berkeley and Los Angeles: University of California Press, 1974. xviii, 326 p. Also paperbound.

Brameld, Theodore. THE CLIMACTIC DECADES: MANDATE TO EDUCATION. Foreword by Kenneth D. Benne. New York: Praeger Publishers, 1970. xiv, 210 p.

Brameld seeks to harmonize, what to some seems to be, the irreconcilable polarities that have manifested themselves in the course of his philosophical development.

Brentano, Franz. ARISTOTLE AND HIS WORLD VIEW. Translated by Rolf George and Roderick M. Chisholm. Introduction by Roderick M. Chisholm. Berkeley and Los Angeles: University of California Press, 1977. 150 p.

Brentano sets forth the essential feature of Aristotle's thought systematically and as a unified whole. Of special importance to the educational philosopher are the essays on truth, intelligence, causality, teleology, interaction of mind and body, preparation for the world beyond, and the comparison of Aristotle's with other world views.

_____. ON THE SEVERAL SENSES OF BEING IN ARISTOTLE. Translated by Rolf A. George. Berkeley and Los Angeles: University of California Press, 1975. 210 p.

Broudy, Harry S. "Sartre's Existentialism and Education: A Bibliography." EDUCATIONAL THEORY 21, no. 2 (1971): 155-77.

Brumbaugh, Robert S., and Lawrence, Nathaniel M. PHILOSOPHERS ON EDUCATION. Boston: Houghton Mifflin, 1963. 211 p. Paperbound.

> The authors chose to examine the thought of two classical figures (Plato, Aristotle), two from the Enlightenment (Rousseau, Kant), and two who lived through the first half of the twentieth century (Dewey, Whitehead) because the philosophy of each of them includes an explicit philosophy of education and has had a great impact on convictions about man and his self-betterment in society.

Buber, Martin. MEETINGS. Edited with introduction and bibliography by Maurice Friedman. La Salle, Ill.: Open Court Publishing, 1973. 115 p.

> The book is important for Buber's final judgments and opinions.

Buckley, William F., ed. DID YOU EVER SEE A DREAM WALKING? American Conservative Thought in the Twentieth Century. Indianapolis: Bobbs-Merrill, 1970.

> Buckley gives a first-rate description of classical conservatism according to G. Wells, John Courtney Murray, F.S. Meyer, M. Oakeshott, A.J. Nock, M. Friedman, W. Kendall, J. Burnham, E. van den Haag, R. Kirk, C. Dawson, E. Voegelin, F.D. Wilhelmsen, and a host of others.

Cahn, Steven Mark. CLASSICS OF WESTERN PHILOSOPHY. Indianapolis: Hackett Publishing, 1977. xi, 1,007 p.

Clark, Mary T., ed. AN AQUINAS READER. Garden City, N.Y.: Doubleday, 1972. 600 p. Bibliog. Paperbound.

> This paperback offers texts and a useful index to some key ideas of Thomas Aquinas.

Copleston, Frederick Charles. CONTEMPORARY PHILOSOPHY: STUDIES OF LOGICAL POSITIVISM AND EXISTENTIALISM. Rev. ed. London: Search Press; Paramus, N.J.: Paulist/Newman Press, 1972. 230 p.

_____. "The History of Philosophy: Relativism and Recurrence." In his PHILOSOPHERS AND PHILOSOPHIES, pp. 17-28. London: Search Press; New York: Barnes and Noble, 1976.

In plotting the advance of what he thought to be the one perennial or true philosophy evolving through successive stages, Copleston grew aware of metahistorical problems which "arise not so much when one is actually writing history of philosophy as when one reflects on the nature and implications of this activity."

Cordaro, Raffaele. LA PEDAGOGIA NEI SUOI PRESUPPOSTI THEORETICI. Florence: Kursaal, 1968. 109 p.

Doig, James C. AQUINAS ON METAPHYSICS: A HISTORICODOCTRINAL STUDY OF THE COMMENTARY ON THE METAPHYSICS. The Hague: Martinus Nijhoff, 1972. 417 p.

Gilson, Etienne. INTRODUCTION A L'ETUDE DE SAINT AUGUSTIN. 4th ed. Paris: J. Vrin, 1969. vii, 370 p.

_____. PHILOSOPHY OF ST. THOMAS AQUINAS. Authorized translation by Edward Bullough from 3d rev. ed. of LE THOMISME. Edited by G.A. Elrington. Folcroft, Pa.: Folcroft Library Editions, 1972; Norwood, Pa.: Norwood Editions, 1975. xv, 287 p.

_____. RECENT PHILOSOPHY: HEGEL TO THE PRESENT. New York: Random House, 1966. 876 p.

_____. UNITY OF PHILOSOPHICAL EXPERIENCE. 1937. Reissue. New York: Charles Scribner's Sons, 1965. xii, 331 p. Paperbound.

Gilson establishes the following principles, each one of which has a special significance for the philosophy of education:

(1) Philosophy always buries its undertakers.

(2) By his very nature, man is a metaphysical animal.

(3) Metaphysics is the knowledge gathered by a naturally trans-cendent reason in its search for the first principles, or first causes, of what is given in sensible experience.

(4) As metaphysics aims at transcending all particular knowledge, no particular science is competent either to solve metaphysical problems, or to judge their metaphysical solutions.

(5) The failures of the metaphysicians flow from their unguarded use of a principle of unity present in the human mind.

(6) Since being is the first principle of all human knowledge, it is a fortiori the first principle of metaphysics.

(7) All the failures of metaphysics should be traced to the fact, that the first principle of human knowledge has been either over-looked or misused by the metaphysicians.

Goodsell, Willystine. THE CONFLICT OF NATURALISM AND HUMANISM. New York: Teachers College, Columbia University, 1910. Reprint. New York: AMS Press, 1972. vii, 183 p.

Heidegger, Martin. THE END OF PHILOSOPHY. Translated by Joan Stambaugh. New York: Harper and Row, 1973. xiv, 110 p.

> The first three chapters are taken from the end of volume 2 of Heidegger's NIETZSCHE (1961) and the fourth from his VORTRAEGE (1954) and AUFSAETZE (1954). Here he considers the analysis of metaphysics as the history of being.

Jaspers, Karl. PHILOSOPHY OF EXISTENCE. Translated from German with introduction by Richard F. Grabau. Philadelphia: University of Pennsylvania Press, 1971. xxvii, 99 p.

Kant, Immanuel. CRITIQUE OF PURE REASON. Translated by F. Max Muller. Garden City, N.Y.: Doubleday, 1966. 543 p. Paperbound.

> The translation incorporates the unabridged first edition together with Kant's revision for the second edition.

Kenny, Anthony, ed. AQUINAS: A COLLECTION OF CRITICAL ESSAYS. 1969. Notre Dame, Ind.: University of Notre Dame Press, 1976. vi, 389 p. Paperbound.

> Among the writers to be noted in this work are Knowles, Geach, McCabe, Ross, Brown, Deck, Kenny, Sheehan, and Grisez.

Klauder, Francis J. THE WONDER OF THE REAL: A SKETCH IN BASIC PHILOSOPHY. Quincy, Mass.: Christopher Publishing House, 1973. 114 p.

Kockelmans, Joseph J., ed. PHENOMENOLOGY: THE PHILOSOPHY OF EDMUND HUSSERL AND ITS INTERPRETATION. Garden City, N.Y.: Doubleday, 1967. 555 p.

Kreyche, Gerald F. THIRTEEN THINKERS: A SAMPLER OF GREAT PHILOSOPHERS. Washington, D.C.: University Press of America, 1976. 131 p. Bibliog. Paperbound.

> This introductory overview, by a philosopher who understands education and its foundations, guides the undergraduate through each philosophical movement from Plato to Sartre. The work is replete with study hints, review study questions, and glossary of basic terms.

Langiulli, Nino, ed. THE EXISTENTIAL TRADITION: SELECTED WRITINGS. New York: Doubleday, 1971. 480 p. Paperbound.

> The essays are by sixteen philosophers of existentialism.

McInerny, Ralph M. ST. THOMAS AQUINAS. Boston: Twayne Publishers, 1977. 197 p. Bibliog., pp. 183-89.

Marcel, Gabriel. THE PHILOSOPHY OF EXISTENTIALISM. 7th ed. Translated by Manya Harari. New York: Philosophical Library, 1956; Citadel Press, 1966. 128 p. Paperbound.

The work is "An Essay in Autobiography" taken from EXISTENTIAL-ISME CHRETIEN, edited by Etienne Gilson.

Maritain, Jacques. A PREFACE TO METAPHYSICS. 1939. Freeport, N.Y.: Books for Libraries, 1971. 152 p.

Marshall, John P. THE TEACHER AND HIS PHILOSOPHY. Lincoln, Nebr.: Professional Educators Publications, 1973. 101 p. Bibliogs. Paperbound.

The relationship of philosophy to teaching and to teachers themselves is highlighted through the examination of idealism, realism, perennialism, pragmatism, and existentialism.

O'Meara, John J., ed. AN AUGUSTINE READER. Garden City, N.Y.: Doubleday, 1973. 556 p. Bibliog.; index. Paperbound.

The readings selected by O'Meara, an acknowledged authority on Augustine, are useful for Augustine's understanding of both philosophy and education.

PHILOSOPHES CRITIQUES D'EUX-MEMES = PHILOSOPHERS ON THEIR OWN WORK = PHILOSOPHISCHE SELBSTBETRACHTUNGEN. 2 vols. Edited by Andre Mercier and Maja Svilar. Federation Internationale des Societes de Philosophie. Bern, Switz.; Frankfort on the Main, W. Ger.; and Munich: Lang, 1975-76.

Volume 1: This volume includes the personal statements of A.C. Ewing, M. Faber, K. Huebner, R. McKeon, J. Passmore, C. Perelman, and J.N. Theodoracopoulos. 1975. xxi, 253 p.

Volume 2: This volume contains the personal statements of P. Caws, H.G. Gadamer, K. Kuypers, F. Lombardi, A. Mercier, H.L. Parsons, and A. Schaff. 1976. 267 p.

The articles appear in two of the following languages: German, English, French, Italian.

Pongratz, Ludwig J., ed. PHILOSOPHIE IN SELBSTDARSTELLUNGEN. [Philosophers present their views]. 3 vols. Hamburg, W. Ger.: Felix Meiner Verlag, 1975-77.

Important contemporary thinkers present their own philosophies and the sources of their thought.

Volume 1: Essays by E. Bloch, J.M. Bochenski, A. Dempf, H. Glockner, H.-E. Hengstenberg, P. Jordan, W. Marx, J. Pieper, H. Plessner. 1975. x, 316 p.

Volume 2: Essays by G. Guenther, D.V. Hildebrand, L. Landgrebe, B. Liebrucks, F. Mayer-Hillebrand, W. Schulz, W. Weischedel, C.V. v. Weizaecker. 1975. vi, 399 p.

Volume 3: Essays by Julius Ebbinghaus, Hans-Georg Gadamer, Heinz Heimsoeth, Erich Heintel, Friedrich Kaulbach, Helmut Kuhn. 1977. iv, 292 p.

Prufer, Thomas. "A Protreptic: What is Philosophy?" In STUDIES IN PHILOSOPHY AND HISTORY OF PHILOSOPHY, edited by John K. Ryan, vol. 2, pp. 1-19. Washington, D.C.: Catholic University of America Press, 1963.

David Tracy recommends this article "for an excellent study of the horizon shifts from classical to medieval to modern and postmodern philosophy."

Romano, Gianbattista. IL PENSIERO PEDAGOGICO DI JACQUES MARITAIN. Palermo, Italy: Galaten, 1970. 183 p.

Royce, Josiah. LECTURES ON MODERN IDEALISM. New foreword by John E. Smith. 1919. Reissue. New Haven, Conn.: Yale University Press, 1964. xvi, 266 p.

Russell, Bertrand. BERTRAND RUSSELL: AN INTRODUCTION. Selections edited by Brian Carr. London: Allen and Unwin, 1975. iii, 149 p.

_____. AN OUTLINE OF PHILOSOPHY. London: Allen and Unwin, 1970. 317 p.

_____. THE PROBLEMS OF PHILOSOPHY. 1912. London and New York: Oxford University Press, 1972. 167 p.

Shanab, Robert Elias Abu, and Weinroth, A. Jay, eds. PRESENT DAY ISSUES IN PHILOSOPHY. Dubuque, Iowa: Kendall/Hunt Publishing, 1971. xix, 385 p.

Vlastos, Gregory, ed. PLATO I: METAPHYSICS AND EPISTEMOLOGY. Garden City, N.Y.: Doubleday, 1971. 320 p. Paperbound.

Wallace, William A. THE ELEMENTS OF PHILOSOPHY: A COMPENDIUM FOR PHILOSOPHERS AND THEOLOGIANS. New York: Alba House, 1977. xx, 338 p.

Wallace summarizes the basic philosophical disciplines of logic, natural philosophy, psychology, metaphysics, epistemology, natural theology, and ethics. Part 2 treats disciplines that have come into being since the scientific revolution. Part 3 is a brief history of Western philosophy. References are indexed to the NEW CATHOLIC ENCYCLOPEDIA and to the fifteenth edition of the ENCYCLOPEDIA BRITANNICA.

Weissman, David. ETERNAL POSSIBILITIES: A NEUTRAL GROUND FOR MEANING AND EXISTENCE. Carbondale: Southern Illinois University Press, 1977. xii, 300 p.

Wilson, John. PHILOSOPHY. London: Heinemann Educational Books, 1968. 124 p.

Wolff, Robert Paul. THE POVERTY OF LIBERALISM. Boston: Beacon Press, 1968. 200 p.

P 3: THE PHILOSOPHY OF THE HUMAN PERSONALITY

Aristotle. ANTHROPOLOGIE/ARISTOTE. Texts selected and translated from Greek by Jean-Claude Fraisse. Paris: Presses Universitaires de France, 1976. 197 p.

_____. DE L'AME. Text established by A. Jannone. Translated from Greek with annotations by Edmond Barbatin. Paris: Le Club Francais du Livre, 1969. xx, 247 p.

ARISTOTLE'S PSYCHOLOGY. Introduction and notes by Edwin Wallace. New York: Arno Press, 1976. 327 p.

Aristotle's texts are made available in both Greek and English.

Barrett, William. IRRATIONAL MAN: A STUDY IN EXISTENTIAL PHILOSOPHY. 1958. New York: Doubleday, 1962. 278 p. Paperbound.

This text should be helpful in familiarizing teachers, who are not too comfortable in the study of philosophy, with the more important existentialist lines of thought.

Cassirer, Ernst. AN ESSAY ON MAN. AN INTRODUCTION TO A PHILOSOPHY OF HUMAN CULTURE. 1944. New Haven: Yale University Press, 1962. 237 p.

Guardini, Romano. THE WORLD AND THE PERSON. Translated from German by Stella Lange. Chicago: Henry Regnery, 1965. ix, 221 p.

The essays dealing with the person represent an outline of the Christian portrait of man. Those that deal with the world stress the relations of man with reality and the tasks that confront him. The final chapter concludes that the true purpose of Providence is not that man may prosper in time but that the new creation and the man of eternity may be made perfect.

Haught, John F. RELIGION AND SELF-ACCEPTANCE. New York: Paulist Press, 1976. vii, 189 p.

Haught, a professor at Georgetown, is a disciple of Lonergan and has presented the "clearest summary yet of the Lonergan paradigm" according to Andrew Greeley, in ADVOCATE (31 March 1978).

Jaspers, Karl. MAN IN THE MODERN AGE. Translated by Eden and Cedar Paul. New York: Doubleday, 1957. viii, 230 p.; London: Routledge and Kegan Paul, 1959. 208 p.

_____. WAY TO WISDOM: AN INTRODUCTION TO PHILOSOPHY. Translated by Ralph Manheim. New Haven: Yale University Press, 1970. 208 p.

Kainz, Howard. THE PHILOSOPHY OF MAN, REVISITED. Washington, D.C.: University Press of America, 1977. 187 p. Paperbound.

Kainz brings recent empirical data to bear on the traditional problems examined in the philosophy of man. It is an important update on discussions over the problem of human nature.

Marcel, Gabriel. THE EXISTENTIAL BACKGROUND OF HUMAN DIGNITY. Cambridge, Mass.: Harvard University Press, 1963. 178 p.

Peterson, Forrest H. A PHILOSOPHY OF MAN AND SOCIETY. New York: Philosophical Library, 1970. xiv, 224 p.

Ryan, John Julian. THE HUMANIZATION OF MAN. New York: Newman Press, 1972. 246 p.

Wandersman, Abraham, et al. HUMANISM AND BEHAVIORISM: DIALOGUE AND GROWTH. Elmsford, N.Y.: Pergamon Press, 1976. 439 p.

The authors invite the reader to a recent intensive debate, between Joseph Wolpe and Sidney Jourard, about humanism and behaviorism. The systematic analysis of each position, together with the discussions from almost a score of scholars who joined the debate, raises some critical issues about underlying diverging philosophies that guide clinical psychologists.

P 4: THE PHILOSOPHY OF INTELLECT

Addis, Laird, and Lewis, Douglas. MOORE AND RYLE: TWO ONTOLOGISTS. The Hague: Martinus Nijhoff; Iowa City: University of Iowa, 1965. v, 184 p.

> Addis observes that Ryle's materialism is a strange fruit of his ontology of mind and is tied to his rejecting the science of man. Lewis accepts Moore's refutation of idealism but thinks Moore has failed to achieve the adequate realistic position he strove so hard to reach. Moore may be mistaken in assuming that predicating truly some characteristic of a material object is an entity which bears the character in question.

Ayer, Alfred Jules. THE CONCEPT OF A PERSON AND OTHER ESSAYS. London: Macmillan, 1963. 272 p.

Corti, Walter Robert, ed. THE PHILOSOPHY OF WILLIAM JAMES. Hamburg, W. Ger.: Felix Meiner Verlag, 1976. 397 p. Bibliography by Charlene Haddock Seigfried.

> Directly related to James's theory of education are the essays by Broyer, Lowe, and Jamali. The other essays shed light on his thinking in philosophy and psychology.

Hitt, William D. "Two Models of Man." AMERICAN PSYCHOLOGIST 24, no. 7 (1969): 651-58. Reprinted in THE HELPING RELATIONSHIP SOURCEBOOK, edited by Donald L. Avila et al., pp. 51-65. Boston: Allyn and Bacon, 1971.

> Hitt states the arguments for and against the behavioristic versus the phenomenological models of man. He concludes both models are useful because each appears to have some truth or evidence. The great importance of each model demands continuous dialogue between behaviorists and phenomenologists.

Jaspers, Karl. REASON AND ANTI-REASON IN OUR TIME. Translated by Stanley Godman. New Haven: Yale University Press, 1952; Hamden, Conn.: Archon Books, 1971. 96 p.

Jones, Howard Mumford. REFLECTIONS ON LEARNING. 1958. Freeport, N.Y.: Books for Libraries Press, 1969. 97 p.

Strawson, P.F. THE BOUNDS OF SENSE: AN ESSAY ON KANT'S CRITIQUE OF PURE REASON. London: Methuen; New York: distributed by Harper and Row, Barnes and Noble, 1975. 296 p.

White, Morton Gabriel, and White, Lucia. THE INTELLECTUAL VERSUS THE CITY: FROM THOMAS JEFFERSON TO FRANK LLOYD WRIGHT. New York: Oxford University Press, 1977. 270 p. Paperbound.

P 5: THE PHILOSOPHY OF WILL AND EMOTION

Cleverly, John F., and Phillips, D.C. FROM LOCKE TO SPOCK: INFLUEN-
TIAL MODELS OF THE CHILD IN WESTERN THOUGHT. Carlton South, Vic.:
Melbourne University Press, 1976. ix, 120 p.

Dobinson, C.H. JEAN-JACQUES ROUSSEAU: HIS THOUGHT AND ITS
RELEVANCE TODAY. London: Methuen; New York: Barnes and Noble,
1969. 146 p.

> Instead of analyzing the works as a whole, Dobinson prefers to
> study, along selected lines of thought, LA NOVELLE HELOISE,
> EMILE, and two essays for the Academy of Dijon. This material
> is of special importance now.

Giarelli, James M. "Lawrence Kohlberg and G.E. Moore on the Naturalistic
Fallacy." EDUCATIONAL THEORY 26, no. 4 (1976): 348-54.

> The author evaluates Kohlberg's use or misuse of the naturalistic
> fallacy against Moore's original understanding of it. Yet Giarelli
> applauds Kohlberg's attempt to reopen the dialogue between phi-
> losophers and psychologists.

May, Rollo. LOVE AND WILL. New York: W.W. Norton, 1969. 352 p.

Neville, Robert C. THE COSMOLOGY OF FREEDOM. New Haven: Yale
University Press, 1974. xi, 385 p.

> Since philosophy has the task to offer a critical vision of the whole
> of things and because freedom is the element basic to philosophic
> culture, what is needed is a comprehensive concept of freedom that
> does justice to the social sciences, metaphysics, ontology, cos-
> mology, and religion. Neville moves toward meeting this need by
> presenting his cosmology of freedom within a full range of human
> experience.

Weiss, Paul. MAN'S FREEDOM. Carbondale: Southern Illinois University
Press, 1967. 335 p. Paperbound.

> This work is an essay on human ethical activity. Weiss actually
> seeks a sounder and more adequate interpretation of nature and
> the human person in order to arrive at a clearer understanding of
> man's essential freedom.

Wild, John Daniel. EXISTENCE AND THE WORLD OF FREEDOM. Englewood
Cliffs, N.J.: Prentice-Hall, 1963. 243 p.

Wilson, J.R.S. EMOTION AND OBJECT. New York: Cambridge University
Press, 1972. 192 p.

P 6: AESTHETICS—THE PHILOSOPHY OF THE BEAUTIFUL

Cavarnos, Constantine. PLATO'S THEORY OF FINE ART. Athens: Astir Publishing, 1973. 98 p.

Dickie, George, and Sclafani, R.J., eds. AESTHETICS: A CRITICAL AN-THOLOGY. New York: St. Martin's Press, 1977. ix, 898 p. Bibliogs.

> The readings are divided into traditional and contemporary theories of art and their critiques, theories of individual arts, the theory of art theory, the death of art, traditional and contemporary theories of the aesthetic and critiques of these theories.

Gilson, Etienne. FORMS AND SUBSTANCES IN THE ARTS. Translated from French by Salvator Attanasio. New York: Charles Scribner's Sons, 1966. 282 p.

> Aesthetics is not calology, whose subject matter is the beautiful as a transcendental of being, but the apprehension of the beautiful as produced by the fine arts. Gilson's concern is to prepare an intelligible frame into which all the particular kinds of beauty produced by each major art may find a place, including even those arts which are still the secret of the future.

Gombrich, Ernst Hans; Hochberg, Julian; and Black, Max. ART, PERCEPTION AND REALITY. Baltimore: Johns Hopkins University Press, 1972. x, 132 p.

Listowel, William. MODERN AESTHETICS: AN HISTORICAL INTRODUCTION. New York: Teachers College Press, 1968. 220 p. Paperbound.

Morawski, Stefan. INQUIRIES INTO THE FUNDAMENTALS OF AESTHETICS. Foreword by Monroe Beardsley. Cambridge: M.I.T. Press, 1974. 392 p.

Nahm, Milton Charles. READINGS IN PHILOSOPHY OF ART AND AESTHETICS. Englewood Cliffs, N.J.: Prentice-Hall, 1975. xvi, 587 p.

Oates, Whitney J. PLATO'S VIEW OF ART. New York: Charles Scribner's Sons, 1972. 81 p.

Osborne, Harold, ed. AESTHETICS. London: Oxford University Press, 1972. 186 p.

Saw, Ruth L. AESTHETICS: AN INTRODUCTION. New York: Doubleday, 1971. 231 p.

Tillman, Frank A., and Cahn, Steven M. PHILOSOPHY OF ART AND AES-THETICS FROM PLATO TO WITTGENSTEIN. New York: Harper and Row, 1969. xiii, 791 p.

P 7: ETHICS—THE PHILOSOPHY OF VALUES

Alston, William P., and Brandt, Richard B., eds. THE PROBLEMS OF PHI-
LOSOPHY: INTRODUCTORY READINGS. 3d ed. Boston: Allyn and Bacon,
1978. 768 p.

> The selections include a balance of classical and contemporary pri-
> mary sources about religious belief, value and obligation, ethical
> appraisal of personal actions and political structures, free will and
> determinism, mind and body, the structure of knowledge, and per-
> ceiving the material world. The problem-oriented collection pre-
> sents the chief reasons for accepting or rejecting positions on these
> issues.

ARISTOTELES ETHICA NICOMACHEA. Edited by I. Bywater with Greek text.
1894. Oxford: Clarendon Press, 1970. 264 p. Edited with introduction and
notes to Greek text by John Burnet. New York: Arno Press, 1973. lii,
502 p.

ARISTOTLE'S ETHICS. Introduction and notes by J.L. Ackrill. London: Faber
and Faber, 1973. 280 p.

Childs, John Lawrence. EDUCATION AND MORALS: AN EXPERIMENTALIST
PHILOSOPHY OF EDUCATION. New York: Appleton-Century-Crofts, 1950.
Reprint. Arno Press, 1971. xiv, 299 p.

> To select ways by which to nurture the young is the moral task of
> the educator. To discharge this moral and deliberate effort the
> educator must study philosophy in relation to education and morals.
> [Cf. Broudy (1967), cited in chapter 13, p. 105].

THE ETHICS OF ARISTOTLE: THE NICOMACHEAN ETHICS. Translated from
Greek by J.A.K. Thomson. Introduction and bibliography by Jonathan Barnes.
Rev. with notes and appendixes by Hugh Tredennick. Harmondsworth, Engl.;
New York: Penguin Books, 1976. 383 p.

Feinberg, Walter. "Ethics and Objectivity--The Effects of the Darwinian Revolution on Educational Reform." EDUCATIONAL THEORY 23, no. 4 (1973):
294-302.

Geffre, Claude, ed. HUMANISM AND CHRISTIANITY. New York: Herder
and Herder, 1973. 137 p.

> The Christological foundations of Christian anthropology are most
> deftly explained by such experts as Domenach, Marin, Cornelis,
> de Waelhens, Granel, Ganoczy, Pannenberg, Crespy, Jolif, Gibson,
> and Labbe. The church must fight consciously against all contem-
> porary forms of injustice and dehumanization.

Johnson, Glen. SOME ETHICAL IMPLICATIONS OF A NATURALISTIC PHI-LOSOPHY OF EDUCATION. New York: Bureau of Publications, Teachers College, Columbia University, 1947. Reprint. New York: AMS Press, 1972. 154 p.

Kamenka, Eugene. THE ETHICAL FOUNDATIONS OF MARXISM. Corrected rev. ed. London: Routledge and Kegan Paul, 1972. 230 p.

Kockelmans, Joseph J., ed. and trans. CONTEMPORARY EUROPEAN ETHICS: SELECTED READINGS. Garden City, N.Y.: Doubleday, Anchor Books, 1972. x, 503 p.

The essays are by Lavelle, Jankelevitch, Marcel, Ricoeur, La Senne, Reiner, Polin, Gusdorf, Kockelmans, Jeanson, Simone de Beauvoir, Hochberg, Heidegger, Bollnow, Steinbuechel, Buber, Bonhoeffer, and Thielicke.

Kohlberg, Lawrence. "From Is to Ought: How to Commit the Naturalistic Fallacy and Get Away with it in the Study of Moral Development." In COGNITIVE DEVELOPMENT AND EPISTEMOLOGY, edited by T. Mischel, pp. 153-235. New York: Academic Press, 1971.

McGann, Thomas F. ETHICS: THEORY AND PRACTICE. Chicago: Loyola University Press, 1971. 135 p.

McLean, George F., ed. ETHICAL WISDOM EAST AND/OR WEST. Proceedings of the American Catholic Philosophical Association, vol. 5. Washington, D.C.: Catholic University of America, 1977. iv, 251 p.

Twenty-two papers center on the metaphysical foundation for ethical wisdom, eastern visions of morality, the western problematics in ethics, and studies involving the thought of Hume, Whitehead, Husserl, and Marx.

Maritain, Jacques. "John Dewey and the Objectivity of Values--the Inconsistency of Absolute Naturalism." In his MORAL PHILOSOPHY: AN HISTORICAL AND CRITICAL SURVEY OF THE GREAT SYSTEMS, pp. 396-418. London: G. Bles; New York: Charles Scribner's Sons, 1964.

This critical analysis, from a neo-Thomist viewpoint, annihilates any concept of an ethics subject to the positive sciences or to the sciences of phenomena alone. In opposition to Dewey, Maritain accepts guidance from these sciences only if they are regulated and controlled from a higher level by the aid of criteria concerned with the conscience proper.

_____. MORAL PHILOSOPHY: AN HISTORICAL AND CRITICAL SURVEY OF THE GREAT SYSTEMS. London: G. Bles; New York: Charles Scribner's Sons, 1964. xii, 468 p.

Among the adventures of reason, Maritain includes analyses of Socrates, Plato, Aristotle, the Stoics and Epicureans, Christianity and philosophy, the ethics of Kant. The section on the great illusions and post-Kantian dialecticism contains critiques of Hegelian idealism, dialectical materialism, positivism and human knowledge, positivism and human conduct. The final section explores moral philosophy's crisis of reorientation in regard to person and liberty, closed and open cosmic reality. The study is thorough and comprehensive.

Warnock, Geoffrey James. THE OBJECT OF MORALITY. London: Methuen; New York: Barnes and Noble, 1971. 168 p.

Warnock, Mary. ETHICS SINCE 1900. 2d ed. London: Oxford University Press, 1966. 220 p.

P 8: PHILOSOPHICAL ANALYSIS—THE PHILOSOPHY OF THOUGHT AND LANGUAGE

Ayer, Alfred Jules. LANGUAGE, TRUTH AND LOGIC. 2d ed. London: Gollancz, 1946. 160 p.

W. Kenneth Richmond calls this a key text.

_____. RUSSELL AND MOORE: THE ANALYTICAL HERITAGE. Cambridge, Mass.: Harvard University Press, 1971. 254 p.

Barth, Hans. TRUTH AND IDEOLOGY. Translated by Frederic Lilge. Introduction by Reinhard Bendix. Berkeley and Los Angeles: University of California Press, 1976. 192 p.

This work traces the origin and transformation of the concept of ideology from Bacon to Marx and Nietzsche. Since Barth contends that "truth does survive beyond its reduction to ideology," he affirms the indispensability of basic human values.

Bernier, Normand R., and Williams, Jack E. BEYOND BELIEFS: IDEOLOGICAL FOUNDATIONS OF AMERICAN EDUCATION. Englewood Cliffs, N.J.: Prentice-Hall, 1973. x, 422 p.

Brown, Leslie Melville. GENERAL PHILOSOPHY IN EDUCATION. New York: McGraw-Hill, 1966. xii, 244 p.

Brown presents, from the perspective of analytic philosophy, the tools of critical thinking and illustrates some of the problems of general philosophy relevant within education such as those of knowing, the nature of mind, freedom and determination, moral evaluations. His purpose is to encourage confidence that originates from a better understanding of self, language, reasoning, and beliefs in order to foster the adaptability needed for facing a continuously changing environment. [See Broudy-Smith (1969), cited in chapter 13, p. 130].

Burke, Kenneth. THE RHETORIC OF RELIGION: STUDIES IN LOGOLOGY. Berkeley and Los Angeles: University of California Press, 1970. vi, 327 p.

Connell, Richard J. LOGICAL ANALYSIS: A NEW APPROACH. Winona, Minn.: St. Mary's College Press, 1973. 472 p.

Fay, Thomas A. HEIDEGGER: THE CRITIQUE OF LOGIC. The Hague: Martinus Nijhoff, 1977. ix, 136 p. Paperbound.

Heidegger has noted that the logic question has been transformed into the language problematic, and thus language constitutes the single most important theme in his later thought. What is involved is nothing less than a total transformation of the way of conceiving the nature of philosophy.

Gellner, Ernest. THE DEVIL IN MODERN PHILOSOPHY. Edited by I.C. Jarvie and Joseph Agassi. London: Routledge and Kegan Paul, 1974. 262 p.

Gellner deals with the school of linguistic analysis in a critical but humorous fashion. He reacts to such individual thinkers as Collingwood, Austin, Ayer, Chomsky, Piaget, and Eysenck. These twenty-one essays span twenty years of thinking on linguistic philosophy, ethics, and the history of ideas.

Grimaldi, William M.A. STUDIES IN THE PHILOSOPHY OF ARISTOTLE'S RHETORIC. Wiesbaden, W. Ger.: Franz Steiner Verlag, 1972. 151 p.

The RHETORIC is studied as a philosophy of human discourse that pertains directly to communication, people, truth, and reality. Because human nature is intellective and appetitive, syllogistic or enthymematic methodology must also function as acts of the whole person--in intellect, will, and affections--before it can lead to both conviction and judgment.

Hare, R.M. PRACTICAL INFERENCES. Berkeley and Los Angeles: University of California Press, 1972. 128 p.

Hedley, W. Eugene. FREEDOM, INQUIRY, AND LANGUAGE. Scranton, Pa.: International Textbook, 1968. xi, 131 p.

Ingle, Dwight Joyce. IS IT REALLY SO? A GUIDE TO CLEAR THINKING. Philadelphia: Westminster Press, 1976. 160 p.

Jaspers, Karl. PLATO, AUGUSTIN, KANT. DREI GRUENDER DES PHILOSO-PHIERENS. Munich: Piper, 1967. 404 p.

Kockelmans, Joseph J., ed. and trans. ON HEIDEGGER AND LANGUAGE. Evanston, Ill.: Northwestern University Press, 1972. xix, 380 p.

Kurtz, Paul, ed. AMERICAN PHILOSOPHY IN THE TWENTIETH CENTURY: A SOURCE BOOK, FROM PRAGMATISM TO PHILOSOPHICAL ANALYSIS. New York: Macmillan, 1966. 573 p.

Leiber, Justin. NOAM CHOMSKY: A PHILOSOPHIC OVERVIEW. Boston: Twayne Publishers, 1975. 172 p.

> Leiber highlights Chomsky's outstanding philosophical contribution that human language comes into being through a universal and innate power in man. This conclusion, which seems to be verified by the fact that language is mastered by children who appear otherwise incapable of comparable intellectual attainments at the time, has implications for epistemology, ethics, politics, and the philosophy of education and is quite revolutionary given the modern philosophical climate.

Lorenz, Konrad. "Analogy as a Source of Knowledge." SCIENCE 185 (July 1974): 229-34.

McShane, Philip, ed. LANGUAGE, TRUTH AND MEANING. Notre Dame, Ind.: University of Notre Dame, 1973. viii, 343 p.

Putnam, Hilary. PHILOSOPHY OF LOGIC. New York: Harper and Row, 1971. 87 p.

Russell, Bertrand. LOGIC AND KNOWLEDGE. Edited by Robert Charles Marsh. New York: G.P. Putnam's Sons, 1971. 382 p.

> The collection includes addresses, essays, and lectures on symbolic and mathematical logic.

Searle, John, ed. THE PHILOSOPHY OF LANGUAGE. London: Oxford University Press, 1971. 149 p.

Strawson, P.F., ed. PHILOSOPHICAL LOGIC. London: Oxford University Press, 1967. 177 p.

_____. STUDIES IN THE PHILOSOPHY OF THOUGHT AND ACTION. London and New York: Oxford University Press, 1968. 230 p.

> The lectures are by Gilbert Ryle and others.

Whorf, Benjamin Lee. LANGUAGE, THOUGHT, AND REALITY. Edited by John B. Carroll. 1956. Foreword by Stuart Chase. Cambridge: M.I.T. Press, 1964. xi, 278 p.

Wojciechowski, Jerzy A. CONCEPTUAL BASIS OF THE CLASSIFICATION OF KNOWLEDGE. Munich: Verlag Dokumentation, 1974. 503 p.

P TR: THE PHILOSOPHY OF RELIGION

Augustine, Saint Aurelius. THE ENCHIRIDION ON FAITH, HOPE, AND LOVE. Edited by Henry Paolucci. South Bend, Ind.: Gateway Editions, 1961. 186 p. Paperbound.

> Written late in the life of Augustine, this work is directed toward supplying any well-educated Roman layman with a comprehensive exposition of the essential teachings of Christianity. The work has important ramifications for developing a Christian philosophy of education.

Bambrough, Renford. REASON, TRUTH AND GOD. London: Methuen, 1969. 164 p.

Barrett, William, and Aiken, Henry D., eds. PHILOSOPHY IN THE TWEN-TIETH CENTURY. 4 vols. New York: Random House, 1962.

> The readings chiefly represent analytic and existentialist thought but are introduced with comprehensive surveys of their influence today.

Brown, Peter Robert Lamont. RELIGION AND SOCIETY IN THE AGE OF SAINT AUGUSTINE. London: Faber and Faber; New York: Harper and Row, 1972. 351 p.

Butler, Edward Cuthbert. WESTERN MYSTICISM: THE TEACHING OF SS. AUGUSTINE, GREGORY, AND BERNARD ON CONTEMPLATION AND THE CONTEMPLATIVE LIFE. New York: Gordon Press, 1975. 288 p.

Caporale, Rocco, and Grumelli, Antonio, eds. THE CULTURE OF UNBELIEF. Berkeley and Los Angeles: University of California Press, 1971. 303 p.

> The studies and proceedings are from the First Symposium on Belief, held at Rome in 1969.

Casotti, Mario. IL PENSIERO PEDAGOGICO DI PADRE GEMELLI. Milan: Editrice Vita e Pensiero, 1961. 108 p.

Cobb, John B., Jr. A CHRISTIAN NATURAL THEOLOGY: BASED ON THE THOUGHT OF ALFRED NORTH WHITEHEAD. Philadelphia: Westminster Press, 1965. 288 p.

Copleston, Frederick Charles. AQUINAS. Baltimore: Penguin, 1955. Reprint. Harmondsworth, Engl.: Penguin Books, 1977. 272 p. Bibliog.

> Copleston introduces Aquinas, the university professor and philosopher-teacher, as one who aimed to show that Christian faith rests on a rational foundation and that the principles of philosophy do not necessarily lead to a view of the world which excludes Christianity implicitly or explicitly. The bibliography (pp. 265-67) is that of the 1955 edition.

_____. "Philosophy and Religion in Judaism and Christianity." In his PHILOSOPHERS AND PHILOSOPHIES, pp. 39-42. London: Search Press; New York: Barnes and Noble, 1976.

> Copleston notes that an approach to religious faith through philosophical reflection on man in his situation can be made that yields an area for fruitful discussion between Jewish and Christian thinkers.

_____. RELIGION AND PHILOSOPHY. Dublin: Gill and Macmillan; London: Macmillan; New York: Barnes and Noble, 1974. x, 195 p.

> Theological and educational reflection have implications, presuppositions, or assumptions that are open to philosophical analysis and discourse. Likewise metaphysics, and the thinking that flows from it, can embody a religious impulse or movement. The conclusions are not intended to be a dogmatic statement of one true metaphysics but rather a tentative development of a possible line of thought.

Dourley, John P. "Jung, Tillich, and Aspects of the Western Christian Development." THOUGHT 52, no. 204 (1977): 18-49.

> The modern mind will remain indebted to Tillich and Jung for their revitalization of man's sense of God's immediate and immanential presence in him. Religion is an inescapable and a most important dimension of life; it enhances life ontologically, spiritually, and psychologically; it relates man to God.

Fackenheim, Emil L. ENCOUNTERS BETWEEN JUDAISM AND MODERN PHILOSOPHY: A PREFACE TO FUTURE JEWISH THOUGHT. New York: Basic Books, 1973. 275 p.

Gilson, Etienne. D'ARISTOTE A DARWIN ET RETOUR: ESSAI SUR QUELQUES CONSTANTES DE LA BIOPHILOSOPHIE. Paris: J. Vrin, 1971. 254 p.

Habermas, Jurgen, KNOWLEDGE AND HUMAN INTEREST. Translated from

German by Jeremy J. Shapiro. Boston: Beacon Press, 1971; London: Heinemann Educational, 1972. xiii, 356 p.

> Habermas speaks of science in its strict meaning, in its hermeneutic significance, and in its critical sense.

Harris, Errol E. ATHEISM AND THEISM. Tulane Studies in Philosophy, vol. 26. New Orleans: Tulane University Press, 1977. xi, 157 p.

Hitchcock, James. THE RECOVERY OF THE SACRED. New York: Seabury Press, 1974. xii, 175 p.

MacKinnon, Edward A., ed. THE PROBLEM OF SCIENTIFIC REALISM. New York: Appleton-Century-Crofts, 1972. 301 p.

Marcel, Gabriel. CINQ PIECES MAJEURES. Paris: Plon, 1973. 550 p.

> The five essays in this book are entitled: "Un Homme de Dieu," "Le Monde casse," "Le Chemin de crete," "La Soif," and "Le Signe de la Croix."

NEW CATHOLIC ENCYCLOPEDIA. 15 vols. New York: McGraw-Hill, 1967.

> The articles on the philosophy of education, philosophy, and related themes are helpful starting points for further reading.

Newman, Cardinal John Henry. THE THEOLOGICAL PAPERS OF JOHN HENRY NEWMAN ON FAITH AND CERTAINTY. Selected and edited by J. Derek Holmes. Introduction by Charles Stephen Dessain. Oxford: Clarendon Press, 1976. xv, 170 p.

Patterson, Robert Leet. THE CONCEPTION OF GOD IN THE PHILOSOPHY OF AQUINAS. Merrick, N.Y.: Richwood Publishing, 1976. 508 p.

Phenix, Philip H. EDUCATION AND THE WORSHIP OF GOD. Philadelphia: Westminster Press, 1966. 192 p.

Radnitsky, Gerard. CONTEMPORARY SCHOOLS OF METASCIENCE. 3d enl. ed. Chicago: Henry Regnery, 1973. xl, 446 p.

Richmond, James. THEOLOGY AND METAPHYSICS. New York: Schocken Books, 1971. 168 p.

Ruse, Michael. THE PHILOSOPHY OF BIOLOGY. London: Hutchinson University Library, 1973. 231 p.

SCIENCE AND SYNTHESIS. An International Colloquium organized by Unesco on the Tenth Anniversary of the Death of Albert Einstein and Teilhard de Chardin. Heidelberg, W. Ger.: Springer-Verlag, 1971. 206 p.

Sellier, Philippe. PASCAL ET SAINT AUGUSTIN. Paris: A. Colin, 1970. 645 p.

Teilhard De Chardin, Pierre. THE PHENOMENON OF MAN. New York: Harper and Row, 1959. 320 p.

Tyrrell, Bernard. BERNARD LONERGAN'S PHILOSOPHY OF GOD. Notre Dame, Ind.: University of Notre Dame Press, 1974. 202 p.

Wallace, William A. EINSTEIN, GALILEO AND AQUINAS. Washington, D.C.: Thomist Press, 1963. 37 p.

> A clearer presentation is not likely to be found. Einstein's message is that the mathematical realism of Galileo, or the space-time absolutism of Newton, are antiquated notions of little profit for the modern scientist. Aquinas answers Galileo by denying that mathematics is the skeleton key that opens all the doors of knowledge; to Einstein, Aquinas would say that physical research and mathematics can jointly lead to conclusive physical proof.

Whitehead, Alfred North. RELIGION IN THE MAKING. 1954. Cleveland: World Publishing, 1967. 154 p.

P NS: THE PHILOSOPHY OF SCIENCE

Ackoff, Russell Lincoln. REDESIGNING THE FUTURE: A SYSTEMS APPROACH TO SOCIETAL PROBLEMS. New York: John Wiley and Sons, 1974. ix, 260 p.

Ayer, Alfred Jules. MAN AS A SUBJECT FOR SCIENCE. London: Athlone Publishers, 1964. 26 p.

Bronowski, Jacob. THE ASCENT OF MAN. Boston: Little, Brown, 1974. 448 p.

_____. NATURE AND KNOWLEDGE: THE PHILOSOPHY OF CONTEMPORARY SCIENCE. Eugene: Oregon State System of Higher Education, 1969. 95 p.

Burks, Arthur W. CHANCE, CAUSE, REASON: AN INQUIRY INTO THE NATURE OF SCIENTIFIC EVIDENCE. Chicago: University of Chicago Press, 1977. xvi, 694.

De Lubac, Henri. THE RELIGION OF TEILHARD DE CHARDIN. Translated from French by Rene Hague. Garden City, N.Y.: Doubleday, 1968. 432 p.

> De Lubac has drawn a complete, unified, discerning picture of the entire range of Teilhardian thought. The soul of de Chardin's effort and of his intellectual quest was the "plainer disclosing of God in the world."

Dreiser, Theodore. NOTES ON LIFE BY THEODORE DREISER. Edited by Marguerite Tjaden and John J. McAleer. University: University of Alabama Press, 1974. xiv, 346 p.

> The editors have compiled Dreiser's philosophical reflections, particularly as they were stimulated by his study of natural science. Following no system of philosophy as such, these notes do reflect Dreiser's intense search and reverence for an ultimate creative Source or Person.

Elkana, Y., ed. THE INTERACTION BETWEEN SCIENCE AND PHILOSOPHY. Atlantic Highlands, N.J.: Humanities Press, 1974. 481 p.

Jaki, Stanley L. THE RELEVANCE OF PHYSICS. Chicago and London: University of Chicago Press, 1966. 2d impression, 1970. vi, 604 p.

> Philosophy remains indispensable in the process of scientific understanding unless knowledge is to revert into a meaningless chaos. Nonquantitative concepts are indispensable for a scientifically productive investigation of things physical; physics investigates the external world by focusing on the simplicity that lies behind its complicatedness but philosophy deals with the inner world so essential to respect for and rounding out the whole truth. Plainly, if one addresses questions to metaphysics, one must listen to the answers of metaphysics for all sciences depend on the acceptance of doctrines that are distinctively metaphysical.

_____. THE ROAD OF SCIENCE AND THE WAYS OF GOD. Chicago: University of Chicago Press, 1978.

> A rational belief in the existence of a creator, or at least an epistemology germane to such a belief, played a crucial role in the rise of science. The author pursues his theme through the thought of Bacon, Descartes, Newton, Hume, Kant, Hegel, Comte, Mach, Planck, and Einstein and suggests that the road of science and the ways to God form a single intellectual avenue.

Kiley, John F. EINSTEIN AND AQUINAS: A RAPPROCHEMENT. Foreword by W.E. Carlo. The Hague: Martinus Nijhoff, 1970. xii, 124 p.

Kockelmans, Joseph J. THE WORLD IN SCIENCE AND PHILOSOPHY. Milwaukee, Wis.: Bruce Publishing, 1969. xx, 184 p.

Kockelmans, Joseph J., and Kisiel, Theodore J., eds. and trans. PHENOME-
NOLOGY AND THE NATURAL SCIENCES: ESSAYS AND TRANSLATIONS.
Evanston, Ill.: Northwestern University Press, 1970. xxi, 520 p.

Pendergast, Richard J. COSMOS. New York: Fordham University Press,
1973. 207 p.

Polanyi, Michael. KNOWING AND BEING: ESSAYS. Edited by Marjorie
Grene. London: Routledge and Kegan Paul; Chicago: University of Chicago
Press, 1969. xvii, 246 p.

Smith, Vincent Edward. SCIENCE AND PHILOSOPHY. Milwaukee, Wis.:
Bruce Publishing, 1965. xiii, 266 p.

_____. THE SCIENCE OF NATURE: AN INTRODUCTION. Milwaukee,
Wis.: Bruce Publishing, 1966. xx, 170 p.

Toulmin, Stephen. PHILOSOPHY OF SCIENCE. Rev. ed. London: Hutchinson University Library, 1967. 160 p.

_____, ed. PHYSICAL REALITY: PHILOSOPHICAL ESSAYS ON TWENTIETH
CENTURY PHYSICS. New York: Harper and Row, 1970. xx, 220 p.

Whitehead, Alfred North. SCIENCE AND THE MODERN WORLD. 1925.
New York: Macmillan, 1967. ix, 212 p.

P HS: THE PHILOSOPHY OF SOCIETY

Adams, Jeremy duQuesnay. THE POPULUS OF AUGUSTINE AND JEROME:
A STUDY IN THE PATRISTIC SENSE OF COMMUNITY. New Haven: Yale
University Press, 1971. viii, 1971.

Bambrough, Renford, ed. PLATO, POPPER AND POLITICS. Cambridge, Mass.:
W. Heffer and Sons; New York: Barnes and Noble, 1967. viii, 219 p.

Birley, Derek, and Dufton, Anne. AN EQUAL CHANCE: EQUALITIES AND
INEQUALITIES OR EDUCATIONAL OPPORTUNITY. London: Routledge and
Kegan Paul, 1971. xi, 211 p.

Chirovsky, Nicholas L. Fr., and Mott, Vincent Valmon. PHILOSOPHICAL
FOUNDATIONS OF ECONOMIC DOCTRINES. Florham Park, N.J.: Florham
Park Press, 1977. vii, 179.

> Chirovsky attempts to demonstrate that philosophy is the leitmotif
> for the heterogeneity of economic thinking. Chapters most pertinent

to the educator are chapter 2 on philosophy and economic thought, chapter 6 on the economics of socialism, and chapter 7 on economic pragmatism. The undue interference of government is also an educational issue.

Evans, C. Stephen. PRESERVING THE PERSON: A LOOK AT THE HUMAN SCIENCES. Downers Grove, Ill.: Intervarsity Press, 1977. 177 p. Paperbound.

Feuer, Lewis Samuel. IDEOLOGY AND THE IDEOLOGISTS. Oxford: Blackwell; New York: Harper and Row, 1975. ix, 220 p.

Hollis, Martin, and Nell, Edward. RATIONAL ECONOMIC MAN: A PHILOSOPHICAL CRITIQUE OF NEOCLASSICAL ECONOMICS. London: Cambridge University Press, 1975. vii, 266 p.

Neoclassical economics (i.e., non-Marxist) is flawed because it is based on the philosophies of pragmatism and positivism. The first third of the book is devoted to the destruction of pragmatism and its principal corollaries, positivism, and linguistic analysis.

Jones, Howard Mumford. AMERICAN HUMANISM: ITS MEANING FOR WORLD SURVIVAL. 1957. Reprint. Westport, Conn.: Greenwood Press, 1972. xvi, 108 p.

_____. EDUCATION AND WORLD TRAGEDY. 1946. Reprint. New York: Greenwood Press, 1969. viii, 178 p.

Kandel, Isaac Leon. THE CULT OF UNCERTAINTY. 1943. Reprint. New York: Arno Press, 1971. x, 129 p.

Karier, Clarence J. "Making the World Safe for Democracy: An Historical Critique of John Dewey's Pragmatic Liberal Philosophy in the Warfare State." EDUCATIONAL THEORY 27, no. 1 (1977): 12-47.

Karier holds Dewey's pragmatic social philosophy partly responsible for turning the liberal American state into a warfare state. He blames Dewey for propounding a pragmatic ethic free of rigid principles that provided the moral dexterity which enabled intellectuals and academic professionals to serve the power structure within the liberal state in twentieth-century America.

McClelland, Peter D. CAUSAL EXPLANATIONS AND MODEL BUILDING IN HISTORY, ECONOMICS AND THE NEW ECONOMIC THEORY. Ithaca, N.Y.: Cornell University Press, 1975. 290 p.

McCoy, Charles Allan, and Playford, John. APOLITICAL POLITICS: A CRITIQUE OF BEHAVIORALISM. New York: Thomas Y. Crowell, 1968. viii, 246 p.

Philosophy

Marcel, Gabriel. MAN AGAINST MASS SOCIETY. Translated from French by G.S. Fraser. Foreword by Donald MacKinnon. Chicago: Henry Regnery, 1962. 273 p. Paperbound.

Marias, Julian. METAPHYSICAL ANTHROPOLOGY: THE EMPIRICAL STRUCTURE OF HUMAN LIFE. Translated by Francis M. Lopez-Morillas. University Park: Pennsylvania State University Press, 1971. 273 p.

May, Rollo, et al. EXISTENCE: A NEW DIMENSION IN PSYCHIATRY AND PSYCHOLOGY. New York: Basic Books, 1958. x, 445 p.

> Chapter 1 is an excellent introduction to the origins and contributions of existential thinking.

Mbiti, John S. AFRICAN RELIGIONS AND PHILOSOPHY. Garden City, N.Y.: Doubleday, 1969. 400 p. Paperbound.

> Mbiti furnishes a comprehensive introduction to the values which permeate important sectors of African life and education. The focus is chiefly religious.

Pye, Lucian W. MAO TSE-TUNG: THE MAN IN THE LEADER. New York: Basic Books, 1976. xviii, 346 p.

Seckinger, Donald S. "Response to Strain." EDUCATIONAL THEORY 27, no. 4 (1977): 322-25.

> Strain is said to ignore the revolutionary aspect of Hegel's thought which posits the inevitable transitoriness of all traditions and institutions. Strain's thought pattern ascription only adds more confusion to an issue that already needs reclarification.

Tafuri, Manfredo. ARCHITECTURE AND UTOPIA: DESIGN AND CAPITALIST DEVELOPMENT. Cambridge: M.I.T. Press, 1976. 184 p.

Taylor, George, and Ayres, N. BORN AND BRED UNEQUAL. Preface by Richard M. Titmuss. Harlow: Longmans, 1969. xii, 132 p.

Thayer, Horace Standish. MEANING AND ACTION: A STUDY OF AMERICAN PRAGMATISM. Indianapolis: Bobbs-Merrill, 1973. xv, 298 p.

Wagar, W. Warren. THE CITY OF MAN: PROPHECIES OF A WORLD CIVILIZATION IN TWENTIETH-CENTURY THOUGHT. 1963. Baltimore: Penguin Books, 1967. xvi, 310 p.

Warnock, Geoffrey James. ENGLISH PHILOSOPHY SINCE 1900. 2d ed. London: Oxford University Press, 1969. 200 p.

Weber, Ronald, ed. AMERICA IN CHANGE: REFLECTIONS ON THE 60'S AND 70'S. Notre Dame, Ind.: University of Notre Dame University, 1972. 238 p. Also paperbound.

This book looks for manifestations of change or cultural shifts among recent American trends in society, religion, philosophy, science, and technology. The conclusions have a relevance to education.

Wellmer, Albrecht. CRITICAL THEORY OF SOCIETY. Translated from German by John Cumming. New York: Herder and Herder, 1971. 139 p.

Yartz, Frank; Hassel, David; and Larson, Allan. PROGRESS AND THE CRISIS OF MAN. Foreword by Robert J. Roth. Chicago: Nelson Hall, 1976. 160 p.

These thinkers in philosophy and political science sketch guidelines for solving the problem of progress and suggest ways of determining the meaning and consequences of these solutions for the future.

P AC: THE PHILOSOPHY OF ART AND CULTURE

ARISTOTLE ON THE ART OF POETRY. Edited by Lane Cooper as an amplified version with supplementary illustrations for students of English. Ithaca, N.Y.: Cornell University Press, 1967. xxix, 100 p.

Barzun, Jacques. THE USE AND ABUSE OF ART. Princeton: Princeton University Press, 1974. 150 p.

Barzun suggests that the present is a period of cultural liquidation of the modern age which began with the Renaissance five hundred years ago. The new art to come is likely to be at first not individual but communal.

Bukala, C.R. "Sartre's Dramatic Philosophical Quest." THOUGHT 48, no. 188 (1973): 79-106.

The underlying structure within all Sartre's writings is reviewed in terms of phenomenology, theater as philosophy, the dramas of human consciousness, freedom, the absence and presence of God, the objectifying look, social structures. Bukala thinks Sartre is looking forward to a convulsion or global upheaval even more dramatic in the future.

Canetti, Elias. DIE GESPALTENE ZUKUNFT. [The cleft future]. Munich: Hanser, 1972. 140 p. Bibliogs., biographies.

These reflections give food for thought: Hitler as seen by Speer, Confucius in his dialogues, Tolstoy as the last of his kind, the Hiroshima chronicle of Dr. Hachiyas, conversations with Theodor W. Adorno, Horst Bienek, and Joachim Schickel.

Cassirer, Ernst. ROUSSEAU, KANT AND GOETHE. Translated by James Gutman et al. Princeton: Princeton University Press, 1970. 98 p.

Codini, Aristodemo. L'ORTENSIO DI CICERONE. GUIDA PER LEGGERE LE CONFESSIONI DI SANT' AGOSTINO. Milan: L. Trevisini, 1972. 200 p.

Engelberg, Edward. THE UNKNOWN DISTANCE: FROM CONSCIOUSNESS TO CONSCIENCE, GOETHE TO CAMUS. Cambridge, Mass.: Harvard University Press, 1972. 288 p.

Erickson, Keith Vincent. ARISTOTLE'S RHETORIC: ESSAYS AND BIBLIOGRAPHY. Ann Arbor, Mich.: University Microfilms, 1974. ii, 306 p.

Gardner, John. ON MORAL FICTION. New York: Basic Books, 1978. 214 p.

> Arguing the case against the postmodernistic position of cultural relativism, Gardner maintains that the victorious position of existentialists, absurdists, positivists and others are not demonstrably more valid than philosophies which hold to the fact of rational goodness. Philosophers ought to shift their focus to the universe that is clearly structured and make order the fundament of intellectual, moral, and aesthetic life.

Hall, James B., and Ulanov, Barry. MODERN CULTURE AND THE ARTS. 2d ed. New York: McGraw-Hill Book Co., 1972. 574 p.

Hanke, John W. MARITAIN'S ONTOLOGY OF THE WORK OF ART. The Hague: Martinus Nijhoff, 1973. 139 p.

Harper, Ralph. THE SEVENTH SOLITUDE: METAPHYSICAL HOMELESSNESS IN KIERKEGAARD, DOSTOEVSKY, AND NIETZSCHE. Baltimore: John Hopkins Press, 1967. 153 p.

Hewison, Robert. JOHN RUSKIN: THE ARGUMENT OF THE EYE. Princeton: Princeton University Press, 1976. 228 p.

> This study of Ruskin's visual imagination tries to show how art history, literary criticism, aesthetics, economics, and philosophy found their relations with the mind of Ruskin.

Marias, Julian. PHILOSOPHY AS DRAMATIC THEORY. Translated by James D. Parsons. University Park: Pennsylvania State University Press, 1971. 307 p.

Maritain, Jacques. ART AND SCHOLASTICISM AND THE FRONTIERS OF POETRY. Translated by Joseph W. Evans. 1962. Notre Dame, Ind.: Notre Dame University Press, 1974. vi, 234 p.

_____. ART AND SCHOLASTICISM, WITH OTHER ESSAYS. Translated from French by J.F. Scanlan. 1930. Freeport, N.Y.: Books for Libraries, 1971. 177 p.

Noon, William T. JOYCE AND AQUINAS. 1957. Hamden, Conn.: Archon Books, 1970. 167 p.

Rover, Thomas Dominic. THE POETICS OF MARITAIN: A THOMISTIC CRITIQUE. Washington, D.C.: Thomist Press, 1965. x, 218 p. Bibliog.

This work offers a comparative analysis of poetics according to Aristotle, St. Thomas Aquinas, and Maritain and concludes with a Thomistic critique of Maritain's interpretations.

Suhl, Benjamin. JEAN-PAUL SARTRE: THE PHILOSOPHER AS LITERARY CRITIC. New York: Columbia University Press, 1971. 311 p.

Chapter 12

THE HISTORICAL PROSPECT

Education and the philosophy of education have more reasons than most other sciences for accepting historic continuity as a principle for their research because these studies are directed more toward the future than the past and are spurred by the hope of making new and startling discoveries. Such history follows up the development of related sciences and sources of thought, traces the lines of contact and divergence among educational theories, shows where one system complements the other, and indicates the directions and quality of advancement over the past. To contemplate education as a bond between generations, to view education as a heritage and assimilative process, is to survey it from the horizon of history. To follow the genealogy and force of educational influences and agencies is to study historical movements and historical values and, though they assume various forms in the course of temporal and causal unfolding, all are actually traceable to the fundamental nature of man. As the basis of all educational endeavors, human persons do remain the same essentially. But, of itself, human nature cannot supply all that is needed to understand the aims, categories, problems, and phenomena of education. This really describes the unique function of the history of education itself and the history of the philosophy of education (Otto Willmann).

WESTERN EDUCATIONAL TRADITIONS

Abercrombie, Nigel. SAINT AUGUSTINE AND FRENCH CLASSICAL THOUGHT. 1938. New York: Russell and Russell, 1972. 123 p.

Adler, Mortimer J., and Van Doren, Charles, eds. GREAT TREASURY OF WESTERN THOUGHT. New York: R.R. Bowker, 1977. 1,771 p.

> This anthology contains some nine thousand memorable passages of the most brilliant minds in western civilization. Major sections concern man, mind, knowledge, education, philosophy, and other themes important to the educator. These are further broken down into more narrowly defined categories. Access to the quotations is facilitated by author, subject, and proper name indexes.

Ballauff, Theodor, et al. PAEDAGOGIK. 3 vols. Freiburg, W. Ger.; Munich: Alber, 1969-73.

Volume 1: FROM THE CLASSICAL TO THE HUMANISTIC AGE.

Volume 2: FROM THE SIXTEENTH TO THE NINETEENTH CENTURY. 1970. 774 p.

Volume 3: THE NINETEENTH-TWENTIETH CENTURY.

Bambara, Gino, ed. ANTOLOGIA DEL PENSIERO PEDAGOGICO MODERNO. Bologna, Italy: Zanichelli, 1969. xi, 418 p.

Bambara includes evaluations and criticisms for use at teacher training institutes and schools of education.

Basile, Carmelo. SISTEMI DI EDUCAZIONE ATTRAVERSO I TEMPI: CRONISTORIA DELL'IDEALE EDUCATIVO DELL'ANTICA GRECIA AI NOSTRI GIORNI. Ascoli Piceno, Italy: G. Cesari, 1968. 97 p.

Bastien, Hermas. VISAGES DE LA SAGESSE. Montreal, Canada: Editions Paulines and A.D.E., 1974. 183 p.

Black, Hugh C.; Lottich, Kenneth V.; and Seckinger, Donald S., eds. THE GREAT EDUCATORS: READINGS FOR LEADERS IN EDUCATION. Chicago: Nelson Hall, 1972. 799 p.

Among the readings are writings by Plato, Dewey, Thucydides, Toynbee, Augustine, Benedict, Cicero, and Jefferson.

Blishen, Edward, ed. ENCYCLOPEDIA OF EDUCATION. New York: Philosophical Library, 1970. xi, 882 p.

Topics are indexed alphabetically. Of special interest to the student are the articles by R.F. Dearden on the philosophy of education (pp. 537-39), Aristotle (p. 41), Dewey (pp. 197-98), Froebel (pp. 284-85), Kant (p. 403), Plato (pp. 546-47), Locke (p. 438), Rousseau (pp. 620-21), and Whitehead (p. 819).

Brubacher, John Seiler. A HISTORY OF THE PROBLEMS OF EDUCATION. 1947. 2d ed. New York: McGraw-Hill, 1966. 659 p.

Burston, W.H. JAMES MILL ON PHILOSOPHY AND EDUCATION. London: Athlone Press; distributed by Humanities Press, 1973. 254 p.

James Mill (1773-1836) was a devotee of Jeremy Bentham and helped spread his philosophy of utilitarianism.

Callot, Emile. LES TROIS MOMENTS DE LA PHILOSOPHIE DE L'HISTOIRE: AUGUSTIN, VICO, HERDER: SITUATION ACTUELLE. Paris: La Pensee Universelle, 1974. 379 p.

Cambon, Jacqueline; Delchet, Richard; and Lefevre, Lucien, eds. ANTHOLO-
GIE DES PEDAGOGUES FRANCAIS CONTEMPORAINS. Paris: Presses Universitaires de France, 1974. 386 p.

Cantor, Norman F., and Klein, Peter L., eds. ANCIENT THOUGHT: PLATO
AND ARISTOTLE. Waltham, Mass.: Blaisdell Publishing, 1969. viii, 194 p.

Cass, Walter J. A PRIMER IN PHILOSOPHY OF EDUCATION: PHILOSOPHIES
OF EDUCATION IN HISTORICAL PERSPECTIVE. Dubuque, Iowa: Kendall/Hunt
Publishing, 1974. xi, 107 p.

Chanel, Emile. TEXTES CLES DE LA PEDAGOGIE MODERNE. Paris: Editions
du Centurion, 1973. 346 p.

Cohen, Arthur Allen, ed. HUMANISTIC EDUCATION AND WESTERN CIVILI-
ZATION. New York: Holt, Rinehart and Winston, 1964. vi, 250 p.

Cole, Percival Richard. A HISTORY OF EDUCATIONAL THOUGHT. Westport, Conn.: Greenwood Press, 1972. x, 316 p.

Copleston, Frederick Charles. PHILOSOPHERS AND PHILOSOPHIES. London:
Search Press; New York: Barnes and Noble, 1976. iv, 184 p.

> Aquinas, Nicholas of Autrecourt, Spinoza, Hegel, Nietzsche,
> Bergson, Sartre, and Ortega Y Gasset are the philosophers studied
> in separate essays. The philosophies focus on the issues of philoso-
> phical knowledge, relativism and recurrence, philosophy and reli-
> gion in Judaism and Christianity, Christianity without belief in God
> (also man, transcendence and the absence of God), and the existen-
> tialist conception of man.

De Aloysio, Francesco. DA DEWEY A JAMES. Rome: Bulzoni Editore, 1972.
251 p.

Donohue, John W. "A Medieval Commentator on Some Aristotelian Educational
Themes." In WISDOM IN DEPTH, edited by Vincent F. Daues, Maurice R.
Holloway, and Leo Sweeney, pp. 80-98. Milwaukee, Wis.: Bruce Publishing,
1966.

> The themes of Aristotelian PAIDEIA and KOINONIA POLITIKE are
> connected with two irreducibly important questions. The first asks
> about the nature of that community which will serve as an ideal
> matrix for the education of the good man. The second asks how the
> individual's personal fulfillment is linked to and dependent upon the
> development of his social capacities and calling to a life of associ-
> ation and partnership with others.

Dupuis, Adrian Maurice. PHILOSOPHY OF EDUCATION IN HISTORICAL PER-SPECTIVE. Chicago: Rand McNally, 1966. ix, 308 p.

> Dupuis combines the discussion of seminal issues with past educa-tional theory and practice with regard to man, knowledge, truth, and value. He finds American pluralism does permit a kind of educational unity amid diversity. Educational conservatism and liberalism provide a framework for examining the basic ideas and principles of educational philosophy.

Erlinghagen, Karl. KATHOLISCHE BILDUNG IM BAROCK. [Catholic educa-tion in the age of baroque culture]. Hanover, Berlin, Darmstadt, and Dortmund: Schroedel, 1972. 230 p.

> Erlinghagen proposes the interesting thesis that European educational institutions and school programs in the days of the baroque responded to countless influences and to any number of pragmatic needs long before a systematic theory of education was able to have any im-pact at all on learning and teaching in the schools. Thus, prag-matic exigencies were far more important than ruminations over educational problems. This proposition evokes possibilities that no philosopher of education may overlook.

Frankena, William K. THREE HISTORICAL PHILOSOPHIES OF EDUCATION. Fair Lawn, N.J.: Scott, Foresman, 1965. 216 p. Bibliog. Paperbound.

> The philosophy of education and its problems are seen from the al-ternative philosophies of Aristotle, Kant, and Dewey and then these are compared on the basic questions of dispositions, aims, and methods.

Gosling, J.C.B. PLATO. London: Routledge and Kegan Paul, 1973. 328 p.

> This work gives the reader an understanding of the relative sound-ness of Plato's arguments and conclusions and their moral, epistem-ological, and metaphysical interconnections. Gosling explores the platonic dialogues quite comprehensively.

Granese, Alberto. DIALETTICA DELL'EDUCAZIONE. Rome: Editori Riuniti, 1976. 277 p.

Gruber, Frederick Charles. HISTORICAL AND CONTEMPORARY PHILOSO-PHIES OF EDUCATION. New York: Thomas Y. Crowell, 1973. viii, 200 p.

_____, ed. FOUNDATIONS FOR A PHILOSOPHY OF EDUCATION. New York: Thomas Y. Crowell, 1961. viii, 322 p.

> By a comparative historical survey of different philosophical schools covering a period of twenty-five centuries, the author encourages students to state a philosophy of their own. Gruber's own choice is the philosophy of relativism.

Harrington, Jack. AIMS OF EDUCATION: EARLY TWENTIETH CENTURY. New York: MSS Information Corp., 1974. 297 p.

Higson, Constance Winifred Jane, ed. SUPPLEMENT TO SOURCES FOR THE HISTORY OF EDUCATION: A LIST OF MATERIAL ADDED TO THE LIBRARIES OF THE INSTITUTES AND SCHOOLS OF EDUCATION, 1965-1974, TOGETHER WITH WORKS FROM CERTAIN UNIVERSITY LIBRARIES. London: Library Association, 1976. x, 221 p.

Khalid, Tanvir. EDUCATION: AN INTRODUCTION TO EDUCATIONAL PHILOSOPHY AND HISTORY. Karachi, Pakistan: National Book Foundation, 1974. xx, 238 p.

Lang, Ossian Herbert. EDUCATIONAL CREEDS OF THE NINETEENTH CENTURY. 1898. Reprint. New York: Arno Press, 1971. vii, 162 p.

Lichtenstein, Ernst. BILDUNGSGESCHICHTLICHE PERSPEKTIVEN: GLAUBE UND BILDING, BILDUNG ALS GESCHICHTLICHE BEGEGNUNG. [Historical perspectives of liberal education: belief and liberal education, liberal education as historical encounter]. Ratingen by Dusseldorf, W. Ger.: Henn, 1962. x, 187 p.

Maritain, Jacques. ON THE PHILOSOPHY OF HISTORY. Edited by Joseph W. Evans. 1952. Clifton, N.J.: Augustus M. Kelley, 1973. 180 p.

_____. THREE REFORMERS: LUTHER, DESCARTES, ROUSSEAU. Westport, Conn.: Greenwood Press, 1970. 234 p.

Markus, Robert Austin. SAECULUM: HISTORY AND SOCIETY IN THE THEOLOGY OF SAINT AUGUSTINE. Cambridge: Cambridge University Press, 1970. ix, 252 p.

Mehl, Bernard. CLASSIC EDUCATIONAL IDEAS FROM SUMERIA TO AMERICA. Columbus, Ohio: Charles E. Merrill Publishing, 1972. x, 220 p.

Meyer, Adolphe E. GRANDMASTERS OF EDUCATIONAL THOUGHT. New York: McGraw-Hill, 1975. ix, 302 p. Paperbound.

> The grandmasters, in the judgment of Meyer, are Socrates, Isocrates, Plato, Aristotle, Quintilian, Augustine, Erasmus, Luther, Loyola, Comenius, Locke, Franklin, Jefferson, Webster, Rush, Knox, Rousseau, Pestalozzi, Herbart, Froebel, Emerson, Parker, and Dewey. The writing spotlights their doctrines and educational ideas.

Ottaviano, Carmelo, and Petrullo, Salvatore. APPUNTI DI PEDAGOGIA CONTEMPORANEA. Catania, Italy: Muglia, 1974. 149 p.

Power, Edward J. EVOLUTION OF EDUCATIONAL DOCTRINE: MAJOR EDUCATIONAL THEORISTS OF THE WESTERN WORLD. New York: Appleton-Century-Crofts, 1969. xiii, 408 p.

Pseudo-Boece. DE DISCIPLINA SCOLARIUM. Critical ed. Introduction and notes by Olga Weijers. Leiden, Netherlands: E.J. Brill, 1976. xiv, 189 p.

> The text is Latin with critical notes in French. The work has importance because it was a standard educational text used in medieval European universities.

Rusk, Robert Robertson. DOCTRINES OF THE GREAT EDUCATORS. Rev. and enl. 3d ed. Melbourne: Macmillan; New York: St. Martin's Press, 1965. vii, 336 p.

> Plato, Quintilian, Elyot, Loyola, Comenius, Milton, Locke, Rousseau, Pestalozzi, Herbart, Froebel, Montessori, and Dewey.

Schaller, Klaus, and Schaefer, Karl-H. BILDUNGSMODELLE UND GESCHICHT-LICHKEIT. EIN REPRETORIUM ZUR GESCHICHTE DER PAEDAGOGIK. [The history and ideals of education: essays toward a history of education]. Hamburg, W. Ger.: Leibniz-Verlag, 1967. 271 p. Bibliogs.

> Beginning with the influence of Wilhelm Dilthey and Otto Willmann, who established the history of education as a scientific and educative discipline, the authors have also edited selected texts for the light they shed on modern educational problems. Their intent is to clarify issues from three perspectives: the intellectual history of education, the history of education as it is mirrored in the spirit of modern research and a new age, and the history of what actually occurs in the schools.

Steenberghen, Fernand van. ARISTOTLE IN THE WEST: THE ORIGINS OF LATIN ARISTOTELIANISM. Translated from French by Leonard Johnston. New York: Humanities Press, 1970. 244 p.

Stephens, J.E., ed. AUBREY ON EDUCATION: A HITHERTO UNPUBLISHED MANUSCRIPT BY THE AUTHOR OF BRIEF LIVES. London: Routledge and Kegan Paul, 1972. xi, 204 p.

> While writing his classic among biographical writings, John Aubrey (1626-97) became acquainted with the thinking of Francis Bacon, John Milton, Thomas Hobbes, and Sir Walter Raleigh. Aubrey offers an historical glimpse into post-Elizabethan English thoughts about education.

Stoops, John A. PHILOSOPHY AND EDUCATION IN WESTERN CIVILIZATION. Danville, Ill.: Interstate Printers and Publishers, 1971. 424 p.

> Stoop contributes summaries and interpretations for schoolmen and churchmen.

Ulmann, Jacques. LA PENSEE EDUCATIVE CONTEMPORAINE. Paris: Presses Universitaires de France, 1976. 157 p.

AMERICAN EDUCATIONAL TRADITIONS

Angell, James Rowland. AMERICAN EDUCATION: ADDRESSES AND ARTICLES. 1937. Reprint. New York: Books for Libraries Press, 1970. 282 p.

Barnes, Ronald E. 1996: A LOOK BACK AT EDUCATIONAL TRANSITIONS. Topeka, Kans.: Transitions, 1976. 16 p. Bibliog.

This is a volume in the series on educational alternatives.

Bayles, Ernest E., and Hood, Bruce L. GROWTH OF AMERICAN EDUCATIONAL THOUGHT AND PRACTICE. New York: Harper and Row, 1966. x, 305 p.

Ben-David, Joseph. AMERICAN HIGHER EDUCATION: DIRECTIONS OLD AND NEW. New York: McGraw-Hill, 1972. 137 p.

The author gives a very modern account of the process of secularization in American higher education.

Best, John Hardin. BENJAMIN FRANKLIN ON EDUCATION. New York: Teachers College, Bureau of Publications, 1962. 174 p.

Brauner, Charles J. AMERICAN EDUCATIONAL THEORY. Englewood Cliffs, N.J.: Prentice-Hall, 1964. ix, 341 p.

_____. THE EVOLUTION OF AMERICAN EDUCATIONAL THEORY. W.H. Cowley, project director. Stanford, Calif.: Stanford University, 1962. xviii, 192 p.

Butler, James Donald. IDEALISM IN EDUCATION. Philosophy of Education Series. New York: Harper and Row, 1966. xii, 144 p.

This insightful study offers a short introduction to idealism as an educational philosophy together with its history. After a critical review of its major tenets, Butler outlines his own philosophy of idealism. The objectives of education, the student's participation, and the school as a social institution in the process of education are important concerns to the idealist.

Carbone, Peter. THE SOCIAL AND EDUCATIONAL THOUGHT OF HAROLD RUGG. Durham, N.C.: Duke University Press, 1977. xi, 225 p. Bibliog.

Using methods of analysis developed in recent analytic philosophy,

Carbone notes that certain shifts in emphasis can be discerned in Rugg's thinking. Rugg still generates considerable controversy and so an appraisal of this social reconstructionist's premises for judging the usefulness of this movement today is instructive in the light of recent social and intellectual history.

Chambliss, Joseph James. THE ORIGINS OF AMERICAN PHILOSOPHY OF EDUCATION. The Hague: Martinus Nijhoff, 1968. viii, 114 p.

Chambliss traces the main currents of philosophical thought in nineteenth century American education and the development of the American philosophy of education as a distinct discipline, 1808–1913.

Cremin, Lawrence Arthur. AMERICAN EDUCATION: SOME NOTES TOWARD A NEW HISTORY. Bloomington, Ind.: Phi Delta Kappa International, 1972. 18 p.

_____. TRADITIONS OF AMERICAN EDUCATION. New York: Basic Books, 1977. ix, 172 p.

Dewey, John. EDUCATION TODAY. Edited with a foreword by Joseph Ratner. New York: G.P. Putnam's Sons, 1940. 370 p. Reprint. New York: Greenwood Press, 1969. xiv, 373 p.

_____. JOHN DEWEY. Edited with an introduction by Malcolm Skilbeck. London: Collier-Macmillan; New York: Macmillan, 1970. vi, 170 p.

Flower, Elizabeth, and Murphey, Murray G. A HISTORY OF PHILOSOPHY IN AMERICA. 2 vols. New York: G.P. Putnam's Sons, 1977. vol. 1, xx, 435.; vol. 2, 463 p.

The authors make clear the fundamental role of the intellect in the making of America. First, they review theoretical links with the Old World, especially the Scottish, German, and English thinkers. Then their attention is given to American colleges and universities for their influence on philosophical and scientific thought. Finally, the remarkable framework of American thought helps locate the special contributions of Jonathan Edwards, Peirce, James, Royce, C.I. Lewis, and other important intellectual leaders.

Gutek, Gerald Lee. THE EDUCATIONAL THEORY OF GEORGE S. COUNTS. Columbus: Ohio State University Press, 1971. xv, 277 p.

Despite his political and educational friendship for the Soviet Union, Counts eventually became a strong opponent to USSR educational policy and thought. Counts came to see the Soviet concentration on science and technology as a serious threat to the

United States and Western Europe. Sheerin calls this study an excellent summary and critique of the work of Counts (see Sheerin entry, p. 263).

Handlin, Oscar. "Education and the American Society." AMERICAN EDUCATION 10, no. 5 (1974): 6-15.

The essay, accompanied by photographs of historical interest, notes the achievements of the American school in shaping a Democratic people. Handlin esteems the impressive contributions of the schools as being "without parallel in the modern world."

Heslep, Robert D. THOMAS JEFFERSON AND EDUCATION. New York: Random House, 1969. 131 p.

"An excellent analysis of Jefferson's educational thought" (Perkinson, see entry, p. 257).

Hiner, N. Ray. "Herbartians, History, and Moral Education." SCHOOL REVIEW 79, no. 4 (1971): 590-601.

Hiner uses the American Herbartian movement to illustrate the way familiar institutions and values were subtly modified in the complex process of transition and adjustment to a more radical and instrumentalistic philosophy of education. Dewey was chiefly instrumental in effecting the transformation.

Kilpatrick, William Heard, ed. THE EDUCATIONAL FRONTIER. New York and London: D. Appleton-Century, 1933. 291 p.

Kneller, George Frederick. "Contemporary Educational Theories." In FOUNDATIONS OF EDUCATION, edited by George F. Kneller, pp. 247-51. New York: John Wiley and Sons, 1971.

Mayer, Frederick. A HISTORY OF EDUCATIONAL THOUGHT. 3d ed. Columbus, Ohio: Charles E. Merrill, 1973. xiii, 557 p.

Rippa, S. Alexander. EDUCATION IN A FREE SOCIETY: AN AMERICAN HISTORY. 3d ed. New York: David McKay, 1976. 436 p. Bibliog. Paperbound.

Rippa considers his historical synopsis to be selective rather than encyclopedic, with topics organized around dominant patterns of educational thought, in order to provide a strong foundation for education in a free society.

Smith, William, ed. THEORIES OF EDUCATION IN EARLY AMERICA, 1655-1819. Indianapolis: Bobbs-Merrill, 1973. xxxvii, 442 p.

Sullivan, Phyllis. "John Dewey's Philosophy of Education." HIGH SCHOOL JOURNAL 40, no. 8 (1966): 391-97. Reprinted in READINGS IN THE FOUN-DATIONS OF EDUCATION, edited by James C. Stone and Frederick W. Schneider, pp. 495-502. 2d ed. New York: Thomas Y. Crowell, 1971.

> Whatever the reader's opinion of John Dewey, the study of his ideas on the principles of education, the function of the school, the curriculum, and the teacher is a very important aspect of the historical and philosophical foundations of education. The chart, comparing traditional with Dewey's progressive education in regard to sixteen issues, is thought provoking.

Thayer, V.T. FORMATIVE IDEAS IN AMERICAN EDUCATION: FROM THE COLONIAL PERIOD TO THE PRESENT. New York: Dodd, Mead, 1965. xii, 394 p.

> The author follows the various schools of American educational philosophy to find their links to the cultural and historical influences that led to their flourishing. Thayer concentrates on the basic con-cepts of man, nature, and the world in change during the last three centuries.

Tyack, David B., ed. TURNING POINTS IN AMERICAN EDUCATIONAL HISTORY. Waltham, Mass.: Blaisdell Publishing, 1967. xiv, 488 p.

Wingo, Glenn Max. THE PHILOSOPHY OF AMERICAN EDUCATION. Lexing-ton, Mass.: D.C. Heath, 1965. 438 p.

H TR: HISTORY OF EDUCATIONAL THOUGHT AND THE PHILOSOPHY OF RELIGION

Benz, Ernst. EVOLUTION AND CHRISTIAN HOPE: MAN'S CONCEPT OF THE FUTURE FROM THE EARLY FATHERS TO TEILHARD DE CHARDIN. Garden City, N.Y.: Doubleday, 1968. 270 p.

Cross, Robert D. THE EMERGENCE OF LIBERAL CATHOLICISM IN AMERICA. Cambridge, Mass.: Harvard University Press, 1958. 328 p.

Leclercq, Jean. THE LOVE OF LEARNING AND THE DESIRE FOR GOD. Translated by Catherine Misrahi. 1961. Rev. ed. New York: Fordham Uni-versity Press, 1974. x, 415 p.

> Chapters of special significance to the philosophy of education are those concerning cult and culture, sacred learning, and liberal studies.

Mohler, James. THE SCHOOL OF JESUS: AN OVERVIEW OF CHRISTIAN EDUCATION YESTERDAY AND TODAY. New York: Alba House, 1973. xii, 279 p.

Winter, Nathan H. JEWISH EDUCATION IN A PLURALIST SOCIETY: SAMSON
BENDERLY AND JEWISH EDUCATION IN THE UNITED STATES. New York:
New York University Press, 1966. xvi, 262 p.

> The fundamental ideas and influence of early twentieth century
> Judaism are examined through the philosophy and activities of
> Samson Benderly. More of this type of study is sorely needed.

H NS: HISTORY OF EDUCATIONAL THOUGHT AND THE
PHILOSOPHY OF SCIENCE

Bronowski, Jacob, and Mazlish, Bruce. THE WESTERN INTELLECTUAL TRADI-
TION, FROM LEONARDO TO HEGEL. Harmondsworth, Engl.: Penguin Books,
1963. 578 p.; Freeport, N.Y.: Books for Libraries Press, 1971. xviii, 522 p.

Dooley, Patrick Kiaran. PRAGMATISM AS HUMANISM: THE PHILOSOPHY
OF WILLIAM JAMES. Chicago: Nelson-Hall, 1974. 232 p.; Totawa, N.J.:
Littlefield, Adams, 1975. xii, 220 p. Bibliog.

> The thematic exposition is orderly and attempts to discover a basic
> consistency in the thought of this important American philosopher
> and educational theorist. The notes, bibliography, and clarity of
> text make it suitable for introductory and supplemental reading.

Kockelmans, Joseph J., ed. PHILOSOPHY OF SCIENCE: HISTORICAL BACK-
GROUND. New York: Free Press, 1968. xiii, 496 p.

White, Morton Gabriel. SCIENCE AND SENTIMENT IN AMERICA: PHILO-
SOPHICAL THOUGHT FROM JONATHAN EDWARDS TO JOHN DEWEY. New
York: Oxford University Press, 1972. viii, 358 p.

H HS: HISTORY OF EDUCATIONAL THOUGHT AND THE
PHILOSOPHY OF SOCIETY

Cassirer, Ernst. THE PLATONIC RENAISSANCE IN ENGLAND. Translated by
James P. Pettegrove. 1953. Reprint. New York: Gordian Press, 1970. vii,
207 p.

Coser, Lewis A. MEN OF IDEAS: A SOCIOLOGIST'S VIEW. New York:
Free Press, 1965. xviii, 374 p.

> Of the three essays, "Settings for Intellectual Life," "Intellectuals
> in the House of Power," and "The Intellectual in Contemporary
> America," the last will probably be of most interest to the philoso-
> pher of education. Coser's sixfold criteria for intellectual behavior
> invite careful reflection.

Counts, George Sylvester. THE AMERICAN ROAD TO CULTURE: A SOCIAL INTERPRETATION OF EDUCATION IN THE UNITED STATES. 1930. Reprint. New York: Arno Press, 1971. xiii, 194 p.

_____. EDUCATION AND AMERICAN CIVILIZATION. 1952. Reprint. Westport, Conn.: Greenwood Press, 1974. xiv, 491 p.

Dray, William H., ed. PHILOSOPHICAL ANALYSIS AND HISTORY. New York: Harper and Row, 1966. 390 p. Paperbound.

Dyson, A.E., and Lovelock, Julian, eds. EDUCATION AND DEMOCRACY. London: Routledge and Kegan Paul, 1975. 308 p.

> In one hundred well-illustrated documents, the authors depict the radical changes that overtook education between 1791 and 1916. Education was becoming more Democratic and gradually produced a democratizing effect on society so that by 1916 the principle of universal education had become accepted. This book helps clarify the changes that have continued to take place especially since education is now no longer the preserve of the wealthy. Contributors to the debate include Robert Owen, J.S. Mill, Engels, Charles Dickens, and Bernard Shaw.

Harlan, Louis R. BOOKER T. WASHINGTON: THE MAKING OF A BLACK LEADER. 1856-1901. New York: Oxford University Press, 1972. xl, 379 p.

Kammen, Michael G., ed. THE CONTRAPUNTAL CIVILIZATION: ESSAYS TOWARD A NEW UNDERSTANDING OF THE AMERICAN EXPERIENCE. New York: Thomas Y. Crowell, 1971. 312 p. Also paperbound.

> The explanations given for the paradoxes, contradictory tendencies, dualisms, and polarities in American thought and life illuminate the dilemmas intrinsic to cultural pluralism. The right to dissent and to be different includes also some tendency toward inefficiency and disintegration.

Kulick, Bruce. THE RISE OF AMERICAN PHILOSOPHY. New Haven: Yale University Press, 1977. 720 p.

> This intellectual history describes the emergence of American pragmatism through the thought of Charles Peirce, William James, Josiah Royce, George Santayana, Alfred North Whitehead, and C.I. Lewis. During the seventy years between the Civil War and the Depression, Harvard established an intellectual community of philosophical dialogue that is intimately related to the formation of the modern university. The philosopher of education must understand this history and this unique relationship if he is to appreciate that, in the United States, philosophy and education often define each other.

May, Henry F. THE ENLIGHTENMENT IN AMERICA. New York: Oxford University Press, 1978. xix, 419 p.

Monmouni, Abdou. EDUCATION IN AFRICA. Translated from French by Phyllis Nauts Ott. Preface by L.J. Lewis. London: Deutsch; New York: Frederick A. Praeger, 1968. 319 p.

Morris, Van Cleve, ed. MODERN MOVEMENTS IN EDUCATIONAL PHILOSO-PHY. Boston: Houghton Mifflin, 1969. xii, 381 p.

Pennar, Jaan; Bakalo, Ivan K.; and Bereday, George Z.F. MODERNIZATION AND DIVERSITY IN SOVIET EDUCATION. New York: Praeger Publishers, 1971. xix, 395 p.

Perkinson, Henry J., ed. TWO HUNDRED YEARS OF AMERICAN EDUCA-TIONAL THOUGHT. New York: David McKay, 1976. xi, 367 p. Paper-bound.

> Perkinson directly engages the reader in critical dialogue with such educators as Franklin, Jefferson, Mann, Emerson, Eliot, B.T. Washington, Dewey, Conant, and the "Romantic Critics": Goodman, Friedenberg, Holt, Kohl, Kozol, Postman, Weingartner, Dennison, Graubard, and Illich. Commentaries include analyses of primary and secondary sources.

Peterson, Merrill D. THOMAS JEFFERSON AND THE NEW NATION. New York: Oxford University Press, 1970. ix, 1,072 p.

Wittig, Horst E., ed. MENSCHENBILDUNG IN JAPAN. [Education in Japan]. Munich, W. Ger., and Basel, Switz.: E. Reinhardt, 1973. 214 p. Bibliog.

> The twenty-two essays by prominent Japanese educators and politi-cal thinkers represent a collegial effort to deepen and to adapt to their culture the educational traditions of Europe. Important themes concern the history and philosophy of education, institutional inno-vations, and pedagogical perspectives. The bibliography contains many sources published in German and English from 1945 to 1971.

H AC: THE HISTORY OF EDUCATIONAL THOUGHT AND THE PHILOSOPHY OF CULTURE

Jones, Howard Mumford, ed. EMERSON ON EDUCATION. New York: Bureau of Publications, Teachers College, Columbia University, 1966. viii, 227 p.

> "Unfortunately this collection contains the synthetic essay 'Education' pieced together from a number of Emerson's writings by his friend and literary executor, James Eliot Cabot. . ." (Perkinson, see entry, p. 257).

Chapter 13

THE SCIENCE OF EDUCATION—THEORY AND RESEARCH

To be versed in the science of education means to be familiar with the principles that order the general work of education as a whole. When principles, taken from the sciences and philosophy itself, are applied to education, the study of education as a whole progresses like any other science through the different stages of meaning or of intellectual abstraction. Education then moves, as Whitehead has noted, from the stage of romance to that of precision and hypothesis until it finally arrives at the perfection of ultimate generalization. In Lonergan's terms and in a somewhat different conception, the conscious and intentional operations of the first stage are expressed in the mode of common sense. This stage is followed by the mode of theory which is controlled by logic and finally a certain autonomy is reached without, however, any loss of the romance or precise meanings of the previous modes or stages. The science of education, therefore, has its own domain in the kingdom of human learning and science not yet so clearly defined yet ever so essential to the harmony and unity of the study of education as a whole. Writings on this subject are sparse. But the following sampling does reveal that the study of education as a science has become a problem uppermost in the minds of some educational philosophers.

Adler, Mortimer J. "In Defense of the Philosophy of Education." In FORTY-FIRST YEARBOOK OF THE NATIONAL SOCIETY FOR THE STUDY OF EDUCATION, PART 1. Edited by Nelson B. Henry, pp. 197-249. Chicago: University of Chicago Press, 1942.

> Since the problems of education have philosophical dimensions, their solutions depend on first principles and their application to the process by which human powers are susceptible to habituation, are made perfect by good habits, and are employed to help men achieve virtue. Ethical knowledge is the one truth, which educational philosophy must presuppose, and is of the greatest importance to all persons engaged in education.

Barnett, George, ed. PHILOSOPHY AND EDUCATIONAL DEVELOPMENT. Boston: Houghton Mifflin, 1966; London: Harrap, 1967. 157 p. Paperbound.

These papers by Aiken, Kaufmann, Scriven, Edel, Bertocci, and Benne concern the development of education as a field of study and an object of scholarly interest to academic man. Among the many contributions philosophy can make to education must be noted its power to expand consciousness, settle value conflicts, refocus the method of rationality, release as an educational good a dialogue addressed to currently central policy and action issues, and project images of potentiality for man.

Belth, Marc. EDUCATION AS A DISCIPLINE: A STUDY OF THE ROLE OF MODELS IN THINKING. Boston: Allyn and Bacon, 1965. xviii, 317 p.

Models have both assumptions and implications that ought to be carefully weighed before these are assumed into an educational philosophy. To distinguish and assess the objective merits of the hypotheses on which models are erected is an essential function of education as a discipline.

Bhattacharya, Srinibas. FOUNDATIONS OF EDUCATION AND EDUCATIONAL RESEARCH. Baroda, India: Acharya Book Depot, 1968. 398 p.

Brezinka, Wolfgang. GRUNDBEGRIFFE DER ERZIEHUNGSWISSENSCHAFT: ANALYSE, KRITIK, VORSCHLAEGE. [Concepts basic to a science of education: analysis, evaluation, recommendations]. 2d ed. Munich: E. Reinhardt, 1975. 246 p.

Broudy, Harry S. BUILDING A PHILOSOPHY OF EDUCATION. 2d ed. Englewood Cliffs, N.J.: Prentice-Hall, 1961. 410 p.

In what is basically an Aristotelian interpretation, modified classical realism considers the questions of man, society, school, and the good life to be the core issues for the study of educational philosophy. Such philosophizing in education involves the aims and curriculum of education, an understanding of human personality, the school in respect to the good life, and values whether economic, aesthetic, moral, or religious. The ultimate standards must be self-determination, self-realization, self-integration, and democracy.

Broudy, Harry S., et al. PHILOSOPHY OF EDUCATION: AN ORGANIZATION OF TOPICS AND SELECTED SOURCES. Urbana: University of Illinois Press, 1967. xii, 287 p. Paperbound.

This comprehensive reference of some two thousand sources makes accessible a systematic and annotated listing of books and articles dealing philosophically with the nature and aims of education, curriculum, organization and policy, and teaching-learning. The organization of topics and materials is intended to indicate the kind of competence needed by those who teach the courses in the philosophy of education. The project is aimed at meeting the challenge of whether it is possible, in some rational and enlightening order, for philosophy of education to concern itself meaningfully with the problems of education.

_____. READINGS IN EDUCATIONAL RESEARCH: PHILOSOPHY OF EDU-CATIONAL RESEARCH. Berkeley, Calif.: McCutchan Publishing; New York: John Wiley and Sons, 1973. xvii, 942 p.

The forty-nine readings in part 2 deal with the theoretical issues involved in a science of education. Educational research faces philosophical problems in observation, inference, testability, causa-tion, models, value judgments, concepts and their clarification, behaviorism, and programmed instruction. Part 1 readings shed light on the conditions necessary for scientific educational research. Of special relevance is the focus on the philosophy of science and its methods.

Busch, Friedrich W., and Raapke, Hans-Dietrich, eds. JOHANN FRIEDRICH HERBART: LEBEN UND WERK IN DIE WIDERSPRUECHEN SEINER ZEIT. [Herbart's life and work in the contradictions of his era]. Oldenburg, W. Ger.: Holzberg, 1976. 136 p.

The editors review the status of research into Herbart's thought and work. The nine analytical essays were read at Oldenburg to cele-brate the two-hundredth anniversary of Herbart's birth (1776-1841).

Cohen, Brenda. EDUCATIONAL THOUGHT: AN INTRODUCTION. London: Macmillan, 1969. 109 p.

Derbolav, Josef. SYSTEMATISCHE PERSPEKTIVEN DER PAEDAGOGIK. [Sys-tematic perspectives of education]. Heidelberg, W. Ger.: Quelle and Meyer, 1971. 183 p.

The seven essays range from educational anthropology, the science of education, pedagogical ethics to the theory of political educa-tion.

Ferre, Frederick. SHAPING THE FUTURE: RESOURCES FOR THE POST-MODERN WORLD. New York: Harper and Row, 1976. 194 p.

Horvath, Tibor. ENCYCLOPEDIA OF HUMAN IDEALS ON ULTIMATE REALITY AND MEANING: A PLAN AND LIST OF TOPICS FOR A NEW ENCYCLO-PEDIA. Toronto, Canada: Tibor Horvath, S.J., 1970, 166 p.

Lassahn, Rudolf. GRUNDRISS EINER ALLGEMEINEN PAEDAGOGIK. [The ground plan for a general theory of education]. Heidelberg, W. Ger.: Quelle and Meyer, 1977. 208 p.

Lassahn analyzes education in its theoretical, anthropological, social, and political dimensions. He gives considerable attention to learning theory and its importance in education.

Lucas, Christopher J. "The Demise of Educational Philosophy." SCHOOL REVIEW 79, no. 2 (1971): 269-81.

While it is axiomatic that thinkers, in a heterogeneous and pluralistic society, need not agree, this fact does not excuse educators from acquiring philosophically grounded convictions about their lifework. Every philosopher of education ought to respond to the imperative of responsible partisanship in order to make positive recommendations in regard to educational theory and practical schooling.

METHODEN ERZIEHUNGSWISSESNSCHAFTLICHER FORSCHUNG. [Methods of educational research]. Edited by Leo Roth in collaboration with Hans-Kark Beckmann. Stuttgart, Berlin, Cologne, and Mainz: Kohlhammer, 1978. 206 p.

The authors discuss educational research within the context of education as a field of scientific theorizing. The focus is centered on the concepts and strategies of research.

Perkinson, Henry J. THE POSSIBILITIES OF ERROR: AN APPROACH TO EDUCATION. New York: David McKay, 1971. 128 p.

Piaget, Jean. TO UNDERSTAND IS TO INVENT: THE FUTURE OF EDUCATION. Translated by George-Anne Roberts. 1973. New York: Penguin Books, 1977. viii, 148 p.

Price, Kingsley. "On Education as a Species of Play." EDUCATIONAL THEORY 27, no. 4 (1977): 253-60.

Price feels that education is not a species of play. We must make up our minds to the fact that education is work, joyful sometimes, but requiring energy to illumine the sojourn of men while on this earth.

Reich, Kersten. THEORIEN DER ALLGEMEINEN DIDAKTIK. [Theories of general education]. Stuttgart, W. Ger.: Klett, 1977. 482 p.

Reich concentrates on the development of educational theory as a domain for research. He examines the theoretical and practical points of departure for and the actual development of German pedagogical thought since 1945. Of special interest are the new directions of research, the relativizing and reductive tendencies of current criticism, and the search for new foundations in the philosophy of education.

Roehrs, Hermann. DIDAKTIK. [The science of education]. Frankfort on the Main, W. Ger.: Akademische Verlagsgesellschaft, 1971. viii, 385 p. Bibliog.

> Five essays discuss the theoretical and scientific foundations of education, three its cultural-humanistic basis, three the principles of curriculum building, three the curriculum as cognitive psychological and social experiences, two the plan of studies as a didactic problem, and six the fundamental problem of methodology and the curriculum. The bibliography (pp. 359-74) is a fine resource for further study.

Rosenow, Eliyahu. "Methods of Research and the Aims of Education." EDUCATIONAL THEORY 26, no. 3 (1976): 279-88.

Sheerin, William E. "Educational Scholarship and the Legacy of George S. Counts." EDUCATIONAL THEORY 26, no. 1 (1976): 107-12.

> "George S. Counts . . . brought bold new initiative to educational thought. His life proved there need be no schism between theorist and practitioner, professional and reformer. First and foremost a teacher, Counts integrated scholarly rigor and a thoroughgoing humanism. His work stands as a model and a challenge to us all" (p. 112).

Smith, Philip G. "The Relation of Philosophy to Education as a Discipline." EDUCATIONAL ADMINISTRATION AND SUPERVISION 46, no. 1 (1960): 41-51.

Taylor, Calvin Walker, et al. DEVELOPMENT OF A THEORY OF EDUCATION FROM PSYCHOLOGICAL AND OTHER BASIC RESEARCH FINDINGS. Salt Lake City: University of Utah, 1964. viii, 193 p.

Vircillo, Domenico. LA PEDAGOGICA E LE SCIENZE DELL' EDUCAZIONE. Messina, Italy: Peloritana, 1973. 425 p.

Wilson, John. PHILOSOPHY AND EDUCATIONAL RESEARCH. Windsor: National Foundation for Educational Research in England and Wales, 1972. x, 133 p.

Xochellis, Panagiotis (Panos). DIE ENTFALTUNG DES WISSENSCHAFTLICHEN PAEDAGOGISCHEN DENKENS. [The development of the science of educational thought]. Ratingen by Dusseldorf, W. Ger.: Henn, 1967. 101 p.

T TR: THE PHILOSOPHY OF RELIGION

Brown, Stuart C. REASON AND RELIGION. Ithaca, N.Y., and London: Cornell University Press, 1977. 315 p.

The essays of these five symposia were prepared for a conference sponsored by the Royal Institute of Philosophy and held at the University of Lancaster in 1975. The essays have been revised for this publication and concern the issues of the intelligibility of the universe, the problem of evil, the rationality of religious belief, meaning and religious language, and immortality.

Kevane, Eugene. CREED AND CATECHETICS. Westminster, Md.: Christian Classics, 1977. xxiii, 319 p.

Kevane presents the catechetical order of religious education as completely distinct from that of the theologies, especially the modern philosophical ones.

Schlesinger, George. RELIGION AND SCIENTIFIC METHOD. Boston: D. Reidel, 1978. 203 p.

Taylor, Marvin J., ed. FOUNDATIONS FOR CHRISTIAN EDUCATION IN AN ERA OF CHANGE. Nashville: Abingdon, 1976. 288 p.

The primary value of these twenty-one essays and selected bibliography since 1966 is to lead the reader into the broad dimensions of Christian education. For example, separate courses could be offered in each of the twenty-one fields identified by chapter headings. The stress on foundations is also interdenominational.

T NS: THE PHILOSOPHY OF SCIENCE

Colodny, Robert G., ed. THE NATURE AND FUNCTION OF SCIENTIFIC THEORIES. Pittsburgh: University of Pittsburgh Press, 1971. 361 p.

Dubin, Robert, ed. THEORY BUILDING: A PRACTICAL GUIDE TO THE CONSTRUCTION AND TESTING OF THEORETICAL MODELS. New York: Free Press, 1969. ix, 298 p.

Feibleman, James K. SCIENTIFIC METHOD: THE HYPTHETICO-EXPERIMENTAL LABORATORY PROCEDURE OF THE PHYSICAL SCIENCES. The Hague: Martinus Nijhoff; New York: Humanities Press, 1972. 246 p.

Harre, R. THE METHOD OF SCIENCE. London: Wykeham Publications; New York: Springer-Verlag, 1971. 120 p.

T HS: THE PHILOSOPHY OF HUMAN SOCIETY AND CULTURE

Buford, Thomas O. TOWARD A PHILOSOPHY OF EDUCATION. New York: Holt, Rinehart and Winston, 1969. ix, 518 p.

Without attempting to develop any philosophical position, Buford divides the readings into The Spirit of Modern American Culture (Parsons, Cassirer, Seeman, Whyte, Marcuse, Jung, Sartre, Bell), Methodological Options for Educational Philosophy (O'Connor, Dewey, Whitehead, Buber), The Philosophy of Learning (Plato, Augustine, Locke, Kant, Hegel, Dewey, Cassirer, Polanyi, Buber), and Cultural Postures and Educational Aims (Maritain, Dewey, Brameld, Polanyi). Annotated references for further study follow each section.

Cunningham, Frank. OBJECTIVITY IN SOCIAL SCIENCE. Toronto: University of Toronto Press, 1973. 154 p.

de Groot, A.D. METHODOLOGY: FOUNDATIONS OF INFERENCE AND RESEARCH IN THE BEHAVIORAL SCIENCES. Translated by J.A.A. Spiekerman. The Hague: Mouton, 1969. 400 p.

Mey, Harold. FIELD-THEORY: A STUDY OF ITS APPLICATION IN THE SOCIAL SCIENCES. New York: St. Martin's Press, 1972. 325 p.

Sanders, William B., ed. THE SOCIOLOGIST AS DETECTIVE. New York: Praeger Publishers, 1974. xiii, 263 p.

Four sections deal with the interview, the survey, the ethnography, and content analysis. This field manual combines an introduction to research, descriptions of several methods, examples of each method in use, and exercises requiring applications of the methods in new situations.

Williams, Raymond. KEYWORDS: A VOCABULARY OF CULTURE AND SOCI-ETY. New York: Oxford University Press, 1976. 286 p.

BIBLIOGRAPHIC RESEARCH AIDS

Brickman, William W. BIBLIOGRAPHICAL ESSAYS ON THE HISTORY AND PHILOSOPHY OF EDUCATION. Norwood, Pa.: Norwood Editions, 1975. x, 185 p.

Brickman includes articles originally published in SCHOOL AND SOCIETY (now INTELLECT). Probably no one in the field of educational philosophy is more familiar than Brickman with what is being published in English and in other languages of the world.

Broudy, Harry S., and Smith, Christina M. PHILOSOPHY OF EDUCATION: AN ORGANIZATION OF TOPICS AND SELECTED SOURCES--SUPPLEMENT, 1969. Urbana: University of Illinois Press, 1969. iv, 139 p.

This supplement extends Broudy's 1967 project by listing an additional 526 items classified according to the schema originally proposed by him. It contains no items taken from general philosophy.

Broudy, Harry S., et al. PHILOSOPHY OF EDUCATION: AN ORGANIZATION OF TOPICS AND SELECTED SOURCES. Urbana: University of Illinois Press, 1967. xii, 287 p. Paperbound.

The bibliographic principles employed here should be applied perhaps to the entire field of the philosophy of education. While the project is far from complete, it is still indicative of what ought to be done rather soon systematically and year by year.

DEUTSCHE BIBLIOGRAPHIE, DAS DEUTSCHE BUCH. Auswahl wichtiger Neuerscheinugung. Frankfort on the Main, W. Ger.: Buchhaendler-Vereinigung GMBH, 1971-- .

This publication appears bi-monthly and covers all subjects including a special section for education (Erziehung, Unterricht, Jugendpflege).

Goodman, Steven E., ed. HANDBOOK ON CONTEMPORARY EDUCATION. New York: R.R. Bowker, 1976. 622 p. Bibliogs.

More than one hundred experts contribute one hundred eighteen articles and reports on current controversies, trends, and developments in the world of education. Each of the eight major areas of educational interest has a bibliography for further reading.

Groothoff, Hans-Hermann, and Stallmann, Martin, eds. NEUES PAEDA-GOGISCHES LEXIKON. 5th ed. Stuttgart and Berlin: Kreuz-Verlag, 1971. 1,346 columns.

More than half of the articles have been rewritten and about one hundred and thirty new essays added. This reference is a proven resource for clarifying definitions, for key ideas, for ready reference to important educational movements.

Jordak, Francis E. A BIBLIOGRAPHICAL SURVEY FOR A FOUNDATION IN PHILOSOPHY. Washington, D.C.: University Press of America, 1978. 250 p. Paperbound.

This reference work is valuable to the philosopher of education because it provides a recent and comprehensive survey of books, periodicals, encyclopedias, reference works, and dictionaries in the field of philosophy.

Krepel, Wayne J., and DuVall, Charles R. EDUCATION AND EDUCATION-RELATED SERIALS: A DIRECTORY. Littleton, Colo.: Libraries Unlimited, 1977. 255 p.

Lacy, A.R. A DICTIONARY OF PHILOSOPHY. New York: Charles Scribner's Sons, 1977. 239 p.

Leistner, Otto. INTERNATIONALE BIBLIOGRAPHIE DER FESTSCHRIFTEN. [International bibliography of festschriften]. Osnabruck, W. Ger.: Biblio-Verlag, 1976. 893 p.

> This bibliography covers the period from 1850 to 1974. Thoroughly indexed according to the names of distinguished persons, institutions, and subject matter, this work explains many foreign terms and expressions together with their German and English equivalents.

Lobies, Jean-Pierre, ed. INDEX BIO-BIBLIOGRAPHICUS NOTORUM HOMINUM. Osnabruck, W. Ger.: Biblio-Verlag, in preparation.

> Part A: Allgemeine Einfuehrung

> Part B: Liste der ausgewerteten bio-bibliographischen Werke 1973

> Part C: Corpus alphabeticum 1. Sectio generalis. Volume 1: A usque ad Aelmerus 1974. v, 960 p.

> Part D: Supplementum

> Part E: Gesamtregister der Verweisungen

> This international work will contain several million names.

Natalis, Ernest. UN QUART DE SIECLE DE LITTERATURE PEDAGOGIQUE. Gembloux, Belgium: Editions J. Duculot, 1971. 766 p.

> The collection includes over fifteen thousand references from 1945 to 1970. Note that the last name of the author is Natalis and not Ernest as given in some sources.

Paulston, Rolland, ed. NON-FORMAL EDUCATION: AN ANNOTATED INTERNATIONAL BIBLIOGRAPHY. Foreword by Don Adams. New York: Praeger Publishers, 1972. 356 p.

> Since many thinkers are considering the need for alternatives to all kinds of formal education, this scholar's tool offers a means of entry into the very important field of nonformal education. The entries number over one thousand.

Powell, John Percival, ed. PHILOSOPHY OF EDUCATION: A SELECT BIBLIOGRAPHY. 2d ed. Manchester, Engl.: Manchester University Press, 1970. xiii, 41 p.

> This bibliography lists twenty-nine book titles and numerous articles of journals published in English that are relevant to both philosophy and philosophy of education.

Richmond, W. Kenneth. THE LITERATURE OF EDUCATION: A CRITICAL

BIBLIOGRAPHY 1945-1970. London: Methuen, 1972. x, 206 p.

> Ten sectors, all with introductions worth reading, of the field of educational studies are represented in this survey: philosophy of education, educational theory, curriculum study, educational psychology, history of education, sociology of education, educational administration, comparative education, economics of education, and educational technology.

VERZEICHNIS LIEFERBARER BUECHER 1977/78. [German books in print]. 3 vols. 7th ed. Frankfort on the Main, W. Ger.: Verlag der Buchhaendler-Vereinigung; Munich: Verlag Dokumentation, 1977-78.

> These volumes contain a wealth of incomparable sources for research in all disciplines and for the philosophy of education.

Wehle, Gerhard, ed. PAEDAGOGIK AKTUELL: LEXIKON PAEDAGOGISCHE SCHLAGWORTE UND BEGRIFFE. [A lexicon of key ideas and catchwords in education]. 3 vols. Munich: Koesel, 1973.

> This resource is a unique aid to intelligent research into the educational literature published in the German language. The German language is endowed with a rich and highly nuanced educational vocabulary and these distinguishing characteristics can be easily lost when carelessly translated by an English term such as "education."
>
> Volume 1: ERZIEHUNG, ERZIEHUNGSWISSENSCHAFT. [Moral education, the science of moral education]. 1973. 205 p.
>
> Volume 2: BILDUNGSFORSCHUNG, BILDUNGSPOLITIK. [Research in intellectual education, educational politics]. 1973. 206 p.
>
> Volume 3: UNTERRICHT, CURRICULUM. 1973. 200 p. Index.
>
> Volume 3 has a complete and very useful index for the entire work.

Williams, Lloyd P. A GLOSSARY OF TERMS FOR STUDENTS OF EDUCATIONAL PHILOSOPHY. Norman: University of Oklahoma Book Exchange, 1965. 16 p.

JUST A BEGINNING . . .

Palisi and Ruzicka are exploring a problem tangentially yet vitally related to the philosophy of education. They wish to determine what effects, if any, an individual's philosophy of life and education has on the quality of helping relationship and on the individuals who benefit from the encounters with self and others. The approach is sometimes experimental, sometimes clinical or purely observational and introspectional.

Palisi, Anthony T. "Effects of Multiplexity, Self-Confidence and Different Clients on the Verbal, Interview Behavior of Counselor Trainees." Doctoral dissertation, Temple University, Ann Arbor, Mich.: University Microfilms, 1973. 351 p.

Palisi, Anthony T., and Ruzicka, Mary F. "Effects of Counselor Trainees' Personality and Philosophy and of Client Type on Interview Dynamics." HUMANIST EDUCATOR 15, no. 3 (1977): 110-20.

> The responses reflected neither a philosophy of human nature (i.e., their view of mankind ranging from positive to negative) nor the effects of client type.

Ruzicka, Mary F. "Effects of Multiplexity, Self-Confidence and Different Clients on the Range of Verbal, Interview Behavior of Counselor Trainees." Doctoral dissertation, Fordham University, Ann Arbor, Mich.: University Microfilms, 1975. 877 p.

> In the dissertations of Palisi and Ruzicka, multiplexity may be defined as the degree to which trainees view mankind as complex and variable. Inspection of the data indicates the more trainees viewed mankind as complex and variable the more their verbal behavior was proportionately indirect or less controlling. In regard to other client-type interactions and the philosophy of the helper, the results are inconclusive.

Ruzicka, Mary F., and Palisi, Anthony T. "Influence of Philosophy and the Need to Control Trainees' Verbal Behavior." HUMANIST EDUCATOR 15, no. 1 (1976): 36-40.

> Neither philosophy nor need to express control over others contributed in any significant way to indexes of direct-indirect trainee talk.

AN AFTERWORD: VENATOR SAPIENTIAE

Norman Perrin, himself a scholar of world repute who has tried to break new ground in New Testament studies, recounts approvingly what his own professor of sacred scripture, the late T.W. Manson, used to tell his students in Manchester, England:

> There are two ways of arriving at viable projects for research--
> either (1) find a conspicuous hole needing to be filled in the current scholarly discussion or (2) find a conclusion of that discussion with which one strongly disagrees.[1]

The forthright carrying out of Manson's directives for learning and researching from first-hand experiences--whether the intellectual adventure be one of problem solving or one of problem finding--may very well put the lie to Whitehead's observation that "the secondhandedness of the learned world is the secret of its mediocrity."[2]

The research required to solve a problem that already has been discovered usually demands complete understanding of the genesis and history of that problem. The value of such truth seeking is all too evident to anyone who has ever wrestled with alternate approaches to learning difficulties or devised a superior reading program. For problem-solving experts of such excellence the field of education will rarely ever want. The present cultural milieu and present schooling practices will most likely continue to foster such truth seeking. One need only observe Whitehead's caution that knowledge does not keep any better than fish! The problem, therefore, "must come to the students, as it were, just drawn out of the sea and with the freshness of its immediate importance." This research scholar succeeds in evoking "into life wisdom and beauty which,

---

1. Cf. Norman Perrin, A MODERN PILGRIMAGE IN NEW TESTAMENT CHRISTOLOGY (Philadelphia: Fortress Press, 1974), p. 4.

2. Cited by J. Sterling Livingston, "Myth of the Well-Educated Manager," HARVARD BUSINESS REVIEW (January-February 1971), 89.

apart from his magic, would remain lost."[3]

A much rarer breed of truth seeker in education, however, is the authentic problem finder. This "truth hunter"[4] habitually scans the horizon for clues and signs of what is yet to be; he seeks the deeper meaning in current changes of thought and method; he identifies crucial situations long before evidence of them can be detected by the most sophisticated information and retrieval systems.[5] This creative and imaginative opportunity finder prospers best in an environment of direct personal engagement with scholars known for their alertness and sensitivity to the frontier demands of education. By guided sorties into important yet mysterious intellectual territories, by brainstorming and speculative pioneering, by critically assessing axiological presumptions, or by dismantling theoretical structures that obstruct any full and genuine understanding of human nature and human behavior, this gifted and perhaps apocalyptic thinker clears the way for the truly great task at hand. He exults in the chase for the truth; discarding models elaborated from purely physical and biological data, he discovers the most important object of search not in "how to do things right"-- for this he does anyway--but in "how to find the right things to do and concentrates resources and efforts on them."[6]

On the adventurous hunt for the right things to do, the problem finder is instinctively aware of the traps lurking in educational models created from principles, assumptions, or even empirical data that conceal dangers to every man. He knows, for example, that behind Freudianism lies a lifeless robot of matter and mechanical energy, that beneath the typology of thought process is imbedded an invariant and fleshless geometry, that in self-actualization and growth theory may lurk in disguise the ironbound denizen of Walden Two. He is satisfied with neither Skinner nor Plato nor the existentialist because he divines over the horizon a richer, a more exciting, a more beautiful vision of man as man. But his chief concern is not the danger. Rather he discloses to colleague and student alike his profound and irrepressible drive to identify key issues that urgently need solving; he shares with all the thrill of the chase; he will eventually--if you live with him long enough--irradiate you with incandescence and his inward vision. Then, the wisdom hunter has made you restless for long nights and days and even years until you, like he himself, are about to catch up with wisdom itself. That, the wisdom hunter always knew and may you grow to learn as well, was all along the right thing to do!

Charles Albert Baatz

3. Alfred North Whitehead, AIMS OF EDUCATION AND OTHER ESSAYS (New York: Free Press, 1967), p. 98.

4. Pythagoras, DIOGENIS LAERTII DE CLARORUM PHILOSOPHORUM VITIS, VIII, 8. The Greeks speak of this truth hunter as "Therates tes aletheias"; the Romans as "Venator Sapientiae"; the Germans as "Jaeger der Wahrheit."

5. Livingston, p. 83.

6. Peter F. Drucker, MANAGING FOR RESULTS (New York: Harper and Row, 1964), p. 5.

AUTHOR INDEX

This index includes authors, editors, translators, compilers, and other contributors to works cited in the text. Numbers refer to page numbers and alphabetization is letter by letter.

Author Index

Author Index

Author Index

Author Index

Author Index

Author Index

Author Index

Author Index

TITLE INDEX

This index includes the titles of all books cited in the text. In some cases titles have been shortened. Numbers refer to page numbers and alphabetization is letter by letter.

A

Title Index

Title Index

Title Index

Title Index

G

Title Index

Title Index

Title Index

Title Index

Title Index

Title Index

Title Index

Title Index

Title Index

SUBJECT INDEX

This index is alphabetized letter by letter and numbers refer to page numbers. Major areas of emphasis within a subject have been underscored.

Subject Index

Anthropology 240
  Christian 228
  cultural 189
  educational 46, 56, 134, 157,
      158, 195, 206-7, 261
    bibliography on 147
Antiintellectualism
  American 109
  attack on Catholic 123
Antrobus, John S. 90
Aquinas, Thomas Saint (Thomism) 7,
      9, 17, 19-20, 30, 35,
      63, 83, 103, 108-9,
      110, 189, 197, 207,
      215, 216, 218, 219,
      220, 221, 234, 236,
      237, 242, 243, 247
  idea of Grace in 121-22
  man's vision of God according to
      73
  realism of 135
  See also Neo-Thomism
Archambault, Reginald D. 48
Architectonics, in describing inter-
      personal relationships 133
Aristotle 7, 9, 17, 20-21, 30,
      63, 118, 133, 152,
      188-89, 190, 192, 204,
      216, 217, 218, 228,
      230, 231, 234, 241,
      242, 243, 246, 247,
      248, 249, 250, 260
  critique of 52
  psychology of 223
Arnold, Matthew 98, 170
Arnstine, Donald 54
Art and culture 7
Art and the arts 181, 195
  and culture 7
  in curriculum design and content
      98-99
  in educational aims and ideals
      78-79
  as an educational foundation 22
  in educational organization and
      policy 170
  influence on educational thought
      7
  nature and ethos of education and
      211-12

philosophy of 241-43
  in the process and methods of
      education 183
  relationship to formal and informal
      educational agencies 150
  relationship to personal agencies
      of teaching and learning
      123-24
  See also Fine arts; Literature;
      Music; Painting; Poetry
Arts (aesthetics). See Aesthetics
Assimilation and accommodation 126
  existential view of 127
Atheism 235
Athens. See Education, Greek
      classical
Atkinson, R.F. 66, 105
Attitudes 90
Aubrey, John 250
Augustine, Saint Aurelius 21-24,
      30, 35, 40, 44, 111,
      135, 172, 193, 197,
      200, 215, 218, 221,
      232, 233, 236, 238,
      242, 245, 246, 249
  challenge to liberal education by
      140
  on immortality 197
  learning theory of 67
  use of Plotinus in understanding
      107
Austin, J.L. 201, 231
Ausubel, David 200
Authoritarianism and antiauthor-
      itarianism 150
  essays on education's lack of 50
Authority 130, 143, 146
  changing face of 46
  concept of 82
Automation, education and 179
Autonomy 133, 140, 191
Axiology. See Ethics and values
Ayer, Alfred Jules 231

B

Bacon, Francis 237, 250
  concept of ideology 230
Baier, Kurt 41, 43
Baker, Bruce F. 45, 46
Baldwin, Rosecranz, 46

Subject Index

Capitalism
  Marxist concept of education in
    167-68
  Marxist concept of man in 133
Career education, reforms in 54
Carnap, Rudolf 143
Caselmann, Ch. 35
Cassirer, Ernst 143, 148
Catholic education 206
  in the age of baroque culture 248
  impact on adult religious behavior
    144
  philosophy of 19, 26-27, 30,
    45, 58, 165, 235
  See also Franciscan education
Catholics
  attack on the antiintellectualism
    of 123
  leftist politics of 128
  liberalism of 254
Catholic universities 94
  role of in a pluralistic society 166
Causality 8, 111, 146, 217, 236
  children's concept of 111
  scientific explanation and 8, 96
  See also Teleology, educational
Caws, P. 221
Chamberlin, J. Gordon 57
Chardin, Teilhard de 73, 237, 254
Charters, W.W., curriculum-making
    devices of 83
Chartism 150
Chicago, University of 159
Child psychology 201
Children 226
  Amish 166
  concept of physical causality by
    111
  rights of 139, 149, 164-65
  See also Boys; Problem children
Childs, John Lawrence 45
China. See Education, Chinese
Chipkin, Israel S. 45
Chomsky, Noam 143, 181, 214,
    231, 232
Christ, Jesus 21, 22
Christian Albrechts University (Keil)
    74-75
Christianity
  Augustine's teaching on the
    morality of 21

concept of education in 8, 19,
    38, 72, 77, 163, 205,
    206, 207, 254, 264
  Dewey's implications for 51
  in India 52
  language and 94
  ethics of 141, 230
    faith in 115
  freedom and 144-45
  humanism of 95, 228
  impact on education 95
  outline of man in 224
  philosophy of 233, 234, 247
  realism in 145
  view of man and society from 131
  See also Anthropology, Christian;
    Catholic education; Church;
    God; Jesus Christ; Luther-
    an Church; Protestantism
Church, as a teacher in Judeo-
    Christian education 8, 9
Cicero 24, 246
Citizenship
  education for 149
  liberal education for 97
Civil rights 155
  increasing concern with 148
  See also Children, rights of
Clark, W. Norris 107
Classical education 77, 186
Classroom management 104. See
    also School discipline
Coffey, Daniel J. 46
Cognitive abilities 89-90, 104,
    110, 111, 187, 200
  critique of child development
    theory based on 66
  epistemology and 102
  importance of in learning 71
  individual differences in 108
  interaction with affective talent
    112
  Jean Piaget's theory of 111
  moral theory of development of
    117
  periods in the development of 89
  procedures for inquiry into 102
  reason as 123
  relationship to organic regulations
    75
  sociology of 123

Subject Index

Culture 65, 128, 131-32, 144
analysis of contemporary American 161, 183
change in 47, 126
in development of individualism 71
educational aspects of 49, 128, 152, 153, 157, 163, 171-72, 263
aims and ideas of education 78-79
curriculum design and content 98-99
educational organization and policy 170
formal and informal educational agencies 150
nature and ethos of education 211-12
personal agencies of teaching and learning 123-24
process and methods of education 183
need of by Americans 65
philosophy of 241-43
history of educational thought and 257
science of education and 264-65
place of literature in 201
science and 146
See also Anthropology, cultural; Relativism, cultural
Cunningham, William Francis 45
Curriculum design and content 8, 19, 26, 34, 38, 42, 49, 58, 59, 81-99, 119, 126, 254, 260, 263
aims of in natural science 74
art and culture in 98-99
bibliography on 112
in community education 148
epistemological aspects of 81-82
in France 83
human aesthetic powers in 92-93, 138
human affective powers in 89-92
human and social sciences in 96-98, 168
human intellective powers in 86-89, 199

human nature and unity in 84-86, 132, 197, 200
implications of Locke's philosophy for 32
importance to educational philosophy 66
in Judaic education 74
metaphysical aspects of 82-84, 153, 154, 179
need to develop for decision making 70
physical and mathematical sciences in 95-96, 122
reform of 43
religion and theology in 94-95
thought and language in 94, 205
values and ethics in 83, 93-94, 125
See also Instructional materials
Cybernetics 180, 189

D

Daley, Leo Charles 57
Danforth Foundation Workshop (1975) 70
Dante Alighieri 173, 217
Darlington Colloquy (1964), papers of 209
Darwin, Charles 148, 234
influence on educational reform 228
view of man changed by 108
Dawson, Christopher 218
Dearden, R.F. 66, 140, 246
de Beauvoir, Simone 203, 229
Debl, Helmut 188
Decision making, curriculum design for 70
Democracy 23, 32
definition of 37
education and 37, 55, 70, 76, 77, 136, 143, 148, 149, 152, 155, 164, 204, 210, 253, 256, 260
conflicts over 51
John Dewey on 54, 146
H.H. Horne on 35
R.B. Perry on 150

Subject Index

Subject Index

Subject Index

Stevenson, C.L. 58
Stoicism 230
Strain, John Paul, critique of 240
Strike, Kenneth A. 41, 46, 54
Structuralism 135
Students
  educational aspirations of 78
  influence of teachers on 123
    long-term 117
  social problems faced by 64
  See also College students
Suarez, Francis 192
Subconsciousness, implications of
    Freud's theory on 107
Sullivan, Phyllis 58
Summerhill 136, 137
Swanger, David, critique of 116
Syllabus of functions 18
Symbolism, the meaning and effect of
    72
Symposium on Belief, First (1969),
    papers of 233
Synthesis 27

T

Tanzania. See Education, Tanzanian
Teacher Corps 183
Teacher education 36, 194
  educational theory in 105, 119
    shortcomings of 17, 83
  humanistic approach to 93, 103
  for Jews 166
  philosophy of education in 33,
    40, 45
  reforms in 43, 54
Teachers 66, 67, 112, 147, 200,
    254
  influence on students 123
    long-term 117
  philosophies of 104, 221
  role of 104
  social problems faced by 64
  See also College teachers
Teaching 26, 29, 39, 44, 59,
    97, 103, 104, 107, 108,
    109, 110, 111, 115,
    173, 174, 260
  in a humanistic manner 176
  implications of Locke's philosophy
    for 32

of liberal arts 24
  logic in 119
  models of in affective education
    114
  as a personal and human act 91
  philosophical models of 119
  principles of 28
  professionalization of 195
  relationship of theories of knowl-
    edge to 62
  scientific basis of 102
  theories and concepts of 101, 119
Teaching methods. See Education,
    process and methods of
Technology 167, 195, 241
  dangers of modern 86
  Dewey on 107
  relationship to values 204
  See also Useful arts
Teleology 217
  educational 197
  See also Causality
Television, educative function of 9
Telfer, Elizabeth 66, 140
Testing. See Evaluation techniques
Theater. See Drama and theater
Theism 235
Theodoracopoulos, J.N. 221
Theology. See Religion and theology
Theory and research 11
Therapeia 34
Thomism. See Aquinas, Thomas; Neo-
    Thomism
Thorndike, Edward Lee 108
  teaching methods of 110
Thought and thinking 61, 126, 171
  approaches to the study of 108
  in curriculum design and content
    94
  in educational aims and ideals
    70-72
  in educational organization and
    policy 165
  nature and ethos of education and
    204-5
  philosophical 172
  philosophy of 230-33
  in the process and methods of edu-
    cation 180-81
  relationship to formal and informal

Subject Index